JOSEPH PEARCE is the author of many books, including *Small is Still Beautiful*, *Solzhenitsyn* and *Tolkien: Man and Myth*. He is currently Writer in Residence at Ave Maria College in Ypsilanti, Michigan.

From the reviews:

'The case for Bellocian revival is made by Joseph Pearce in a beguiling and sympathetic biography based on his private correspondence and memories of his descendants.'

JOHN COONEY, *Irish Independent*

'Pearce's principal achievement is to sketch in and dramatize the two worlds in which Belloc operated: on the one hand a "Georgian" quintessence made up of beer, briar pipes, long walks, drinking songs and Sussex by the Sea; on the other the salons of inter-war literary Catholicism, descending from the aristocratic redoubts of Lady Lovat and Maurice Baring to H. V. Morton, "Beachcomber" and the apologists of the popular press.' D. J. TAYLOR, *TLS*

'Joseph Pearce's portrait makes an excellent starting-point,'

JOHN GROSS, *Sunday Telegraph*

'An enjoyable read.' CRISPIN JACKSON, *Tablet*

'A good account of the sheer diversity of the man's activities.'

MELANIE MCDONAGH, *Evening Standard*

'Thoroughly recommended, thoughtful without being heavy, and giving a vivid portrait of Belloc the man,'

JOHN POLLOCK, *Church of England Newspaper*

D1421530

OLD THUNDER

A Life of Hilaire Belloc

JOSEPH PEARCE

HarperCollins*Publishers*

HarperCollins*Publishers*
77–85 Fulham Palace Road,
Hammersmith, London w6 8jb

www.**fire**and**water**.com

This paperback edition 2003
1 3 5 7 9 10 8 6 4 2

First published in Great Britain by
HarperCollins*Publishers* 2002

ISBN 0 00 274096 6

Typeset in Postscript Linotype Minion by
Rowland Phototypesetting Ltd,
Bury St Edmunds, Suffolk
Printed and bound in Great Britain by
Clays Ltd, St Ives plc

For James Catford,
In lasting gratitude for the faith he has always shown in my work

CONTENTS

CONTENTS

ACKNOWLEDGEMENTS

I have been truly blessed during my work on this volume to have received the help and co-operation of several of Belloc's descendents. I enjoyed many delightful hours in the presence of his granddaughter, Sister Emmanuel Mary, nee Marianne Jebb, amidst the idyllic tranquility of the convent of the Canonesses of St Augustine, the order she joined in 1945. A similarly fruitful visit was enjoyed in the company of Rom Philip Jebb, Belloc's grandson, at Downside Abbey, and with Zita Caldecott, another granddaughter, in her London flat, nestled in the shadow of Westminster Cathedral. The Earl of Iddesleigh and Edward Northcote, grandsons of Marie Belloc Lowndes, offered their time and their anecdotal memories. Barbara Wall and Bob Copper were also kind enough to share their memories with me. Chloe Blackburn, daughter of the artist Sir James Gunn, shared her fond reminiscences of her father's friendship with Belloc and Chesterton. I am particularly indebted to Zita Caldecott, Chloe Blackburn and Miranda Mackintosh for the loan of many letters to and from Belloc, the quotations from which have enriched this volume considerably.

Apart from the unique insights offered by the aforementioned, my work has been assisted greatly by those academics and devotees of Belloc who have assisted me in my research. Kim Leslie, chief archivist at the West Sussex Record Office in Chichester, was utterly selfless in making many previously unpublished letters available to me, as were Grahame and Gill Clough at the Belloc Study Centre, also in Sussex. Mike Hennessy allowed me access to his own exhaustive research into Belloc's parliamentary career, and I am grateful to William Griffiths and Alan Davidson for their knowledge and their support. Gerard Tracey, Archivist at the Birmingham Oratory, was very helpful in assisting my efforts to piece together the missing details of Belloc's schooldays at the Oratory school.

Further afield, I have been the beneficiary of the fruits of the diligent labour of a number of American academics. Dale Ahlquist spent several hours trawling through the Special Collections in the O'Shaugnessy-Frey Library at the University of St Thomas in St Paul, Minnesota. During his endeavours on my behalf he was assisted by Jim Kellen, the Librarian responsible for the Special Collections. Nicholas Scheetz, Manuscripts Librarian at Georgetown University Library, was generous with his time, and his patience, as he guided me through the Belloc material at Georgetown. Marty Barringer, Associate University Librarian, responsible for the Special Collections and Archives at Georgetown, was also very helpful, as was my friend and colleague on the *Saint Austin Review*, Father James V. Schall.

By far the greatest collection of Belloc material is to be found at Boston College, and I have to thank several people for their valuable assistance. Robert K. O'Neill, Father Frank Vye, John Atteberry and, most particularly, Peter Kreeft, were all most helpful in making the material at Boston College available to me.

Others who have assisted in sundry ways include Father Fessio at the Ignatius Press and Amy Boucher-Pye at HarperCollins. Penultimately, and emphatically, I must thank my wife, Susannah, who assisted me in multifarious ways throughout the months in which this labour of love was in preparation. Ultimately, however, I must conclude with a confession of all the sins of omission that I have doubtless committed in leaving out many other people who have assisted my efforts on this volume. To these unsung heroes and heroines I offer my sincerest gratitude and my heartfelt apologies for my failure to acknowledge their efforts individually.

ONE

Cradle Refugee

STORM CLOUDS GATHERED OMINOUSLY over the village of La
Celle Saint Cloud, 12 miles outside Paris, on 27 July 1870. By four
o'clock in the afternoon, as Elizabeth Belloc was in the final stages of
childbirth, a violent thunderstorm heralded the arrival into the world of
her son. Thereafter, whenever his mercurial temperament erupted into
anger she would call him Old Thunder in reminiscence of the tempest
which had accompanied his birth.[1]

The baby's father, Louis-Marie, recorded the event in his wife's small
engagement book. '*Mercredi, 27 Juillet: C'est aujour-d'hui à 4 h. [1/4] qu'est
né un beau gros garçon que je nommerai Joseph Hilaire Pierre.*'[2] Two days
later his intention was formalized when Joseph Hilaire Pierre's birth was
registered in the presence of Jean-Baptiste Thomas Huilier, a local school-
master, and Pierre Antoine Lemaire, a doctor.[3] Louis-Marie had tried to
contact Dr Lemaire during his wife's confinement, but the 72-year-old
doctor, a former physician to Louis XVIII, was nowhere to be found.
Hilaire had been delivered by the midwife, Mercy Baker, who conveyed
the news of the birth to one of Elizabeth Belloc's friends. 'I was alone,
and I brought the baby into the world. The doctor . . . did not arrive
until the event was quite over, and the baby washed and dressed.'[4]

The storm clouds that had gathered on the afternoon of 27 July were
portentous of more than the birth of the poet. A week earlier, on 19 July,
France had declared war on Prussia. On 30 July, in the first serious
engagement of the Franco-Prussian War, the French army launched an
offensive at Saarbrücken. The town was recaptured by the Germans on
6 August. On the same day the advancing Prussian army inflicted heavy
defeats on the French at Wörth and Forbach. The war had begun badly
– and worse was to follow. From 9 August, the Prussian army began its
relentless advance through France, capturing Reims on 5 September.
Within days of her son's birth, Elizabeth Belloc watched a procession of

1

gun carriages pass by her house on their way to reinforce the retreating French lines.[5] Blissfully ignorant, the newborn child could not know that this baptism of fire would leave an indelible mark on his life.

Belloc's birth also coincided with the culmination of the Vatican Council in Rome which, in July 1870, had declared the doctrine of papal infallibility. Ironically, or perhaps aptly, the proclamation of the Pope's infallibility in the spiritual sphere coincided with a dramatic confirmation of his vulnerability in the sphere of politics. Following the outbreak of the Franco-Prussian War, the French garrison which had been protecting Rome was withdrawn by Napoleon III. In September the soldiers of Victor Emmanuel entered the Eternal City, crushing the papacy's temporal power at the very moment in history that its spiritual power had been solemnly asserted.

Paradoxically, the Pope, in being humbled, would be exalted. Until his death in 1878, Pius IX, as the defiant 'prisoner of the Vatican', enjoyed a degree of personal popularity without parallel in the history of the modern papacy. Furthermore, in the midst of tribulation, the ageing Pope was consoled by the missionary expansion of Catholicism around the world.

This pivotal moment in the history of Christendom would also leave its mark on the future life of the child being born in its midst. As a champion of the Church Militant in a hostile secular society, Belloc would sometimes exhibit à siege mentality akin to the defiance of Pius IX. In 1864 the Pope had published an encyclical denouncing the principal errors of the age, amongst which was the very suggestion that the Church could or should reconcile itself to 'progress', liberalism or modern industrial 'civilization'. Similarly, the Vatican Council, in its resolute opposition to many aspects of modern life, had effectively declared war on the secular states of the industrialized world. *Pro Ecclesia contra mundum* appeared to be the battle cry of both Pius IX and the Council he summoned. It was a battle cry with which Belloc would feel entirely at home.

A more obvious and immediate influence on the newborn child was that of his own family. His father's origins were steeped in romance. Louis Belloc's maternal grandfather, Colonel Jacques Swanton, was descended from a family of Irish Protestants from County Cork, where the place now known as Ballydehob used to be called Swantonstown. The French connection had begun when Jacques Swanton's uncle had fled to the continent after killing his opponent in a duel. He later became a Catholic and afterwards a priest. Colonel Swanton was one of the last serving officers of the Berwick (Stuart Irish) Brigade before its dissolution, and was a Dean of the Order of St Louis, described by Hilaire's sister, Marie Belloc Lowndes, as 'one of the greatest orders of chivalry in Europe'.[6] He served in the Royalist army prior to the Revolution, but afterwards fought in Napoleon's early campaigns.

His daughter, Louise, pursued a literary vocation. In 1823 she published a French translation of the Irish Melodies and her life of Byron was published with a preface by Stendhal. She went on to write children's books and translated contemporary English and American novels into French. One of her books was awarded the Monthyon Prize of the French Academy.[7] Against the wishes of her father, Louise married the well-known painter Jean Hilaire Belloc, who would immortalize their love in a memorable portrait of his wife that would be exhibited in the Louvre.

If the newborn child could claim a rich literary and artistic inheritance on his father's side of the family, his maternal antecedents were equally impressive. His mother Elizabeth Parkes, known to everyone as Bessie, was the great-granddaughter of the scientist Joseph Priestley who, as an early pioneer in the chemistry of gases, was one of the first discoverers of oxygen. Priestley, like his great-great-grandson, was no stranger to controversy. In 1791 his reply to Burke's *Reflections on the French Revolution* so incensed public opinion that a mob attacked his house in Birmingham and destroyed its contents.

Bessie's father, Joseph Parkes, a solicitor by profession, devoted much of his time and energy to the cause of political radicalism. His political and literary contacts were extensive and, through him, his daughter came to know many of the leading lights of Victorian London. He was a friend of Henry Brougham, George Grote and John Stuart Mill, and was a frequenter of Samuel Rogers's famous breakfasts, to which Bessie was sometimes invited. Bessie counted both Thackeray and Trollope amongst her friends, the former of whom, relishing the company of Liberal politicians, would often dine at the Parkes's family home in Wimpole Street. Bessie corresponded with George Sand, and she travelled to Yorkshire with Elizabeth Gaskell when the latter was working on her life of Charlotte Brontë. Bessie's own love for the Brontës was evident in a letter to a friend in which she declared the superiority of their novels to those of George Eliot. Eliot's books contained 'wisdom, wit, tenderness, an amazing knowledge of human nature, high principle of a very deep kind' – everything 'except genius . . . I consider that her books are conglomerate rocks, not granite or crystal. There is more of the living burning fire of genius in one page of *Wuthering Heights* than in the whole of *Romola* or *Daniel Deronda*.'[8]

In spite of Bessie's reservations about Eliot's work, she counted her as one of her friends. 'My father was much attached to her,' Bessie would recall in her memoirs, adding that 'whenever any special celebrity was invited to dinner, such as Thackeray', her father 'was never content' unless he could secure Eliot's attendance also.'[9] Bessie remembered George Eliot descending the great staircase of the house in Wimpole Street. 'She would talk and laugh softly, and look up into my father's face respectfully, while the light of the bright hall lamp shone on the waving masses of her hair, and the black velvet fell in folds about her feet.'[10]

It is not clear to what extent Eliot's agnosticism had undermined the lukewarm Unitarianism of Bessie's parents. There is little doubt, however, that many of Joseph Parkes's circle of friends were deeply antithetical towards Christianity. George Grote, John Stuart Mill and George Eliot were great advocates of the Positivist ideas of the French philosopher Auguste Comte, who claimed, amongst other things, that since the existence of God was unprovable, humanity, idolized in the abstract, should look to itself as the only meaningful guiding force.

Evidently, Bessie Parkes found such a creed unsatisfactory. Inspired by a desire to know more about the history of the Reformation, she visited 'Dr Manning of Bayswater', the future Cardinal Archbishop of Westminster. Manning was 'perfectly polite' and 'spoke with the most measured chilly calmness ... as if perfectly conscious of the Comtist influence then taking possession of English Society'.[11] Bessie felt convinced that Manning was not very impressed with her, a precocious young woman caught up with the heresies of the age, but she, nonetheless, was greatly impressed by him. 'I do not think he had any suspicion that I was so impressed and overpowered by his intellect, that when I left the room and the house I ran nearly all the way home, with the sense that I was fleeing from an overmastering brain, and that I dreaded it.'[12] Like the protagonist in Francis Thompson's poem 'The Hound of Heaven', Bessie's efforts to flee were futile. From that moment on, she became increasingly convinced that Comte, Mill, Grote and Eliot were no match for the 'overmastering brain' that she had encountered in Bayswater. To the surprise of many of her father's circle, she was received into the Catholic Church in 1864. The impact of this fateful or providential act on the life of her son, as yet unborn, is inestimable. Indeed, it is scarcely conceivable that the figure of Hilaire Belloc, as the following century would know him, could have existed if his mother had not succumbed to the powerful combination of faith and reason that she had discovered in the mind of Manning.

Bessie's conversion does not appear to have affected any of her old friendships adversely. She continued to move in the same religiously sceptical and politically radical circles, and in the spring of 1867 she travelled to France with Barbara Bodichon, the noted watercolour painter and campaigner for women's rights who, in the words of Marie Belloc Lowndes, 'had come to feel no belief in any form of revealed religion'.[13] The two women rented a small chalet in the grounds of the house in La Celle Saint Cloud where the recently widowed Louise Swanton Belloc lived with her son Louis. Bessie and Louis became engaged within weeks of their first meeting and were married on 19 September 1867 in the old church of St James, Spanish Place in London. The newly married couple settled in the English capital and it was here, in August of the following year, that their daughter Marie Elizabeth was born.

As much as he was delighted with the birth of his daughter, Louis Belloc earnestly desired a son. He also hoped that his next child would be born in France. Consequently, when he learnt that Bessie was going to have another baby, he made arrangements for a return to his native land. Bessie was aware of her husband's wishes, and before leaving London she wrote to his mother of her hopes for the future. 'Ah, dearest Maman, how happy I should be if I could give my Louis a son, and you another Hilaire Belloc! But if this is not to be, then I shall gladly welcome a second Louise Swanton, who will be, if my prayers are answered, in every way a replica of the beloved grandmother after whom she will be named.'[14]

The parents' joy at the birth of 'another Hilaire Belloc' five years after the death of his grandparental namesake was tempered by the anxiety caused by further French defeats in the war. 'We are very anxious today,' Bessie wrote to her mother on 9 August, '. . . the bad news came to the village yesterday.' In response to the growing emergency, the young men of France were answering the call to arms. Louis's two nephews had both joined the army and Bessie informed her mother that heavy artillery had been passing the house all through the morning. 'Although the Emperor is said to have taken a hasty pretext to declare war, I believe it was inevitable, and that Bismarck meant it all along . . . Should France be beaten – which God forbid – the whole balance of Europe will crash into shivers.'[15]

Even by the most pessimistic estimates, nobody could have predicted the speed of the Prussian advance or the shocking suddenness of the French capitulation. Within weeks of Belloc's birth his parents were forced to make hasty plans to evacuate their home. They fled to Paris, the 12-mile journey taking five hours in the stifling heat of August, and, following the fall of Reims on 5 September and anxious appeals from Mrs Parkes and Madame Swanton Belloc, who had already left the country, Louis agreed reluctantly to take his wife and children to England. They caught the last train from Paris to Dieppe. The decision to leave France almost certainly saved the life of the six-week-old baby. During the siege of Paris, which lasted all through the winter until the triumphant entry of the Prussian army into the city on 1 March 1871, almost every child under three years old perished from malnutrition.

The Bellocs moved into the Parkes's house on Wimpole Street and studied the newspapers for any news of the war. They learned from *The Times* that the houses in the neighbourhood of La Celle Saint Cloud were 'fast disappearing' under heavy bombardment from Prussian artillery on the surrounding hills. After the French surrender in the spring of 1871, Bessie and Louis returned to France to survey the damage to their family home. Although the structure of the house was intact, its contents had been vandalized. The German soldiers had taken 'great delight in breaking everything that was breakable, including all the kitchen pottery', and it took four men to clear the filth and rubbish from the lower part of the house. The eighteenth-century portraits hanging in the bedrooms were disfigured or destroyed, daubed in ink with moustaches and beards, or simply torn up. Others had been used for target practice. A portrait of Madame Belloc's mother, with several bullet holes in the painted breast, was discovered stuffing up a broken window. Paintings of Colonel Swanton and Madame Belloc's late husband Hilaire had simply disappeared, presumably stolen and sent to Germany.[16] Many papers and manuscripts were also lost, including two letters of Lord Byron and several pages of the manuscript of *Childe Harold*. Madame Belloc was particularly saddened by the disappearance of the letters her husband had written to her on the rare occasions they had been parted.

Devastated at the scale of the damage, Bessie wrote disconsolately to a friend, 'I am beginning to wonder if we shall ever be able to live in either of our two houses again. The wreck and devastation baffles description. Do you remember your sister's wedding present to me? It was a fine old china tray. Various pieces of it were found ... yesterday, in what I can only describe as a dunghill.'[17]

The plunder of his family's possessions was destined to fall like a shadow across the life of the child who, as a cradle refugee, had so narrowly escaped having his life extinguished scarcely before it had begun. The ghosts of the Franco-Prussian War would haunt Belloc always, fuelling his love for France and his lifelong antipathy to Prussianism. Ironically, he would never be able to forget the devastation that he was too young to remember.

TWO

An Anglo-French Childhood

IN DECEMBER 1871, Louis, Bessie and their two children moved to 11 Great College Street in Westminster. Bessie had inherited the lease of the house, together with the substantial sum of £20,000, from the estate of her uncle, Josiah Parkes, who had died the previous August. On 5 January 1872, Bessie informed Madame Belloc that the family were settling in well and were 'so comfortable and happy in our little house'.[1] Her air of optimism was understandable. In the wake of the turmoil and upheaval of the previous 18 months, she must have relished the prospect of a peaceful and secure future. Within eight months, however, her comfort and happiness would be shattered by the sudden death of her husband.

The family returned to La Celle Saint Cloud for several months in the summer. On 6 August, Louis and Bessie left the two-year-old Hilaire and four-year-old Marie with their nurse while they travelled to the Massif Central to visit some friends. When they returned 12 days later, Louis, complaining of feeling fatigued, retired to his room. He slept all through the next day and, when efforts to waken him proved fruitless, the doctor and priest were sent for. He died, without regaining consciousness, shortly before midnight on 19 August. He was 42 years old.

On the following morning Bessie bathed and dressed her two children and took them in to see their father. Marie described this episode as 'the first clear memory of my life'. She recalled seeing her father lying, as she thought, asleep, and being told by her mother that she and her brother should look at their father very carefully and kiss his hand because he was going to heaven and she wished them never to forget him.[2] Although this incident made a lasting impression on Marie, it is likely that Hilaire was too young to remember it. 'Little Marie evidently knows something is wrong, for she cries sadly,' Bessie wrote to her mother on the same morning. 'Poor little Hilaire is too young to know what his loss will mean to him.'[3] Once again Belloc's life was destined to be haunted by the ghosts of events he was not able to recall.

The funeral took place on 22 August. Bessie walked immediately behind the coffin, holding Hilaire by the hand, and was followed by Madame Belloc, holding Marie's hand. Following the Requiem Mass in the village church, the procession made its way to the cemetery. Once there, Bessie turned her back on the open grave, knelt down, and put an arm round each of the children so that they would not see the lowering of the coffin. After everyone else had left the cemetery, Bessie approached the open grave and threw flowers onto the coffin.

Over the following months, Bessie struggled to contain her grief. Her mother wrote to Madame Belloc that she was 'so terribly anxious about her',[4] and it was not until March of the following year that Bessie felt able to confide in a friend that she was finally emerging from the shadow of desolation.

> There are some days when the great change, the great sorrow, seems to press on me peculiarly; and this has been the first feeling of the warm spring-time, coming round to the summer again. I sometimes wonder if you have any idea of what this year has been to me – but, as time goes on, I feel more and more inclined to bury it out of sight silently.[5]

Her efforts to put the grief behind her had been helped by a meeting with Manning, whom she had not seen since that eventful meeting prior to her conversion almost a decade earlier. Since then Manning had succeeded Cardinal Wiseman as Archbishop of Westminster and would soon be named cardinal by the ageing Pope Pius IX. Manning counselled her sternly, telling her that grief is a luxury which, if too much indulged in, becomes injurious to the character. As at their previous meeting, Manning's uncompromising mind impressed Bessie tremendously. She resolved to control her grief, accept her sorrow and rebuild her life. Outwardly she seemed to succeed in doing so, but her daughter recalled that she never mentioned her husband's name, even in extreme old age, without her eyes filling with tears.[6]

At times Bessie struggled with a deep sense of inadequacy with regard to her parental duties, sensing her inability to fill the vacuum left in her children's life by the absence of their father. 'Hilaire would ride on my shoulders this evening, just as if I had been the father I am not; and at last I had to put the poor little creature down on the floor. My strength had given way, and I felt as if it were symbolical of the whole position.'[7]

The absence of a father in Belloc's life, and its lasting legacy, was discussed with probing succinctness by his biographer Robert Speaight. 'Had Louis Belloc survived,' Speaight suggested, 'his son would have been a Frenchman with an English mother instead of being an Englishman with a French father.'[8] Nonetheless, Louis's absence remained a powerful presence in Belloc's life. The son's loyalty to the unremembered father would foster in him a love for France that was accentuated occasionally to the point of caricature. As an Englishman with a French father he could never quite belong to, or integrate with, the French nation that he loved and admired so dearly. On occasion, as Maurice Baring and some of Belloc's other friends would discover, his Frenchness could be forced and even falsified by an affectation – often utterly unconscious in its expression – that was uncharacteristic of any full-blooded Frenchman. In his published works this sometimes translated into a slightly too shrill defence of the cause of France and a slightly too damning condemnation of her enemies.

The Anglo-French dimension in Belloc's childhood was nurtured by his mother's decision to divide her time between her English and French homes. Whereas most of the year was spent in London, the summers were invariably spent at La Celle Saint Cloud. In November 1874 Bessie decided to let the house in Great College Street, and she and the children moved to her ageing mother's house in Wimpole Street. Soon afterwards Hilaire was sent to a preparatory school in Hampstead. It was, however, the long summer months in France that fired Hilaire's imagination and filled him with many of the Gallic influences and impressions that would colour his personality. Writing of the effect of these summers in France, Marie wrote that she and Hilaire 'loved our French home dearly'. Yet, tellingly, she added that, although she and her brother spoke French well, 'at no point could we have been actually taken for French children'.[9]

In the autumn of 1877 Bessie Belloc suffered a further severe blow which plunged her once more into grief and uncertainty. In October her mother died quite suddenly after a very short illness. According to Marie, 'Eliza Parkes, even in extreme old age, was certainly indispensable to her daughter's welfare, and to what peace, if not happiness, my mother should have been able to enjoy, during the years following my father's death.'[10] The seven-year-old Hilaire's efforts to console his distressed mother and to come to terms with his grandmother's death were expressed in words of precocious innocence. 'My darling Mama, I am very sorry Grandmama is Dead and that I shall never see her again. I send you a text, God is love.'[11]

Bessie's unhappiness in the wake of her mother's death was exacerbated by a catastrophic turn of events with regard to her finances. A stockbroker friend of her mother's had lost £20,000 of Bessie's money, the inheritance she had received from her uncle, in rash speculations. Having crashed so dramatically from affluence to poverty, she had little option but to sell the lease of the house in Westminster.

Bessie decided to leave London and rented a house in Slindon, a quiet, secluded and picturesque Sussex village nestling peacefully in a fold of the South Downs, four miles from Arundel. In such financially troubled but apparently tranquil circumstances, Hilaire Belloc moved into the first of his Sussex homes on 22 July 1878, five days before his eighth birthday. It would herald the commencement of a lifelong love affair with this particular corner of England. Thereafter the county of Sussex would vie with the charms of France in his affections.

Four months before the move to Slindon, while his mother was in the throes of the panic caused by the loss of her fortune, Belloc was inspired by the loss of HMS *Eurydice*, which had foundered off the coast of the Isle of Wight on 24 March 1878, to write some fine juvenile verse. This maritime disaster, which had also inspired Gerard Manley Hopkins to compose one of his best-known poems, had moved Hilaire to the composition of poetry which belied the fact that he was still only seven years old. Bessie, understandably proud of her son's ability to master rhyme, metre and refrain with such consummate ease, sent this and other examples of his verse to her old tutor, Lucy Field, whose effusive reply on 11 April must have cheered her careworn heart. 'I do not wonder that you are proud of your Boy's talents, and it is almost incredible that he could manage sense, sentiment and metre as he has done in the little poems you send us ... I feel quite alarmed at his precocity ...'[12]

Belloc's sister would refer to the poem on the loss of the *Eurydice* as 'a vivid, solemn picture of that awful shipwreck', adding that her brother's juvenile verses were 'astonishing as to both thought and diction in a child of his age'.[13] She also records that Hilaire learned *The Lays of Ancient Rome* by heart, for his own pleasure, when he was only five years old.[14] Remarkably, other verses composed by Belloc in his childhood illustrate a deep sense of the powerful presence of Time and the melancholic tension it creates between endurance and erosion. 'The Nameless Knight', written when he was nine, and another poem about a medieval ruin near Slindon, written a year later, convey a degree of saddened solemnity, rooted in tradition, which prefigure later works such as 'Ha'nacker Mill'.

Another hallmark of the adult that was being stamped onto the child at this time was a love for walking, a passion which had been awakened by the move to Slindon. Beginning with modest walks into the hills with his mother, Belloc was soon embarking on his first long-distance trek, a walk of several days along the roof of the Sussex Downs from Petersfield to Beachy Head. Since landscape and history were always intertwined in Belloc's mind, his love for Sussex would have been coloured by the close proximity to Slindon of Arundel Castle, ancient seat of the Dukes of Norfolk, which served as the living symbol of the survival of English Catholicism during the years of persecution. Arundel was, in many respects, the symbolic capital of recusant England, a fact that had been significantly reinforced in 1870 by the construction of the impressive new church of St Philip Neri. Although there was a Catholic church in Slindon, Bessie sometimes took the children to Mass or Benediction at this imposing church which towers over the town, a potent image of the Catholic Revival heralded by the conversions of Manning and Newman. Living history, its triumphs and its tragedies, its crucifixions and its resurrections, was already exerting its monumental power on Belloc's inquisitive mind.

In a letter to Barbara Bodichon at the end of 1880, Bessie lamented the passing of another 'sad and tragic year'. She had lost two other close friends, Mary Merryweather and Mademoiselle de Montgolfier, 'such landmarks in my life', and was further saddened by the death of her old friend George Eliot. She had seen her less frequently in recent years, taking Hilaire with her on the last occasion that she had visited, but had 'thought of her often'.[15]

On 6 September 1880 Bessie wrote to John Henry Newman, who had been named cardinal during the previous year by the new Pope, Leo XIII. Writing from Paris, she expressed her hope that Cardinal Newman would accept Hilaire as a pupil at the Oratory School at Edgbaston, near Birmingham, over which he presided. She informed him that her son was the great-grandson of Joseph Priestley and that he had 'a pronounced taste for all natural science'. Hilaire was 'a good little boy' whose religious instruction had been commenced by Father Arden of the Dominican Priory, Haverstock Hill.[16]

Newman invited Bessie to come to see him and the subsequent interview was evidently a success. Bessie wrote delightedly from Edgbaston to a friend: 'Nurse and I brought Hilary here and have launched the dear thing at the Oratory School,' adding that her son was 'very delighted to go'.[17] Hilaire's first letter from the Oratory to his sister, who was at a convent school at Mayfield in Sussex, spoke of the 'rather long hours' that the boys kept at the school. They rose each day at 6.30 in time for daily Mass an hour later. Lessons commenced immediately after Mass and continued until nine o'clock in the evening, with breaks for breakfast, dinner and 'play'.[18] His letters home to his mother, or to his sister at Mayfield, are full of the daily life at the school. He boasts of running over two miles and not feeling 'any the worse for it', of climbing a smooth pole 18 feet high, of learning to skate in the winter, and of playing cricket which was 'awful fun' in the summer.[19] He continued to write poetry and, a month after his arrival, sent his mother a poem entitled 'Bravery', inspired by Napoleon's retreat from Moscow – a theme to which he would return at much greater length, and with memorable results, many years later.[20] His favourite authors, judging by the books he was reading when he first arrived at Edgbaston, included Sir Walter Scott and Jules Verne. He was also much impressed by Milton's *Paradise Lost*.

During the Easter holidays of 1881, Bessie took Hilaire to Wales, from whence he wrote excitedly to his sister of his pony-trekking adventures on Snowdon when his mount had 'danced and capered in a very nasty place betwixt two precipices'. Bessie enjoyed the time spent with her son and remained astounded by his precocity. 'He is a little flame, pouring out poems, parodies, calculations, metaphysics, till I am frightened to hear him. He knows more Welsh in a week than I have ever known.'[21]

On 6 November 1881, Hilaire's last surviving grandparent, Madame Belloc, died in France at the age of 84. Her popularity was reflected in the fact that a thousand people were present at her Requiem. 'I feel as if a great light and power has been extinguished,' Bessie wrote from La Celle Saint Cloud. 'What she was to me there are no words to tell, and she was far the noblest and best human being I have ever known.'[22]

Madame Belloc's death compounded Bessie's sense of loss. Earlier in the year, with the memory of recently deceased friends fresh in her mind, she had confided to Barbara Bodichon her secret desire for the relative peace and seclusion of the religious life. 'When I first became a widow I used to tell myself that if my children married early I might join the Sisters of Charity if, that is, they would be willing to take me. I did not think I should be too old at sixty. I had decided to give all my possessions to my children.'[23] Bessie's grief-stricken faith was clearly tormented by a spiritual restlessness that her son would inherit. She yearned for a peace that the world seemed incapable of providing. This restlessness was evident in her efforts to convey the tenets of her faith to her children:

> I have been telling the children tonight that serving God means something active, not only what they call 'being good'. It is so difficult to help children to serve; and yet I believe it would remove half the difficulty of making them 'good'. Human creatures can't poise. Even the wild bird cannot do it for more than a moment; and the spiritual wings not even for that moment.[24]

It would be wrong to imply from these words, or from her expressed desire for the cloister, that Belloc's mother was over-assiduous, or even fanatical, in her desire to teach the Catholic Faith to her children. Marie states unequivocally in her memoirs that, beyond simple morning and evening prayers and Mass attendance on Sundays, she and her brother were not 'taught' religion as children.[25]

In May 1882, Father John Norris, the headmaster of the Oratory School – whom Belloc would describe more than 40 years later as the wisest man he'd ever known[26] – wrote to inform Bessie that her son would be making his First Communion on Corpus Christi of that year: '. . . he is preparing himself for it very nicely and thoughtfully, and Fr Pope, who is instructing him, is very much pleased with him.'[27] According to Marie, her brother's religion meant 'a great deal to him' during his schooldays, a view which would seem to be verified by a letter from Belloc, presumably written shortly after Corpus Christi. 'My first Communion has made a great difference to me, there is always something by me in the Blessed Sacrament, something to place entire confidence in, which is the really great want I have felt here.'[28]

Many years later, on 14 April 1938, Belloc recalled his First Communion across the chasm of more than half a century. His words in old age were a reiteration of those of his boyhood, indicating that the vision of the truth accepted at the Oratory appears to have remained throughout his life. If, however, the truth of the words remained, the facts surrounding them seem to have become muddled in his mind by the passage of time. Writing to his goddaughter Cecilia Pollen, the grandchild of one of his friends from his schooldays at the Oratory, he expressed delight that she was about to take her First Communion, pronouncing that it was 'very great and good news!': 'I made my First Communion an enormous number of years ago. It was this same day, Holy Thursday, in 1884, when I was 14. When you get to be as old as I am you will remember your First Communion as though it were yesterday, because it is so great a day in one's life.'[29]

Clearly the forgetfulness that would characterize the last years of Belloc's life had confused the facts of the matter. He might have been received on a Thursday, even a holy one, because Corpus Christi, a moveable feast, always falls on a Thursday, but it was not usual for First Communions to be celebrated during Holy Week, making Holy (Maundy) Thursday far less likely than Corpus Christi. Furthermore, if he had been received on Holy Thursday 1884, he would not have been 14, as he claimed, but 13. In fact, as records at the Birmingham Oratory confirm, he did not receive his First Communion on either of the Thursdays in question but on the Sunday within the octave of Corpus Christi, 11 June 1882, several weeks before his twelfth birthday, at a Mass celebrated at the St Joseph's altar of the old Oratory church by Father Paul Eaglesim.[30] This, perhaps, is a timely reminder that essential truth remains even when the 'facts' may lie. The latter might have become confused in the old man's mind, but the truth shone forth through the haze and fog of the years. The old man and his younger self remained united in the belief that the First Communion had made 'a great difference' and that the Blessed Sacrament was 'something to place entire confidence in'.

Belloc's enthusiastic approach to his faith at the Oratory School was further in evidence in letters to his sister. Referring to a religious Retreat, he remarked that 'I like it but a great many boys don't', adding that he kept a notebook 'of all that is said and enlarge on it on my own account'. The same letter referred to 'a very wonderful sermon' on the Resurrection, illustrating a piety that was surely unusual in boys of his age. He also appeared to have inklings of mystical theology beyond that which one would expect of a boy who was not yet 13. Commenting in a letter to his mother of how he found it easier to 'pray beautifully' on days when the school chapel was 'all a beautiful grey' in the evening light, and when 'the sanctuary lamp looks so bright and yet lights up so small a space', he expounded on the 'essence of God' in beauty and love.

> I think that beauty and love, and things which people generally look down upon as not stoic or heroic, are the essence of heroism and manly feeling, and this because they are the essence of God as we hear of Him and understand Him. I felt this in chapel today, that the light feeling which proceeds from love or something beautiful, is not a feeling that will pass, but the happiness of angels in the love of God. Have you ever felt that in one of those beautiful churches, Notre

Dame or St Ouen, how one loves the beauty around one so much
that one is convinced that it was the grace of God, as well as man,
that helped to build that church?[31]

The spirit that permeated these words was also the inspiration for 'Notre
Dame', a poem that he enclosed with this letter. The poem laments
that 'Notre Dame' is, to some, merely 'a memory of the past', of 'a faith
that . . . has fled'. To others she is 'a poem wrought in stone' or a 'tinted
light' in old stained-glass windows breathing 'a spirit lost and dead'.
For the poet, however, she is 'my people and my land', signifying that,
in the boy's mind, the Church Mystical was also the Church Militant, a
crusading spirit that forges nations and cultures. These are the first sparks
of Belloc's emerging conviction that Europe was inextricably bound to
the Catholic Faith in chains of duty and love, deriving its beauty, its
meaning and ultimately its very existence from God and His Church.
More specifically, however, since the poem refers to the Gaul and the
Frank, and to the Mother of Christ as 'Notre Dame' and not as 'Our
Lady', the poet's people and his land are clearly the French and France.
In his vision of the Immaculate Conception the boy had conceived an
embryonic nationalism.

Apart from loyalty to the memory of his father, Belloc's nationalism
was also rooted in a desire to honour his French ancestry. His great aunt,
Madame Bibron, known to Hilaire and his sister as 'Tante Jenny' and the
only surviving sister of their grandfather, Hilaire Belloc, wrote to him
when he was still only 10 years old of the importance of his family and
of his duty to France. Although she loved him for his own sake, she also
loved him 'because you are the grandson of my brother, a man who was
distinguished by his talents, by his devotion to his family and friends,
and last, though not in any sense least, by his services to the country he
loved so truly during his long arduous life. These, dear Hilaire, are your
letters of nobility.'[32]

Belloc was well aware that his paternal grandmother had wished
ardently for a boy when he was born and that she had wanted him to be
named Hilaire after his famous grandfather. He was all too aware of the
'letters of nobility' of which his aunt spoke. Indeed, he carried his nobility
with pride, treasuring any stories he could glean about his distinguished
forebear. Marie recalled that her brother 'delighted' in any 'family tradition concerning our painter grandfather'. He was particularly impressed
by the story that his grandfather had been taken as a child to Paris in the

middle of the Revolution and that he had been taken to a window so that he could see Danton on his way to the scaffold.[33]

With such a welter of passion and pride welling up inside his youthful conscience, it is perhaps of little surprise that Belloc felt a deep sympathy for Paul Déroulède and his *Ligue des Patriotes* who were calling for an avenging war against Prussia following the humiliation of 1870. Marie Belloc shared her brother's sympathies, paying tribute to Déroulède as a Frenchman who 'gave up his whole life, and of what money he had, to the then onerous task of keeping alight what had become in his country a thin and flickering flame of patriotism'.

> That flame he not only kept alive, but caused to burn more and more brightly for forty-four years, in the face of strong official opposition, and the often angry disapproval of all those belonging to what must be termed, for want of a better term, his own class. By all the educated Frenchmen of his day he was regarded as a dangerous crank who desired to embroil his country with a neighbour whose one wish was to live with her in amity and peace. The kinder of his critics considered him ... as the arch type of tiresome idealist who spends an idle life tilting at windmills. He was naturally loathed, as well as feared, by the venal politicians who knew they had in him a watchful and implacable enemy. He was even looked at askance by the chiefs of the French Army, then still smarting from the knowledge that the professional soldiers had been found wanting in the summer of 1870. When Déroulède was mentioned in the Paris press, which was seldom, the mention always took the form of an attack, and always the attack was made in contemptuous terms.[34]

It is possible that Marie's sympathy for such an unpopular figure might have been due, at least in part, to the fact that she counted him as a friend. Déroulède's mother lived at Croissy, not far from La Celle Saint Cloud, and the Bellocs – Bessie, Marie and Hilaire – met him on their regular visits to Croissy during their summer sojourns in France. It would, however, be a trifle simplistic to ascribe Hilaire's and Marie's support for Déroulède purely on grounds of friendship. Hilaire's consistent antagonism towards the influence of Prussia, which was always unequivocal in its vehemence throughout his life, indicates a deeply ingrained desire to defend France from the expansionist designs of her neighbour. Thirty years later, when a recalcitrant Prussia found itself at war with both France and Britain, Hilaire and Marie would proclaim it as a vindication of Déroulède's vision of the inevitability of a future war.

Hilaire and Marie both became members of the *Ligue des Patriotes*, and Marie subscribed to its weekly paper *Le Drapeau*. Hilaire chose a more active role and attended some of Déroulède's meetings during his visits to France. Bessie was as sympathetic to Déroulède's cause as her children and, on one occasion, she accompanied both of them to a mass rally of the *Ligue des Patriotes* on the Champ-de-Mars in Paris.

Belloc, still barely a teenager, was already beginning to display the volatility and the love of controversy that would characterize his adult years. At the most impressionable period of his life he was dividing his time, and his loyalty, between the peaceful surroundings of the Oratory School, under the benign guidance of the quintessential Englishman Cardinal Newman, and the embattled barricades of nationalist politics, under the explosive influence of the fiery Frenchman Paul Déroulède. With such a powerful cocktail working on his youth, the precocious child was already revealing glimpses of the extraordinary man.

THREE

First Love

B ELLOC'S EDUCATION AT THE ORATORY SCHOOL furnished him
with a lifelong love for the classics. On 2 October 1882 he wrote
enthusiastically to his mother of Euripides' *Alcestis* and described his studies
of Virgil as 'very delightful'.[1] A month later he waxed lyrical on the timeless
quality of classical literature. 'The more one reads and understands the
ancients, the more one understands that they were men very like us. I
feel so sympathetic with them for the feelings they felt were so pure,
undisturbed by the factions and Party quarrels of today so innocent and
yet so grand.'[2] On 16 November he wrote of his devotion to Homer:

> I am getting fonder and fonder of those 'mighty minds' of old who put
> forth the affections and beauty of life so wonderfully. There are some
> passages in the Iliad which make me thrill with pleasure . . . And my
> chief pleasure is that they are so real, the old Heroes; and want of any
> kind is always filled up by the sympathizing Character of Homer . . .[3]

In a letter to his mother on 26 April 1883 the 12-year-old Belloc contrasted
his admiration for Homer with his evident disdain for the prevailing
scepticism of Victorian philosophy. 'After the ridiculous theories which
everyone preaches now, that no such thing as love exists without selfish-
ness,' it was 'quite refreshing' to read Homer. The Greeks 'were noble
because their whole system was founded on love of *something*, to Socrates
it was the Unknown God, and in Homer's time I think it was the love
of that power they did not understand which enabled them to love the
beautiful around them'.[4]

If the precocious schoolboy was able to detect the philosophical significance of the classics, he was equally able to find political parallels
between the ancient and the modern. Thus, for instance, Cicero was 'just
like a man speaking in Parliament only rather more excitable'.[5]

Echoes of his mother's influence are clearly discernible in this early blossoming of Belloc's interest in politics and philosophy. Bessie had grown up amid the philosophical speculations and political radicalism of her father's friends and she seems to have imparted much of her experience to her son. He had also inherited her love for contemporary literature, finding time to read 'a good deal' of Tennyson in the midst of his studies, describing the current poet laureate's *The Princess* as 'a kind of cross between Homer and Heaven'.[6]

Robert Speaight referred to the 'incalculable debt' that Belloc owed to the Oratory School for its having imbued him with a love for the classics.[7] It was a debt that Belloc freely admitted. Nearly half a century later, in a letter dated 20 January 1932, he would write: 'As for the Classics *all* my generation ought to thank God that they were well whipped into them – for Latin and Greek are *tasks* for boys and it is as tasks and discipline that they take root. Then in later life they bear a glorious fruit.'[8]

At the Prize Day for 1884 Belloc became the first boy under 14 to win the Second Norfolk Prize, awarded for superlative achievement in the classics. He also won the first English Prize and the Fourth Form Prize. 'Hilary has gained a most extraordinary series of prizes,' Bessie wrote proudly in her diary. 'It was pleasant to see the old Cardinal stand up and present them. Very imposing did the old man look with his white hair falling on his scarlet cape. As to my laddie, he took his successes very modestly.'[9] Bessie recorded that Newman was not at table for the banquet which followed the prize-giving, but that he was present later for the school's annual Latin play, which, that year, was the *Aulularia* of Plautus. Belloc's performance as the female character, Staphyla, was praised in a review of the play published in a local newspaper in which the reviewer opined that Belloc was not only 'splendidly "made up"', but that he had 'evinced genuine talent'.[10]

Belloc's success continued with further accolades at the following year's Prize Day. 'Hilary has got the Mathematical prize: £7 of books,' Bessie informed Barbara Bodichon in July 1885. 'It is a great honour, for last year he took the highest classical prize possible to his place in the school.'[11]

In 1886 Belloc won the English Prize and also the debating prizes, the latter of which he shared with his friend James Hope, 'both of whom', according to the headmaster, had 'taken great interest in the debates and devoted considerable time and study to the getting up of the subjects on which discussion had taken place'.[12] Hope, who would later become Deputy Speaker of the House of Commons, was probably Belloc's closest friend during his schooldays and their friendship would remain for the rest of their lives. 'I wonder what is generally thought of friendship?' Belloc had written as an 11-year-old, soon after his arrival at the Oratory School and shortly after he and Hope had become friends. 'I think it is the brightest angel Earth has, perhaps Heaven also.'[13] These surprisingly mature sentiments were a fleeting foretaste of Belloc's oft-quoted lines from his 'Dedicatory Ode' that there was 'nothing worth the wear of winning but laughter and the love of friends'.

Every year the young Hilaire would spend part of his summer holidays at Heron's Ghyll, near Crowborough in Sussex, where James Hope and his three sisters lived with their grandmother, the Dowager Duchess of Norfolk. During these visits Belloc naturally became friends with Hope's sisters, the eldest of whom became his first love.

It is not clear to what extent Belloc's feelings for Minna Hope were reciprocated. She was eight years older than him, which would seem to preclude any reciprocal feelings on her part, and the few surviving letters show that she was more mature, and possibly more deliberately distant, in her approach to their friendship. Belloc's letters to her from the Oratory are full of references to daily life at the school. He tells her of his receiving 'a whack on the head' with a cricket ball and his frustration that the mild concussion it had caused had resulted in the doctor forbidding him anything in which 'my brain may be excited!' This included a ban on all books and, which was particularly frustrating, his enforced withdrawal from the examination for the Religious Instruction prize.[14] He shared his love of the classics with her, enthusing over Horace and Sophocles, and paying homage to the beauties of the Greek language which 'positively *sings* even in a dusty room in Birmingham'.[15] Minna's knowledge of Greek was minimal, but she was well versed in Latin and her reply, which was peppered with Latin quotations from Horace, demonstrated an obvious affinity of literary interests.[16] This, however, does not suggest any romantic affinity and there is scanty evidence to suggest any depth of feeling on Minna's part.

An exchange of letters in May 1887[17] seems to indicate that Belloc may have made clumsy efforts at making his amorous feelings known during a visit to Heron's Ghyll in the Easter holidays. In the circumspect wording of Minna's letter, written from the Convent of the Sacred Heart in Roehampton on 6 May,[18] there is, however, little evidence of what Speaight referred to as 'the gropings of calf-love'.[19] Minna alludes to her 'sympathy' and to Belloc's 'difficulties' and there are suggestions of some form of intimacy in her mild admonishments. Yet there are also hints that she may have rejected his advances.

I do really feel for you more than I can well say ... You must remember not to take anything I say to you as preaching, what I say to you would apply every bit as well to myself. Do you try, I wonder, mentally to put yourself into other people's shoes and judge things from their point of view? Would it not sometimes be the better way to try and understand and perhaps help them even though they may not understand you? One gains so much from shifting one's position and learning to look at life through other people's windows.[20]

These words, if not exactly patronizing, are almost motherly in tone and it is only in Belloc's reply that a more detailed picture begins to emerge:

You had a great deal to say to me, and I have a great deal to say to you. Imprimis, I think you got very near what I was thinking of last holidays, only I don't think you quite know how it made me feel at the time ...

Do you know, when you tell me that which you have told me in your letter it makes me a little bit sad. I scarcely know how to answer because I scarcely know how you meant me to understand you ... You see of course when you tell me that after two years you found a difference of relations it pulls me down a little, and when you tell me that you regret it, it makes me think that the state of things did not exist ...

You are the only person who ever helped me or whom I ever cared to be helped by ... And so when your letter takes the form, I may have misunderstood it, of regret for a new state of things in a friendship, it makes me a little bit sad, for I don't see, selfish that I am, how I am to get along alone after all. You see, it may have been my fault, but I took your friendship not as a help only, for one doesn't pick up one's friends but one's mind takes hold of them and won't let them go. I am afraid all this is great bosh to you and I only wish I could put it more clearly, I only mean that it would take me down a bit to think that our friendship was not as before.

Now what really bothered me during the holidays was this; I couldn't say what I wanted to say, because I thought it would sound ridiculous. There were a number of things I wished to tell you, and I half told you one ... but I had no courage to tell you anything else. But now I will tell you just simply this, that either my morbidness or my self-sufficiency prevents my keeping a friend's friendship, and you know when one cares for anyone, it's hard to find that they find you a bore ...[21]

Only a draft of this letter exists and it is possible, since it ends in mid-sentence, that it remained both unfinished and unsent. Either way, the forced restraint and the scarcely suppressed sentiments convey a tension in which the words left unwritten seem to scream from the silence between the lines. Certainly the sense of rejection is all too obvious in the manner in which the 16-year-old boy's pain-pricked pride, smarting at the loss of his first and largely unrequited love, shows sorrowfully through each and every line.

Marie Belloc Lowndes, acknowledging that Minna Hope was her brother's first love, conjectures that she might have been the inspiration for a fine early verse in which the boy poet ponders the nature of his love.[22] Indeed, since Belloc made reference to his 'poetical compositions' in his letters to Minna,[23] it is possible that he even sent her a copy of it. Perhaps he hoped that he could utter poetically by proxy what he was unable to say personally in her presence. If so, one suspects that Minna, more mature and detached than her young admirer, would have greeted his work with mild amusement.

The short-lived and seemingly one-sided love affair faded before it had flourished. Minna would later marry the distinguished diplomat Sir Nicholas O'Connor, and Belloc would marry the one woman who would totally eclipse all others in his affections.

Apart from the time spent at Heron's Ghyll, the bulk of the summer holidays was still spent with his mother and sister at La Celle Saint Cloud. Belloc acquired a penny-farthing bicycle and used it to explore the French countryside. The enduring power of France in general, and La Celle Saint Cloud in particular, to fire his imagination was in evidence in a long story, *Buzenval*, that he probably wrote while he was still at the Oratory, although it would not be published until May 1888. Its theme, significantly, was the Franco-Prussian War.

Belloc's love for France, epitomized by his active support for Paul Déroulède and his *Ligue des Patriotes*, was tempered, if not necessarily compromised, by the lure of England. By the beginning of 1887 England appeared more enticing than ever. On 14 February, presumably in response to the suggestion that he might consider studying in France once he left the Oratory School, he wrote a long letter to his mother insisting on his desire to remain in England.

I write this letter for one purpose only, and that a very definite one. I wish you to act upon its information, it is absolutely final. For my

profession, ceteris Paribus, I choose England. I speak English, I wish
to write in English ... I want to live in England. In an English
profession I believe I shall gain a place in English writing. I love my
country but I cannot bear the cosmopolitan folly which is destroying
the Frank and Gaul in our class. I dislike the life of a Paris student.
My desire is to make a name in literature and as I can write in English,
I choose England if it be possible ... For my country – France, for
my patriotism – France; for my society and money and field of work
– the country of Minna.[24]

Quoting this letter in her memoir of her brother, Marie Belloc Lowndes
wrote that 'the last word perhaps gives the clue to this impassioned
outburst'.[25] Penned appropriately on St Valentine's Day, Belloc's letter
was written as the 16-year-old approached the zenith of his infatuation
with Minna Hope. Two months later his lovelorn hopes would be dashed
on the rocks of her indifference. For the time being, however, Minna was
the centre of his universe. She was more important than France, whereas
England was merely 'the country of Minna'.

Belloc left the Oratory School at the end of the summer term in 1887,
having passed with honours the London Matriculation. 'I believe I am
the second who had got honours of all who have matriculated from the
Oratory since it began,' he wrote proudly to his mother, adding with a
touch of one-upmanship, 'I think I passed higher than the other.'[26] Obviously delighted with his achievement, the school's headmaster, Father
John Norris, presented him with a copy of *The Imitation of Christ*. There
was also an interview with the then very aged Cardinal Newman, who
signed and presented a copy of his book, *The Dream of Gerontius*, to the
school's star pupil.

The triumph of Belloc's academic achievement was overshadowed by
the tragedy, for so it seemed to his battered boyish pride, of his rejection
by Minna. In her absence, England, 'the country of Minna', lost its attraction and France, his country of birth, once again gained the ascendancy.
'When Hilaire was seventeen,' wrote Marie Belloc Lowndes, 'he underwent
a complete *volte-face*, and earnestly begged Bessie to allow him to enter
the Collége Stanislas in Paris with a view to joining the French navy.'[27]
'I tore myself up by the roots deliberately after I left school at the age of
17,' Belloc would write 53 years later.[28] In fact, he had been torn up by
the roots by the failure of his first love. His next love, beckoning beyond
the horizon, would be his last.

FOUR

'Youth Gave You to Me'

Belloc's sudden desire to enter the Collége Stanislas was regarded as foolish by some members of the French side of his family. His cousin, René Millet, warned Bessie that her son was to all intents and purposes an Englishman and that any attempt to turn himself into a Frenchman would be doomed to failure.[1] Similar misgivings were expressed by Father Norris. Although both he and Cardinal Newman wrote fine testimonials to Hilaire's character and abilities, Father Norris questioned his former pupil's 'present decision', adding that he thought 'a safer and more solid career would have opened out to him in this country'.[2] In spite of such cautionary advice, Bessie agreed to her son's wishes and he entered the Collége Stanislas in October 1887.

The Collége was run by the Marist fathers on strict disciplinarian lines. The Abbé Ernest Dimnet, who taught there in later years after the Marists had been banished by the anti-clerical government of Combes, painted a vivid picture of the system that Belloc would have experienced upon his arrival.

> The Marists had invented a system, still maintained, whereby every mark given in class was converted into 'points' which really were the college currency. Studious boys were affluent, lazy ones were penurious. With a given number of points you could buy your Sunday outing, a monthly play-day or a day or two extra vacation at Christmas or Easter. So was virtue rewarded while remissness looked on.[3]

Although the Collége laid especial emphasis on literature and mathematics, two subjects at which he excelled, Belloc was never comfortable with the high degree of regimentation. Particularly irksome was the rule forbidding boys from leaving the precincts of the college except when accompanied by an approved escort. Belloc knew Paris well and longed to stroll through the Jardin du Luxembourg, scarcely two minutes' walk away, or to explore the bohemian enticements of the Quartier Latin, only a few minutes further on. It was intolerable to have such delights within walking distance and yet find them forbidden. Resenting such restrictions, he was soon perceiving the college as a prison and began to plan his escape. Having saved enough pocket money for his return to England, he simply walked out of the building, clad in his distinctive cadet's uniform, and went back to London. His mother and sister were shocked by his unannounced arrival at their home on Great College Street, and Marie recalled that they were 'filled with dismay and apprehension as to what he would decide to do next'.[4]

Having given up any notion of a seafaring career, Belloc decided to try his hand on the land. He trained as a land agent at a farm near Bury, a beautiful Sussex village tucked between the banks of the Arun and the foot of the Downs. This proved equally unfruitful and unsatisfying and, abandoning the land also, he travelled to Ireland in the summer of 1888, seeking to escape from an intolerable present and fearing the contemplation of an uncertain future. 'I remember in what mood and with what view of the future I rowed a boat upon an Irish river in the month of August 1888,' he would recall wistfully in a letter to Maurice Baring many years later.[5]

Alone with his doubts and uncertainties amid the beauties of the Irish landscape, Belloc's restless spirit began to rekindle the hope of a literary career. In the previous May his story *Buzenval* had been published in *Merry England*, the magazine edited by Wilfrid and Alice Meynell, in an issue that also heralded the first publication of 'Dream Tryst' by the unknown poet Francis Thompson.

Belloc had sent some of his own poems to Father Matthew Russell, S.J., editor of the *Irish Monthly*, and was delighted when one of his sonnets was published in the November 1888 edition. Entitled 'To Regret', the sonnet laments a lost love, presumably Minna Hope, and longs for her return, not on the 'soul-crushing wings' of 'sudden memory' but 'in life'.[6] The March 1889 edition contained another sonnet, 'Mixed Metaphors', that displayed early signs of the poet's emerging sense of satire.[7]

In his correspondence with Father Russell, Belloc confessed a degree of financial insecurity that would be prophetic of much of the remainder of his life. Over the following half a century he would often find himself writing from financial necessity, frequently using the pen to ward off penury.

To tell you the truth my only motive in thus trying to appear at an age when one's work, if healthy, must be imperfect, was to begin to earn a little. When one has been brought up in the way of knowing how many pence make a shilling (especially when two women have to live on the common fund) one desires at least the beginnings of gain. So that I now ask if you would read in the regular way a prose story of mine; I can quite understand how valueless Rhythm and English are on the market. But something in the way of story sells better.[8]

Financial constraints forced Belloc to seek employment in an architect's office at the end of 1888, where he learned draughtsmanship and applied mechanics. Aware of his responsibility to contribute to the 'common fund', he wrote with forced optimism to his mother and sister in March 1889 from his lodgings in Bloomsbury that it was 'very interesting work'.[9] In fact, as he would later confess to his mother, he was very unhappy at the time and 'at war with most of my world'.[10]

During these months he sought an escape from the claustrophobic confines of what he called 'my little room in Bloomsbury' by visiting the ageing Cardinal Manning.[11] Presumably Belloc would have been aware of his mother's deep admiration for Manning and he would probably have known of the influential part that Manning had played in her conversion to the Catholic Faith 25 years earlier. In fact, it is likely that it was only through Bessie's intercession that Manning had agreed initially to receive her son. Thereafter, however, it seems that the elderly cardinal had taken a liking to the 18-year-old youth, because they seem to have met regularly during 1889.

Manning's influence on Belloc was profound. His ultramontanism was an inspiration, and his political radicalism a rallying cry. Manning was not only an unequivocal defender of the Pope, he was an outspoken champion of the poor. For the impressionable youth, whose own background was rooted in the philosophy of the Church and in the politics of the French Revolution, the combination of traditionalism and radicalism that Manning preached was a potent one.

Even as a septuagenarian, Cardinal Manning had remained actively involved in the social aspects of his ministry. In 1885 he had been a member of the royal commission on the housing of the poor, and in the following year was appointed to the royal commission on education. His social vision was gaining international recognition and in 1891 would prove to be influential to the teaching enshrined in Pope Leo XIII's famous encyclical *Rerum Novarum*. This encyclical would itself become the inspiration for Belloc's preaching of the socio-economic creed that, many years later, would become known as distributism.

Belloc confessed his debt to Manning in *The Cruise of the Nona*.

> It was my custom during my first days in London, as a very young man ... to call upon the Cardinal as regularly as he would receive me; and during those brief interviews I heard from him many things which I have had later occasion to test by the experience of human life ... and Manning did seem to me (and still seems to me) much the greatest Englishman of his time. He was certainly the greatest of all that band, small but immensely significant, who, in the Victorian period, so rose above their fellows, pre-eminent in will and in intelligence, as not only to perceive, but even to accept the Faith.[12]

One particular phrase of Manning's so impressed the young Belloc that it changed for ever the way he viewed the world of human affairs. The cardinal told him that all human conflict was ultimately theological, a 'dogmatic assertion of truth', as Belloc described it, which bewildered him at the time but which 'came to possess for me a universal meaning so profound that it reached to the very roots of political action'.[13]

Even while Manning was imparting his 'dogmatic assertions' to his young disciple, he was called upon to put his words of wisdom into practice. In August 1889 the London dockers went on strike to protest against their conditions of work and to obtain an extra penny on their wages of five pence an hour. The strikers were led by Ben Tillett and John Burns, both of whom were friends of the cardinal, and Manning agreed to act as an intermediary between the strikers and their employers. He used all his powers of persuasion on the directors, who reluctantly agreed to consider the strikers' demands 'if they came through Cardinal Manning'.[14] Speaking of his negotiations with the directors, Manning stated, 'I never in my life preached to so impenitent a congregation.'[15] After weeks of delicate negotiation, Manning finally obtained for the dockers the bare justice for which they had asked, and, on 14 September, 'the Cardinal's Peace' was signed. Some consider this Manning's finest hour and it certainly illustrated the eminent place that the 81-year-old cardinal had come to occupy in the public mind.

Belloc retained vivid memories of 'the great London Dock Strike'. 'Well do I remember the fevers of that struggle!' he exclaimed in 1925.

I was but nineteen years of age; it was my delight to follow the intense passions of the time.

It was a time when men who have since been caught in the net of professional politics, and have lost their souls, went down to speak fiercely at street corners, and to light in the hearts of broken men the flame of human dignity ...

I remember the great mobs that followed John Burns, and how I myself would go miles through the East End to hear him; and I remember that great whirlpool of men in Trafalgar Square on the most critical day when he and others accepted imprisonment. There is nothing now for which men would act so; no one now has a creed; therefore, I call that time of my youth a better time.[16]

In late August or early September, at the height of the Dock Strike, Belloc departed for France as the 'cycling correspondent' of the *Pall Mall Gazette*, having abandoned his job in the architect's office for the prospects of a career in journalism. His appointment to a paid position with the *Pall Mall Gazette* was secured at the instigation of his sister, who already worked for the magazine and was on good terms with its editor, W.T. Stead. His brief was to travel through France talking to 'typical Frenchmen' about the volatile nature of that nation's politics.

Belloc's departure for the continent coincided with the arrival of three American ladies in London, one of whom was destined to break his heart even more devastatingly than had Minna Hope. Mrs Ellen Hogan, the widow of Joseph Smethwick Hogan of Napa, California, was visiting Europe with two of her daughters, Elizabeth and Elodie. The younger of the two daughters, Elodie, who was still only 19 and who had never previously visited Europe, kept a diary of their visit.[17] On 15 August they had left 'dear old Ireland', the birthplace of both her parents, and proceeded to explore England. On 3 September they visited the offices of the *Pall Mall Gazette* where they met Marie Belloc, 'a charming chic little French damoiselle' who 'was kinder to us than one woman is generally to another'. Inevitably, the conversation included a discussion of the Great Dock Strike, the subject on everybody's mind, and Elodie recorded that Marie, echoing her brother's position, told them that 'the strikers are good people'.

Marie invited the three Americans to tea. She told them of her mother's friendship with George Eliot and Cardinal Manning and offered to try to arrange a meeting with the latter. 'Now, at last, I shall meet someone who knew George Eliot,' Elodie wrote excitedly. 'We were promised an interview with Mr Stead tomorrow and a visit to Cardinal Manning some day soon. How lucky we are!' On the following afternoon they had tea with Bessie, having met W.T. Stead in the morning, and Elodie was delighted to meet 'Madame B – one of George Eliot's best friends'.

After they had once more met with Bessie and Marie for tea on the following day, Elodie recorded her impressions of 'Madame Belloc'. She had 'a strong personality' and was 'sweet & endearing'. Marie accompanied the three Americans to Westminster for their audience with Cardinal Manning, and it says much for the ageing cardinal's prodigious energy that he managed to find time to meet them even though he was in the midst of negotiating an end to the dockers' strike.

Having struck up such a warm friendship, Bessie, Marie and the three Americans decided to visit Paris together, departing on 24 September and travelling via Newhaven and Dieppe. Hilaire, still touring the French provinces on his bicycle, is not mentioned in Elodie's diary so it seems he was not able to rendezvous with his mother, sister and their companions. He would, however, have sympathized with Elodie's positive impressions of Paris: 'Paris – la belle France & O but it is so beautiful; no anvil leaden skies or smutty atmosphere, but sunshine & a sky like our own – the very bluest & such white luminous clouds, sailing around between the high strait narrow houses.'

After Ellen Hogan and her two daughters had returned to the United States, Elodie wrote to thank Bessie and Marie for their hospitality, expressing 'an undying remembrance of all the love and kindness and sweetness which you both gave to us ... strangers whom you took in, whom you sheltered, and to whom you gave unquestionable love and friendship. Ah, dearest Madame Belloc and Marie, we shall only be dust when we forget you.'[18]

With such a bond of friendship it was only natural that they should renew their acquaintance when Ellen, Elodie and Elizabeth stopped in London on the return leg of a pilgrimage to Rome and Lourdes in the spring of 1890. During one of their regular visits to Great College Street, Belloc walked into the room and was introduced to the three Americans. Elodie at that time would be described by the American novelist Gertrude Atherton as 'a beautiful creature, with hair like polished mahogany, eyes of a dark, rich blue, delicate regular features ... She had neither figure nor style, and dressed abominably, but with a face like that it little mattered, and she also possessed the twin gifts of personality and charm.'[19] Belloc took one look at her and determined that she should be his wife.

Shortly after this fateful meeting, Mrs Hogan received news that one of her sons was ill. She decided to cut short her stay and head home to California. Elodie and Elizabeth were deeply disappointed at the thought of leaving London so soon and sought to persuade their mother to allow them to remain behind. She agreed after Bessie had told her that they could stay at Great College Street as her guests. Both sisters were deeply religious and, during their stay, they went to daily Mass at the old Jesuit church in Horseferry Road. Elodie, in particular, believed she had a religious vocation and intended to join the Sisters of Charity as soon as she returned to America. Belloc had other ideas. Almost daily he acted as her guide to the London sights and he spoke to her of his confused ambitions to make his mark in literature. She listened to this intense 19-year-old and began to perceive in him a greatness that she would recall in a letter to Father Russell more than 20 years later.

> Years and years ago ... I met him; and considering my complete indifference during those days, indifference and virginal scorn for the whole masculine world, I marvel at my own insight! for I plainly foresaw all his power and I realized the greatness of his soul. As he has gone on from year to year achieving and accomplishing, I have never been surprised. It is only my girlish vision of him and faith in him being realized.[20]

Put more prosaically, she had fallen in love with him – as he had with her. One day, Elodie plucked up the courage to seize his hand and kiss it. '"What an awful girl" the prudes and propers would say and with some justice. Now weren't you shocked that a young woman's democratic enthusiasm should run so away with her? I think you must have nearly fainted, Honey-bun.'[21]

Although Elodie and Elizabeth extended the length of their stay in England, they were only delaying the inevitable. As the date of their departure loomed, Elodie and Hilaire spoke confusedly about their feelings for each other and of their plans for the future. Hilaire, as restless and reckless as ever, saw no obstacles to their marriage that could not be simply swept aside, including the objections of Elodie's mother who remained convinced that her daughter was called to the religious life, and the objections of his own mother who believed that he was too young to contemplate an engagement. Elodie, however, was far less certain. Loyalty to her mother's wishes and a lingering confusion over whether she still had a religious vocation resulted in the triumph of doubt over decisiveness.

In such a maelstrom of muddled emotions the two lovers were severed in the summer of 1890 by several thousand miles of ocean, mountain and desert. Undaunted, Belloc told Elodie that even such a distance was no barrier to his love, and he spoke of his plans to travel to California to see her.

In spite of such bravura, Belloc must have wondered, as he and Elodie said their final farewells, whether he would ever set eyes on her again. His hopes and his fears found expression in a sonnet, 'Her Youth', presumably written for Elodie during the early days of their relationship, in which the poet refuses to believe that the love he has found will be lost.

> Youth gave you to me, but I'll not believe
> That Youth will, taking his quick self, take you.

Once before, he had loved and lost and now he seemed to be looking at the spectre of lost love once again. Yet, haunted by an unfathomable future, he harnessed the hope of a cherished happy ending.

FIVE

Editor and Tramp

AT THE END OF JULY 1890, possibly as a means of coping with his grief at Elodie's departure, Belloc left for France. In a little over a week he had travelled, presumably on foot but possibly by bicycle, from La Celle Saint Cloud, through Paris, Reims, Sedan and Luxembourg to Metz in the German-occupied region of Alsace-Lorraine, a distance of about 200 miles. He wrote to Elodie from Château-Thierry, *en route* from Paris to Reims, and again upon his arrival in Metz. 'I have done two silly, silly things,' he wrote from Metz on 6 August. 'I have not written to you for at least a week [and] I have gone into Alsace-Lorraine! You know the Germans took away Alsace-Lorraine from us in 1871 and you know of course that we are going to take it back...'[1]

The letter is peppered with the politics of the *Ligue des Patriotes* and displays Belloc's interest in military logistics and his prophecy, *à la* Déroulède, of impending war:

I shall be lucky if I do not get into Prison or something; for I go about talking French in a loud voice and telling everybody not to forget France – a dear & beloved country which will come some day & take them back again to herself. Germans do not like this sort of behaviour. What fun it would be if they would lock me up! But I shall have no such luck Elodie (which rhymes with melody) – I have not the pluck to pick a quarrel with one of the officers & short of that I do not think they would stop one doing anything. There are 23,000 German soldiers in the town alone! ... all believing that they will cross the frontier in a year or two. They probably will, & if they do there will be such a big fight outside Nancy, where we have 30,000 ... to meet them ...

All about me men are speaking French & all about me German soldiers – and I hear distant war songs & loud cannon & rifle fire, snapping and volleying like a cart over heavy stones, I hear them but

I am a prophet – & all these others are blind. I see old France rising again as young as her old age itself – as old as her magnificent youth. You & I & France are young Elodie . . . So is my heart. So are my hopes for the country. There will be some good verse out of this journey sooner or later.

Politics aside, Belloc's letter from Metz was clearly intended to woo his beloved. Throughout its pages the young idealist's romantic nationalism is blended, almost incongruously, with romantic love:

I have written all sorts of foolish things to you – foolish because I ought to have waited to see how they would be received. – But it is such a long, long time to wait a month for one's answers – & such a long long way from France & England to San Francisco.

And yet Honey-bun, Tiddlywinks, though I have no answer – it is a pleasant thing to write to you . . .

Good bye – Elodie – good night – It is always night when I write to you . . . So again good night – If I could follow the night round her long whirl around the bend of the earth – at last I should come to you. But I cannot follow the night. She goes too quick.

Do not forget me altogether.

Write often.

As a postscript, Belloc appended 'the last verse of a pretty little poem I have written to you which you shall have'.

Presumably it was this remarkable blend of poetry, politics and prophecy that had so beguiled Elodie during their halcyon summer in London and which had convinced her of Belloc's 'greatness of soul'. He must have hoped, as he poured himself out onto the pages of this and other letters to her, that the spell would not be broken by her return to California.

Belloc's letter from Metz also contained a reference to 'my Review', suggesting that he had discussed with Elodie his plans to establish an independent literary journal. He was still in his teens when plans for the launch of the magazine were put in place and barely 20 when the first issue of the *Paternoster Review* was published in October 1890. His co-editor was A.H. Pollen, a friend from his schooldays at the Oratory, and the project was financed by other friends, including James Hope. Its principal aim, apart from giving voice to new literary talent, was to declare 'open war' on

a certain number of men who for mere effect have dared to introduce into literature and into art views which make men morbid, tired, unhappy. A time was, quite a little time ago, when men refused these views as unhealthy and almost immoral. The Paternoster looks back to it; but, above all, looks forward to the future time when these views shall be regarded not as unhealthy ones to be avoided by the individual, but as insane ones, intolerable to all.[2]

With unabashed precocity, Belloc set about trying to sign up well-known literary figures to the *Paternoster*'s somewhat draconian anti-decadent stance. He took the liberty of calling unannounced at Wilfrid Scawen Blunt's Sussex home and, finding him away or possibly simply 'unavailable', wrote him a letter requesting an article from him on Egypt. 'I trust I am not presuming too much upon your kindness in hoping you will accede to our request.'[3] By way of adding weight to the request, Belloc assured him that the review already counted Coventry Patmore and George Meredith 'and many others' among its contributors. In fact, according to Marie, who assisted her brother in the launch of the review, the first list of subscribers and contributors also included Cardinal Manning; the Duke of Norfolk; Aubrey de Vere, Irish poet and Catholic convert; F.C. Burnand, the editor of *Punch*; W.T. Stead, editor of the *Pall Mall Gazette*; F.W. Farrar, the clergyman and writer who had been recently appointed chaplain to the House of Commons, and St George Mivart, the famous Catholic biologist.

With such an array of *prominenti* offering their support to the project, it is little wonder that Belloc could write confidently to his mother in September about the *Paternoster*'s prospects. 'We are having a great success – £60 of advertisements already! We are getting 6 guineas a page all round – quite beyond what we expected. Our first number is very strong . . .'[4] The first issue contained an article on India by the Marquess of Ripon, an ex-Viceroy of India and a convert to Catholicism, and an account by the publisher and writer Charles Kegan Paul of his last visit to Henry Parry Liddon before the latter's sudden death at Weston-super-Mare earlier in the year. The issue also contained the last photograph to be taken of Cardinal Newman before his death on 11 August.

The impact of the *Paternoster Review* and the extent of its initial circulation could be gauged from a letter written by Gertrude Bell to Belloc's co-editor, Arthur Pollen, on 28 September.

I saw it (the Paternoster) yesterday on a bookstall at Windermere and its attractive appearance caught my attention even before I had realized that it was the Review. Need I add that I fell upon it at once and found that its inner pages did not belie the promise of its outer? . . .

The man at the bookstall said 'I like the look of this paper. I am sure it will sell. I am very pleased with it myself.'[5]

All was not as well as it seemed, however, and there are hints, in the impatient tone of Belloc's letter to Wilfrid Blunt after the latter had failed to deliver his promised article, of the impending financial crisis that would kill the *Paternoster* in its infancy.

> I am very much disappointed that you should not see your way to giving us your article for our first number, and I feel it all the more when I consider how difficult it is when one is starting to secure that confidence which the established Reviews inspire in their contributors.
>
> I see however that many things might make it unwise of you to publish an article of this importance at any moment but the particular one chosen by yourself for political reasons, and await that moment hoping that when it comes we shall be on a footing firm enough to promise you an audience . . .
>
> . . . it may be a matter of literary interest to you to watch the gradual decline & fall of our magazine . . .[6]

Considering Belloc's brusqueness, it is perhaps surprising that, according to Marie, the friendship between her brother and Blunt actually began from this unpromising correspondence.[7] It would last until Blunt's death more than 30 years later. Interestingly, Belloc concluded his irritable letter to Blunt by requesting that Blunt introduce him to William Morris. 'He is a man for whom I have always had the greatest reverence in his writing, & whose work once all but converted me to approach the Great Beast of Socialism. I should much like to know him.'

The *Paternoster Review* could hardly be said to have set the literary world alight, but there were, nonetheless, one or two notable highlights before its untimely demise after only six issues. The second issue contained a poem, 'The Riddle of Men', by George Meredith, and an article by Barthélèmy Saint-Hilaire. Issue three, the December 1890 edition, contained the first signed contribution by Belloc, a short story entitled 'Bona Mors'. The January 1891 edition contained a review by Cardinal Manning of General William Booth's newly published book *Darkest England*, in which Booth described the work of the Salvation Army in London's East End and elsewhere. 'Let him try his hand, and if he fail let others do better,' wrote Manning. 'Above all it is intolerable to hinder General

Booth in feeding the starving and reclaiming the criminal of this day because in the next generation a normal state of capital and labour may provide employment for posterity. In the meanwhile, must they starve?'

Although Belloc's ill-fated journal may not have set literary England alight, it was quite literally set alight in Turkey, where copies of it were burned publicly in protest at an article in defence of the Armenians. Thus, after a brief blaze of controversy, the *Paternoster Review* burned itself out on the embers of indifference. According to Marie, its demise was 'a bitter blow to Hilaire's pride'.[8]

Throughout the months of the *Paternoster Review*'s brief life, Belloc had continued to correspond with Elodie. She remained confused about her feelings for him and continued to struggle with the idea of entering a convent. Gertrude Atherton, a friend who would later become a well-known novelist, remembered her sitting on the edge of her bed one morning and 'crying into a cup of cocoa'.[9] She wanted, and she did not want, to become a nun. She was praying that Belloc would not come out to California as he had promised, but could not help hoping that he would. Something of her confusion was evident in a distraught letter to Belloc.

> Darling, Do not ask me to be frank with you – it looks so as if you thought I am not. I could not bear to tell you sooner and believe me darling I was not conscious that I put so much sorrow in my letters to you. Don't tell me I'm morbid; I am not. I love you dear and I am so afraid of the future. And I have suffered so much on your account. I am not blind – you see I am an unhappy girl, and I keep putting my misery on you, Honey Bun. If we were only near to each other, there is so much we could say and ink and paper are of so little worth.[10]

Belloc concurred wholeheartedly with the sentiments of the last sentence of this letter and, early in 1891, resolved to rectify the situation by travelling to California to see her. Since, however, both his mother and hers opposed the prospect of their becoming engaged, he knew that he would have to proceed by stealth. On the pretext of wishing to visit his Priestley cousins in Philadelphia, he borrowed 20 pounds from one of his mother's friends and sold everything of value that he owned to pay for his passage to the United States. After he had sailed, Bessie discovered with horror that his prize volumes, including the copy of *The Dream of Gerontius* signed by

Newman, were on sale in an Oxford Street bookshop. She immediately bought them back.

After visiting his Priestley cousins for a few days, Belloc embarked upon his real purpose in coming to America – the quest to reach Elodie in San Francisco. His epic journey to California has become almost legendary, and a myth has emerged that he trekked penniless across the North American continent from east to west, almost exclusively on foot. The source for these romantic embellishments springs largely from Belloc's account of his exploits in *The Contrast*, published 30 years later, and from an account in a letter to his friend George Wyndham that Belloc wrote in February 1910. In the latter, Belloc informed Wyndham that he had made his way on foot 'for lack of a railway ticket along the Denver and Rio Grande':

> through the deserts and threading odd and deep canyons by way of the railway embankment, seeing trains go by with people in them and sleeping out and trudging on next morning and marvelling at the rocks and the new sights and sleeping in unexpected houses and so on, with no end but getting somehow to Denver and selling pictures on the way and wondering about things that don't matter and writing verse in one's head and losing money at cards on the Cimarron and then having none and so limping into Canyon City and then getting money again and walking over the shoulder of Pike's Peak down on to the Florente and landing up at night in a goods wagon – and so on to the end.[11]

This particular letter has been quoted without question by Belloc's biographers, who recount with evident relish how he also gambled his way from saloon to saloon down the Ohio River to Cincinnati, and how 'he set out to tramp his way across the United States of America'.[12] Yet Edward Northcote, grandson of Marie Belloc Lowndes, laments the 'mistake that, when Belloc went to America, he tramped across the United States'.[13] He cites a postcard that Belloc sent to Marie in which he states quite clearly that the journey had been made by train: 'Night and a day, and night and a day to Omaha, Nebraska, and night and a day, and night and a day to California.' Certainly Belloc stopped off in Omaha during his visit to the United States, because he refers to it in *The Path to Rome* as a place where the food was particularly poorly cooked,[14] but he also mentions in the same book 'an old man in a valley called the Curicante in Colorado' who gave him practical advice on path-finding in the local mountains:

I wish I had space to tell all about this old man, who gave me hospitality out there. He was from New England and was lonely, and had brought out at great expense a musical box to cheer him. Of this he was very proud, and though it only played four silly hymn tunes, yet, as he and I listened to it, heavy tears came into his eyes and light tears into mine, because these tunes reminded him of his home. But I have not time to do more than mention him . . .[15]

Clearly such anecdotal evidence proves that Belloc did indeed spend some time trekking through Colorado, as he claimed, yet, equally clearly, he did not 'tramp his way across the United States'. In February 1891, shortly after his arrival in the States, Belloc had written to his mother from Brooklyn to say that he had 'ample money to get to California where I expect your reply'.[16] A few days later he was in Philadelphia and, by 10 March, had reached California. It is possible, therefore, that, as Edward Northcote maintains, he caught the direct train to San Francisco.

Belloc's first letter from California bubbled with enthusiasm. The people drank wine, 'which is necessary to salvation', and were 'healthy in mind, chivalrous and brave'. California was 'made for the future' and would soon have its own 'great artists and poets: and Elodie is here – worth many journeys'.[17]

Within days of his arrival, however, Belloc's bubble had burst upon the rock-like resolve of Mrs Hogan to thwart his amorous intentions. Although Elodie's mother treated him with civility, mindful of the hospitality that her daughters had received at the hands of Madame Belloc during the previous summer, she was determined that Belloc's efforts to woo her daughter would not prevail. Even though Belloc had travelled 6,000 miles to see Elodie, the two would-be lovers were soon reduced to passing notes surreptitiously to each other via Gertrude Atherton. Under such circumstances progress was impossible and Belloc soon realized that Elodie would not openly defy her mother. Reluctantly he left California with no more than a vague promise that Elodie would think his proposal over and send him a reply at a later date. In fact, after he left and as she later confessed to him, Elodie had collapsed with grief at the prospect of losing him. 'I cried myself blind and ill and almost insane.'[18]

Having left California empty-handed and with a head filled with frustrated aspirations and dented dreams, Belloc made his way aimlessly back across the vast expanse of the United States. It was then, it seems, that his tramping really began. More than 30 years later he would describe his trek 'from the Pacific to the crest of the Sierras through Colorado', i.e.

eastward, as one of the 'prodigious walks' of his life.[19] This was the epic journey recalled to George Wyndham when he wrote of having made his way on foot 'for lack of a railway ticket'. He had hurried to Elodie as directly as possible with the 'ample money' he had at his disposal at the start of his quest. He now ambled away from her with no particular goal in mind and with severely diminished resources. From Grand Junction, Colorado, in the midst of the Southern Rocky Mountains, he wrote to his mother of the sheer vastness of the terrain through which he had trudged: 'All the mountains have become confused to me, they are 1,500 miles broad! And between the ranges nothing but deserts of sand. I am earning a little money . . .'[20]

He lost the money again at cards, 'playing against more cunning and older men', and was forced to earn his food and his lodging *en route* by selling sketches of the ranches that he came across. It was presumably in this way that he had befriended the old man with the music box. The haphazard nature of his great trek was conveyed in a letter to Maurice Baring in 1909 in which he romanticized about 'how I saw the Sierra Nevada against the dawn of Easter 1891 . . . how I walked from the green river to Canyon City all across Colorado and drew pictures for Agricultural Men'. Finally, once more penurious, he 'borrowed more money from an unknown man and got to Chicago'.[21]

The return journey from west to east took over a month to complete and resembles in metaphoric microcosm the heroic retreat of Napoleon's army from Moscow, an event that always retained the power to excite Belloc's imagination. His own retreat from the disappointments of California ended at Montclair in New Jersey on 30 April 1891, from whence he learned of the final defeat of his quest.

> My dearest Mother, Elodie's refusal came today. It is very final and definite and I must accept it. I shall in all probability leave this country for England next Wednesday, May 6, getting to London on May 15. You must be a good friend to me, for I have been hit very hard indeed, harder than I thought I could be hit – and you are evidently the best friend I have. I shall want to go to the country when I get back to England. Perhaps you can come with me? I have answered Elodie. Your affectionate son, Hilaire Belloc.[22]

SIX

Soldier and Scholar

B ESSIE BELLOC WAS 'DEEPLY DISTRESSED' by her son's state of mind when he returned to England.[1] Throughout the summer she looked on helplessly as he grieved silently and sullenly. Finally, on 2 October 1891, Bessie decided to intervene. She wrote to Elodie from La Celle Saint Cloud beseeching her to 'cross the Atlantic and come and see me quietly at Slindon'.

> I have already told you more than eight months ago that I only desire to know what is really in your mind; and if you really love my son, you certainly ought not to enter the religious life. Any reasonable priest, indeed any priest, would tell you the same. There is nothing wrong with your love for each other, and I cannot in the least understand the misery which you cause the one to the other. Pray, my dear child, do not waste your life and his, in a struggle of feeling which seems to me quite wrong and useless, and if you do love him, follow the love simply, as God's will, and come over to me.[2]

Elodie's reply has not survived, if in fact she did reply. She certainly did not do as Bessie suggested. Outwardly at least, she appeared as determined to enter the religious life as ever, although her primary motivation for doing so may have had more to do with a desire to honour the wishes and the memory of her mother, who had died suddenly and quite unexpectedly less than two months after Belloc's departure, than with any purely selfless desire to give herself to God in poverty, chastity and obedience.

Belloc responded to his loss of Elodie in much the same way that, four years earlier, he had responded to the failure of his first love for Minna Hope. He ran away to France, this time to volunteer for military service with the French army. Yet the need to escape from the emotional turmoil wrought by Elodie's rejection was coupled with a more complex desire to serve the calling of his nationality. If he wished to remain a French citizen, then military service was compulsory. Added to this practical necessity was his acute sense of military tradition, inherited from the forebears on his father's side, from his short but poignant taste of French militarism at the Collége Stanislas, from the painful and lingering psychological hangover of the French defeat in the Franco-Prussian War and, last but not least, from the enduring influence of Déroulède and the *Ligue des Patriotes*.

Bessie had vigorously opposed the idea that her son should serve in the French army, fearing in the short term that the venture might prove as disastrous as the aborted naval adventure at the Collége Stanislas. In the longer term she feared that French military service would brand her son, for the rest of his life, as a foreigner in the eyes of the English. Belloc would later reflect ruefully that in this she would prove to be correct.

Belloc received his *feuille d'appel* on 9 November and joined the 10th Battery of the 8th Regiment of Artillery at Toul five days later. Toul was only 35 miles south of Metz, the German-occupied town from which Belloc had written to Elodie in August 1890. Like Metz it was in a permanent state of preparation for war and the young recruit must have felt acutely the close proximity of the hated Prussian foe. As a front-line town, Toul had taken on great importance. Its civilian population numbered a mere 7,000 and was swamped by the 16,000-strong garrison. For every adult man in Toul there were at least six soldiers, producing 'a peculiar effect' as Belloc observed in a letter to his mother on 20 November.[3]

The rigours of his basic training failed to exorcise thoughts of Elodie from his mind. '*If anything comes from America*, pray send it on at once,' he wrote on 15 December. 'Do not keep anything back. I have lost here a little photograph which I had kept sixteen months and it gives me great pain.'[4]

In January 1892 he learned of Cardinal Manning's death. 'It has given me a great shock. Of course he was certain to die sooner or later; he was so old and feeble – but I would have liked to see him again before he died. He was always very sympathetic to me.'[5] In honour of the cardinal's memory he wrote some verses 'to the poor' which he hoped would be published in the Oratory School magazine.

For all his sense of duty towards France, Belloc did not relish his time in the French artillery. He was determined from the very outset to obtain the dispensation to which he was entitled as the only son of a widow. This would enable him to be discharged after only 12-months' service instead of the usual three years. He endured rather than enjoyed the soldier's life, although he gained a great deal of pleasure from that part of the training that involved riding. 'We are already riding every kind of horse, without stirrups – jumping and getting on and off at the gallop. They teach the men very thoroughly here.'[6] Above all, the fact that he had become 'by statute a French citizen for a whole year', as he put it to his mother,[7] could not disguise the fact that he was ultimately an Englishman with a French father, not a Frenchman with an English mother. His French, although fluent, was not *au naturel* and he was painfully aware that this marked him as a 'foreigner' in the eyes of his comrades. Never was this more apparent than during the march to Châlons-sur-Marne for manoeuvres in July 1892, when his battery had encamped for the evening in a small village.

> That night I sat at a peasant's table and heard my four stable-companions understanding everything, and evidently in their world and at home, although they were conscripts. This turned me silent, and I sat away from the light, looking at the fire, and drying myself by its logs. As I heard their laughter I remembered Sussex and the woods above Arun, and I felt myself to be in exile.[8]

Perhaps it was on this march that Belloc composed his poem '*En Bivouac*', in which his sense of exile is transfused with the pangs of his exile from Elodie. Addressed to the woman he had not seen for 18 months, every line is haunted by her presence as the poet was haunted by her invisible omnipresence. She comes 'without a human sound', while his comrades lie asleep 'on the firelit ground' all around him, bringing with her his soul. He feels her 'holy hands' signing his forehead with the cross and when he sleeps he sees her 'dim eyes', demanding and mysterious, 'hungry as death' but 'very far'.[9]

As Belloc approached the end of his military service, his cousin René Millet suggested that he should consider becoming an interpreter in the French army. His Anglo-French background would seem to have made him an ideal candidate for such a job, but Belloc was now intent on a return to England. 'As to the interpreter scheme I would not dream of such a life as a permanency,' he wrote to his mother on 15 August. 'My whole ambition is in politics and letters.'[10]

His mother and sister were concerned that he would continue to drift aimlessly following his discharge from the army and, with this fear in mind, Marie set about raising the money to enable him to go to Oxford. Belloc wrote to her excitedly,

As to Oxford, I shall certainly jump at it. I am afraid you have misunderstood my gadding about the world. I have two or three principles which I could not change. I had, in California, what a call is to other men, and what I would have died for! And in my service of France an equally sacred idea which I have kept to and played out to what is practically the end – unless there should be a war. The classics, and the society of my equals, is just what I now most desire.[11]

Having passed the entrance examination in December, mainly on his English essay about poetry, Belloc went up to Balliol College in January 1893. His impact on his peers was both immediate and pronounced, as was recalled by his friend and fellow undergraduate E.C. Bentley, who would later achieve fame as the author of the bestselling detective novel *Trent's Last Case*.

When Hilaire Belloc came to Oxford ... a little older in years and far older in the world's ways than the usual undergraduate, a fresh spirit began to work in the intellectual life of England. His immense personal magnetism, his cascade of ideas, of talk, of fervid oratory, his exuberant and irreverent humour, his love of bodily activity and adventure, carried all before them.[12]

F.Y. Eccles, another contemporary, remembered that he and his friends 'never tired' of asking Belloc to tell them of his experiences in the United States or France. 'He would talk about himself without the slightest trace of boasting; but he talked, as he talked about everything else, with a frankness and a spontaneity, as admirable as they are rare. It was no doubt this marvellous facility of speech which made Hilaire Belloc's reputation at Oxford.' Eccles also recalled Belloc as 'the gayest of companions' who laughed, sang and feasted as vivaciously as he talked. Although he was not interested in team sports, he was 'indefatigable on foot, on horseback, or in the water' and was 'especially keen on sailing and canoeing up the river . . .'[13]

Perhaps the most vibrant evocation of Belloc's irrepressibility at Oxford was given by Edward Thomas in 1906. He recalled standing with a companion at the foot of Boars Hill one afternoon in May when they were disturbed by a high tenor voice lifted on the air:

> 'S'ils tombent, nos jeunes héros,
> La France en produit de nouveaux,
> Contre vous tous prêts à se batter
> Aux armes, citoyens!'

A bicycle swept by, down a steep hill, guided, so far as it was guided at all, by the spirit of the Spring, winged by the south wind, crowned by superb white clouds, and singing that song in a whirl of golden dust. 'That was Belloc,' said my companion, as he lay by the roadside trembling from the shock of that wild career. It was Belloc; and it still is.[14]

The most legendary of all Belloc's physical feats as an undergraduate was his epic walk from Carfax, in the centre of Oxford, to Marble Arch, in the centre of London, which, in the company of fellow undergraduate Anthony Henley, he is said to have achieved in only 11 and a half hours. Not surprisingly, this broke all previous records and almost defies belief. Yet Belloc's grandson, Dom Philip Jebb, certainly remembers Belloc, in old age, boasting about breaking the record.[15]

It was, however, in his skill as an orator at the Oxford Union that Belloc's real claim to fame as an undergraduate resides. His contemporaries appear almost unanimous in their judgement that he was the greatest orator of his generation, outshining speakers as gifted as F.E. Smith and John Simon in Union debates. Basil Mathews described what was presumably Belloc's maiden speech at the Union early in 1893:

> It was one of those rare nights in the Oxford Union when new men are discovered. Simon had denounced the Turk in Thessaly and Smith had held up the Oriental in admiration. Men whispered to each other of the future Gladstone and Dizzy whom Oxford was to give to the nation. No one would be fool enough to speak after such brilliant rhetoric . . . Suddenly a young man rose and walked to the table. He was broad of shoulder and trod the floor confidently. A chin that was almost grim in its young strength was surmounted by a large squarely-built face. Over his forehead and absurdly experienced eyes, dark hair fell stiffly. As he rose, men started up and began to leave the house; at his first sentence they paused and looked at him – and sat down again. By the end of his third sentence, with a few waves of his powerful hands, and a touch of unconscious magnetism and conscious strength, the speeches of J.A. Simon and F.E. Smith were as though they had never been. For twenty minutes the new orator, Mr Hilaire Belloc, who was soon to sit in the seat of Gladstone, Salisbury, Milner, Curzon and Asquith, as President of the Union, held his audience breathless.[16]

According to F.Y. Eccles, Belloc's speeches at the Union 'astonished, then captivated and dazzled his audience':

He spoke with great fluency, without the slightest hesitation and without any blurring of his words ... But above all there was inspiration and there was movement. Towards the end he kindled to his theme, and we were kindled by him. I can still see him, standing upright in the great debating hall. He was of medium height, but powerfully built ... He had a wide forehead and a determined chin ... You wondered whether he was English or French. Those who took him for a Frenchman on the strength of his surname were as surprised as any. The style and the diction were beyond reproach, and nothing in his accent, except a slightly guttural pronunciation of his r's, betrayed his foreign birth. Only an occasional gesture, and a bell-like timbre in his voice at certain moments suggested that he was not of purely English blood.[17]

E.C. Bentley recalled Belloc's 'immense popularity with the Union audience', his 'unstudied and spontaneous' eloquence which 'poured from him' in his 'slightly husky voice'. Echoing the impression of Mathews and Eccles that Belloc exuded physical strength and vigour as he spoke, Bentley recalled his 'sturdy figure, tough looking, high-shouldered ... very unlike an undergraduate; very unlike an intellectual, but with force of mind and character written all over him. Magnetized, we drank in his words.'[18]

Edward Thomas remembered Belloc as 'a stiff, small, heroic figure, with a mouth that might sway armies, a voice as sweet as Helicon, as irresistible and continuous as Niagara, pouring forth praise of the English aristocracy and the Independent Labour Party, to a house that believes or disbelieves, and applauds'.[19] In fact, Thomas's memory was somewhat amiss. Belloc generally attacked the aristocracy during Union debates, from a specifically French Republican stance, and, when the policy of the Independent Labour Party was debated, he opposed it vigorously. 'How could Collectivism work,' he exclaimed, 'without a military despotism? How could it work with the existing attitude of the individual conscience unchanged? In fact, it involves Theft in its inception, and Tyranny in its execution, and for neither is Society yet ready.'[20] Belloc was already cutting through the cant of left and right and countering it with a beguiling combination of radicalism and libertarianism, learned from Cardinal Manning and Pope Leo XIII, that would come to fruition as the creed of distributism many years later.

Possibly the most memorable of all the tributes to Belloc's oratory prowess was paid by his rival at the Union, John Simon. Writing in the Sunday Times more than half a century later, after a notable career in both politics and law which included terms of office as attorney-general, home secretary, foreign secretary, chancellor of the exchequer and lord chancellor, Viscount Simon remembered 'the part played in Union debates by some of my friends' during his years as an undergraduate.

> Hilaire Belloc, then a history scholar of Balliol, was our star performer ... and I agree with Lord Birkenhead that he was 'undoubtedly a great orator'. The full tones of his resonant deep-pitched voice might have come from the throat of his hero, Danton. His wider range and his imaginative outlook, together with the intensity of the feelings to which he gave utterance, made an unforgettable impression.[21]

The impression, though always unforgettable, was not always favourable. A Union debate in October 1893 roused the undergraduate magazine the *Isis* to observe plaintively,

> Mr Belloc, Balliol, who had already taken a fair share in the conversational rhetoric of the debate, spoke as a Roman Catholic, a Frenchman and a Democrat. He abused the aristocracy, of whom he has quite primitive ideas, he abused the Church [of England] and he abused the preceding speaker. He cannot help being eloquent and whatever he says must always be listened to, for it is always interesting and well said. But it is a pity he does not always confine himself to the question at issue.[22]

A year later, in October 1894, Belloc opposed the Bishop of Chester's licensing scheme with a display of rhetorical logic that offered a premonition of the fire and bombast so characteristic of his later writing. Efforts to inhibit the abuse of alcohol through licensing was, Belloc insisted, 'like putting a thermometer in front of the fire to make the weather warmer. Opportunity has little to do with drunkenness. Drunkenness is due to the desire for getting drunk.'[23]

On 24 November 1894 Belloc surpassed himself in the debate on which the choice for the new President of the Oxford Union would largely depend. In spite of its uninspiring subject, the London School Board Election, his performance prompted the *Isis* to praise his forceful eloquence effusively in its following edition: 'A consistent view of almost every subject, based on intelligent and broad principles; an elaboration of forcible and easily comprehended argument; an appropriateness of phraseology adorned by an appositeness of analogy and delivered with an irresistible vehemence of utterance – each of these Mr Belloc has in greater abundance than any other member of the Society.'[24] Evidently most of the *Isis*'s readers agreed with this appraisal, because Belloc was elected to the presidency with 327 votes against 196 for F.R.C. Bruce, the other candidate, succeeding F.E. Smith to the prestigious position that represented the pinnacle of undergraduate achievement at Oxford.

Bessie Belloc travelled to Oxford to hear her son make his inaugural speech and was overwhelmed to be told by two different dons that he was the best speaker the Union had had since Gladstone.[25] 'Hilaire's success at Oxford . . . brought Bessie the first gleams of real happiness that she had enjoyed since our father's death,' wrote Marie Belloc Lowndes.[26]

On 19 January 1895 the *Isis* published a pen portrait of the Union's new President:

> . . . for a time there was a tendency to regard Mr Belloc as a windy rhetorician with one speech, until he proved by happy efforts of humour, and convincing arguments dispassionately searching the most various provinces of politics and debate, that he was equally master of all styles and topics . . .
>
> From Mr Belloc you get a speech different from anything else you will hear in the Union . . . and Mr Belloc, almost alone of Union speakers, makes converts . . .
>
> His heart is so ostentatiously on his sleeve that you suspect that it is large enough for some to be under his waistcoat too. But the freedom of his conversation is admirable; he scintillates with enthusiasm on all things – boats, riding, Shakespeare, running across country, Balliol – and some others in camera.
>
> Among other tastes should be mentioned a liking for – Burgundy, sunshine, tobacco, music, Rabelais, good verse, non-typical Frenchmen, beggars, Irishmen, gas-lamps, pretty stories, Gothic architecture, similes, and all good fellowship: and a hatred for – Oxford tradesmen, the Proctorial system, affectation, prudery, English weather, silence, the German Emperor, modernity, hero-worship . . . Socialists and oligarchs.
>
> There roughly you have the President portrayed. Only one College turns out a school of men whose brains are not turned to muscle, nor their thews to flap-doodle; but even Balliol has seldom before numbered among her trophies such a combination as the familiar figure with the big dark cloak, soft hat, and bludgeon, known to his friends as 'Peter'.

The most flattering allusion to Belloc's triumphs at the Oxford Union appeared in the *Pall Mall Gazette*. Declaring that Belloc had made 'the best speech of the night' during a debate on the motion 'that this House would welcome a European war', the *Gazette* described him as 'the Balliol Demosthenes'.[27] Although the description obviously flattered, it did not entirely deceive. Demosthenes, the greatest of the Greek orators, had lost his father at an early age and his inheritance was subsequently lost by the neglect of his guardians. It is therefore likely that Belloc would have seen an amusing aptness in the comparison.

In June 1895 Belloc sat for his Schools and gained a First Class Honours, but it says much for the heights he had reached as an undergraduate that there was something almost anti-climactic in the culmination of his time at Balliol with the attainment of a First in History. His friend W.R. Titterton would write many years later that Belloc had 'gained high academic honours, and thought nothing of them. What pleased him more was that he became President of the Union.'[28] For all the experience he had already crammed into his 25 years of life – as editor, tramp, soldier and scholar – nothing had given Belloc more satisfaction than the laurel with which he had been crowned as the Balliol Demosthenes.

SEVEN

Survivals and New Arrivals

I N JULY 1895 BELLOC SAT FOR a Prize Fellowship at All Souls College. Following his academic success in gaining a First during the previous month, and in the wake of the praise that had surrounded his election to the presidency of the Oxford Union, he approached the examination basking in an almost nonchalant self-confidence, possibly approaching the blasé. He was, therefore, devastated when he failed to get elected and nurtured a resentment towards the examiners for the rest of his life. He always maintained that he had been rejected for his 'militant Catholicism',[1] a claim that is difficult either to prove or disprove. He was competing with 22 other first-rate scholars, of which only two were elected, so it is perhaps likely that he was simply not chosen on grounds of perceived merit, or its lack. Yet it is interesting to note that the historian H.A.L. Fisher claimed that Belloc injured his chances by a prolonged eulogy of St Louis and that he had annoyed the examiners by placing a statue of the Blessed Virgin on the desk where he was writing.[2] Ultimately, as A.N. Wilson explained, the method by which a Prize Fellow is chosen is 'famously whimsical':

> Each candidate is required to write a number of essays in subjects of his choice, and to show an aptitude for languages. But much, too, depends, on his social demeanour. Each candidate is invited to dinner and assessed; for it is a private society, and the fellows might feel entitled to decide, however clever a man may be, that they do not want him as a member of what was, and is, a rather intellectual gentleman's club.[3]

It seems, therefore, that Belloc was not chosen because he was simply not liked, for whatever reason, by those responsible for making the selection. It is likely, for instance, that his radical political views would have made him suspect to the learned elders of an institution rooted in preserving the status quo, and it is certain that his scathing attacks on the aristocracy would have echoed discordantly around the hallowed halls of enshrined elitism. There was no doubt, too, that anti-Catholic prejudice was still rife at Oxford and that Belloc's faith could well have been held against him. Finally, the examiners would have been aware of his meteoric rise to the presidency of the Union and it is possible that they might have sought to bring the opinionated upstart down to earth. Consequently, and ironically, Belloc's very success might have been the cause of his failure. There are certainly suggestions of this in the memoirs of Sir Charles Osman, one of his examiners, who was surely alluding to Belloc in these acerbically supercilious recollections:

> Far the most interesting kind of examination in which I have ever taken part was the annual competition for the All Souls Fellowships . . . The number of candidates was never very great, and all (with few exceptions) were picked men – there were only a few whose judgement of their own capacity was hopelessly optimistic, and rested on 'Union' oratory, or popularity among their own particular or literary or political clique, won by persistent self-assertion. These candidates gave little trouble when pinned down to the rather searching questions set before them – though I have known one or two who did give the fellows some little annoyance in the smoking-room, where they tried to sparkle, or to demonstrate that they were men of the world or epigrammists.[4]

Throughout his time as an undergraduate, Belloc had continued to correspond with Elodie who, since her mother's death, had been suspended in a state of ambivalence. She still spoke of her desire for the cloister, yet simultaneously wrote impassioned letters to Belloc: '. . . do not you believe but that I have loved you and held to you and believed in you and hoped for you all the time?' she pleaded on New Year's Day 1894.[5] Three months later, on the third anniversary of Belloc's arrival in California, Elodie wrote to him in a spirit of self-reproach for having broken his heart.

> It is three years ago today since you arrived in San Francisco . . . Hilaire, darling, do not think that I forget or can forget. During these long days that have gone by without letters from you . . . I have been so near you, so with you all the time . . . But my heart is so full of memory . . . that I hardly know what to say. Only this – I love you and I hope for you and I pray for you and I remember you. And I care for you so much. I know all those griefs of your dear soul and I love you for them. And also, darling, all these years and all the dark

and all the misery have not touched you where you rest sweet, secure and known in my heart. But I cannot bear to think of all I have caused you to suffer. Do not, for our loves' sake, believe that I have been only selfish . . . I am frightened by so many things and I almost persuade myself that it is for your happiness and final good that I go away. And yet I know you love me – tell me, Honey, – dear friend of my heart, why do I vacillate and change so?[6]

Throughout the following months Belloc was sinking most of his emotional energy into his studies, his undergraduate friends and his brilliant displays at the Oxford Union. As his reputation shone more brightly, it seemed that his feelings for Elodie were dimmed. Elodie's distress at this was evident in a letter written in July 1894.

A few days ago I received a letter from you and in it was the unkindest word you ever said to me . . . You told me that I had no right to speak to you of hope and energy and success and hope in life. Well, I have a right to speak of those things to you. You say I do not love you, that I do not remember you. I only laugh at that. You cannot see me. You cannot be with me now. But you have seen me and you have been with me and if you do not know me now, judge me by your memories of me while we were together . . .[7]

Perhaps it was the growing awareness that her place in Belloc's heart had diminished that prompted Elodie, at last, to try her vocation with the Sisters of Charity. In April 1895, while Belloc was preoccupied with his studies for the impending final examinations, she wrote to inform him of her decision and to effectively put an end to their relationship.

My own and best friend . . . The superior of the American branch of the Sisters of Charity is in San Francisco. I shall probably go to Baltimore with her where I shall go into the Mount Hope Hospital. At least, that is where I am to postulate. Elizabeth begs me to stay a month longer – that would allow me to hear from you again. But I think I shall have gone before a month . . .

I realize now, darling Hilary, that I have done you a grave wrong in asking you to wait . . . In addition to all the pain that I have given you I have no possible right to jeopardize your welfare in the world. I know all that dearest old Hun. So I leave you absolutely free. Let me go. Whistle me down the wind and if things go wrong with me I shall face them as well as I can . . .

Dearest Hun, do not believe that I am as heartless as this reads. I have suffered so much and so have you that it seems rather good to be getting down to certainties – even such certainties as these . . .

God be good to you all the time – better to you than I have been. Lovingly, Elodie.[8]

Elodie entered St Joseph's Central House of the Sisters of Charity at Emmitsburg, Maryland, in October 1895. The 'certainties', however, were not as she had expected. Several weeks later she left the convent, certain, at last, that she had no calling to the religious life. It is likely that she had discussed her lingering love for Belloc with the Vincentian father who was the priest-director to the nuns and postulants at the convent. Perhaps she had shown him Belloc's letters and been told by the priest that the author of such letters was clearly in love with her. Possibly he even advised her to pursue her love for him rather than her thoughts of a vocation with the Sisters of Charity. Whatever the reason, she wrote to Belloc to tell him that she had failed to prove her vocation.

Surprised by the news, Belloc cabled her imperatively, perhaps impatiently, on 24 January 1896 in terms that tersely implied an ultimatum: 'Elodie write plans won't wait.'[9]

She replied on 1 February:

Darling,

Ever since I wrote you at the beginning of the week I have been thinking of our future . . . Things have been so vague and indefinite between us, dearest, that I really know little of your affairs. It may be difficult for you to come to California without incurring debt or jeopardizing your place in Oxford. If either thing be probable, would it be any comfort to you, darling, if I offered to go to England to you, in order to save you the expense and time of so long a trip?

. . . Oh dear heart, God give me the light and strength to be only a help and comfort to you, forever, and in all things . . .

I shall wait anxiously to hear from you. I shall be so glad to see your dear writing again.[10]

Belloc needed no further encouragement. With quixotic rashness he immediately made plans to sail to the United States. The financing of such a trip could have been problematic had his sister not once again provided much needed assistance. She had married Frederic Lowndes, a journalist with *The Times*, at Brompton Oratory on 9 January and the couple had taken over the lease of Bessie's house on Great College Street. This not only helped to pay for the voyage, it enabled Bessie to accompany her son when he sailed to New York in April. The trip was also financed in part by a series of University Extension Lectures that Belloc had been engaged to deliver in Philadelphia, Baltimore and New Orleans. These brought him a weekly income of £20 which, as he wrote contentedly to Marie, 'is not too bad'.[11]

At the beginning of May, Bessie remained in Philadelphia with her relatives while her son travelled to New Orleans. He wrote to her of 'how bi-lingual the town is' and how the hotel in which he was staying was 'pure French'. The country round about was 'all swamp'. 'All night there were zig-zags of light through the woods, coming from fireflies which swarm as gnats do in England.'[12] It is easy to imagine Belloc gazing out at the zig-zags of light and thinking of Elodie as she awaited his arrival in California, hundreds of miles to the west. At last, after years of confused and frustrating procrastination, they were to be together. Elodie had written to him in New York on Good Friday:

> I shall never stop being good to you, beloved. Because love of you means to me to help you and comfort you and do your will, to keep eternally near you ... Won't we have a time 'getting acquainted'? It is quite wonderful to think of. It is like the old Kings and princesses who had to woo by proxy. Our proxy has been the post man alas![13]

Belloc finally arrived in San Francisco in the middle of May. To his distress he discovered that Elodie was dangerously ill, apparently the result of a nervous breakdown brought on by the emotional strains of the previous year. For Belloc, too, the strain had proved too much. On seeing her for the first time in five years, and finding her in such a distressing condition, he 'went to pieces. I suppose every man does that once or twice in his life, but I hope never again to suffer from a collapse of the kind. It is worse than drink – one is afraid of delirium.'[14] This candid confession was made on 28 May to his friend J.S. Phillimore. To his mother, 10 days earlier, he had been somewhat more circumspect about his own collapse, stating simply that he had been 'terribly fatigued with the journey and am just picking up again', but he was considerably less secretive about Elodie's condition.

> Elodie was at death's door while you and I were in New York – they sat up with her ten days and nights. But she is now in full convalescence. I have seen her doctor and had a long talk with him – it seems the breakdown was due to that experiment in Maryland – he says she has an excellent constitution and that as she gets well she will be

stronger than ever. She takes little walks with me every day, and I go to Mass with Elizabeth.[15]

Belloc had not been in the habit of attending Mass daily, but the discipline of daily attendance with Elodie's sister, coupled with his relief and joy at finally being reunited with his love, appears to have honed his faith to a degree of intensity which almost constituted a religious conversion, or at least a reversion to the childlike faith that had been diluted by his worldly successes in Oxford. In his letter to Phillimore he discussed 'the shock of readjustment after all the wreck of these five years' and intimated that the shock had produced a salutary effect.

> God brings a man to knowledge in any one of a thousand paths, but I feel as though I had not understood the Mother Rome until these days. Her immense tradition and power putting into insignificance the ill-working and over-momentum of the hierarchy of the moment. That is the one thing here which is holding and moulding the new chaos they have made. The Mass and the Sacraments are the same: and I tell you it is like home to me to hear the Mumbo-Jumbo of the young priests and the venerable common sense of the old Fathers: and to be able to pray at Our Lady's altar and to find my childhood again.
>
> I had no conception till I got here of what these five years had been. My soul had frozen – a little more and I should have done nothing with my life.[16]

Belloc's letter concluded with a note of gratitude to Phillimore for a gift of $100 which 'will form the most useful of wedding presents', suggesting that Belloc had already proposed to Elodie and that he had been accepted. As soon as he arrived, plans were set in motion for their marriage. The days of doubt were over and he was determined that they should not be separated again, except in death.

The date of their wedding was set for 15 June. In the meantime, while Elodie continued to convalesce, Belloc took a short walking holiday in the Diablo mountains and the San Joaquin valley outside San Francisco. On 7 June he wrote to her from 'a Place called Priests', somewhere beyond the Tuolumne River in the vicinity of what is now the Yosemite National Park. The letter was decorated with a sketch of the mountainous terrain through which he had trekked.

> My darling,
>   I broke myself all up today by walking without knowing how hot it was: I walked right through the middle of the day and began to

feel dead when I got to a house where a thermometer was kept and found it was 98[DEG] in the shade! ... I waited till 4 and then came up the steep hill called Rattlesnake or Priests Hill. It is a deep mountain gorge with this house at the top of it. From a knoll above one has a wonderful view – I went up and saw the sunset and took two sketches which you shall see with your two beautiful eyes.

They are good sketches as are all that I have taken on this trip. One could see Diablo clearly – right over the St Joaquin Valley and over miles and miles of foothill ranges ...

Multitudinous beasts inhabit this wild place and croak and chirrup and sing and hiss in the hot long evening.[17]

Apparently the 'multitudinous beasts' kept him awake, because he wrote on the following evening that he had slept 'hardly at all by reason of the evil man-eating beasts, man & wife for all I know, certainly industriously harmonious in getting their food'. He went on:

I have made twenty-six miles today and am therefore dog-healthy-sleepy tired ... I started at half past four and have gone through – oh! Honey! just such a country. The Hills have changed to mountains steep and immensely high all covered thick with huge high firs ... Up here it is cool for the first time. The right kind of coolness ... the cool of a summer evening.

Earlier in the day he had bathed in a river, 'but (a funny thing) in all that twenty-six miles not a house had any liquor – and how I longed for beer!'[18]

His wanderings over, Hilaire Belloc was married to Elodie Hogan on 15 June 1896 at St John the Baptist Church in Napa. The officiant was Father Maurice D. Slattery, the elderly Irish priest who had celebrated the Requiem Mass for Elodie's mother five years earlier. The witnesses were Elodie's brother and sister, Henry and Elizabeth.[19] 'We have been married in as Catholic a way as could be,' Belloc wrote to his mother on the following day. 'With a Nuptial Mass and Communion and all sorts of rites and benedictions by an old priest called Slattery; he stands in great awe of your having met the Archbishop.'[20]

After a short honeymoon at Geysers in Sonoma County, a few miles from Napa, the newly married couple began their preparations for a return to England. They travelled to the east coast and visited Philadelphia for a few days in early July and then set sail for Europe. Before settling down in Oxford, where a friend had taken rooms for them at 5 Bath Place,

Hilaire and Elodie spent a few days in London. Marie Belloc Lowndes gave an account of her first meeting with her brother and sister-in-law after their return.

> There are certain moments in life that remain immortal. Such a moment was that when, looking out of the middle window of my drawing-room, I saw a hansom cab draw up before the door and my brother and Elodie leap – for leap was the word – out of it.
>
> During her youth my sister-in-law, who was two years younger than myself, attracted admiration and interest in every gathering where she happened to be. During her stay with us, two young men I had regarded as my special friends had been so taken with her as to arouse my brother's jealousy.[21]

Marie is fulsome in her praise for her sister-in-law's beauty, suggesting that Elodie's union with Belloc had hastened her recovery. She had 'a graceful figure ... but her principal beauty was a mass of red-gold hair, and she had the translucent-looking white skin which occasionally accompanies red-gold hair'. Her expressive face 'always betrayed what she was thinking, and she possessed a strong, at times an exuberant, sense of humour'.[22]

Marie gave Elodie a white satin gown as a wedding present, because it was customary for a bride to wear a white dress at dinner parties for the first few months after her marriage, and Marie was anxious 'that Hilaire's wife should appear, in the critical eyes of the Oxford ladies, in what they would regard as the right kind of evening dress'.[23] The stunning impression that Elodie was to make in such circles was recounted to Marie by 'a famous don' who told her that 'when she had suddenly appeared in a room filled with the then staid, no longer young, ladies, who at that time formed the feminine part of Oxford society', she had reminded him of Raphael's beautiful portrait of the Fornarina which hangs in the Louvre, 'though there was in Elodie's countenance a far greater glow'.[24] 'As a matter of fact,' wrote Marie, 'I think Elodie was far better looking than the Fornarina. She looked much younger and for years retained – even after her children were born – a girlish grace and charm of appearance.'[25]

After they settled in Oxford in September 1896, Belloc found regular employment as a lecturer for the University Extension. He also supplemented his income in the intervals between lectures by privately coaching students. Yet his future prospects were somewhat precarious. 'I have a prospect of work lecturing – nothing enormous,' he had written to Phillimore, adding wistfully, 'I wish to God they had given me the All Souls.'[26]

His failure to secure the Fellowship had cast a shadow over the future and, perhaps partly in desperation, he began to hope once more for a literary career. His first volume of poems, *Verses and Sonnets*, had been published in the previous March and was largely ignored by critics and public alike. 'I do not think that this book excited a ripple of attention at the time,' observed Maurice Baring, 'and yet some of the poems in it have lived, and are now found in many anthologies, whereas the verse which at this time was received with a clamour of applause is nearly all of it not only dead, but buried and completely forgotten.'[27]

The volume contained many sonnets inspired by Belloc's long and torrid love affair with Elodie, and possibly remnants of verse conceived during his earlier infatuation with Minna Hope. 'Her Music' employs the play upon 'Elodie' and 'melody' that had first been mentioned by Belloc in his letter from German-occupied Metz on 6 August 1890 when their love was young. Others such as 'Her Faith', 'Her Gift in the Garden' and 'Her Youth' are a testament to the love that had served as his muse throughout the preceding five years. 'The Poor of London', which sits uncomfortably amid the love sonnets, had been written early in 1892 in honour of Cardinal Manning. The sonnet sequence to the 'Twelve Months' owes a transparently obvious debt to the poet's youthful enthusiasm for the Elizabethans, and to Shakespeare specifically, whereas the sonnet 'Love and Honour' betrays shades of Donne and Milton. Such derivativeness is scarcely avoidable in a young poet and is probably beneficial to the development of an authentically individual voice. Certainly there is much in the volume that is suggestive of a promise still to be fulfilled.

It was, however, the next volume of verse, published in November 1996, which heralded the arrival of Belloc as a versifier of renown. *The Bad Child's Book of Beasts*, a volume of cautionary verse for children written by Belloc and illustrated by Basil Blackwood, sold 4,000 copies within the first three months of publication. This particular book, as Robert Speaight perceptively remarked, established 'Belloc's popularity, as distinct from his reputation'.[28]

Belloc was delighted at the book's instant success. 'I was not able to send you a copy of *The Bad Child's Book of Beasts*,' he wrote to his mother on 1 December, 'because the first edition sold out *at once* on my return to Oxford, four days after publication'.[29] A second edition was rushed into print and also sold out in a matter of days. On 13 December he wrote excitedly to his mother that an American edition was being planned, for which he and Basil Blackwood had been paid £30 in advance. Such additional income was most welcome as a supplement to Belloc's meagre earnings as a lecturer, and he was hopeful in early December of being raised to the position of Staff Lecturer in the University Extension, a promotion that would have doubled his salary. Yet, mindful of the lingering disappointment over the All Souls Fellowship, he added somewhat sceptically in a letter to his mother that the promotion was 'unlikely' because 'it would give cause of jealousy to many older men'.[30]

Future prospects of employment were becoming a more urgent cause for concern as Belloc and Elodie looked forward expectantly to starting a family. Their naiveté in sexual matters had evidently caused a degree of frustration in the early months of their marriage and, on at least one occasion, this had boiled over into anger on Belloc's part. 'You must excuse my very cross-ness,' he wrote from Derby on one of his regular lecture trips to the Midlands and the north. 'I am very sorry indeed, sweetheart, but it comes from little physical matters in which we will both grow wiser.'[31]

When Elodie became pregnant in December 1896 it was a symbolic crowning of a love affair that had not only survived but which had finally surmounted all obstacles. It was also the symbolic crowning of a year that had heralded Belloc's arrival on the literary scene. As the new year dawned, husband and wife could look forward expectantly to a new arrival who was the first fruit of their own survival.

EIGHT

Baring and Buchan

H ILAIRE AND ELODIE spent the first three months of 1897 in the United States, where Belloc embarked on a rigorously demanding lecture tour. He gave 100 lectures in 15 towns and cities in New Jersey, Pennsylvania and Delaware, speaking on subjects ranging from the French Revolution to the Crusades. Returning to England in April, Belloc continued to speak occasionally at the Oxford Union. On 6 May he spoke in a debate on the British government's foreign policy in Europe alongside such notable Union orators as F.E. Smith, F.W. Hirst and John Buchan. He outshone them all. The *Isis* declared his speech to be 'considerably greater than any Englishman present' could 'imagine himself capable of delivering'.[1] These appearances further enhanced Belloc's reputation as an orator, ensuring that what became known as 'a Belloc night' at the Union was always very well attended.

The measure of Belloc's influence in Oxford had been exhibited earlier in the year by the publication of *Essays in Liberalism* by Six Oxford Men. The 'Men' in question were Belloc, J.L. Hammond, F.W. Hirst, P.J. Macdonnell, J.S. Phillimore and John Simon. Phillimore and Hirst, in their introduction to the volume, described Belloc as 'the leading spirit' amongst them and they expressed their admiration 'for his kindling eloquence, his liberal enthusiasm and his practical idealism'.[2] The six 'liberals' were not, however, as united as Phillimore's and Hirst's introduction might have implied, and Belloc, far from being a 'leading spirit', was already showing signs of marching stridently in directions that the others would prove reluctant to follow. The underlying tension between the views espoused by Belloc in *Essays in Liberalism* and those expressed by his co-contributors was detected by a reviewer in the *Isis*: 'Mr Belloc is in all his ideas a Frenchman and has never fully appreciated the character of the English people.' Perceptively, the reviewer also noted that the 'liberal' views of the six essayists 'do not correspond to those of any recognized section of the Liberal Party'.[3] Similarly, a review in the *Academy* detected strange discrepancies between Belloc's statement of first principles and the 'Manchesterian economics' of Hirst's essay which followed it. Another critic believed that Hammond's essay sat uncomfortably beside the others because of its apparent drift towards socialism.[4]

If, however, there was no clear cohesion between the various visions of 'Liberalism' put forth by the 'Six Men', Belloc's own essay for the volume, 'The Liberal Tradition', exhibited both a cohesive and a coherent riposte to those liberals who advocated a powerful welfare state. Belloc's essay held aloft an ideal of freedom that was rooted in the economic and political independence of the 'individual possessor and producer of wealth'.[5] Although his essay paid lip service to Liberalism's antecedents, such as Charles James Fox, Richard Cobden and John Bright, Belloc's real inspiration, apart from the social doctrine of the Catholic Church, was the rural radical William Cobbett. Belloc shared Cobbett's view that the 'community' of Old England had been undermined by the emergence of a powerful plutocracy in the wake of the Protestant Reformation. He devoted most of his essay to the question of land reform, emphasizing the need for a substantial yeoman class that would provide the nation with 'a strength and a kind of promised permanence which purely industrial aggregations could never afford'.[6]

Belloc's essay represented an early example of the socio-political creed that would later emerge as distributism. Integral to such a creed was a deeply ingrained aversion to the squalor, ugliness and dehumanizing tendencies of urban industrialism. Thus we find Belloc complaining to his mother on 24 June 1897 that the northern counties had been 'spoilt in every way by the commercial necessities of England'. He was in the midst of a short walking holiday in County Durham and observed that, although the city of Durham itself was 'especially fine' and had 'the finest group of buildings I have seen in England . . . all around it are collieries and dirt'.[7]

Belloc found refuge from the ugliness of the industrial conurbations in the open country that stretched beyond its reach. Walking in the Cheviot Hills on the borders of England and Scotland, he sought solace in the beauties and contours of the landscape. 'I have taken many sketches and hope to take many more before I get to Edinburgh,' he wrote.[8] Here, as in the United States, France and wherever else he travelled, Belloc was invariably accompanied by a sketch-pad. As he ventured out on foot in virgin territory he would draw the array of newly discovered vistas with an eye and a dexterity of line that served as a testimony to his inheritance as the grandson of a famous painter.[9]

Shortly before his trip to the north, Belloc had made the acquaintance of a young man who was destined to be a lifelong friend. Maurice Baring was not an Oxford man, having been educated at Trinity College, Cambridge, but he was staying in the city in the summer of 1897 to be coached in Latin and arithmetic prior to his entry into the Diplomatic Service. Baring knew many of the same undergraduates as Belloc, particularly those of the new Balliol generation, and it was through these mutual acquaintances that the two men first met.

On 31 May 1897 Baring had described Belloc as 'a brilliant orator and conversationalist ... who lives by his wits',[10] presumably after he had witnessed one of Belloc's speeches at the Oxford Union. Yet at their first meeting, in the presence of Basil Blackwood, Belloc had told him that he would 'most certainly go to hell',[11] after which Baring understandably thought it unlikely that they would ever be friends. Nonetheless, he still concluded from 'the first moment I saw him that he was a remarkable man'.[12] Soon, however, Belloc was praising Baring's sonnets, even going so far as to copy one of them in order to attach it to the back of a picture hanging in his room. He also approved of a number of parodies, written by Baring in French, of several French authors. Belloc translated these to the pupils he was coaching before asking them to translate them back into French.

The earliest extant letter sent by Belloc to Baring, dated 5 July 1897, was written in verse.[13] Its tone was both affable and convivial, indicating a warming of their relationship in the weeks following their less than promising first meeting. Thereafter Belloc was a regular guest at the riotous gatherings held in Baring's rooms on King Edward Street.

> People would come in through the window, and siphons would sometimes be hurled across the room; but nobody was ever wounded. The ham would be slapped and butter thrown to the ceiling, where it stuck. Piles of chairs would be placed in a.pinnacle, one on top of the other, over Arthur Stanley, and someone would climb to the top of this airy Babel and drop ink down on him through the seats of the chairs. Songs were sung; port was drunk and thrown about the room. Indeed we had a special brand of port, which was called throwing port, for the purpose ... [T]he evenings would finish in long talks, the endless serious talks of youth, ranging over every topic from Transubstantiation to Toggers, and from the last row with the Junior Dean to Predestination and Free-will. We were all discovering things for each other and opening for each other unguessed-of doors.[14]

Another regular guest at these 'wonderful supper parties' was Donald Tovey, then a music scholar studying under Parry at Balliol, who would play Wagnerian settings of stories he had found in *Punch*, or explain to the assembled revellers how bad, musically, were the *Hymns Ancient and Modern*. Belloc, for his part, 'discoursed on the Jewish Peril, the Catholic Church, the *Chanson de Roland*, Ronsard, and the Pyrenees with indescribable gusto and vehemence'.[15]

During the long summer afternoons and evenings the same group would take a punt and drift downstream 'in tangled backwaters', bathing and diving into the cooling river whenever the fancy took them and passing the idle hours in 'inconsequent conversation'. They read aloud to each other from *Alice in Wonderland*, from a volume of Swinburne, and, surprisingly, from the works of H.G. Wells.[16] Belloc was, in fact, an early admirer of Wells, in stark contrast to his later aversion to all things Wellsian. 'My brother,' wrote Marie Belloc Lowndes, 'was the first person who spoke to me of Wells's work, and he praised him more highly than I ever heard him praise any writer of our day.'[17] Baring described these sojourns in 'the wandering, lazy punt' as the 'best of all' his memories of Oxford,[18] and Belloc, 12 years later, would look back fondly on 'how at Balliol I punted about with you in a punt'.[19] Such were the sun-drenched memories upon which their deep and lasting friendship was launched.

On 23 September 1897, Elodie gave birth to a son. He was named Louis after his paternal grandfather, much to Bessie's delight. 'The Boy is the dearest thing in the universe,' Elodie wrote to Bessie. 'He is amiable and sweet and quiet and sleeps well and we hardly know he is here until food time comes! Then a cry comes from Israel! I am sure he grows every hour and is so well, by God's grace.'[20]

Louis had been born in the family home at 36 Holywell in the heart of Oxford, described by Marie Belloc Lowndes as 'one of the smallest townhouses I have ever seen'.[21] Elodie was now growing restless in Oxford and hoped for a home in the country. During her pregnancy she had been optimistic about the prospects of moving to a more rural setting before the summer was over. 'We are going to have a cottage – a home somewhere,' she had written to Bessie. 'It will be permanent and a home indeed.'[22] The dream did not materialize. Belloc's precarious income showed no immediate signs of improvement, making any move to 'a cottage' too costly to contemplate.

The financial anxieties were alleviated somewhat by the continuing success of 'the Beast Book', as Belloc dubbed *The Bad Child's Book of*

Beasts, which was still 'selling like wild fire'.[23] Not surprisingly, Belloc sought to emulate its success by giving his public, and his publisher, more of the same. *More Beasts (for Worse Children)* was published in November 1897, *The Modern Traveller* appeared in November 1898, and *A Moral Alphabet* in November 1899, all illustrated delightfully by Basil Blackwood. The success of these volumes resulted in Belloc being bracketed as a writer of comic verse and of little else. The *Academy* ranked him as being equal to Lewis Carroll and superior to Edward Lear. A good book of nonsense, it declared, was 'as rare as a visit from the angels'.[24] *The Spectator* devoted a long article to Belloc's comic verse on 26 December 1897, repeating the comparison with Edward Lear and observing that 'books of nonsense' were 'the best cures in the world' for the 'laughter of fools'. The praise, though welcome and no doubt beneficial to sales, missed the vital point that the whimsical wit and cautionary moralizing in Belloc's comic verse was never purely 'nonsense'.

In December 1898, Belloc's publisher Edward Arnold put out a volume of comic verse entitled *Tails with a Twist* by a writer using the pseudonym 'A Belgian Hare'. This was, in fact, Lord Alfred Douglas, who had returned to London only a month earlier following his voluntary exile in the wake of his involvement in the scandals that had led to Oscar Wilde's downfall. Douglas's volume bore remarkable similarities to Belloc's 'Beast Books' – similarities that were made more manifest by the fact that they shared the same publisher. Although Douglas's book enjoyed 'a considerable success',[25] there were inevitable charges of plagiarism. In 1928 Douglas defended himself from such charges with an amazing display of chutzpah in which he implied that Belloc had actually plagiarized *him.*

> I once wrote a book of pure nonsense; it was called *Tails with a Twist,* and achieved great successes, among them the flattering but (to me) not altogether satisfactory one of being very closely imitated by Mr Hilaire Belloc, in a book which he called *The Bad Child's Book of Beasts.* This book actually appeared before *Tails with a Twist,* but most of the rhymes contained in my book had been written at least two years before Mr Belloc's, and were widely known and quoted at Oxford, where Mr Belloc was my contemporary, and in other places.[26]

Belloc was tiring of his increasingly lightweight reputation as the writer of comic verse and began pursuing meatier material. *The Modern Traveller,* with its gibes against British imperialism and stock-market speculators, already hinted that his comic verse was closer to political satire than to populist 'nonsense'. This aspect of the poem was warmly received by Arthur Quiller-Couch in his review of *The Modern Traveller* for the *Speaker*. It was no surprise, he wrote, that a poem which set out to expose '*The Daily Menace*' should have been coolly received in certain quarters of the press. Maurice Baring, writing to Belloc on 15 November 1898, stated that *The Modern Traveller* was 'the wittiest verse that has appeared since Byron's *Vision of Judgement*', adding that 'in this line you can do anything'.[27]

The political dimension was also to the fore in Belloc's study of Danton, his first volume of prose, which was published in March 1899. In the judgement of Robert Speaight, the publication of *Danton* 'proved beyond all cavil that if Belloc had lost a Fellowship England had gained an historian'.[28] Nonetheless, the historian could hardly help but continue to regret the loss of the Fellowship when he pondered his pecuniary position, particularly now that he had another child to support following the birth of his and Elodie's first daughter, Eleanor, on 14 July 1899. 'I am full of work,' he wrote plaintively to a friend a fortnight before Eleanor's birth, but added that it was 'not lucrative'.

> You will be glad to hear that the publishers ask me for many books but sorry to hear that no man can live upon books alone; exactly 30,410 of my books are in the hands of the public and my total earnings therefrom in three years is £500! i.e. £150 to £175 a year.[29]

With the spectre of penury looming alarmingly over the horizon, Belloc decided to apply for the vacant Professorship of History at Glasgow. He had not reckoned, however, on the levels of sectarianism in Scottish academia, and was incensed when he received a letter from the Principal of Glasgow University informing him that his religion would be an absolute bar to election. At first he was minded to stand for election in defiance of such an ultimatum, but was persuaded not to do so by Elodie. Reluctantly he withdrew his application, retreating, as he put it to John Phillimore, 'for the first time in my life'.

> It is very sad . . . I have fits of depression when I consider that there is no future for me, but again I am merry when I consider the folly, wickedness and immense complexity of the world. It is borne in upon me that before I die I shall write a play or poem or novel, for the sense of comedy grows in me daily.[30]

During this troubled period, Belloc continued to make the occasional speech at the Oxford Union. Father H.E.G. Rope remembered him as 'vigorous', 'confident' and 'outspoken' during his appearances at the Union between 1898 and 1900, adding that 'he waved his pencil like a conductor's baton'.[31] He was also a member of the Horace Club, founded in 1898 by John Buchan, Raymond Asquith, H.T. Baker and A.C. Medd, at which, ostensibly, the members would read their own poems but at which, in practice, they often laughed and drank the night away. Apart from Belloc and the Club's founders, other members included Lucian Oldershaw and John Phillimore. Among its honorary members the Horace Club could claim Maurice Baring, Laurence Binyon, F.Y. Eccles and Sir Rennell Rodd.

Belloc's relationship with John Buchan, who had been elected as President of the Oxford Union in November 1898, was particularly close at this time. Their bond of friendship would have been strengthened still further in 1899 when Buchan, like Belloc, was refused a Fellowship at All Souls. 'Most people are very indignant at John Buchan being passed over,' wrote Raymond Asquith, 'he is certainly a much more brilliant man than either of the others . . .'[32] Taffy Boulter, who shared a room with Buchan at 41 High Street, remembered Belloc shouting from the street below: 'Buchan, have you any beer up there? Very well, I'll come up.'[33] Buchan, in union with Belloc, had moved at the Oxford Union that 'the popular literature of today is a sign of national degradation'.[34] Yet, according to Boulter, Buchan was 'not a very good speaker – not anything like as fluent as F.E. Smith or Belloc'.[35]

Belloc certainly read his poems 'The South Country' and 'West Sussex Drinking Song' to the Horace Club, but it is not known to what extent he involved himself with their more vigorous activities. These included, according to Buchan, canoeing as far as they could between dawn and dusk; walking to London or Cambridge in 24 hours; riding across country on a compass course, regardless of back gardens or flooded rivers; sleeping out of doors, and scrambling over Oxford roofs.[36] As a member of the Club's inner sanctum it seems unlikely that the almost obsessively outward-bound Belloc was not an enthusiastic participant in at least some of these exciting expeditions.

In spite of such lively diversions, and the stimulating friendship of the likes of Maurice Baring and John Buchan, Belloc was growing tired of, and disillusioned with, Oxford. Increasingly he was beginning to view the city of dreaming spires as the city of broken dreams. It was time for a fresh start. As the year and the century drew to a close, he made plans to move home – not to a cottage in the country, as Elodie had hoped, but to a house in London.

Baring and Chesterton

O N 18 DECEMBER 1899 Elodie was making plans for her last Christmas in Oxford: 'I am going to give dear little Louis a real Christmas,'
she wrote to Bessie. 'I am getting a tree for him and for a few other little
ones on Sunday; then on Christmas Day I shall light the tree up again
for six or seven of the tiny Nazareth House babies.'[1] Her husband was
not at home as Elodie wrote this letter to her mother-in-law; on Monday,
18 December he was in London checking out their new home. 'All day I
have been laying siege to Cheyne Walk & at the end of the day have got
the key! I am just off now to do all my inspection by candlelight.'[2] He
spent the whole of the following day at the house and, possibly unwisely
considering his uncertain finances, decided that he wanted to acquire the
adjoining property also. 'Prepare yourself for many arguments (chiefly
connected with question of piercing through wall) in favour of taking . . .
extra rooms next door,' he wrote to Elodie. 'I will however discuss this
with you.'[3] The following day he met the 'electric light man' and then
returned to Oxford enthused about the prospect of starting a new life at
104 Cheyne Walk on the Chelsea Embankment, no doubt telling Elodie,
as he would later tell his mother, of the 'wonderful views up and down
the river' that could be seen from the upstairs windows.[4]

Shortly after Hilaire, Elodie and their two small children had moved
in, early in January 1900, Belloc wrote to his mother that they had fixed
up 'a scratch bedroom where we sleep'. His own work was being squeezed
in between 'the intervals of business and buying locks and keys'.[5]

Belloc's 'own work' at this time was centred on the writing of two
books, one on Paris and the other on Robespierre. He was also writing
'a good deal of verse', hoping to get it published in the *Speaker*, which
was now under the editorship of his friend J. L. Hammond.[6]

In early February Belloc travelled to Paris, ostensibly perhaps to gain
material for his book on the city. During his visit he met up with Maurice

Baring who had been living in the French capital as a diplomat since January of the previous year. They visited the Louvre, where Belloc probably took great delight in showing Baring his grandfather's paintings, and the Concert Rouge. They went to Vespers at St Sulpice and to Benediction at Notre Dame. Then, during a tour of the city on the top of an omnibus, Belloc discoursed effusively about Paris in general and Danton in particular. 'Hilaire pointed out to me Danton's house, and Danton's prison, and Danton's café and Danton's *kegelbahn* and Danton's tobacconist. I daresay he didn't know anything about it: but I have the faith that swallows archaeologists.'[7]

Maurice Baring was fluent in the language and thoroughly *au fait* with the culture of France. This was evident not merely from his position in the Diplomatic Service but from the lengthy correspondence he had precipitated in the *Saturday Review* during the previous year in which he had championed the suggestive qualities of the French language. It is interesting, therefore, that Baring should perceive that Belloc was not as French as many of his friends and enemies believed. On the contrary, he was 'very un-French when seen in France. In fact his gallicism is an untrained pose. His Catholicism is a political opinion: he is really brutally agnostic. His gallicism too is a political opinion; it is Anti-Daily Mailism.'[8]

There is much in these words that probes to the very core of both men. Years later, Belloc would reveal in a letter to Baring that he did not believe the French language possessed the suggestive qualities which Baring had championed,[9] and perhaps Baring had already guessed as much by February 1900. Certainly he had regretted encouraging Belloc to join in the correspondence to the *Saturday Review*, believing that he would 'spoil the argument'.[10] Perhaps, in their conversations with French acquaintances during the visit to Paris, Belloc had betrayed a bluntness, and a blindness to nuance, that Baring had detected.

There was, however, much in Baring's assessment that revealed his own inability to judge Belloc's character objectively. His failure to perceive the genuine nature of Belloc's Catholic faith was the result of the bluntness and blindness of his own anti-Catholic prejudices. At this time, Baring felt a great hostility towards what he saw as the oppressive nature of Catholicism in the politics of Italy and France, and there seems little doubt that he was projecting his own prejudices when reaching his jaundiced view of Belloc's faith. Following his own conversion to Catholicism in 1909 he would understand Belloc, both as a man and as a Catholic, very differently.

At first sight he seems to you entirely wrong-headed; at second sight and after due reflection, you think he is impossibly wrong-headed with patches and flashes of sense, and what a pity! . . . and then after years, ten years, fifteen years, it suddenly dawns on you sometime, not that he has always been right but that he has sometimes been right about the very points where you thought him most wrong and most wrong-headed.[11]

Years later, in *Have You Anything to Declare?*, the last book he ever published, Baring would illustrate the futility of his initial efforts to judge the nature of Belloc's faith:

It is utterly futile to write about the Christian faith from the outside. A good example of this is the extremely conscientious novel by Mrs Humphry Ward called *Helbeck of Bannisdale*. It is a study of Catholicism from the outside, and the author has taken scrupulous pains to make it accurate, detailed and exhaustive. The only drawback is that, not being able to see the matter from the inside, she misses the whole point.[12]

In spite of their differences, Belloc's and Baring's friendship was cemented by the time they spent together in Paris. 'I like him immensely and think him full of brilliances and delightful to be with,' Baring wrote to a friend at the time of the visit.[13]

Belloc's *Paris* was published by Edward Arnold in May. 'It is a good, good book, explanatory of the city as is none other,' Belloc would write proudly in a letter to a friend.[14] By and large, the critics agreed with the author's judgement, and the book proved very popular with people crossing to France for the great Paris Exhibition of 1900. Yet, as Belloc had confessed during the previous summer, 'no man can live on books alone'.

His and Elodie's finances looked as frail as ever in the spring of 1900, calling into question the decision to take on the lease of the house in Chelsea and also Belloc's decision, taken several months earlier, to give up lecturing in order to concentrate on literature. In desperation, he contemplated emigrating to California. 'Yes, darling, we must think carefully over the Californian matter,' Elodie wrote to him. She was, however, not very enamoured with the idea. 'If it can be avoided I do not want to bring Louis up as an American . . . Have you thought seriously of being called to the Bar in the Fall, if by hook or by crook we could get the fees?'[15] In the event, neither emigration to the United States nor a call to the Bar would come to the rescue. Instead Belloc would muddle along

precariously, increasingly forced by financial necessity to write not for
love but for money.

Early in April 1900 Belloc attended a political meeting at the studio
of the artist Archie MacGregor in Bedford Park. This had been organized
as a protest against Britain's role in the Boer War, a conflict that was
bringing down the final curtain, somewhat ignominiously, on the reign
of Queen Victoria and which had incurred the ire of a small but vocal
anti-imperialist and pro-Boer minority. In retrospect, this meeting's principal importance is that it seems to have been the first occasion at which
Belloc and G.K. Chesterton were present under the same roof at the
same time. The immediate impact of Belloc's oratory on the 25-year-old
Chesterton was evident in a letter that Chesterton wrote to Frances Blogg,
his fiancée.

> You hate political speeches: therefore you would not have hated
> Belloc's. The moment he began to speak one felt lifted out of the
> stuffy fumes of forty-times repeated arguments into really thoughtful
> and noble and original reflections on history and character. When I
> tell you that he talked about (1) the English aristocracy (2) the effects
> of agricultural depression on their morality (3) his dog (4) the Battle
> of Sadowa (5) the Puritan Revolution in England (6) the luxury of
> the Roman Antonines (7) a particular friend of his who had by an
> infamous job received a political post he was utterly unfit for (8) the
> comic papers of Australia (9) the mortal sins of the Roman Catholic
> Church – you may have some conception of the amount of his space
> that was left for the motion before the house. It lasted for half-an-hour
> and I thought it was five minutes.[16]

Chesterton was clearly bowled over by Belloc's performance, feeling the
force of his words like 'a cavalry charge'. He obviously detected, amid
the medley of themes upon which Belloc had touched, the presence of a
kindred spirit.

According to W.R. Titterton, a friend in later years of both men,
Chesterton had written a letter to 'a mutual friend, a discerning friend',
presumably shortly after the meeting in MacGregor's studio, saying that
he would like to meet Belloc.[17] An element of mystery surrounds the
identity of this mutual friend. From the conflicting reports of Belloc's
and Chesterton's first meeting, it is unclear whether they were introduced
by E.C. Bentley or Lucian Oldershaw. The former had first met Belloc at
the end of 1893 when both men had sat for the Brackenbury history

scholarship. Bentley had found himself sitting opposite Belloc, 'who fell upon each paper and tore it limb from limb with ... startling rapidity'.[18] He was not surprised when Belloc won the scholarship. Lucian Oldershaw had also met Belloc in Oxford, where both men were members of the Horace Club. Oldershaw was now sharing rooms with Belloc's friend J.L. Hammond, editor of the *Speaker*. Bentley and Oldershaw had both been friends with Chesterton since their schooldays together at St Paul's. It is clear, therefore, that either could have been the 'mutual friend' who, in introducing Belloc to Chesterton, would not only be responsible for launching one of the most famous literary friendships of the new century but would also become the catalyst responsible for the cultural-political chimera that George Bernard Shaw would parody as the 'Chesterbelloc'.

Oldershaw claimed the distinction for himself and put its immense importance into perspective: 'I lost Gilbert first when I introduced him to Belloc, next when he married Frances, and finally when he joined the Catholic Church ... I rejoiced, though perhaps with a maternal sadness, at all these fulfilments.'[19]

The most famous account of that fabled first meeting was given by Chesterton in his *Autobiography*. He had arranged to meet Oldershaw in a little French restaurant in Soho, the Mont Blanc in Gerrard Street, one of the 'delightful little dens off Leicester Square, where in those days a man could get a half-bottle of perfectly good red wine for sixpence'.[20] Oldershaw entered,

> followed by a sturdy man with a stiff straw hat of the period tilted over his eyes, which emphasized the peculiar length and strength of his chin. He had a high-shouldered way of wearing a coat so that it looked like a heavy overcoat, and instantly reminded me of the pictures of Napoleon; and, for some vague reason, especially of the pictures of Napoleon on horseback. But his eyes, not without anxiety, had that distant keenness that is seen in the eyes of sailors; and there was something about his walk that has even been compared to a sailor's roll ... He sat down heavily on one of the benches and began to talk at once about some controversy or other ...
>
> As Belloc went on talking, he every now and then volleyed out very provocative parentheses on the subject of religion ... All this amused me very much, but I was already conscious of a curious undercurrent of sympathy with him, which many of those who were similarly amused did not feel ... It was from that dingy little Soho café, as

from a cave of witchcraft, that there emerged the quadruped, the twiformed monster Mr Shaw has nicknamed the Chesterbelloc.[21]

A lesser-known account is given by Chesterton in his introduction to *Hilaire Belloc: The Man and his Work*, in which Belloc is described as arriving with 'his arms and pockets ... stuffed with French Nationalist and French Atheist newspapers':

> When I first met Belloc he remarked to the friend who introduced us that he was in low spirits. His low spirits were and are much more uproarious and enlivening than anybody else's high spirits. He talked into the night, and left behind in it a glowing track of good things ...
> ... What he brought into our dream was his Roman appetite for reality and for reason in action, and when he came to the door there entered with him the smell of danger.[22]

'Reason in action' and the 'smell of danger': in these words Chesterton had unlocked one of the secrets that so attracted him to Belloc. Whereas Chesterton would often live out his imagined desire for danger and his hunger for action through the medium of his art, particularly in fictional fantasies such as *The Man Who Was Thursday*, *The Napoleon of Notting Hill*, *The Ball and the Cross*, *The Flying Inn* and the Father Brown stories, Belloc was a man of action who not only dreamed of the adventure but was himself the adventurer. Chesterton imagined the bravery of battle; Belloc had been a soldier in the French artillery. Chesterton imagined the exhilaration of exploring wild frontiers; Belloc had walked across mountainous terrain in the United States, discovering the 'Wild West' in the 1890s. As Robert Speaight observed, Chesterton's 'imagination was stronger than Belloc's ... But they needed the Attic salt of Belloc's realism; Chesterton's fantasy required Belloc's fact.'[23]

More important still, the 'reason in action' and the 'smell of danger' that attracted Chesterton to Belloc had a metaphysical dimension. Chesterton was grappling uncertainly with religious truths in the abstract while Belloc lived religious truth ritually. He not only professed a faith, he practised it. Titterton believed that the last of these attractions would have a profound influence on Chesterton's subsequent spiritual development.

> Chesterton was already a near-Catholic, brimful of Catholic beliefs, but without a leg to stand on – or rather with nowhere to put those huge legs. And Belloc was firmly planted on a rock. Chesterton was romantic, Belloc was Roman, as romance was once. Since the one man was fixed and the other fluid, it was natural that Belloc should

give the strength of Roman iron to Chesterton's vivid Gothic romance. It was not for many years after this that G.K.C. acknowledged himself a Catholic; but he did then and there in truth become one.[24]

Belloc told Maisie Ward, Chesterton's friend and biographer, that he believed 'the chief thing he had done for Chesterton when they first met was to open his eyes to reality'.[25] Meanwhile Chesterton, with customary humour and humility, once remarked that 'Belloc suggests a classic temple, while I am only a sort of Gothic gargoyle.'[26] Nonetheless, it would be a trifle simplistic – and utterly incorrect – to suggest that Chesterton was little more than a disciple of Belloc. He was much more than that. Yet it would be equally erroneous to underestimate the profound importance to Chesterton of the first meeting with Belloc in the little Soho restaurant sometime during the spring of 1900. The subsequent friendship would be valuable to both men and invaluable to the Catholic Literary Revival in the twentieth century, of which they were at once the instigators and the inspiration. 'More than any other man, Belloc made the English-speaking Catholic world in which all of us live,' wrote the Catholic publisher Frank Sheed in 1953. 'There was Chesterton, of course, but then Belloc had so much to do with the making of Chesterton and Chesterton not much with the making of Belloc.'[27]

TEN

Romeward Bound

S HORTLY AFTER THE MOVE TO LONDON, Elodie received the devastating news that her sister Elizabeth had died in childbirth. 'Elizabeth's death was a fearful blow to Elodie,' Marie Belloc Lowndes remembered. It was 'the one great sorrow of her life'.[1] Elodie wrote to Bessie:

> For twenty years and more Elizabeth and I have been close friends, so near to each other. We always understood everything. I feel as if I had been suddenly deprived of one of the powers of my soul. It has made me ill and miserable. I take refuge in constant prayers for her for I know she is somewhere watching and knowing. That strong heroic soul that left her body in doing her duty has not gone out. What a blessing it is to be even the worst and humblest child of the Church.[2]

Elodie was herself pregnant when she heard of her sister's death and, on 17 November 1900, she gave birth to her second daughter. She was baptized Elizabeth.

As the year drew to a close, Belloc was still struggling to finish his book on Robespierre, a volume that would finally be published in November of the following year. Yet even as he worked on this book, the inspiration for a new one was germinating. On New Year's Eve he wrote excitedly to a friend:

> I am going to walk on a kind of pilgrimage from Toul (which was my old garrison town) to Rome next Easter and on my way I shall write down whatever occurs to me to write – what proportion will deal with landscape, what with architecture, what with people and what with general subjects I can't yet tell – it will be as the spirit moves me . . .[3]

On the following day, Belloc wrote optimistically to another friend, E.S.P. Haynes, about the birth of a new century.

> You are rather gloomy about what you facetiously term the New Century. Last night there was a midnight Mass and I had Communion ... but then there was a similar Mass last year, so I suppose 1900 is without question and infallibly a kind of Buffer Year. God bless you! You take things too hard, especially great whacking things like centuries ...
>
> If any damn fool Editors had asked me what the greatest perils of the century were likely to be I should have answered that their own damn fool habit of asking such questions was the greatest annoyance.
>
> Farewell. If by any chance you meet a man who thinks that the century whose first year is now so happily and gloriously concluded ... will see the end of the Church, the Republic, the habit of drinking in Inns or the human relaxation of laughter, tell him from me that he is wrong.[4]

Belloc's flippancy aside, the sense that the new century was ringing out the old and heralding the dawn of a new epoch was heightened three weeks later, on 22 January 1901, with the death of Queen Victoria. Her reign, which had lasted for 63 years, had seemed to symbolize the imperial dignity of Britain's position in the world. Even those with Republican sympathies or those not normally tempted to jingoism were affected profoundly by news of her death. Belloc was no exception. His obituary of the Queen, published in the *Speaker*, was considered by Chesterton to be the best of all the dozens of obituaries that peppered the press. Belloc wrote:

> It is a commonplace to call her good, and it is a little the fashion to be weary of the private virtues or to leave them unmentioned. But that commonplace has been of inestimable value to our nation and that wearying subject has appealed so forcibly to the world that we have received through her in these last days, a little to our astonishment and very much to our comfort, a universal benediction.[5]

It was, however, of another and older Empire, and another and greater benediction, that Belloc was thinking as he began to make plans for his epic walk to Rome. Poverty precluded any prospect of embarking on his journey in the manner of taking the Grand Tour, even assuming that he would have wished for such luxury, and dictated that he would have to forgo such 'necessities' as motorized transport, comfortable lodgings and a gourmet's taste for food and drink. He would, in fact, be forced to tramp in the manner of a beggar as he had done in Colorado 10 years earlier. Yet it would be wrong to assume that such a prospect filled him with dread. On the contrary, he relished the challenge. He was undertaking the trek not as a tourist but as a pilgrim and, as he made clear in an essay entitled 'The Idea of a Pilgrimage', published five years later, a pilgrimage 'must not be untroublesome'.

> It would be a contradiction of pilgrimage to seek to make the journey short and vapid, merely consuming the mind for nothing, as is our modern habit . . . That is not the spirit of pilgrimage at all. The pilgrim is humble and devout, and human, and charitable, and ready to smile and admire; therefore he should comprehend the whole of his way, the people in it, and the hills and the clouds, and the habits of the various cities. And as to the method of doing this, we may go bicycling (though that is a little flurried) or driving (though that is luxurious and dangerous, because it brings us constantly against servants and flattery); but the best way of all is on foot, where one is a man like any other man, with the sky above one, and the road beneath, and the world on every side, and time to see all.[6]

Belloc's impulsive plan to drop everything in order to tramp across Europe, leaving behind a wife and three young children, brought a degree of opposition from his mother. Belloc was unmoved. He agreed that he could not afford to neglect his journalistic commitments, particularly the 'enormous amount of work' he was currently doing for the *Daily News* which sometimes earned him £14 a week, but he insisted that there was 'nothing permanent' in such work. 'There is more of a future in good literature for me . . . than there can be in journalism. Moreover, my literary work raises my journalistic prices immensely.'[7]

Finances were so stretched at this time that, according to his great-nephew Edward Northcote, Belloc had to beg his sister for money to help with the costs of his pilgrimage.[8] Undeterred by all objections and obstacles, pecuniary or parental, he set off for Paris in early June 1901, from whence he proceeded by train to Toul. The following day being the Feast of Corpus Christi, Belloc went to morning Mass and spent the remainder of the day renewing his acquaintance with the town in which he had done his military service. In the evening he started to walk up the valley of the Moselle. His 'path to Rome' had begun.

The spirit in which he embarked on the journey was epitomized in the opening pages of *The Path to Rome*, the book that was destined to make his pilgrimage immortal.

> One day as I was wandering over the world I came upon the valley where I was born, and stopping there a moment ... what should I note (after so many years) but the old tumble-down and gaping church ... all scraped, white, rebuilt, noble and new, as though it had been finished yesterday ... I entered, and there saw that all within was as new, accurate, and excellent as the outer part; and this pleased me as much as though a fortune had been left to us all; for one's native place is the shell of one's soul, and one's church is the kernel of that nut.
>
> Moreover, saying my prayers there, I noticed behind the high altar a statue of Our Lady, so extraordinary and so different from all I had ever seen before, so much the spirit of my valley, that I was quite taken out of myself and vowed a vow there to go to Rome on Pilgrimage and see all Europe which the Christian Faith has saved ...[9]

As Belloc wended his way southwards towards the Swiss border, he worried about his family's finances. He wrote to Elodie, who was becoming alarmed at their lack of funds, to reassure her that he was due 65 pounds for delivery of the manuscript of Robespierre, which he had finally completed in Paris on the day before setting off for Toul. He was also owed seven guineas from the *Daily News*, and 12 pounds 10 shillings from the London University Extension for whom he was now lecturing. Such was the precarious nature of Elodie's position that she could not cash a cheque until this money was received, nor could she send the five pounds that Belloc would need by the time he reached Milan.

Mindful of the scarcity of resources, Belloc travelled as cheaply as possible, rarely paying more than a franc for his night's lodging. At the small Swiss town of Brienz, however, after he had walked about 270 miles, he enjoyed the extravagance of 'a magnificent great meal' of six courses, with cognac, vermouth and a cigar, which cost him the princely sum of two shillings and 11 pence.[10] Thus fortified, he began the long, arduous ascent of the Alps. On 15 June he reached the top of the Grimsel Pass where he huddled against the freezing wind as the sleet fell relentlessly. It was his and Elodie's fifth wedding anniversary, and it is hard to imagine that he did not wish he had remained safely at home with her and the children as he trudged doggedly through the snow. By the time he emerged on the south side of the Alps at Como, he was so fatigued that he was forced to take the train for the final few miles into Milan. It was from here on 18 June, clearly relieved to have found the refuge and comforts of the city, that Belloc recounted the hardships of his Alpine adventure in a letter home to Elodie.

> I have all your letters & the five pounds which is an enormous relief. I wasted two days trying to force the Alps without going round one of the regular passes but it was no good. There was a terrific snowstorm & I nearly perished with cold. The guide refused to go on & I had to take the road again. The St Gotthard of all vulgar and traditional routes. This waste of time resulted in waste of money too & at Airolo at the bottom of the St Gotthard I found I had but f12.50 left! And Milan more than 80 miles away! I made a terrific effort, marched to some miles past Lugano in one day; lunched at Como this morning & got in here with exactly four pence; it was a tight squeeze.
>
> It is . . . bitterly cold. I could sleep out in the woods in France but here in Lombardy it is impossible. I tried it last night & found it far too cold – but I got a bed at an Inn that only cost sixpence!
>
> I have not yet seen a map so as to know where I shall pass in Tuscany, but when I do get a map I will wire to you where to post. I am tired and shall rest here the best part of a day. I have seen the Cathedral which I think magnificent. It is astonishing how bad the photographs make it seem! But the best thing I have yet seen is the Cathedral at Como. That is quite marvellous.[11]

Concerns over money continued to dog his steps and he was disappointed to learn from Elodie that the 65 pounds had not been forthcoming from the publisher for the delivery of his book on Robespierre. 'I finished the book specially to get the money,' he wrote plaintively.[12] There was also more than a hint of economy in the manner in which he almost apologized to Elodie for spending four francs on a meal: 'As I have been living like a Pig for two days on Bread & Sausage I went to an Hotel tonight & paid 4 fr for a perfectly *filthy* dinner.'[13]

Having acquired a map and planned his route, he informed Elodie that he would collect his next mail from her at Siena. Setting off south-wards once again, he was singularly unimpressed with the unseasonably cold conditions and with the dreariness of the Lombard Plain with its 'wet rice growing out of stagnant water'.[14] At Piacenza, cold and weary, he complained that he would 'give sixpence for a fire'.[15] It was not until he reached Fornovo di Taro, a few miles south-west of Parma, that his spirits warmed with the weather.

I am now at Fornovo in the first hills of the Apennines. It is rather warmer than yesterday and less chance of rain. I crossed the river Tari [sic] with great difficulty as it is in flood. I had a man to show me the ford, but it was up to my waist & more & a very strong current ... It is a wide valley, nearly a mile, through which in dry weather goes a small trickle of water but now there are several deep streams ... after all this rain ... The river valley points straight at the Alps & one sees them on the horizon like a very sharp high cloud that does not change.[16]

In *The Path to Rome* Belloc recounted with more than a hint of exaggeration that the current of the Taro had 'rushed and foamed past me, coming nearly to my neck'.[17] By contrast, his vision of the Alps corresponded pretty closely to the impression conveyed at the time to Elodie: 'There were sharp white clouds on the far northern horizon, low down above the uncertain edge of the world. I looked again and found they did not move. Then I knew they were the Alps.'[18]

By way of familiarizing Elodie with the landscape in which he was walking, he told her that the countryside south of Parma reminded him of 'the stony flats under Diablo' in her native California where he had walked in the days before their wedding.[19] After he had climbed out of the valley and into the mountains he trekked for three days along the ridge of the Apennines, heading south towards Lucca.

I am at the very top of the Apennines in a great glade of chestnut trees, having just climbed up the last wall that separates the Adriatic from the Mediterranean. For the last three days there has been no road but only mule paths and (what is very irritating) no bridges over the rivers! I have had to wade through 5 and it is a long job as one has to poke about with one's stick for a ford. The fords are about three or four foot deep. The paths are very deceitful & it takes a long time to find one's way.[20]

By now the weather had changed and the days were hot. Having learned his lesson the hard way five years earlier in California, Belloc did not attempt to walk when the sun was at its hottest, resting between the hours of ten and four. Descending at last, he stayed at an inn halfway down the mountain, somewhere north of Bagni di Lucca. 'I am at a little inn where there is a young priest and a lot of people on a terrace under a vine. It is delightful ...'[21] The letter concludes with the first suggestions of homesickness. 'God bless you my darling little wife. I am hardly myself after being so long away from my kind & good wife. I hope to have lots of news from you at Siena.'

At Bagni di Lucca he decided to make a detour through Lucca to the south-west rather than heading due south to Pescia as he had originally planned. 'It is much easier as there is a plain but it is about 5 miles out of my way.'[22] In Lucca he visited the Duomo di San Martino, sending to Elodie a picture postcard of the tomb of Ilaria del Carreto by Jacopo della Quercia, which is situated in the cathedral's north transept. Scrawled on the top left corner of the photograph, Belloc had written simply: 'Now at *Lucca* all well. I send you this from Lucca for its beauty.'[23]

As the weather got warmer, and the walker got wearier, the temptation to look for short cuts grew stronger. 'Now & then I have taken advantage of the train in the heat. 10 miles to Lucca & another 10 to this place but it does not break my walk.'[24] 'This place' was Siena, which Belloc thought was 'wonderful'. He went to Mass in 'a funny kind of chapel behind the Cathedral' and began to look forward expectantly to the impending completion of his pilgrimage. 'I am just 100 miles from Rome as the crow flies or (say) 130 by road. I walk in the morning & evening & rest in the day.'[25]

Belloc's letter from Siena is most interesting for its discourse on politics and the Church, not least because it suggests that his opinions were not as many perceived them to be.

People are very silly to say that the Church is different in different countries. It is just the same. But Italy does not [vanish/vanquish?] me as it does most Englishmen. It has been dead. I think it is rising now & I am very glad to see all their democratic movement – though for a generation or so it is bound to be anti-clerical. But Italy has been dead & I have no great passion for dead and putrefying things. Italy will depend upon France. If the French are wise, as I think they are, & carefully avoid war (as England did for seventy years) they will lead Europe & all the Latin race will grow up in their shadow. I read the papers with the greatest interest. I do not think it is wise to exaggerate the power of the Freemasons or the Jews. The Priests certainly exaggerate it.[26]

Possibly the key to understanding the enigmatic politics that underpin these peripatetic ramblings is to be found in a few lines that Belloc inscribed in his own copy of *The Path to Rome* some years later, probably in 1908: 'When you have reconciled these two things – I mean the high stoicism of the Republic and the humility of the Church (for they can co-exist) then you will have the perfect state.'[27]

From Acquapendente, 15 miles to the west of Orvieto, Belloc wrote the briefest of notes to Elodie. 'I am 60 miles from the Capital of the World. It is hot & I walk at night. The country is all dried up.'[28] His words conveyed nothing of the romantic tale recounted with mischievous relish in *The Path to Rome*.

> I was in some despair at the sight of that valley, which had to be crossed before I could reach the town of Acquapendente, or Hanging-water, which I knew to lie somewhere on the hills beyond. The sun was conquering me, and I was looking hopelessly for a place to sleep, when a cart drawn by two oxen at about one mile an hour came creaking by. The driver was asleep, his head on the shady side. The devil tempted me, and without one struggle against temptation, nay with cynical and congratulatory feelings, I jumped up behind, and putting my head also on the shady side (there were soft sacks for a bed) I very soon was pleasantly asleep.
>
> We lay side by side for hour after hour, and the day rose on to noon; the sun beat upon our feet, but our heads were in the shade and we slept heavily a good and honest sleep ... And the heat grew, and sleep came out of that hot sun more surely than it does out of the night air in the north.[29]

At long last, after 22 exhausting days, Belloc arrived in Rome on 29 June. He was just in time to hear Mass on the Feast of Saints Peter and Paul. His first impressions of the city were mixed. The buildings and monuments were smaller than he had imagined and he was decidedly unimpressed with the quality of the stone out of which most of the monuments were built. 'It seemed to me almost squalid. I know why this was. I had seen too many photographs and drawings which left the material to my imagination, and I imagined everything to be of marble and to shine.'[30] The Tiber was also a disappointment. 'I was astonished that it seemed to be made of mud. I had expected, I know not why, a stream clear because it was famous.'[31] The legend of the Seven Hills also evaporated under the cold gaze of reality. 'I could hardly distinguish any hills in the city, let alone seven: and the Capitol gave me no impression of height or of steepness.'[32] On the other hand, he was greatly impressed by St Paul's Outside the Walls, declaring that it proved 'the Italians alone of modern men can make a modern thing as nobly as their fathers did'. He also found the quality of the choral music in the churches 'most astounding

. . . almost supernatural', and was surprised that, amid so much 'building and statuary and ornament, so little was bad' and that 'one came upon so little that shocked a reasonable taste'.[33]

Most impressive of all that he saw in Rome was St Peter's itself. He was awe-struck by the sheer scale of the Basilica, rendered dumb by the beauty of the mosaics, and 'moved as by a vision when I saw that splendid bronze recumbent figure in the Chapel of the Blessed Sacrament . . . where the Middle Ages and the Renaissance meet'. He was also 'puzzled to come round the corner of a pillar and to see the memorial and the tablet to the Stuart kings'.

> It takes a young man a long time to get rid of the falsehoods he has been taught as I had been taught history at Oxford (if teaching it may be called). I could not yet conceive of the rightful kings of England, in their exile, as being what they were. From that first glimpse of that small memorial I began to recover a right perspective.[34]

Belloc's greatest wish upon reaching Rome was to meet the ageing Pope Leo XIII, then in his ninety-first year. Leo XIII was one of Belloc's heroes. His encyclical *Rerum Novarum*, published in 1891, had shaped many of Belloc's own views on politics and the economy; the Pope's action, three years later, to constrain the French clergy and monarchists to accept the Republic would have found in Belloc's Catholic republicanism an assenting voice; the encyclical of 1896 pronouncing Anglican orders invalid would have been similarly well received, as would have been the Pope's condemnation of the heresy of Americanism, the new Modernism that believed that the Church, at least in its external life, should move with the times. On the last of these, Belloc would have agreed with Chesterton's famous maxim that what was needed was not a Church that moved with the world but a Church that would move the world.

From the beginning, Belloc's efforts to obtain an audience with the Pope were fraught with difficulty. Writing to Elodie, he explained that he had planned to leave Rome on 1 July, only two days after his arrival, but he had been told that the Pope could not see him until 6 July. He resolved to remain in Rome until the audience.

> How as everyone has been telling me that it is impossible to see the Pope at all now, I jumped at this chance. Of course a week is a loss of quite ten pounds & it makes it a long time to be away from England but on the other hand it would be a great pity to miss such a unique

opportunity in one's life. So after some hesitation I determined to remain.[35]

Deeply disappointed, he wrote to Elodie on 7 July informing her that an error had ruined his hopes of seeing the Pope. 'By a most unfortunate & unbusinesslike piece of folly on the part of the Vatican officials the man sent to tell me to come at 5 yesterday never delivered his message! I went again today and they said they could not let me see the Pope again for 10 days so it is impossible.' Clearly both angry and frustrated, he complained that 'the same thing happened to a French republican deputy who failed to get an audience on the day that *4 Protestant American tourists* were taken to the Pope'.[36] The depth of his disappointment can be gauged by the fact that he could still write with wistful regret 33 years later that 'Leo XIII had sent for me but some ass who got the message delivered it too late ... Thus I missed the greatest of Popes since the Reformation.'[37]

Regrets aside, Belloc's two primary goals as he set out to walk to Rome were both achieved. Physically and spiritually, he had made his pilgrimage and had fulfilled his vow. Artistically, he would produce the 'good literature' which had been his purpose, and his defence against his mother's objections to him undertaking the adventure in the first place. 'This *Path to Rome* is a jolly book to write. No research, no bother, no style, no anything. I just write straight ahead as fast as I can and stick in all that comes into my head.'[38] The pilgrimage produced poetry as well as prose, inspiring the dash and dare of 'The End of the Road', arguably the finest of all his verse. Furthermore, according to Dom Philip Jebb, former abbot of Downside and Belloc's grandson, the passages about the Alps in *The Path to Rome* mark its author as a genuine mystic.[39]

The Path to Rome, published in April 1902, would eventually sell more than 100,000 copies, and is still reprinted regularly to this day. Something of its spirit, and perhaps part of the secret of its success, was captured by Chesterton in a review he wrote for *The World* in which Belloc's rumbustious *joi de vivre* is contrasted with the fashionable artificiality of the Decadents:

> *The Path to Rome* is the product of the actual and genuine buoyancy and thoughtlessness of a rich intellect ... The dandies in *The Green Carnation* stand on their heads for the same reason that the dandies in Bond Street stand on their feet – because it is the thing that is done; but they do it with the same expression of fixed despair on

their faces, the expression of fixed despair which you will find everywhere and always on the faces of frivolous people and men of pleasure.
He will be a lucky man who can escape out of that world of freezing
folly into the flaming and reverberating folly of *The Path to Rome*.[40]

Many other critics were almost as fulsome in their praise as Chesterton.
Reviewers in periodicals as diverse as the *Athenaeum*, the *Literary World*,
the *Daily Chronicle*, the *Manchester Guardian* and the *New York Times*
queued up to salute the exciting new author, comparing his literary credentials to writers as rare and distinguished as Burton, Butler, Cobbett,
Heine, Rabelais, Sterne, Stevenson and Walton. Perhaps, however, nobody
has summed up the importance of the classic work inspired by Belloc's
classic walk better than his friend, admirer and biographer, Robert
Speaight.

> More than any other book he ever wrote, *The Path to Rome* made
> Belloc's name; more than any other, it has been lovingly thumbed
> and pondered. It was a new kind of book, just as Belloc was a new
> kind of man. It gave a vital personality, rich and complex, bracing
> and abundant, to the tired Edwardian world. Above all, it brought
> back the sense of Europe, physical and spiritual, into English letters.
> Vividly and personally experienced, the centuries returned.[41]

There is evidence that Belloc himself believed that *The Path to Rome*
represented not merely one of his finest books but possibly the summit
of all his achievement. Inscribed in his own personal copy of the book,
dated 29 May 1904, two years after its publication, are the words: 'I wrote
this book for the glory of God.' Four years later, on the Feast of the
Epiphany, he inscribed in the same volume the final wistful lines of a
Ballade, the first part of which was presumably never written:

> Alas! I never shall so write again!
> *Envoi*
> Prince, bow yourself to God and bow to Time,
> Which is God's servant for the use of men,
> To bend them to his purpose sublime.
> Alas! I never shall so write again.[42]

ELEVEN

The South Country

I N MAY 1901 'The South Country' and 'West Sussex Drinking Song', two of Belloc's verses praising the corner of England that was closest to his heart, were published in *The Book of the Horace Club*. Other contributors to the volume included Raymond Asquith, Laurence Binyon, John Buchan, J.S. Phillimore and Owen Seaman. Even in such illustrious company Belloc's verses shone forth confidently. 'The South Country' eulogized 'the great hills' of Sussex with a melancholy passion that offered a foretaste of later laments such as 'Ha'nacker Mill', whereas 'West Sussex Drinking Song', with its self-proclaimed 'rousing chorus' and its celebration of the 'good Beer at Haslemere' and the 'good brew in Amberley too', imbibed a different spirit entirely, at least on the babbling surface. There was, however, a paradoxical connection between the nostalgic reveries of the former poem and the rumbustious revelry of the latter. In their differing moods and modes of expression, both poems were a celebration of that 'laughter and the love of friends' which offered consolation to the melancholy spirit. 'I loved you for your sad face,' Elodie had told Belloc before they were married,[1] and this inner sadness is visible in much of his verse, either candidly confessed as in 'The South Country', or carelessly concealed as in the 'Drinking Song', in which the poet's sad eyes are laughing.

In the summer of 1901 Belloc, together with his friend Arthur Stanley, acquired the *Nona*, a nine-ton cutter. During the years ahead, in the company of friends who shared his passion for sailing, he would often take refuge in the *Nona*, gaining the same solace from the rolling waves of the sea as he gained from the rolling hills of Sussex. In April 1902, the month in which *The Path to Rome* was published, he was granted a certificate of naturalization as a British citizen, further proof, if proof were needed, that he was primarily an Englishman with a French father, not a Frenchman with an English mother. Yet, as though to emphasize the French dimension, Belloc spent a large part of the same month in Paris mixing with the students of the Sorbonne and drinking with workmen in the Rue Mouffletard, just outside the university. He talked politics and was heartened to discover that the younger generation were looking for 'a Socialism that may be brotherly and French – not Collectivism'.[2]

In June and July the whole family left Chelsea for the little farm of Gossmarks[3] at the south end of Ashurst Common. Belloc had rented rooms at the farm so that he and Elodie, who was heavily pregnant with Hilary, their fourth child, could rest in the peaceful surroundings of their beloved Sussex. Eleanor was not quite three at the time, but she retained vivid memories of the long family holiday. In particular, she recalled her 18-month-old sister's lucky escape from being crushed by a sewing machine that had been perched precariously on a table in the garden. 'Nannie was making clothes for us in the garden under the apple trees – Louis and I were fighting each other as usual and Elizabeth was tottering around near the insecure sewing table when, with a heave-ho, down it came with a dull thud on the grass. Her baby sobs and cries were only from fear, for she was uninjured.'[4] Eleanor also recalled of this holiday that it was the first time she had heard a cuckoo and the first time she had seen her father riding a bicycle.

When he wasn't returning to London at weekends to attend social gatherings such as a Balliol dinner and a 'literary celebration' at the Fisher-Unwins,[5] Belloc seems to have spent much of the holiday exploring the Adur valley on his bicycle. He also took the opportunity to renew his friendship with Wilfrid Scawen Blunt.

> May I not make your acquaintance again? It is easy for me to come the short distance between my cottage & Crabbet Park. It is about seventeen miles – an hour a half [sic] of good road. I should very much like to call because you have encouraged me in praising my book. I am quite sure that when one is beginning praise helps to make good work, I do not know how it is later or when, or if, one succeeds. I suppose praise then becomes mechanical and bad.[6]

On 29 October 1902, according to his own account in *The Four Men*, Belloc was 'sitting in the "George" at Robertsbridge, drinking that port of theirs and staring at the fire',[7] when he was overcome with a nostalgic desire to see again the Arun valley, on the other side of Sussex, where he had spent so many happy days in his childhood. It was then that he resolved to walk the length of Sussex, from east to west, in homage to the soil of the South Country. It is, however, unclear whether he actually walked the 75 miles from Robertsbridge on the Kent-Sussex border to the borders of Hampshire between 30 October and 2 November, as he claimed in *The Four Men*, or whether he undertook the journey some years later.

The book was not published until 1912 and when he began work on it, possibly as early as 1907, he envisaged calling it 'The County of Sussex'. In 1909 he told Maurice Baring that it would describe 'myself and three other characters walking through the county: the other characters are really supernatural beings, a poet, a sailor and Grizzlebeard himself: they only turn out to be supernatural beings when we get to the town of Liss, which is just over the Hampshire border'.[8] Since he embellished his journey with imaginary characters it does not seem fanciful that he also invented the dates on which the journey was made. Indeed, it is possible, perhaps probable, that the journey itself was a figment of the writer's imagination. It is clear that he knew almost every inch of the way and had evidently walked most of the route at various times, even if he had never walked the whole route at one time. Whatever the facts of the matter, the truth is that Belloc, in writing *The Four Men*, provided a metaphysical path through Sussex to accompany his path to Rome, a secular pilgrimage conveying a soul's love for the soil of his native land. Home, like Rome, was a 'holy place' and *The Four Men* is full of spiritual premonitions of 'the character of enduring things' amid the decay of time.

And as a man will paint with a peculiar passion a face which he is only permitted to see for a little time, so will one passionately set down one's own horizon and one's fields before they are forgotten and have become a different thing. Therefore it is that I have put down in writing what happened to me now so many years ago, when I met first one man and then another, and we four bound ourselves together and walked through all your land, Sussex, from end to end. For many years I have meant to write it down and have not; nor would I write it down now, or issue the book at all, Sussex, did I not know that you, who must like all created things decay, might with the rest of us be very near your ending. For I know very well in my mind that a day will come when the holy place shall perish and all the people of it and never more be what they were. But before that day comes, Sussex, may your earth cover me, and may some loud-voiced priest from Arundel, or Grinstead, or Crawley, or Storrington, but best of all from home, have sung Do Mi Fa Sol above my bones.[9]

If the walk across Sussex that inspired *The Four Men* could have been a figment of the author's imagination, there was nothing imaginary about the walk that inspired the writing of *The Old Road*, an account of Belloc's pilgrimage, late in December 1902, from Winchester to Canterbury, following the traces of the Pilgrims' Way. After a trek of 120 miles, made in the company of two companions, Belloc arrived at the West Gate of Canterbury on 29 December, the feast day of St Thomas à Becket and the anniversary of his martyrdom.

Throughout 1903 Belloc turned his attention to politics, setting his sights on Parliament. Initially he sought adoption as the Liberal candidate for Dover, but his hopes were dashed when the parish priest came forward to embrace him at the adoption meeting. Belloc was convinced that the priest's embrace had been akin to a kiss of death to his chances. The subsequent rejection only served to remind him of, and embitter him still further towards, the sort of anti-Catholic prejudice that he was convinced had been the reason for his failure to get a Fellowship at Oxford.

Undaunted by this early setback, he began to employ his wit and his oratory prowess in the service of his political aspirations. Shawn Bullock wrote in the *Chicago Evening Post* of one of Belloc's speeches:

> Personally, I do not think that Belloc's talents fit him for great public service, nor am I convinced that his convictions lead him in that direction; but no matter. Two full hours of his company convinced me of his genius ... He rose to speak on French fiction. Once or twice he sighted the subject – but a word turned him – and off he went rambling delightfully, talking about his experiences as a conscript, his dealings with the French peasant, his adventures everywhere, his ideas, his opinions, his beliefs. And the talk was splendid ... it flooded us all, just carried us off our solid British feet and left us gasping.[10]

A more prosaic description was offered by Vincent Baynes who described Belloc, during an appearance at the Pharos Club, probably in June 1903, as 'a youngish dark man, with expressive eyes, a pointed chin, a frequent smile, and a conversational manner resembling his books'.[11]

Belloc's oratory also beguiled the young J.C. Squire, then an undergraduate at St John's College, Cambridge. Encountering Belloc for the first time, Squire recalled 'little of the lecture except that Belloc had made him laugh uproariously'.[12] Thereafter, Belloc exerted a profound and lasting influence over Squire, and the two men, years later, became good friends. Squire was responsible for probably the funniest parody of Belloc ever written, a parody that was described by Squire's biographer as 'arguably the best Squire ever wrote ... at which Belloc himself used to laugh loudly and frequently'. One can indeed imagine Belloc chuckling with delight as he read the final verse of Squire's parody in which his own verses are affectionately lampooned.

> So Sussex men, wherever you be,
> *Hey diddle, Ho diddle, Do.*
> I pray you sing this song with me,
> *Hey diddle, Ho diddle, Do;*
> That of all the shires she is the queen,
> And they sell at the 'Chequers' on Chanctonbury Green
> The very best beer that ever was seen,
> *Hey Dominus, Domine, Dominum, Domini,*
> *Domino, Domino.*[13]

The potent cocktail of beer, Belloc and Sussex was certainly in evidence in the summer of 1903 during Belloc's first meeting with Reginald and Charlotte Balfour. The Balfours had recently moved to the village of Ford and were lunching at the Bridge Hotel at Arundel, a few miles from their new home. '*The Path to Rome* had not long been published, and they were reading it with admiration,' recounts their daughter Clare Sheppard in her memoir, *Lobsters at Littlehampton*.

> At another table a group of people were talking animatedly, dominated by a square-set young man with brown hair and very blue eyes. His voice was not loud but extraordinarily clear. My father and mother sat in silence and exchanged glances; they were enthralled by the torrent of wit and originality that poured from his lips as he darted from one subject to another. It could only have been the author of *The Path to Rome*.[14]

A few days later Belloc called on them in a pony trap, 'and a friendship sprang up that was to last for the rest of their lives'. The relationship was probably influential in Charlotte Balfour's decision, the following year, to be received into the Catholic Church.

The reason why Belloc was to be found at the Bridge Hotel in Arundel was that he had rented 'Bleak House' in nearby Slindon, the village in which he had spent so much of his childhood. As with the previous summer, the whole family had uprooted from Chelsea to enjoy a rural retreat. Eleanor, now four years old, recalled a visit from G.K. Chesterton and his wife to the house.

> Gilbert and H.B. seemed to talk the whole time. We children could not understand one word of the torrent. H.B. was lying on the lawn with head pillowed on his arm. Talk, talk, talk! We heard it through the bushes, where we were up to mischief as usual. Elizabeth had now joined Louis and me for fun in the garden and Hilary was a year old.[15]

Perhaps the torrent of talk between Belloc and Chesterton in the garden at Slindon centred on their plans to collaborate on a short satire on Tariff Reform, at that time a burning political issue. The chief advocate of Reform, Joseph Chamberlain, was on the verge of resigning from office in the government so that he could concentrate on his personal crusade for imperial preference and protectionism. His resignation in September 1903 coincided with Belloc's satire, *The Great Inquiry*, which was illustrated by Chesterton. This was the first of what would become known in later years as the 'Chesterbellocs', books written by Belloc with Chesterton's illustrations.

A more successful satire, both in terms of sales and in terms of the critical acclaim it received, was *Caliban's Guide to Letters*, published earlier in the summer. Consisting of a series of literary lampoons, many of which had been previously published in the *Speaker*, it suffers, like most satire, from having its edge blunted by the passage of time. Even today, however, occasional glimpses of the wit that delighted Belloc's audiences whenever he spoke – whether from a public platform, or in the relative privacy of a dinner party, or round the table at an inn – shine forth splendidly. His contemporaries, closer to the topicality of Belloc's subject, and therefore closer to the joke, were more fulsome in their praise. Maurice Baring was a great admirer, believing that 'young journalists' should study it carefully, that they should 'read, mark, learn and inwardly digest, as the Collect says'.[16] H.G. Wells had also read Belloc's satire with evident satisfaction. On 19 September 1903 he wrote to Arnold Bennett to suggest light-heartedly that passages in Bennett's latest book, *How to Become an Author*, 'read like a parody of Dr Caliban'.[17]

In the autumn of 1903 a fire caused widespread damage to the Bellocs' Chelsea home when the nurse accidentally dropped a lamp in the nursery. She grabbed baby Hilary from the wicker cradle on the floor as the flames took hold. Elodie, who had just returned home with her husband from a party, ran to wake Eleanor and Elizabeth from the room next door. 'I woke with the noise of sundry alarming sounds,' remembered Eleanor, 'there were hurried footsteps and orders given in frightened voices. Suddenly our door flew open wide, the passage light streamed in and Mamma, in a long silk dress and with her hat on, swept in followed by Annie the cook.'[18]

Having evacuated the children, they watched helplessly as the fire took hold. Belloc, with the assistance of some passers-by, did his best to keep the flames at bay until the engines arrived. By the time the fire was finally extinguished, however, both rooms had been badly damaged and all the children's clothes had been destroyed. The full drama was encapsulated by Belloc's sister Marie, who recounted to her mother the account she had heard from Elodie: 'The nurse seems to have saved the children's lives by her energy and sense. The baby's cot was already in flames when she snatched the child out.'[19] Greatly relieved that a far worse disaster had been averted, Elodie had Masses said in thanksgiving that everyone had survived the inferno without injury.[20]

Within weeks of the fire, Belloc was struck down by illness. On 26 October 1903, he wrote apologetically to Wilfrid Scawen Blunt that his delay in writing was due to a collapse in health.

What happened was that I had, in the interval, a fit of influenza not of the ordinary kind but quite virulent. I could do nothing at all. I could not think or remember; it was the nastiest illness I ever had.

The consequence was everything got wildly out of order, & it was only last night that I went through a mass of papers & sorted what arrears I had got into.[21]

The following year, Belloc was struck down by what his sister described as 'the worst misfortune' to befall him in all his years in London, 'the one serious illness of Hilaire's early life'.[22] At one stage, he was so dangerously ill that a distraught Elodie phoned Marie to say that she thought her husband was close to death. The family doctor also believed that Belloc was terminally ill, remarking to Marie that it was a tragedy 'that such a fine young man should be dying, leaving a wife and so many little children'.[23] A priest was called and the last rites were administered. Belloc 'wept with gratitude and begged for the Sacrament himself', Elodie told Charlotte Balfour.[24] Finally, after many anxious days, the family's deepest fears began to subside. Having passed through the worst of the illness, Belloc's recuperation was remarkably fast and within weeks he was as fit and strong as ever. 'H. Belloc has been very ill, but is better thank God,'

Frances Chesterton recorded in her diary on New Year's Eve 1904.[25]

Belloc's period of convalescence was spent in North Africa, gathering the impressions that would come to fruition in his book *Esto Perpetua*, published the following year. He also seems to have spent the time pondering his future, and that of his family, because, as soon as he returned to England in February 1905, he made plans to leave London for Sussex. His decision, however, was not motivated principally by a desire to live in Sussex but by the necessity of leaving London. 'I was driven by real – and even dangerous – poverty,' he explained to Charlotte Balfour years later. 'I was earning not a quarter of the absolute minimum income necessary to the meanest household of our sort, and my earnings were decreasing.'[26]

By Easter 1905 the family was installed at Courthill Farm, a Georgian house on the edge of Belloc's beloved Slindon, which was leased on a short-term basis until a more permanent residence could be found. Elodie was overjoyed to find herself living the life of a countrywoman in Sussex, writing excitedly to a friend of the 'great kitchen garden full of cabbages and cauliflowers'.

> . . . the other beds are set out with peas, beans, French beans, radishes, lettuces, and for later times and such gross palates as mine, potatoes, turnips, carrots, parsnips and heaps of onions. We have gooseberries, strawberries and currants to come by the bushel if we have no frost. Also in the orchard apples, cherries, pears, with a dozen great hazel nut trees as the place stands where once a wonderful forest was.

They were the proud possessors of nine hens, two cocks, 17 chicks and 'two darling pigs whom we call Ruskin and Carlyle'. There were no flowers because the previous occupants had neglected the flower garden, but Elodie had put in some wallflowers and had planted nasturtiums, sweet peas and candytufts. The view was 'like heaven' to her. 'Great forests of wonderful beeches and firs and beyond the blue line of the Downs.'[27]

Elodie's blissful account of the family's *vita nuova* in Sussex suggests that she might have been instrumental in persuading her husband to uproot from London. Perhaps she had wanted to settle in Slindon ever since the family's summer holiday in the village two years previously. She knew that Slindon's special place in her husband's heart would make it a more enticing prospect than anywhere else, enabling him to sever his emotional ties with London and its invigorating, stimulating society with less difficulty.

Belloc certainly missed the city and would return frequently to the laughter and the love of friends that it offered, but he was as much in love with their new home as was his wife. Soon after the family's arrival at Courthill Farm, he acquired a mare called 'Monster', 'a steady sturdy chestnut cob', with whom he began to explore the surrounding countryside and the majestic Downs beyond. Not far away was Halnacker Hill, a place that would wield a mystical power over him, inspiring one of the most haunting poems of the twentieth century. Even if he did not fully realize it at the time, he was where he belonged. He had come home. The South Country that he had always loved had become the country in which, for the remainder of his life, he would always live. Sussex had claimed him as her own.

The Chesterbelloc

IN THE SPRING OF 1904 G.K. Chesterton dedicated his first novel, *The Napoleon of Notting Hill*, to Belloc. 'I am lost in my effort to choose which thing I must most thank you for – the book, the inscription or the glorious dedication!' Elodie wrote to Chesterton on 5 April.

> My loyalty to you and my memories of Slindon drive me towards the book; my egotism and my violence and my security in the soundness of my views in all things drive me towards the inscription in which you have so sweetly and so kindly included me; my passionate love of Liberty and my mild Irish belief in the final victory of all the good over the miserable muddy muggy streams of evil that drop under our unhappy noses (here and in Holy France) and the love for my beloved Man and the joy that I always have when he is recognized drive me to the dedication. I beg you and Frances to come and tell me which is the thing of all these three that should make me most happy.[1]

It is likely that Chesterton had a specific motive for dedicating *The Napoleon of Notting Hill* to Belloc, aside from the obvious and genuine expression of friendship. The novel's central theme was the perennial struggle of small communities and small nations to survive and express themselves in the face of the encroachment of the centralizing tendency of monolithic Power, a subject inspired, at least in part, by the author's political discussions with Belloc. In this context, Chesterton's initial impression of Belloc, on the occasion of their first meeting four years earlier, is worth recalling. Belloc's sturdy and keen appearance had 'instantly reminded' Chesterton 'of the pictures of Napoleon; and, for some vague reason, especially of the pictures of Napoleon on horseback'.[2] It seems probable, therefore, that the 'Napoleon' of the novel's title was a fantastic and fictionalized remodelling of Chesterton's romantic vision of Belloc – a vision that he had described in verse following their first meeting. Belloc was the 'furious Frenchman' who 'comes with his clarions and his drums' and who was 'bursting on our flanks ... For Belloc never comes but to conquer or to fall.'[3]

If the novel's 'Napoleon' was distinctly Bellocian, its 'Notting Hill' was avowedly Chestertonian. Notting Hill and its environs was the area of London in which Chesterton had spent the happiest of childhoods; it was to him as sacred in memory and as sacramental in significance as was Sussex to Belloc. From its very core, therefore, in its title as in the libertarian nature of its plot, *The Napoleon of Notting Hill* was a product of the 'Chesterbelloc', the nickname invented by Bernard Shaw for 'the twiformed monster' that Belloc's and Chesterton's friendship, politics and art presented and represented to the reading public.

During the Bellocs' final year in London, prior to their move to Sussex, they and the Chestertons were near neighbours. The Bellocs' Chelsea home was situated only a few yards from Battersea Bridge, on the opposite side of the Thames from Battersea where the Chestertons had lived since shortly after their marriage in June 1901. A sketch map drawn by Chesterton, probably in 1902, shows the site of both homes depicted by crude figures marked 'GKC' and 'Belloc'. About half way between, Chesterton had marked the site of a public house with the words 'beer excellent' beneath.[4] It is a safe assumption that this particular hostelry had been selected as a mutually convenient meeting place. The close proximity of friends such as Chesterton, and the opportunity it presented for frequent meetings, would have been one of the aspects of the move from London most irksome to Belloc's naturally gregarious temperament.

Three weeks after Elodie had penned her grateful letter to Chesterton, she and Belloc paid a visit to Gilbert and Frances in Battersea. 'The Bellocs ... came here to dinner,' Frances Chesterton recorded in her diary on 27 April. 'Hilaire in great form, recited his own poetry with great enthusiasm the whole evening.'[5] The Chestertons were also frequent visitors to Chelsea, their arrival always being greeted with enthusiasm by the Belloc children. Eleanor recalled:

> Frances had a deep tenderness of heart for children and a great understanding of them. She gave me the first carnation I had ever seen – it was in her buttonhole – and I carry the undimmed magic of its scent and beauty to this day. It had to be left for the night when I was put to bed – but I only parted from it having seen it safely in a cup of water and put into the doll's house.

Eleanor also retained a vision of Chesterton as 'a vivid memory making his puppets come to life for us in the nursery, sitting perilously on a chair far too small for his vast form and rumbling out romances and feuds, at which he laughed almost more than we did'.[6] She also recalled her own father's dexterity in the art of paper-folding, remembering how she and the other Belloc children were enthralled by the 'delightful paper birds which flapped their wings and beautiful little paper boxes which fitted into each other' that their father crafted for them in the nursery at Cheyne Walk.[7]

Belloc's and Chesterton's circle of literary friends was widened considerably during 1904 through their regular attendance at the Tuesday luncheons hosted by Edward Garnett at the Mont Blanc restaurant on Gerrard Street in Soho. At these lively gatherings they met, amongst others, Ford Madox Ford, W.H. Hudson, J.D. Beresford, H.M. Tomlinson, Thomas Seccombe, Joseph Conrad, Arthur Marwood, R.H. Mottram, John Galsworthy, Edward Thomas and W.H. Davies. According to Mottram's account of one such Tuesday gathering, Belloc, 'bowler-hatted' and seated immediately to Garnett's left, dominated the conversation, 'talking like a machine-gun between draughts of wine'.[8]

In May 1904, *Avril*, Belloc's collection of essays on the poetry of the French Renaissance, was published. It was, in the estimation of Robert Speaight, 'the best introduction to its subject in the English language', due, he believed, to Belloc's intense knowledge of, and love for, the period and the culture of which he wrote. 'Belloc not only knew these poets, but he understood the civilization that produced them. He was inside them in a way that he could never have been inside – for example – the English Metaphysicals.'[9]

Speaight's perceptive judgement struck at the very heart of Belloc's singular place in Anglo-French culture. Predominantly English, he needed nonetheless to immerse himself periodically in the culture of his beloved France. He was not merely culturally ambidextrous but culturally amphibious, requiring regular immersion and refreshment in the holy waters springing from his love for an idealized Gallic Christendom. In the weeks before the publication of *Avril* he and Elodie left their children with friends in Brittany and departed on a touring holiday of France. On 22 March he wrote to his mother from Beauvais, north of Paris, enthusing about the 'heavenly' day they had spent travelling through 'the most delightful country'. The cathedral at Beauvais gave 'the greatest impression of height of any building in the world' and could boast 'the highest nave in Europe'. From Beauvais they planned to proceed to Chantilly. 'Elodie enjoys this very much. She has had few holidays.'[10] It seems, in fact, from a letter that Elodie wrote to Chesterton soon after she and Belloc had returned to England in early April, that she shared her husband's highly infectious love for France and her people. She babbled effusively of 'Holy France', and her

> happy blessed people who have high horizons ... and who work in the fields and who sleep at night and who go to Mass and say their Rosaries in trains and behind their market-stalls. May God give back to England some such strong hold upon her own heroic soil ... These precious Frogs (I call them so lovingly) hold securely to their land, their country, their very God by a silky film like a spider's web.[11]

With his vociferous allegiance to the Church Militant and his intense loyalty to the people and culture of France, it would seem that Belloc was a singularly unlikely candidate for the English Parliament. Yet in May 1904, the very same month in which he had displayed his love for the French Renaissance with the publication of *Avril*, he presented himself for adoption as the Liberal candidate for South Salford, an industrial suburb of Manchester with a large working-class population. Having been accepted by the Salford Selection Committee, he appeared before the Executive and General Council of the local Liberal Association, the body charged with the ultimate responsibility for either accepting or rejecting his candidacy. In his speech to the Council, he stated his personal position on several of the most pressing political issues of the day. He opposed the Education Act (1902) on the ground that 'there is no right more sacred than the right of a parent to have his children educated in the religious influence which seems to him the most important part of his life'. Such a stance was in tune with the Nonconformist roots of Liberalism, but reflected Belloc's own desire to defend Catholic schools from State interference.

On the question of Temperance Reform, Belloc's celebrated love for French wine and English ale would seem to place him at loggerheads with the Nonconformist abstainers in the ranks of his adoptive party. He overcame any such difficulty by siding with them against the wealthy brewing interests.

> Before the brewing monopoly arose England was not a drunken country ... In those days the publican managing his own house – the man, that is, who is now put forward as the victim of our policy – was the only person directly concerned in obtaining licences. At the present moment the vast majority of publicans throughout England are the servants, and probably the debtors also, of a small and very wealthy clique whose power it is our business to destroy.[12]

Belloc also touched upon the question of Chinese Labour in South Africa and Home Rule in Ireland, declaring himself opposed to the former and in favour of the latter. On the burning issue of Tariff Reform, he subscribed to the gospel of Free Trade, the official position of the Liberal Party, and opposed the Protectionism being advocated by Joseph Chamberlain and others. Finally, as though to predict and pre-empt the anti-Catholic prejudice that his candidature might provoke, he nailed his colours candidly and firmly to his religious mast.

> My religion is of course of greater moment to me by far than my politics, or than any other interest could be, and if I had to choose between two policies, one of which would certainly injure my religion and the other as certainly advance it, I would not for a moment hesitate between the two.[13]

In spite of such candour, or possibly because of it, Belloc was adopted unanimously as the Liberal candidate. His adoption served to further widen his circle of acquaintances. He met Lloyd George at the annual dinner of the Palmerston Club, but, as if to prophesy his future alienation from the Liberal mainstream, he disapproved strongly of Lloyd George's vision of the 'nanny state', and he had little sympathy with the policies of the deceased statesman after whom the club was named. From the outset, Belloc was a peculiarly uncomfortable Liberal. After he had entertained the members of the Palmerston Club with what Speaight described as 'a brilliant speech about nothing at all', he sat, probably in sullen silence, as Lloyd George 'played the heavy statesman'.[14] For the moment, however, he found it easy and convenient to ignore such differences. Warmed by the glow of his emergent political ambition, he could afford to be optimistic about his future and that of the party that had adopted him as one of their own. At the annual meeting of the National Liberal Federation in Manchester, of which Augustine Birrell was the chairman, Belloc moved a vote of confidence in the party and expressed his belief that the Liberals would win the next election and that 'the ancient soul of Britain, a thing in some peril, would thereby be delivered'.[15] Afterwards, on 18 May, he wrote contentedly to his mother:

> I was getting tired of being refused in so many places on account of my religion ... The chances are against me, but it has already done me a great deal of good that I should be standing. It has helped the sale of my books and has suddenly made the provincial press in the north of England acquainted with my name.[16]

The degree to which Belloc was always the unlikeliest of Liberals was highlighted a few months later with the publication of *Emmanuel Burden*, his first novel. A scathing and sometimes overly subtle satire of the cynical, self-serving relationship between cosmopolitan finance and jingoistic political imperialism, it seethes beneath its tensely restrained surface in a most non-Liberal fashion. The eponymous villain's partners in crime are, significantly, a speculative aristocrat and an 'international' Jewish financier. Together they dupe the hapless Emmanuel Burden into investing in a shady 'development' scheme in Africa. Suggestions of bigotry and beguiling sagacity are interwoven into a literary fabric at once both caustically coarse and satirically smooth. The effect on the reader is beguilement, bemusement or both. Certainly Belloc's friend Lord Basil Blackwood appeared both beguiled by the sharpness of its wit and bemused – and even offended – by the bluntness of its message. 'My dear Belloc,' he wrote on 10 November 1904, a few weeks after the novel's publication on 23 September,

> I am very slowly and with great delight reading 'Mr Burden'. I think it is your masterpiece. I am sorry of course that you should always harp on the same string . . . That is, eternal mockery and denunciation of the rich. I also think that it is a pity to impute baseness and personal interest to every one who follows ideals with regard to the destiny of England as a wide-world-power. I know that's your hobby & you share it in common with the demagogues of Trafalgar Square . . . but on this common place base you have erected a most original structure & I have rarely been so diverted before as I am now reading this biography. I can't congratulate you too warmly.
>
> It's a book one will always be able to take up & to read a page or two because on every page there is a chunk of wit. I think the pictures too are excellent & the titles printed under them are of quite superfine wit, I suppose they are yours . . . I must say I have been most genuinely amused by it.
>
> Enough for the present, if only you could be persuaded to change your strings, if only you were able to curb your petty jealousy of those who are richer & more prosperous than yourself!!! I am as poor as you but I am not perpetually writhing under the knowledge that others – a limited few – are rich and well.[17]

Belloc's satires in general, and his *Emmanuel Burden* in particular, were destined to have a pronounced, profound and enduring influence on the young Rupert Brooke who, at the time of the novel's publication, was a

17-year-old pupil at Rugby. Brooke wrote a paper on Belloc in which he opined with youthful bravura that Belloc's style was 'free, limber, and bubbling with a pleasant pride' and that his prose was 'properly self-conscious indeed and wilful, but not too artificial'. Like a good garment, his style draped 'to reveal, not to conceal, his figure'.[18] According to Brooke's biographer Robert Pearsall, this appraisal of Belloc's style 'accurately describes the style for which Brooke was working, and runs significantly opposite to the Decadent style'.[19]

Another of Brooke's biographers, Christopher Hassall, stated that Belloc was 'already a big influence in Brooke's life' and concurred with Pearsall that Brooke's admiration for Belloc was linked to his disdain for the Decadents. This was evident in a paper by the young Brooke entitled 'Political Satire in English Verse' in which Belloc is compared favourably with, and is seen as a natural successor to, such satirists as Rochester, Marvell, Butler, Dryden and Swift. 'I am thankful for such robust people, thinking of the swarms of decadent and immunized maggots that now swarm over the putrescent corpse of English literature. We moderns are like invalids sitting in a darkened room, afraid of our own shadows and speaking in Maeterlinckian whispers. I thank God when someone shouts or laughs or swears aloud.'[20] Clearly Brooke considered Belloc's robustness an antidote to the effete posturings of the Decadents and quoted with approval the following phrase from *Emmanuel Burden*: 'To see him open his umbrella was to comprehend England from the Reform Bill to Home Rule.' The phrase inspired Brooke to write a satire of his own on the English middle class in the person of a figure whom he decided to call 'John Rump'.[21]

Ironically perhaps, Belloc failed to share the high opinion that Blackwood, Brooke and others had about *Emmanuel Burden*. In later years he came to consider the illustrations that Blackwood thought so 'excellent' far better than the novel itself. There were 34 illustrations, all drawn by Chesterton, making it the second of the so-called 'Chesterbellocs' following their earlier collaboration on *The Great Inquiry*. Belloc expressed his high opinion of his friend's artistic gifts many years later in an essay in which he paid homage to Chesterton's 'drawing of character upon paper' and the 'striking . . . power of perception' that it represented.

It is more living, more real, more the human being itself, than anything called character-drawing by the literary method. More real and more living than any of those found in that art which he himself so intensely admired in the older writers who were the subject of his study and his enthusiasm. He would, with a soft pencil capable of giving every gradation in emphasis from the lightest touch to the dead black point and line, set down, in gestures that were like caresses sometime, sometime like commands, sometimes like rapier-thrusts, the whole of what a man or woman was; and he would get the whole thing down on the paper with the rapidity which only comes from complete possession . . .

No one else has done this, even among the few who have attempted to illustrate their own work . . . and the unique thing was unique not only through its miraculous exuberance, but through its perception of reality.[22]

Having expressed so forcefully his admiration for Chesterton's artistic powers, it is hardly surprising that Belloc came to rely on Chesterton's illustrations not merely as adornments for his future novels but as the very source of their inspiration. Dorothy Collins, Chesterton's secretary for six of the eleven 'Chesterbellocs', remembered Belloc's debt to his friend.

Belloc needed Chesterton, and would come like a whirlwind with the plot of one of his satirical novels, saying that he could not possibly write the story until Gilbert had drawn the pictures. They would go into the study after lunch and for the length of a hilarious afternoon they would be closeted together. At tea-time they would emerge, Belloc triumphant with twenty-five illustrations for his book. The characters had come to life through the medium of the drawings.[23]

Belloc's creative dependence on Chesterton, at least so far as his satirical novels were concerned, indicated a subtle evolutionary change in their relationship. Although Belloc's initial impact on Chesterton could still resonate strongly enough four years after the event to provide a crucial ingredient for *The Napoleon of Notting Hill*, Chesterton's own emerging influence on Belloc was becoming ever more important and apparent as the years passed. In later years, Belloc would describe Chesterton as 'the Master'[24] and would consider him 'a thinker so profound and so direct that he had no equal'.[25] Such judgements must throw into question Frank Sheed's statement that 'Belloc had so much to do with the making of Chesterton and Chesterton not much with the making of Belloc.' If, as Sheed suggests, Chesterton did have little to do with the making of Belloc, he was destined nonetheless to become ever more important as a creative and sustaining force in his life.

THIRTEEN

The Party System

T HE FIFTH AND FINAL of the Belloc children was born in October
1904. Chesterton was asked to be the boy's godfather and the baby
was baptized Peter Gilbert in his honour.[1] It was a fitting tribute from
Belloc to his and Chesterton's friendship.

In the weeks following the baby's birth, Belloc's daily schedule was
so hectic that he became ever more frequently the absentee father, leaving
Elodie and the five children, all of whom were under eight years old,
while he travelled the country simultaneously pursuing his literary and
political careers. The following itinerary of a week in early November
1904 epitomizes the burden of work under which he was labouring.

> This week I dictated two articles on Monday morning, lunched in
> the train, gave an afternoon lecture at Reigate, dined in Norwood
> with an admirer of *Emmanuel Burden*, and lectured at Dulwich the
> same night, wrote another article on Tuesday morning, took the
> express on Tuesday at 3 o'clock for Chesterfield, lectured in Chester-
> field, left Chesterfield before eight on Wednesday, gave two political
> speeches Wednesday afternoon and evening in my constituency, went
> out to stop with the Barlows the night in Cheshire, came back to
> Manchester on Thursday; wrote two notes on the war for 'Outlook'
> and one note for the Speaker, sent four telegrams and wrote eighteen
> letters; then I gave another longer and most effective political speech in
> my constituency in the evening, was back in London Friday afternoon,
> dictated some more stuff and more letters, and am now upon this
> blessed occasion ending my fifth letter after dictating a review of
> Rose's 'Napoleonic Studies'.[2]

It is little surprise that this high-pressured lifestyle immediately preceded
Belloc's utter physical collapse and the subsequent life-threatening illness.[3]
It is also hardly surprising that Elodie greeted their final escape to the
seclusion of Slindon in the following spring with almost ecstatic relief.

Her letters to friends from Courthill Farm convey the joy of a troubled spirit liberated from the pressures of London life into the pleasures of a kitchen garden overlooked by the distant and peaceful splendour of the Downs.

The children also enjoyed their new life in the country, Eleanor's memoirs bearing witness to their salad-day adventures on the green and wooded slopes surrounding the village. It was in Slindon's small Catholic church, only two fields away from Courthill Farm up a steep hillside, that seven-year-old Louis first served Mass, having been taught the Latin responses by Father Wheelhan, the parish priest. Belloc looked on proudly as his eldest child, in blue cassock and white cotta, served at the altar. 'It gave my father such pleasure that Sunday,' recalled Eleanor, 'that he seemed overjoyed and, following Louis into the sacristy after Mass, brought him out into the church and gave him a golden sovereign, while we all began to hop about like happy fleas . . .'[4]

Like his wife, Belloc also derived a great deal of peace from the family's new life in Slindon, escaping to the hills on foot or astride Monster, his cob. Yet his spirit was too restless to remain in Sussex for extended periods. He needed the stimulation of the city as an escape from the rustications of the country just as he had needed the country as an escape from the city. He had been elected to the Reform Club on 9 March 1905 and this would become like a home from home during his frequent visits to London.

Belloc was also committed to making regular visits north to his constituency in Salford, preparing the ground for what he hoped would be his eventual election to Parliament. Following Balfour's resignation in December 1905 and the subsequent dissolution of Parliament, all Belloc's considerable energy was directed to the election campaign.

South Salford was, at the election of 1906, what would now be called a marginal constituency. The sitting Conservative Member, J. Greville Groves, had won the seat from the Liberals at the previous election with a precarious majority of 1,227. With so much at stake and so few votes likely to separate the two candidates, the Conservatives quickly resorted to the crudest of tactics in their efforts to retain the seat. Playing on popular prejudice, they adopted the slogan 'Don't vote for a Frenchman and a Catholic'. Faced with such an affront to his faith and to the blood of his father, Belloc decided to come out fighting. He chose a Catholic school as the venue for his first public meeting and decided to ignore the warnings of the local Catholic clergy that he would be wise to skirt the religious question and concentrate on other, less contentious issues. Disregarding their advice, he rose to address the packed audience as follows: 'Gentlemen, I am a Catholic. As far as possible, I go to Mass every day. This [taking his beads out of his pocket] is a rosary. As far as possible, I kneel down and tell these beads every day. If you reject me on account of my religion, I shall thank God that He has spared me the indignity of being your representative.'[5] For a few seemingly endless moments there was a hush of utter astonishment – followed by a thunderclap of applause.

Belloc had confronted the religious bigotry head-on, but he still had to face the xenophobic nature of the Conservative campaign against him. J. Greville Groves was part of the wealthy brewing company Groves and Whitnall, which owned no fewer than 100 pubs in the area. As such, Groves could claim to be 'a Salford lad' whereas his opponent could barely even claim to be English. Seizing this obvious advantage, his supporters scrawled up the following rhyme on the walls around the town, hoping to gain politically what the verse evidently lacked poetically.

> A Frenchman there was named Hilaire
> And René – the names make you stare;
> He wished to be Salford MP
> But they wanted no foreigners there.

In his autobiography, Chesterton recounted how Belloc dealt with xenophobic hecklers during the Salford campaign, illustrating his friend's debating skills and the manner in which he could instantly turn defence into attack.

Salford was a poor and popular constituency, in which there were many strata of simple and provincial people, retaining the prejudices of our great-grandfathers; one of them being the touching belief that anybody with a French name could be made to cower and grovel by any allusion to the Battle of Waterloo. This was probably the only battle of which the heckler himself had ever heard; and his information about it was limited to the partly inaccurate statement that it was won by the English. He therefore used to call out at intervals, 'Who won Waterloo?' And Belloc would affect to take this with grave exactitude, as a technical question put to him upon a tactical problem, and would reply with the laborious lucidity of a lecturer, 'The issue of Waterloo was ultimately determined, chiefly by Colborne's manoeuvre in the centre, supported by the effects of Van der Smitzen's battery earlier in the engagement. The Prussian failure in synchrony was not sufficiently extensive, etc.' And then, while the unfortunate patriot in the audience was still endeavouring to grapple with this unexpected growth of complexity in the problem he had propounded, Belloc would suddenly change his own note to the ringing directness of the demagogue, would openly boast of the blood of the Pyrenean soldier who had followed the revolutionary army of Napoleon, and risen in its ranks, through all the victories that established a code of justice all over a continent and restored citizenship to civilization. 'It is good democratic blood; and I am not ashamed of it.'[6]

In a similarly robust counteroffensive, Belloc announced defiantly that his 'good democratic' French blood was better than that of the equally French, though aristocratic, Lord Lansdowne, foreign secretary in Balfour's government and leader of the Unionists in the House of Lords. Nonetheless, Belloc insisted that he was 'no foreigner, but an Englishman who talks a Radicalism which is not talked in any other country but England'.[7] Evidently, the working-class voters of Salford agreed because, on polling day, 13 January 1906, he was elected by a slim majority of 852.

Belloc's radicalism at this time was so fierce that, in his victory speech, he chose to associate himself with the radical platform of John Burns, the Labour politician and MP for Battersea, rather than with any mainstream Liberal politician. Not for the first or last time, he was exhibiting a distinctly un-Liberal 'liberalism'. He told a journalist for the *Manchester Guardian* that he had fought on a programme which 'some of my friends thought was too strong, but which was not quite strong enough for my convictions'.[8] Faced with such rhetoric, it was scarcely surprising that 'the routed Tories could find only two words to express their dismay: "Belloc's in!"'[9] Yet one suspects that there were a number of leading MPs of Belloc's own party who, listening uneasily to the words of the loose canon who had just been elected to sit amongst them in the House of Commons, were silently echoing their opponents' dismay. Their fears must have been confirmed on 22 February when Belloc chose the controversial issue of imported Chinese labour in South Africa as the subject of his maiden speech in Parliament. The speech was short, lasting only eight minutes, but contained a number of statements that were more embarrassing to the government of which he was a member than to the opposition.

During the election campaign, the Liberals had criticized the Conservative government's authorization in 1904 of the recruitment and mass importation of cheap Chinese labour to work in the goldmines of the

Transvaal. In a campaign speech at the Albert Hall on 21 December, the Liberal leader Henry Campbell-Bannerman announced that the Liberals would 'stop forthwith the recruitment and embarkation of coolies in China and their importation into South Africa'.[10] Subsequently, however, he was persuaded to limit his prohibition to the future issuance of licences, not to the use of licences already issued, amidst fears that the government would be forced, in law, to compensate the mine owners if existing licences entitling the importation of a further 14,000 Chinese labourers were revoked. Belloc was not happy with this compromise, asserting that it amounted to a breach of his party's campaign promises. He demanded that the government commenced the repatriation of the labourers within three months and that the mine owners be made to pay the cost.

The fact that his maiden speech had been a source of embarrassment to his own party was confessed, almost gleefully, to Maurice Baring five days later:

> The *Morning Post*, naturally trying to hurt the Government, said that I alone of the Liberals had shown courage. *The Times* said in a leader that what I had said was 'dangerous rant'. The Liberal papers keep an ominous silence – being cowardly, but I, my dear Maurice, continue to dance in the sunlight and to sing like the gaslight. For instance, even today I leaped up in my seat and asked a question of the Government which gave them the greatest possible annoyance, to wit, whether it was not a fact that Kaffir labour was increasing steadily until the Chinese labour was brought in, and has since been decreasing. It is a fact.[11]

The question on 27 February that had caused the government 'the greatest possible annoyance' was a supplementary to a question on Kaffir labour in the Transvaal 'which Churchill avoided answering'.[12]

The choice of this particular issue as a launch pad for Belloc's parliamentary career was linked to his entrenched opposition to imperialism in general and to the role of the mine owners in South Africa in particular. He had always been a vociferous opponent of Britain's role in the Boer War, which he believed had been fought at the instigation of the powerful mine owners in order to protect their commercial interests. In his maiden speech he had referred to them as 'those men whom England hated from the bottom of the heart', to whom England owed 'the loss of its military prestige', and who 'had captured the press and who talked of themselves as Britishers yet would not allow an Englishman to express a free opinion in this country'.[13] For Belloc, the issue of cheap imported Chinese labour was a further example of the manipulative power of big business. He insisted, during a further debate on the issue in April, that the shortage of labour used by the mine owners to justify the importation of Chinese labourers had been deliberately created by the forced lowering of wages. It was nothing less than a cynical attempt to undercut the wages of native labourers. He was also concerned with the way that the Chinese labourers were being treated, asking in Parliament whether rumours that they were being routinely flogged were true. His concerns were shared by other MPs, most notably by Lloyd George, who declared that the importation of Chinese labour had 'brought back slavery to the British Empire'.[14]

On a more humorous note, Belloc supported the Pure Beer Bill, a Private Member's Bill that was debated in the House of Commons on 16 March. He claimed that 'in the constituency he represented a number of people had died from drinking impure beer. What was still more important, for electoral purposes, a great number survived.' It is easy to discern that Belloc's wit was pointed, albeit light-heartedly, in the direction of J. Greville Groves, the wealthy brewer, his opponent in the recent election, who owned many of the pubs in his constituency. Warming to his subject, Belloc argued that foreign ingredients were more likely to cause illness and addiction and even suggested, with hyperbolic tongue in cheek, that the question of pure beer was the overriding issue on which most Members had been returned. 'There are very few nights,' he declared, 'when I do not go to bed after drinking a pint or two of beer.' He admitted that, in making such a confession and in supporting the bill, he had hopelessly offended all the teetotallers in his constituency, and then added, amid gales of laughter, 'There are eight of them.'[15]

His rumbustiousness failed to amuse many of the MPs of his own party, nearly half of whom were members of Nonconformist congregations with strong sympathies towards the Temperance movement. The bill was rejected by 65 votes. Needless to say, those friends with whom Belloc regularly imbibed were delighted with his words. 'I congratulate you on your speech on Beer,' Maurice Baring wrote. 'I agree with every word of it.'[16] *Punch*, predictably, was more than happy to join in the fun:

> True, there are hardy souls among us still
> Convinced adherents of the foaming beaker,
> Like that MP who nightly takes his fill
> Two pints of bitter, as he told the Speaker.[17]

Apart from Chinese labour in South Africa, the issue that roused Belloc to the most impassioned rhetoric during his first session in Parliament was the debate surrounding the Education Bill. His defence of Catholic schools from any suggestion of encroachments upon their independence by the State was forthright and uncompromising: 'The honourable Member for Louth made use of the word "moderate", and I have also heard the word "compromise" mentioned as regards the Catholic schools. I cannot too emphatically point out that those two words are absolutely meaningless when the House of Commons is dealing with the Catholic Faith. The House may tyrannically insist on their having less, but English Catholics cannot be content with less for their Catholic children than Catholic schools with Catholic teachers teaching Catholic religion.'

This speech, delivered on 7 May 1906, exhibited Belloc at his most robust and most fiery. It also represented an early indication of his determination to expose the bias that had distorted the facts of English history. He complained that no proper history was taught in the universities and public schools, otherwise people would know that 'since Diocletian nothing can compare with the persecution of the Catholic people of this country by the wealthy and official classes.' He continued: 'It has not been a popular persecution, but a cold, deliberate and bloody persecution on the part of the men who got hold of the land of the country after the dissolution of the monasteries. Can you wonder after two centuries of such suffering we emerged a wholly distinct and highly homogenous body?' The Catholic minority in England, having suffered so much for their faith, were not about to surrender it.

'It is true, not only of myself but of every Catholic in England, that the preservation of the Catholic schools is far and away the first of the political controversies in which he may be engaged. I should not hesitate for a moment, if I found it impossible satisfactorily to represent my constituency, and yet to stand, as I do, for my religion, as to what course I should take. A political career is nothing to us compared with our religion; nor is wealth. Catholics must have their rights on some general principle, and that principle is the right of the parent to have his child instructed, immersed in the religion for the glory and defence of which he brought that child into the world. The Catholics feel that they are in a sense exiles in this country, misunderstood both in regard to their vices and their virtues; and so long as they retain that feeling, they demand the right of maintaining the things for which they have struggled so long and so bitterly.'[18]

Having embarrassed the government of which he was ostensibly a member in his maiden speech, Belloc now found himself at loggerheads with it over its plans for education reform. As a man of principle who put the practice of his faith before his party loyalty, he soon found himself increasingly alienated by the party system. 'I cannot stand the House,' he wrote, disgruntled, to Wilfrid Scawen Blunt on 9 November.[19] Two months later, on 27 January 1907, barely a year after being elected, he wrote to Blunt about his disillusionment with parliamentary politics. He said he was 'continually absent' in the north 'delivering lectures that cost me more than they bring in' and making 'speeches that get me into trouble', adding plaintively that 'the political incapacity of the country is incredible! I can see little object in the House of Commons except to advertise work. It does not govern; it does not even discuss. It is completely futile.'[20]

Friends and Disciples

THROUGHOUT THE EARLY MONTHS OF 1906, away from the publicity and controversy caused by his speeches in Parliament, Belloc managed to find time with Elodie to search for a new home in rural Sussex. They journeyed from village to village on a large bicycle, Belloc in the saddle and Elodie in a wicker trailer. Altogether, according to Marie Belloc Lowndes, they considered 80 houses.[1] Eventually they found an old farmhouse on the edge of the village of Shipley, several miles from Horsham. Set amid five acres of land, with a magnificent windmill attached and overlooked by a splendid twelfth-century church, it claimed their hearts as soon as they set eyes on it. Entering the large living room, which at one time had been the village shop, they 'danced a dance of joy together' at having discovered the home of their dreams.[2]

The oldest parts of the house were held together by dark oak beams and dated from the fourteenth century, whereas the newest parts were modern extensions built as recently as 1890. Its 11 gables were so similar, however, that the distinction between the old and the new was not as obvious to the untrained eye as might be expected. This was King's Land, destined to be the home of Hilaire and Elodie Belloc for the remainder of their respective lives.

On 9 March, Elodie informed a friend that they had 'bought a place of our own in Sussex. A lovely old long brick house. We have to do a lot to it – but we hope to be settled in there during the summer.'[3] In the event, the house had so much that needed doing to it that they did not finally move in until 22 August. It was 'exactly suitable to oneself', Belloc wrote to Desmond MacCarthy several years later, 'though of a kind that no one else would like'. It had been 'such a bargain', at only 1,000 pounds, 'because not every modern man would care to live in a house which was planned as it is, and also because most townsmen coming to it and finding no water supply and not appreciating that a full water system, well, pump, cistern, closets and all could be put in for £100 were put off.'[4]

Belloc's eye for a bargain was driven by financial necessity. Two letters to Maurice Baring, written in February and March 1906, illustrate the precarious nature of his finances, which he described as 'very grave indeed ... No one will give me any sort of salaried post, and it is extremely difficult to earn under the conditions of the House of Commons.'

> I am tired out of piecing together a livelihood by little special efforts of the brain. I want regular work and regular pay. No one dreams of giving it to me. I try to start a good *radical* weekly which just now would boom. No one will hear of it. No one will even give me a literary page to review. It is like being in a large room with fifty doors and all of them locked. I lie awake at night full of black thoughts. I am miserable.
>
> It is quite ridiculous. First Oxford wouldn't give me work and now after all these efforts London won't.[5]

Six months later, on 20 September, Belloc finally succeeded in securing salaried employment, as literary editor of the *Morning Post*. The position did little to alleviate the family's finances, however, and five weeks later Belloc was again complaining to Baring about his 'worry and care and debt, especially debt'.[6] It seems clear that his friends sometimes offered financial assistance, lending him money at times of particular need. 'I am increasingly burdened and worried about the sum of money which I owe you – £300 – but I cannot get my hands on it,' he wrote to Chesterton. 'I have received nothing for months and I cannot get anybody who owes me money to pay me.'[7]

Maurice Baring's friendship was more important to Belloc than ever by 1906, even though they met infrequently due to Baring's posting to Russia on diplomatic service. Baring's letters from St Petersburg or Moscow – often written in verse, as were Belloc's replies – display the candour of kindred spirits rejoicing in a shared approach to life. The two men also admired each other's work. 'I think your verse is as good as Pope's,' Baring wrote on 20 March, 'and that you might write a poem like the "Rape of the Lock" half satirical with passages of real beauty in it. I wish you would do so.'[8] Baring was also greatly moved by Belloc's praise for some of his own sonnets.

> Do you really think my sonnets are good? I wonder. I was fearfully snubbed the other day for publishing a book of verse at all by a high

English official – he said it was ridiculous. He hadn't read it and didn't mean to; but he said this before fifteen people after dinner and they all laughed and I felt a bloody fool. In France nobody thinks it odd if you write verse, or here either – they talk about it naturally; and in England it was so until the reign of Charles II and even later I suppose, and then the damned Puritans cast their stinking tarpaulin of respectability over their filthy vices and pretended to be virtuous. They will surely be damned. Bless you Hilaire and thank you for your Sonnet which has more strength and dignity than anything I ever wrote.[9]

It is tempting to detect more than a hint of Belloc's bellicose influence in Baring's damning indictment of Puritanism, and there is little doubting Belloc's role in bringing Baring closer to the Church during the nine years since they had first met. Baring's questioning approach to matters of faith was illustrated in his enigmatic ending to one of his letters to Belloc from Russia: 'I am till Death and perhaps beyond, Yours . . .'[10]

Belloc's influence on another of his long-standing friends bore spiritual fruit in 1906 when John Phillimore was received into the Catholic Church. Phillimore, three years Belloc's junior, had been an Oxford contemporary from Christ Church who, with Belloc, had become involved in the circle of like-minded friends associated with the *Speaker*. Later in life, he would become Professor of Greek at Glasgow University, playing host to Belloc whenever the latter's lecturing engagements took him north of the border. Phillimore was one of the first visitors to King's Land in the summer of 1906, cycling over from his home at Shedfield in Hampshire. He and Belloc panelled the dining room in new oak, after which 'beer was consumed and songs were sung'.[11] In an undated letter to Phillimore, probably written at around the time of his reception into the Church, Belloc poured forth, with disarming candour, his own understanding of the Faith they now shared.

The Catholic Church is a thing of which a man never despairs or is ashamed. Faith goes and comes, not (as the decayed world about us pretends) with certain waves of the intelligence, but as our ardour in the service of God, our chastity, our love of God and his creation, our fighting of our special sins, goes and comes. Faith goes and comes. You think it gone for ever (you go to Mass, but you think it gone for ever), then in a miraculous moment it returns. In early manhood one wonders at this, in maturity one laughs at such vicissitudes . . . But the Church is permanent. You know what our Lord said: He said

'I have conquered the world' ... With every necessity, with every apparition of tangible human and positive truth the Faith returns triumphant. By that, believe me, the world has been saved. All that great scheme is not a mist or a growth, but a thing outside ourselves and time.[12]

Belloc also befriended George Wyndham, the Conservative MP for Dover, at around this time, the only deep friendship he formed from all the acquaintances he made in the House of Commons. Belloc admired Wyndham for the boldness of his Land Reforms in Ireland under the Balfour administration, and for his scholarship, writing years later that he considered him the most intelligent man he had ever met.[13] The two men enjoyed walking tours together in France before Wyndham's sudden and untimely death in June 1913.

Belloc's friendship with Chesterton continued undiminished and, on 6 September 1906, he wrote a letter to him in which he included his famous Ballade with its refrain that Chesterton was 'The only man I regularly read'.[14] Later the same month Belloc was in Rome, sending a postcard of St Peter's Square and addressing it ostensibly to his youngest son 'Master Peter Belloc', who, approaching his second birthday, would be unable to read it: 'This is the great church of the great Saint Peter, the patron of mammy's little baby Lamb. Peter, my lamb, could easily be lost in it and it is too big for him to walk about it in one day!'[15]

The first Christmas at King's Land was remembered with fondness by Eleanor, then seven years old, who recalled being told mysteriously that 'Father Christmas had chosen an unusual place for his tree'. The children were led out of the house into the December darkness, following their mother who carried a lantern to light the way. Reaching the mill, they climbed the ladder to the main entrance with their father's help and discovered 'with breathless excitement ... the tree glowing with candles, twinkling tinsel and coloured balls'.

I was given a delectable blue satin bag of chocolates which seemed a celestial climax to a perfect evening. I offered one to Papa. He was near the tree staring at it wide-eyed and far away. He did not at first hear me in the happy youthful hum and din of squealing children, but when he did he bent and put a large hand into the bag, coming out of some far dream! He thanked me warmly, stroked my face and put the chocolate into his mouth; and I longed to know what it had for a 'centre'! But I saw he was 'far away' again and looking at the tree with a rapt expression – I wonder what he was thinking about?[16]

As the year drew to a close, Belloc had much to contemplate as he gazed distantly into the candlelit tree, pondering perhaps the many changes that the old year had heralded.

His election to Parliament in the previous January had promised much but delivered little in terms of finances or fulfilment. It was a triumph tinged by disillusionment. He had in fact ended the year very much as he had begun it, by aggravating and alienating his own party colleagues. In a letter to the *Manchester Guardian* he had demanded a public audit of the party funds, claiming that 'whenever a Government makes a fool of itself, especially a Liberal Government, one may be pretty certain that it is due to the pressure of one of the big subscribers'.[17] Much to the chagrin of his Liberal colleagues, Belloc would return to this thorny issue in February 1908, moving in the House of Commons that the secret party funds be publicly audited. Again, in 1927, he would write an essay entitled 'Audit the Party Funds' for the journal *The Nineteenth Century and After*. When this was republished in booklet form by the Aylesford Press in 1992, Father Brocard Sewell wrote of its enduring relevance: 'If such an audit were published today it would be sure to reveal some interesting names, just as it would have done in the twenties. The law of libel inhibits conjectures; but among such names there would surely be that of . . . the late Robert Maxwell, a personality who might have stepped out from the pages of a novel by Belloc.'[18]

On the domestic level, the year had been dominated by the purchase and renovation of King's Land, a small corner of Sussex destined to secure a special place in his and Elodie's affections. The year had also seen the publication of several books that appeared to epitomize the way that he perceived the world and, for that matter, the way that the world was beginning to perceive him. *Sussex*, published by A. & C. Black, was an illustrated guide to the county with which Belloc's name was already synonymous, and *An Open Letter on the Decay of Faith*, published by Burns and Oates, was further evidence of Belloc's emergence as a self-proclaimed *fidei defensor* ready at the slightest provocation to wield his pen in defence of the Church Militant.

Much as he had gazed beyond the Christmas party games of his children into the visionary distance of the candlelit tree, Belloc, in his *Open Letter on the Decay of Faith*, was gazing beyond the particularities of party politics into the religious heart of humanity. In the essential scheme of things, party politics were peripheral and therefore ephemeral; only the truths of religion were central and therefore perennial.

The enormous evils from which we are suffering, the degradation of our fellow-citizens, the accursed domination of our plutocracy is in the act of settlement. But after that? Will there not remain the chief problem of the soul? Shall we not still smell what Chesterton so admirably calls 'the unmistakable smell of the pit', shall we not still need salvation with a need greater than the need for water on a parched day? And will there not remain among us – since we are a civilized people . . . the record of the faith?

The *Open Letter* also introduces the concept of 'a Europe of the Faith', a recurring motif in Belloc's work.

I desire you to remember that we are Europe; we are a great people. The faith is not an accident among us, nor an imposition, nor a garment; it is bone of our bone and flesh of our flesh: it is a philosophy made by and making ourselves. We have adorned, explained, enlarged it; we have given it visible form. This is the service we Europeans have done to God. In return He has made us Christians.

Perhaps, however, the final book of 1906 was also the finest. *Hills and the Sea*, published by Methuen on 11 October, was a collection of essays, all of which had been previously published in sundry journals ranging from the *Speaker* and the *Morning Post* to the *Daily News* and the *Evening Standard*. As the very title of the volume suggests, *Hills and the Sea* was a miscellany of Bellocian prose full of the peripatetic ramblings of the restless pilgrim and the saline observations of the seasoned sailor. The former predominates in essays such as 'The Pyrenean Hive', 'The First Day's March', 'The Idea of a Pilgrimage' or 'The Inn of the Margeride', while the latter comes to the fore in 'The North Sea', 'The Sea-Wall of the Wash', 'The Looe Stream' or 'The Harbour in the North'.

'For many people,' wrote Robert Speaight, '*Hills and the Sea* will be their favourite among Belloc's collected essays; certainly, if we only had this book to go by, we should place him among the finest essayists in the English language.'[19] Few would argue with such a judgement, but it is scarcely sufficient as an insight into the power and popularity of these essays. The secret of the book's success lies not so much in the potency of the prose as in the power of the person who emerges from the pages. It is not the writing but the writer that rises, phoenix-like, as master of the hills and the sea.

It is a well-worn and worn-out cliché to say that a man is larger than life. No man is larger than life. Some men are, however, larger than the literature they produce and Belloc was such a man. To say as much is not to minimize the literature but to magnify the man. The unconscious and uncanny influence he wielded on his friends and contemporaries – on Chesterton, Baring, Phillimore and others – was matched by an even more uncanny ability to inspire a sense of discipleship in a younger generation of aspiring writers.

'Belloc treated younger men, until he knew them well, with a formal courtesy which was rather attractive,' recalled Arnold Lunn, who had first met Belloc sometime between 1907 and 1911 while still an undergraduate at Oxford. Describing himself as 'an agnostic with an Anglican background', Lunn had nonetheless 'read and been fascinated by *The Path to Rome*', a book destined to have an enduring influence throughout his life. Half a century later he would claim that it 'remains to this day my favourite book' and that he had always made a point of re-reading it every year.

> Belloc's aggressive Catholicism in this, as in his other books, alternately irritated and attracted me. I was at first bewildered by his rationalism, by his reiterated insistence on reason as the secure foundation of the Catholic faith . . . and it was Belloc's emphasis on reason which encouraged me to investigate the case for the Church, if only to discover whether Belloc's insistence on reason was a private whimsy of his own or orthodox Catholicism.

It was, therefore, as a grudging, reluctant disciple that Lunn had first met Belloc. 'I told him how much I loved *The Path to Rome*, and he said something to the effect that he had sold the copyright for a ridiculously small sum.' Belloc also found time to discourse on the irrational roots of rationalism, sowing further seeds of doubt into Lunn's youthful agnosticism. 'He talked about the curious illusion of so many who described themselves as "rationalists" that their beliefs are anchored in reason, rather than in an uncritical faith in the dogma that miracles do not occur.'[20]

In his autobiography, Lunn recounts an amusing incident in which his discipleship of Belloc almost landed him in serious trouble. Having purchased a volume of Belloc's verse from Blackwell's bookshop in Oxford, he took it with him when he and a friend went to dine at the Clarendon.

> Over the port we took it in turns to read and declaim Belloc's poems, and the effect of poetry and port was exhilarating. We were particularly pleased with the poem which began:

Remote and ineffectual Don
That dared attack my Chesterton . . .

After we had read this poem to each other more than once it occurred to me that the poem should be recited without further delay to a don in my own college, Balliol, who had spoken disparagingly of Chesterton and who might, for all I knew, be the don who had provoked Belloc. I therefore returned to Balliol and serenaded the don under his windows, and it might have been better for me had he been 'remote and ineffectual'. So far from being remote he was very much on the spot. Somewhat chastened by our interview, I wrote to Belloc next day to describe the effect of his poetry.[21]

It was clear from Belloc's reply that he was delighted that his 'Lines to a Don' had produced such a subversive effect at his old college. 'This is as it should be and warms my heart! Verse is intended to produce that sort of effect – notably in Balliol, when, in my time, we read and wrote it continually, and, when it seemed insufficient, added music to it, and when that failed, drink.'[22]

One of Lunn's acquaintances at Balliol was Ronald Knox. They were exact contemporaries, both being born in 1888. Knox, like Lunn, had fallen under the spell of the Chesterbelloc, although in Knox's case it was Chesterton rather than Belloc who had cast the spell. Knox recalled, as one of his 'indelible memories' of the many debates he attended at the Oxford Union, 'Hilaire Belloc waggling a cigar between his fingers as he demolished the House of Lords'.[23] Knox would eventually convert to Catholicism under Chesterton's benign influence and, many years later as a Catholic priest, he would receive Lunn into the Church, the latter finally succumbing to Belloc's appeal to reason.

Meanwhile, at Cambridge, Rupert Brooke remained as much under Belloc's influence as ever. In May 1907 he finally met his hero in the flesh and was evidently greatly impressed. 'Last night I went to a private small society in Pembroke where Hilaire Belloc came and read a paper and talked and drank beer – all in great measure. He was vastly entertaining.' Belloc's paper and his replies to questions were 'all magnificent to hear'. At the end of the evening Brooke walked Belloc back to his lodgings, a distance of about a mile, finding that his mentor was 'wonderfully drunk and talked all the way'.[24]

A year earlier, Brooke had been slightly disappointed by Belloc's *Esto Perpetua*:

I had expected something like 'The Path to Rome', and was therefore disappointed ... it is historical, descriptive, quite interesting, the expression of an unusual view. But it is not Belloc. I miss that grave and fantastic irresponsibility; it is a clever book which might have been written by any of several men; I wanted one that only one could have made.[25]

Presumably, Brooke's faith in Belloc would have been restored with the publication of *Hills and the Sea*, a book 'that only one could have made'. Either way, his admiration for his literary role model had been clearly confirmed and reinforced by his meeting with him. Others of Brooke's generation would be similarly touched by the beguiling influence of Belloc's powerful literary personality. Young men such as David Jones, Ivor Gurney, Siegfried Sassoon and Edward Thomas, all destined to achieve immortality with Brooke in the ranks of the 'war poets', would each succumb to Belloc's powers. As a writer of both poetry and prose, or as an indomitable defier of Parliament and defender of the Faith, Belloc could now count alongside his many friends a growing circle of disciples.

FIFTEEN

Love and Laughter

THE FINAL YEARS OF THE EDWARDIAN ERA were possibly the happiest of Belloc's life. He had achieved a high degree of celebrity without actively seeking it, and without the financial rewards that so often accompany it – fame without fortune. The absence of material fortune notwithstanding, his irrepressible *joie de vivre* remained undimmed. He enjoyed the laughter and the love of friends that were always so essential to him, and, most important of all, he and Elodie were very happy together, more so than ever now that they had finally found themselves a true home at King's Land.

'You are my beloved & I shall not go to bed without saluting you,' Belloc wrote to Elodie from Chesterton's home in Battersea on the evening of 28 March 1907.[1] The letter was addressed to her 'c/o Mrs Leigh-Smith, 2 Morpeth Terrace, Westminster, SW', suggesting that Elodie was also staying in London at the time. This was unusual. Elodie was never happier than when she was at home at King's Land with her children and her garden, and she strayed from its seclusion and sanctuary as rarely as possible. She had grown so fond of the garden that Belloc had built her a brick path along which she set about planting flowers and herbs. Belloc had written to Phillimore on 1 March beseeching him to 'write to the Mistress of this Honourable House and inform her of how *Lavender, Rosemary, Bergamot, Burrage, Anisette, Crème-de-menthe* and *Grand Marnier* may be grown: as also *Old Man, London Pride, Angelique, Lemon Plant, Scented Poplar* and others'. Continuing in similarly frivolous vein, he asked him 'to write Elodie on Annuals, bi-ennials, perennials (the hardy things!) and even millenials – but anyhow, write to her on FLOWERS for BORDERING PATHS'.[2]

'I never dress for dinner here,' Elodie wrote to a friend on 15 June, 'I just change my bodice or such-like. The days are long and quiet . . . Most people would find it dull – but I adore it . . . It is like Heaven, thank

God.'³ Apart from the hours spent in the garden, Elodie filled the long, quiet days with a good deal of reading. From the gleanings arranged in her scrapbook it would appear that her reading included the works of such divergent writers as Froissart, Whitman, Emily Brontë, Coventry Patmore, Ambrose Bierce, Matthew Arnold, Alice Meynell, St Bernard of Clairvaux and Robert Louis Stevenson. She also found time to teach the Catechism to two Catholic boys from the village.

Elodie's faith was a great support to Belloc. 'It is almost impossible for anyone to whom God has not given it to suffer, to know what it is for two militant and convinced Catholics to live in our world in England,' Elodie wrote to the Jesuit Father Matthew Russell on 4 June, but Hilaire's 'love and his companionship and the security of the Faith' were 'an unmerited reward' for such suffering.⁴ The degree to which Elodie was a 'militant and convinced' Catholic was evident from the fact that she placed a crucifix on a low beam at King's Land 'so that the infidel must bow to the crucifix'.⁵ Her faith, and her sense of spiritual exile, was again in evidence in a letter to Madame Belloc in which she recounted a trip to the priory at Storrington for a Mass at which there 'were eight little angels to make their First Holy Communion ... Hilary and I and the whole churchful all went to Holy Communion after the little ones, and my one overwhelming emotion was the wonderful unity of the Church, and what a holy Home she is to us weary exiles.'⁶

Perhaps it was this visit to Storrington that inspired Belloc's memorable poem, 'Courtesy'.

> On Monks I did in Storrington fall,
> They took me straight into their Hall;
> I saw Three Pictures on a wall,
> And Courtesy was in them all.

It says much for Belloc's peace of mind at this time that he was finding a flood of inspiration to write some of his finest verse. 'Tell Phillimore I have written one good poem every day for now 4 months,' he wrote to a friend on House of Commons notepaper on 8 March.⁷ When these poems – or at least some of them – were published, Belloc dedicated the volume, appropriately in verse, 'to John Swinnerton Phillimore'. Amongst the poems included in *Verses*, published by Duckworth in 1910, were his intoxicating 'Drinking Song on the Excellence of Burgundy Wine' and his 'Dedicatory Ode' with its oft-quoted celebration of 'laughter and the love of friends'.

During this period of contentment Belloc also produced the work for which he is most remembered. *Cautionary Tales for Children*, published in 1907 by Eveleigh Nash and illustrated by Basil Blackwood, was a return to the genre of children's verse that had made him known to the general reading public a decade earlier. Mindful of the lucrative commercial success of *The Bad Child's Book of Beasts* and *More Beasts (for Worse Children)*, it is likely that he undertook the writing of this new volume for purely mercenary motives, hoping to emulate his previous success and alleviate his finances. Yet if Belloc's position had pushed him into pecuniary servitude, his less than selfless motives for writing the book did not curtail his creative gifts. The cautionary tales – of Jim, who ran away from nurse and was eaten by a lion; of Matilda, who told such dreadful lies and was burned to death; of Godolphin Horne, who was cursed with the sin of pride and became a bootblack; of Rebecca, who slammed doors for fun and perished miserably; and of Algernon, who played with a loaded gun and, on missing his sister, was reprimanded by his father – are timeless classics of comic verse.

The *Cautionary Tales for Children* were purportedly 'designed for the admonition of children between the ages of eight and fourteen years'. In fact, they have been admired by 'children' from eight to eighty. The book's popular success was assisted greatly in the months following publication by the famous contralto Clara Butt, who sang the *Cautionary Tales* to sell-out audiences up and down the country. In recent years, Stephen Fry's audio-recordings of the *Tales* have popularized them to a whole new audience, confirming their timeless quality. It might be unjust that Belloc is sometimes only remembered for these comic verses, but it is nonetheless true that he deserves to be known as one of the great comic poets, equal and arguably superior to Lewis Carroll and Edward Lear.

Belloc inadvertently made the comparison between his own work and that of Lewis Carroll in his essay on 'Children's Books' published in the *New Witness* several years later.

As to the element of morals, we have already had the prime element of injustice to be put right. That you must always have, because the sense of justice is the basis of any moral teaching, and it is especially the clearest thing in a child's creed. It is, for instance, the weakness of Lewis Carroll's books that the man did not love justice and that you have no iniquity redressed, but unfortunately a little spitefulness now and then against the sense of justice. For the world in which he lived was at once a privileged and a timid world. But one may fearlessly adventure into plain moral teaching of all kinds and please an audience of children immensely thereby, so long as the thing is done through the vehicle of a story. For instance, one may show the misadventures of a coward or a boastful man to the great delight of children, and in connection with this it is always well to put in a good dose of violence.[8]

Far more prosaic, in every sense of the word, were two books of historical topography on which Belloc was working at this time. *The Historic Thames* was published in 1907, with coloured illustrations by the well-known watercolour artist A.R. Quinton. It was published as one of a series of books, edited by Edward Thomas, under the collective title *The Heart of England*. Thomas had invited Belloc to contribute to the series during one of the star-studded literary gatherings at the Mont Blanc restaurant in Soho. Belloc's arid approach to his subject, scholarly and somewhat laboured, was coloured and lightened by Quinton's realistic but romantically stylized watercolours. Quinton contributed some 60 paintings to the special limited edition of the book, all of which were exhibited by the Royal Society of British Artists.

The other work, *The Pyrenees*, was the fruit of Belloc's love affair with the mountain range that separates France and Spain. He had explored the Pyrenean peaks on foot on several occasions, capturing their melancholy and mystical spirit evocatively and immortally in the succinct brilliance of 'Tarantella', possibly his finest poem. *The Pyrenees*, however, has more the taste of a textbook than the flavour of any mystical memory. The magic and majesty, so potent in 'Tarantella', has to compete in *The Pyrenees* with technical details of how one should set about exploring the mountains. Robert Speaight described the book as 'much the best guide' to the Pyrenees that exists, but one feels nonetheless that Belloc's undoubted genius is being squandered when he contents himself with the penning of guidebooks, however good they may be.

Belloc's most recent trip to the Pyrenees, at the time he wrote the book, had been in September 1907, when he had crossed the mountains on foot intending to walk the length of Spain all the way to Seville. Spain, however, defeated him. Having arrived, utterly exhausted, in Madrid, he wrote dramatically and dejectedly to Baring of his experiences.

Yes, at last! Madrid! But at what cost! All the way burning deserts from the Pyrenees onwards and my Christ! What cooking! Never again! Next time on a mule, or in a Litter, or even in a train. But never again on foot across those brown Sahara plains and those form-less, treeless hills. I have added to my knowledge and I am a fuller man. I know now what is meant by 'Dura Iberiae Tellus' as also by the 'Reconquista'. Great God what a march. I am off home. It is not to be endured. I had meant to run to earth the great-granddaughter of Carmen in Seville, but it was not for me. The country has defeated me as it did Napoleon and sundry others. What an ugly country, a curious place, more like the moon than the earth . . .

I have had enough of Spain. I have crossed the Pyrenees by a difficult col that makes me sick to think of even now, so steep it was and so precipitous for one on foot and all alone . . .[9]

In October 1907, Pope Pius X issued his famous encyclical *Pascendi*, con-demning Modernism. Belloc, recently returned from staunchly Catholic Spain, was delighted with the Pope's decisive and definitive response to the Modernist crisis in the Church. 'Have you seen the Pope's gentle remarks to Modernists?' he enquired of a friend on 8 October. 'They are indeed noble! . . . He gently hints that they can't think – which is true. The old Heretics had guts, notably Calvin, and could think like the Devil, who inspired them. But the Modernists are inspired by a little minor he-devil with one Eye and a stammer, and the result is poor.'[10]

In September 1908 a Congress of leading Modernists was held at Storrington, deep in the very heart of Belloc's 'South Country'. The pres-ence of George Tyrrell, Henri Bremond and Maud Petre on his own doorstep might have been expected to incur the wrath of the 'furious Frenchman'. Instead it simply induced a good deal of mirth. In a letter to Baring, Belloc claimed that Maud Petre had written a book to prove that God was not a 'Person' but a 'Vagueness' and illustrated the difference between the two conceptions with an amusing sketch. In similar mischiev-ous mood, he played punningly with the names 'Peter' and 'Petre' in conversation with William Temple: 'They think we've got the text wrong, and that what Our Blessed Lord really said was "Thou art Maud Petre, and upon this rock I will build My Church".'[11]

There was, perhaps, more than a hint of Belloc's anti-Modernist influ-ence in Chesterton's lengthy debate with Robert Dell, a leading Modernist, in the *Church Socialist Quarterly* in 1909. Chesterton's article in the January edition contrasted the solid 'Tree' of Tradition with the vague 'Cloud' of Modernism, clearly paralleling Belloc's distinction between the 'Person' and the 'Vagueness' of God.

Belloc's clinically Thomist mind was merely baffling to those not so endowed. Max Beerbohm lamented Belloc's 'conviction that there was only a single lane to Heaven', and linked it to what he termed 'blind spots' akin to irrational tribalism. Thus, for instance, when Beerbohm was told that Belloc had been to a cricket match he remarked, with a caustic wit of which Belloc himself would no doubt have approved, that Belloc probably believed 'that the only good wicket-keeper in the history of the game was a Frenchman and a Roman Catholic'.[12] In spite of their 'blind spots', Beerbohm loved and admired both Belloc and Chesterton, describing them as 'delightful men': 'Such enormous gusto, you know, such gaiety, and feeling for life.'[13]

Beerbohm equalled Belloc and Chesterton in gusto and gaiety and shared not only their *joie de vivre* but their friendship. He recalled Belloc's high-pitched singing voice, so surprising in one so sturdy of build, and told Edmund Wilson how Belloc used to sing French hunting songs in a sweet and exquisite way: 'It was rather like a very large nightingale.'[14] Beerbohm's wit was a match for both Belloc and Chesterton and he lampooned them both to hilarious effect. His parody of Bellocian poetry and prose, published in *A Christmas Garland* in 1912, is little short of brilliant. Similarly, his caricature of Belloc and Chesterton, published in 1907, encapsulates the way that the Chesterbelloc was perceived by the public at large. It shows a gargantuan Chesterton seated at a table swigging heartily from a tankard of ale. Opposite him, a tiny Belloc, standing tiptoe on the chair in order to match Chesterton's height, gesticulates forcefully with one hand, endeavouring to make a point, while the other hand embraces a foaming tankard. It is captioned: 'Mr Hilaire Belloc, striving to win Mr Gilbert Chesterton over from the errors of Geneva.'[15] Images such as this were typical of the myth and the mirth surrounding the Chesterbelloc, intoxicating images that would cause H.G. Wells to complain that 'Chesterton and Belloc have surrounded Catholicism with a kind of boozy halo.'[16]

Whereas Beerbohm laughed with, and loved, both halves of the Chesterbelloc, Wells increasingly loved the one and loathed the other. On 11 January 1908 he wrote in the *New Age* that he cherished Chesterton's company, desiring to 'drink limitless old October from handsome flagons' with him and 'argue mightily about Pride (his weak point) and the nature of Deity'. Belloc, however, was not welcome. 'Chesterton often – but never by any chance Belloc. Belloc I admire beyond measure, but there is a sort of partisan viciousness about Belloc that bars him . . .' Years later, Wells and Belloc would cross swords in an embittered battle in which

Belloc would exhibit every aspect of his 'partisan viciousness'. For the present, however, their differences were tempered by civility and mutual respect. 'You write wonderfully,' Wells wrote to Belloc on 12 October 1908, complimenting him for a recent article in the *Morning Post*. 'I think indeed you write English as well as any man alive.'[17]

In a later issue of the *New Age*, George Bernard Shaw wrote:

> Wells has written ... about Chesterton and Belloc without stopping to consider what Chesterton and Belloc is. This sounds like bad grammar; but I know what I am about. Chesterton and Belloc is a conspiracy, and a most dangerous one at that. Not a viciously intended one: quite the contrary. It is a game of make-believe of the sort which all imaginative grown-up children love to play ...
>
> Now at first sight it would seem that it does not lie with me to rebuke this sort of make-believe. The celebrated G.B.S. is about as real as a pantomime ostrich. But it is less alluring than the Chesterton-Belloc chimera, because as they have four legs to move the thing with, whereas I have only two, they can produce the quadrupedal illusion, which is the popular feature of your pantomime beast.[18]

Shaw's essay, entitled 'The Chesterbelloc: A Lampoon', was intended to suggest that Chesterton and Belloc were now seen so synonymously that they formed two halves of 'a very amusing pantomime elephant'. Yet Shaw was only stating the obvious in an amusingly imaginative way, christening a literary friendship that was already firmly enshrined in the public imagination, as Beerbohm's caricature of the previous year had demonstrated.

Not everyone was amused by Shaw's lampoon. Maurice Baring wrote to Chesterton from Moscow to say that he 'hated GBS's article on you and Hilaire', believing it to be 'rude, beastly and untrue'.[19] Chesterton, however, seemed amused by it and referred to it good-naturedly in his autobiography.[20]

Chesterton's *Autobiography* also refers to a memorable day, recorded in Elodie's diary as being 3 January 1908, on which he and his wife, during a visit to King's Land, accompanied Hilaire and Elodie in a quest to find the source of the River Arun.

> Among the memories that are blown back to me, as by a wind over the Downs, is that of the winter day when Belloc dragged us through Sussex to find the source of the Arun. The company included his wife and mine ... We did find the place where the Arun rose in the hills;

and it was indeed, of all the sights I have seen, one of the most beautiful; I might almost say the most classical. For it rose in a (partly frozen) pool in a small grove of slender trees, silver with the frost, that looked somehow like the pale and delicate pillars of a temple.[21]

Chesterton's account omitted to mention the presence of Maurice Baring, the fifth member of the party. According to the entry in Elodie's diary, Baring had arrived from London by taxi at lunchtime, joining the Chestertons who had returned to King's Land with Belloc on the previous day. 'We all had great fun over our lunch & in the afternoon we all taximotred [sic] up to Hammer's Ponds to see the sources of the Arun. It was unspeakably lovely. It still freezes. Maurice Baring stayed all night.'[22]

After their icily aesthetic experiences at the Arun's source, the party retreated to the warmth of a nearby inn where large tumblers of hot rum were consumed. Returning to King's Land, they said the Litany of Loretto in the upstairs room which the Bellocs had recently converted into a chapel, complete with altar, tabernacle and a large missal with its oak stand. Solemnities concluded, the frivolities resumed and Chesterton recalled Belloc 'continually flinging open the door and rushing out to a telescope in the garden (it was already a frosty starlight) and loudly hallooing to the ladies to come and see God making energy'. It seems, from Chesterton's delightful account, that Belloc was in a particularly jolly mood, volleying out lines at regular intervals from a verse by Mary Elizabeth Coleridge that he had recently discovered:

> We were young, we were merry, we were very very wise,
> And the doors stood open at our feast;
> When there passed us a woman with the west in her eyes
> And a man with his back to the east.

The day's festivities 'terminated with a magnificent feast of wine, and all ended in a glow of gaiety; but,' Chesterton added, writing almost 30 years after the event, 'there lingers a sort of legend of that day in winter . . .'[23]

Chesterton recounts 'another rather ridiculous private incident' in his *Autobiography* which 'involved the meeting of Belloc and a very famous and distinguished author'. The author in question was Henry James and the meeting occurred during 1908 in Rye, on the Sussex coast, where Chesterton and his wife had rented a house for a short holiday. James lived next door and, when he learned of the Chestertons' arrival, decided to pay them a visit. Chesterton described his first impressions of the 65-year-old American novelist, 'a very stately and courteous old gentleman' in a 'formal frock-coat', and he likened his visit to 'a very stately call of state'. All of a sudden the puritanical decorum was shattered by a noise resembling that of 'an impatient fog-horn'. It was Belloc, bellowing for beer and bacon. His arrival was something of a surprise because Chesterton was under the impression that Belloc was in France, 'walking with a friend of his in the Foreign Office, a co-religionist of one of the old Catholic families'. They had, however, 'by some miscalculation . . . found themselves in the middle of their travels entirely without money'.

> Their clothes collapsed and they managed to get into some workmen's slops. They had no razors and could not afford a shave. They must have saved their last penny to re-cross the sea . . . They arrived, roaring for food and drink and derisively accusing each other of having secretly washed, in violation of an implied contract between tramps. In this fashion they burst in upon the balanced tea-cup and tentative sentence of Mr Henry James.
>
> Henry James had a name for being subtle; but I think that situation was too subtle for him. I doubt to this day whether he, of all men, did not miss the irony of the best comedy in which he ever played a part. He left America because he loved Europe, and all that was meant by England or France; the gentry, the gallantry, the tradition of lineage and locality, the life that had been lived beneath old portraits in oak-panelled rooms. And there, on the other side of the tea-table, was Europe, was the old thing that made France and England, the posterity of the English squires and the French soldiers; ragged, unshaven, shouting for beer, shameless above all shades of poverty and wealth; sprawling, indifferent, secure. And what looked across at it was still the Puritan refinement of Boston; and the space it looked across was wider than the Atlantic.[24]

Chesterton's love for Belloc is obvious from his affectionate rendition of this humorous, if somewhat embarrassing, episode. Maurice Baring, too, shared Chesterton's deep affection for their mutual friend. 'Maurice Baring loves King's Land,' Elodie had written in her diary on 3 January 1908, and his frequent visits were enjoyed not merely by her husband but also by her children. 'Maurice organized delightfully rough games,' remembered Eleanor, 'and we often rode on his back, either with him on all fours on the drawing-room floor rapidly in and out of the furniture, or at great and dangerous speed round the garden. He dearly loved a frolic and enjoyed our answering delight. His eyes were shining and he allowed us to stroke his bald head.'[25]

If Baring 'dearly loved a frolic', so did Belloc and Chesterton, and tales abound of their riotous exploits. It was around this time that Belloc and Chesterton attended a party in Soho, organized by the Liberal MP Charles Masterman. 'At dinner they all abandoned themselves to childish enjoyment,' wrote Maisie Ward in *Return to Chesterton*. 'They wore paper caps. They romped round the table. At midnight they were thrown out. Then up rose Belloc with the remark: "I have anticipated this moment and am ready for it."' At Belloc's prompting the party-goers hailed taxis and drove off to Maurice Baring's flat 'where a stupendous supper awaited them'. By four o'clock in the morning, Belloc was standing on one chair and Chesterton on another, each engaged in impassioned argument with the other in the mock-manner of soapbox orators, while the rest of the revellers roared their approval, or otherwise, from the sidelines.[26] Such evenings were always more important to their participants than the frivolities might suggest. As many of Belloc's and Chesterton's essays and poems would testify, love and laughter were linked in a mystical unity. Beyond the mere love of laughter was to be found the laughter of love.

SIXTEEN

Religion and Politics

O N 1 AUGUST 1907 Belloc had written to A.C. Benson expressing great admiration for the latter's brother, the convert-priest and bestselling novelist R.H. Benson. Belloc wrote that he had met him once or twice 'and liked him enormously' and confessed a great sympathy for Benson's historical novels. 'It is quite on the cards that he will be the man to write some day a book to give us some sort of idea what happened in England between 1520 and 1560.'[1] In the event, Benson's early death in 1914 meant that he would never fulfil Belloc's hopes. Instead, increasingly frustrated at the Protestant bias of the Whig historians, Belloc began to study the period himself. In 1908 *The Catholic Church and Historical Truth*, Belloc's first foray into the contentious world of religion and history, was published. In later years he would publish studies of key figures of the sixteenth and seventeenth centuries, such as Wolsey, Cromwell, James I, Charles II and Cranmer. His *How the Reformation Happened*, published in 1928, would represent his attempt to put the whole period into context. In 1908, however, he was more concerned with the relationship between religion and politics than with his later fixation on questions of history.

Early in the year, as previously mentioned, he inscribed his own copy of *The Path to Rome* with a succinct statement of his personal political philosophy. 'When you have reconciled these two things – I mean the high stoicism of the Republic and the humility of the Church (for they can co-exist) then you will have the perfect state.'[2] Such idealism sat uncomfortably on the backbenches of Parliament. On 19 February 1908, Belloc moved 'that this House regrets the secrecy under which political funds are accumulated and administered and regards such secrecy as a peril to its privileges and character'. Three weeks later he informed Maurice Baring, almost casually, that he 'went to the House' and 'voted against the Government' as though he were a dutiful member of His Majesty's Opposition, not a dissenting and disillusioned member of the government itself.[3] At best, Belloc must have appeared to his parliamentary colleagues on the government benches as something of a maverick; at worst he would have seemed a positive liability.

Belloc's jaded vision of parliamentary politics inspired two more satirical novels, *Mr Clutterbuck's Election* and *A Change in the Cabinet*, published in 1908 and 1909 respectively. These were written in haste and in haphazard fashion, most of the former being dictated at a stretch in Holy Week, possibly to mollify the effects of abstinence. For the first time, Belloc wrote to Maurice Baring on 13 April 1908, he had given up drinking beer or wine in Holy Week:

> ... partly to see what this is like, partly in memory of the Passion, and partly to strengthen my will which has lately had bulgy spots on it.
>
> I have now gone through thirty-six hours of this ordeal, and very interesting and curious it is ... The mind and body sink to a lower plane and become fit for contemplation rather than for action: the sense of humour is also singularly weakened.[4]

In later years Belloc extended his abstinence to the whole of Lent, drinking crates of ginger beer instead of his customary Burgundy. 'I have become a Protestant and am drinking no wine during Lent, with the most terrible results to my soul which is in permanent despair,' he wrote to Chesterton in 1912. 'I now see what a fool everybody is, a truth which, until now the fumes of fermented liquor had hidden from me.'[5]

It is a little curious, considering that he had spent most of Holy Week writing a satirical novel, that Belloc should confess to Baring that abstinence had 'singularly weakened' his sense of humour. Perhaps this explains why *Mr Clutterbuck's Election* does not rate amongst Belloc's better books. Perhaps, indeed, the novel would have been better, and funnier, if he had waited until Easter. *A Change in the Cabinet* was written in similar haste. Belloc told Wilfrid Scawen Blunt that it 'was run up in such a scramble (seven days) without a touch of the pen & so purely for money that I was ashamed of it, & when the press let off by blaming it I agreed'. Blunt, however, had enjoyed the book and, possibly prompted by his friend's positive response, Belloc moderated his self-criticism. 'But the later reviews are much more favourable & your letter puts me in heart again.'[6]

More successful than his satirical novels were the volumes of essays published at regular intervals during this period; essays *On Nothing* in

1908, *On Everything* in 1909 and *On Anything* and *On Something* in 1910. These illustrate Belloc's undoubted position as one of the twentieth century's foremost and most gifted essayists. They also illustrate not only his Catholicism in all its various guises, but also his catholicity of taste on anything, everything and even, most beguilingly, on nothing in particular. Thus, for instance, he writes 'On the Pleasure of Taking Up One's Pen', 'On Ignorance', 'On Tea', 'On Them', 'On Death', 'On Unknown People', 'On Thruppenny Bits', 'On Experience', 'On Immortality', 'On Sacramental Things', 'On Song', 'On the Rights of Property', 'On Old Towns', 'On High Places' and, appropriately enough at the conclusion of one of the volumes, 'On Coming to an End'. In the pages of these volumes one discovers, in the absence of any autobiography, more about Belloc the man than is discernible in any of his other works, with the exception of some of his verses or those hauntingly personal pilgrimages of the soul, *The Path to Rome*, *The Cruise of the Nona* and *The Four Men*.

Nonetheless, and in spite of their evident success as literature, Belloc wrote many of these essays for purely mercenary motives. They were written, for the most part, for publications such as the *Morning Post*, the *Westminster Gazette* or the *Manchester Guardian* to stave off the ever-present threat of poverty. He had a young family to support and a large house in need of much renovation. His precarious position was put poignantly in December 1907 in a letter to Wilfrid Scawen Blunt.

> I have built myself a new chimney & a flagged floor is next to be built. Then I shall heal the Hall above the floor, then I shall write yet another Pot-Boiler & build stables. Such is the life of man: it is a getting & a spending.
>
> I have this consolation, that I produce nothing (for words are nothing) but that I cause things to exist, bricks & stone & now & all in the right shape.[7]

Aside from the ruminations of his essays, and a brief return to the subject of history with the publication in October 1908 of *The Eye-Witness*, a series of historical scenic miniatures, Belloc remained preoccupied with politics. Two pamphlets for the Catholic Truth Society, *An Examination of Socialism* (1908) and *The Church and Socialism* (1909), indicated that he had broken decisively with all Marxian and pseudo-Marxian alternatives to capitalism. Instead, his radicalism was distinctly Catholic, in the sense that it adhered to the Church's social teaching as preached by Pope Leo XIII in *Rerum Novarum* and by the hero of his youth, Cardinal Manning.

On 18 November 1908, at a public debate held at the Surrey Masonic Hall in Camberwell, Belloc and Chesterton argued against socialism from a radical Christian perspective while Shaw and Chesterton's brother, Cecil, argued for it.

In *The Church and Socialism* Belloc described 'modern industrial society' as 'evil beyond expression, cruel, unjust, cowardly and horribly insecure'. Socialism offered what purported to be 'an obvious and simple remedy', the abolition of private property in land and in the means of production and its replacement by centralized State control: 'let all become workmen of the State, which shall have absolute economic control over the lives of all and preserve to all security and sufficiency'.

> Why does the Church, to which this modern industrial society is loathsome, and which is combating it with all her might; why does the Church, which continually points to the abominations of our great cities as a proof of what men come to by abandoning her; why does the Church, whose every doctrine is offended and denied by this evil, reject the solution offered?[8]

Ultimately, Belloc maintained, the socialist solution was rooted in 'the same false philosophy of life' that had caused the problem in the first place and 'which is now attempting to remedy its own errors by the introduction of a remedy still reposing on the same false philosophy: the remedy of collectivism'. The problem resided in private property being *collected* into the hands of too few people.

> . . . first the great landlord of the 'Reformation' rising on the ruins of religion was economically dominant, next the merchant capitalist reached the head of affairs, until now more and more the mere gambler or the mere swindler enjoys supreme economic power in our diseased and moribund economic society. It was precisely because the old European sense of personal connection between the owner and the thing owned was repudiated and lost when the true conception of life was repudiated and lost with the loss of the Faith, that these monstrous financial fortunes which are the very negation of property at last arose.[9]

The Church's solution was the opposite of collectivism in its capitalist or communist form. Instead of collecting property into the hands of a privileged few, whether the 'few' be powerful 'private' plutocrats or equally powerful 'public' bureaucrats, it should be returned to the hands of the 'many', creating 'a society of highly divided properties bound together by free co-operative organizations'.[10] Later, under Belloc's and Chesterton's patronage, this solution, or creed, would become known to a growing number of its adherents in England as 'distributism'. In the language of the social teaching of the Church, applicable worldwide, it has become known as the principle of subsidiarity.

Chesterton openly confessed that Belloc had converted him to the distributist creed. 'You were the founder and father of this mission,' he would write in an 'Open Letter' to Belloc 15 years later; 'we were the converts but you were the missionary . . . you first revealed the truth both to its greater and its lesser servants . . . Great will be your glory if England breathes again.'[11]

In spite of the Roman roots of Belloc's political vision, Chesterton envisaged him as a natural heir to the quintessentially English radicalism of William Cobbett. 'In Mr Chesterton's view,' wrote the critic R. Ellis Roberts in his review of Chesterton's *William Cobbett*, 'Cobbett stood for England: England unindustrialized, self-sufficient, relying on a basis of agriculture and sound commerce for her prosperity, with no desire for inflation.'[12] In his efforts to mould Belloc into Cobbett's image, Chesterton was at pains to claim Belloc's 'English' credentials. 'Belloc, with the French surname, looked much more like an Englishman; indeed he ended by being the one solitary but symbolic Englishman really looking like the traditional John Bull . . . he looked exactly like what all English farmers ought to look like; and was, as it were, a better portrait of Cobbett than Cobbett was.'[13]

Others failed to share Chesterton's vision of Belloc's Englishness. The sight of Belloc, as recalled by Father H.E.G. Rope, delivering a speech in fluent French at the Westminster Eucharistic Congress in the Albert Hall in 1908 did not exactly suggest the image of a latter-day Cobbett.[14] In spite of Belloc's love for Sussex, the most English of counties, for real ale, the most English of drinks, and for Chesterton, the most English of writers, many still perceived the 'furious' or curious 'Frenchman' as an outsider. The humorists of *Punch*, playing on this popular perception, preferred to emphasize Belloc's exotic roots and esoteric interests as a means of highlighting his unlikely credentials as a Member of Parliament for Salford.

Inquiries at the House of Commons elicited the fact that Mr Belloc is the most hardworked of our younger Parliamentarians. The week-end brings him no respite from his labours, as he invariably spends it in the grimy heart of Salford among his constituents, where he conducts classes in military history, conversational French, mediaeval theology, and thorough Bass. As Mr Belloc has expressed it in a touching couplet:

> French is my heart and loyal and sincere
> Is, and shall be, my love of British beer.[15]

Finally, making the predictable and seemingly almost compulsory link between Belloc and Chesterton, *Punch* suggested that Belloc should name his new novel 'The Man who was Thirsty'.

Ironically, it was Belloc's 'love of British beer', far more than his interest in military history or medieval theology, which incurred the wrath of his constituency party. 'It is taking me all my time to keep the peace here,' Belloc's agent Charles Goodwin wrote on 2 December 1908. 'We had a meeting last night, and a resolution was passed regretting your vote on the Licensing Bill. The rank and file keep forgiving you your antagonism to the Government ever since you were elected, but the temper exhibited last night indicated that they are getting fed up with your policy – which they don't understand.'[16] Belloc was undaunted and unrepentant, replying defiantly that he was 'absolutely certain that a man representing a working-class constituency is safe in regarding a certain number of fads as poison to his constituents; Teetotalism is one, and without doubt Women's Suffrage is another'.[17]

His attitude to the teetotalitarian puritanism of the Temperance movement and to the embryonic feminism of the suffragettes was linked to a deep-rooted belief that both 'fads' were inspired by the patronizing, or in the latter case the matronizing, assumption that working-class prejudice and ignorance could be steamrollered by 'enlightened' views. He believed that this 'nanny-knows-best' mentality led to the welfare or nanny state which itself was inimical to the true freedom of the majority. Yet Belloc's opposition to female suffrage went far deeper than any mistrust of superciliousness and elitism in public affairs. Furthermore, and contrary to popular assumptions, his opposition had nothing to do with the chauvinistic or misogynistic prejudices that are sometimes ascribed to him. His speech in Parliament on 11 July 1910 in relation to the Second Reading of the Parliamentary Franchise (Women) Bill was characterized by a desire to distance himself from 'those whom I shall support with my vote'.

'No one, I notice,' he said, 'has remarked, and that is to the honour of human nature, and even to the nature of politicians, that women are excluded from public action of this kind by a lack of intelligence. I have never met but one category of men who had of women the opinion that their intelligence was inferior to men. That category is only to be found amongst the very young unmarried men. As their experience of life increases the judgement of men with regard to the intelligence of women passes from reverence to stupor, and from stupor to terror. When the honourable Member for Clitheroe proposed that we should recognize the intelligence of women from the fact that they wrote books, I confess it turned me cold. There is perhaps nothing which an educated man or a woman can do which requires less intelligence than the writing of a book.'

Having dismissed any argument arising from the ability of women to fulfil 'the merely trivial function, nearly always done for money or notoriety, of writing a book', he went on to state that 'the argument drawn from physical force' against female suffrage was 'equally baseless . . . The idea that a State ultimately reposes in physical force is the uttermost nonsense. The fate of countries and of empires has been decided in the general run by the common sense and traditional and continuous will of the community . . . The ultimate sanction of physical force is not the ultimate sanction of society . . . Something much more complex, much more deep, and much more worthy of our natures is at the basis of our society.'

He also countered the argument that female suffrage would affect the political life of the country, either positively or negatively, by insisting that the party system would continue to serve the present oligarchy regardless of any additions to the electoral roll. 'I am sorry to say there is no more hope of changing the nature of English politics by that than there is by the anger, satire and indignation which have been used for generations. They will go on precisely as before.'

Belloc's reason for opposing female suffrage was not, therefore, linked to any of the stereotypical presumptions. On the contrary, he did not believe that women should keep out of politics because it was beyond them but because it was *beneath* them: 'If the House will look at society as it is now organized, and see what we do and what we refrain from doing, they will find that it is the view of the wife and mother, acting sporadically and not collectively, which, on the whole, determines the complexion and the nature of the society in which we live.'

The role of motherhood in underpinning the healthy fabric of society would, he said, be undermined if women were to take on masculine functions. The subtle matriarchy at the heart of the family, and therefore at the heart of society, was threatened by such a measure. It is on this firmly feminine ground that Belloc based his opposition to female suffrage. It is a view that is doubtless unfashionable, as it is doubtless unfathomable to modernist and postmodernist prejudices, but it is not a view that can be dismissed easily as bigoted or narrow minded.

Ultimately Belloc's views on female suffrage, like his views on everything else, were coloured by his religious faith. In his speech he had alluded to the words of 'a man with a profound knowledge of human nature' who had said, when told that religion was dying, that 'you will never lose religion in society, or even change it, until the loss or the change is apparent amongst the women'. Women were the anchors that kept humanity from drifting into treacherous and uncharted waters; but this was so only for as long as the anchors were attached to the ship of faith, the Church. As always, and as he had stated specifically as soon as he had entered Parliament, Belloc's religion and his politics were inextricably bound together. The one only existed to serve the other. Religion explained the dignity of humanity; politics, properly practised, was merely the politeness that humanity's dignity demanded.

SEVENTEEN

Farewell to Parliament

Maurice Baring's reception into the Catholic Church at Brompton Oratory on 1 February 1909 was one of the great joys of Belloc's life. 'It is an immense thing,' he wrote to Charlotte Balfour. 'They are coming in like a gathering army from all manner of directions, all manner of men each bringing some new force: that of Maurice is his amazing accuracy of mind which proceeds from his great virtue of truth. I am profoundly grateful!'[1]

Baring's friendship had always been a source of peace and consolation to Belloc, and his conversion must have strengthened still further the kinship of spirit between the two men. Throughout 1909 Belloc spilled out his mounting political frustrations to Baring. 'The House of Commons is hypocritical and dull beyond words, and membership of it is a tremendous price to pay for the little advantages of being able (very rarely) to expose a scandal or to emphasize a point of public interest.'[2]

Belloc's high profile in Parliament made him an obvious target for the political cartoonists of *Punch*. On 31 March 1909, *Punch* published a caricature of Belloc by Edward Reed that accentuated his girth and referred to the fact 'that the Hon. Member fills a considerable space in the literary world'. Shortly after its publication, Belloc ran into W.H. Hudson at Victoria station. Hudson told him that he had just been laughing at the caricature. 'Ah, yes,' Belloc replied, clearly unamused, 'I've heard about it. Very funny, no doubt, but I don't much like his caricatures – they are so vulgar.' 'That's what we all say, is it not, when we are hurt!' Hudson remarked to George Gissing when reporting the incident, before adding sympathetically that he agreed with Belloc that 'the *Punch* man is rather beastly at times . . .'[3]

Belloc's sensitivity to personal attack was evident in another letter to Baring in which he expressed his misgivings about the forthcoming general election.

I am very dejected about the approaching election. I don't want to stand. I detest the vulgar futility of the whole business and the grave risks to which are attached no proportionate reward. So anxious are most people to get into Parliament that they will do anything to oust an opponent, and I have really no desire to be mixed up with such hatreds, or to see myself placarded on the walls in twenty ridiculous attitudes, and with any number of false statements or suggestions attached to my name. It is a perfectly beastly trade.[4]

As the election loomed, Belloc grew ever more pessimistic about his chances of re-election, predicting that his slim majority would be over-turned and that he would be defeated by a little over 900 votes. 'I really cannot see where my chance comes in,' he lamented to Baring. 'I bewilder so many people by not being "party"; I directly offend so many more by refusing to have anything to do with teetotalism, vegetarianism, suffrag-ism, Buddhism, and Scientific Monism, that whole belts of people who voted for me last time will vote against me this time.'[5] In what amounted to an implicit admission that his position on the Liberal benches was becoming increasingly and absurdly incongruous, he expressed his belief that most 'healthy people' who agreed with his opinions would vote Conservative.

In the event, Belloc's pessimism was unfounded. On polling day in the general election, 15 January 1910, he was re-elected with a reduced majority of only 314 votes, the narrowest of victorious margins, but victori-ous nonetheless. Cecil Chesterton wrote to him on the following day, 'to let you know how much your victory has delighted me. Your opinions and mine are not identical, but at least your return proves that political honesty is not always punished even in our dirty political system.'[6]

On 18 January Belloc wrote to a member of his campaign team in Salford, enclosing a letter of thanks to the electorate, and expressing his concerns that 'the halving of my little majority will mean a very strenuous attack next time'. Physically, the campaign had proved exhausting. 'I have got a temperature and my voice has gone altogether . . .'[7]

Meanwhile, with the trials and tribulations of the election campaign behind him, the 'Honourable Member' continued to fill 'a considerable space in the literary world'. According to Robert Blatchford, writing in the *Clarion* on 26 November 1909, he was a thing 'more precious than all the coroneted bald heads in the House of Peers; a really excellent writer of English prose'. Blatchford's appraisal would have earned Rupert Brooke's approval. The latter's admiration for Belloc remained undiminished even though he was now moving in the decidedly un-Bellocian orbit of Blooms-bury. At Brooke's invitation, Belloc gave a long monologue to a small private gathering in Cambridge that included Lytton Strachey and John Maynard Keynes.[8] He spoke at Harrow School on 'The Growth of London', eliciting the less than flattering description from L.P. Hartley, one of the 15-year-olds who comprised his audience, that he was 'a funny looking fellow . . . inclined to corpulence with a red face'.[9] Belloc was also present at a *bouts-rîmes* party hosted by Ford Madox Ford, at which the guests competed to compose a poem against the clock using set rhyme-words. Belloc won the second prize. Other guests included David Garnett, the youngest person present, and Ezra Pound who, in Garnett's words, 'had just appeared in literary London, wearing one ear-ring, which was considered very scandalous by certain ladies'.[10]

Belloc's prodigious literary output continued apace. *Marie Antoinette*, published in October 1909, had taken five years to write and was a 'pro-longed, minute and tiresome labour'. He wrote to Maurice Baring that the book was 'more learned than I had imagined myself to be', but that he was not entirely happy with the results. It was 'stodgy with good passages just like a suet pudding with plums, which is the very worst thing one can say of anybody's style'.[11]

In 1910, apart from two volumes of essays, *On Anything* and *On Something*, a new satirical political novel, *Pongo and the Bull*, and a new volume of *Verses*, Belloc's publications included a controversial pamphlet for the Catholic Truth Society on 'The Ferrer Case'. This related the case of Francisco Ferrer, a Catalonian anarchist who was executed by the Spanish authorities in October 1909 following a violent uprising in Bar-celona. As with the anarchist and communist uprisings a quarter of a century later, the politically inspired violence in Spain was aimed largely at the Church. In the riots of 1909, which Ferrer was found guilty of inciting, churches and convents were burned to the ground, graves were violated and the bodies of the dead exhumed and defiled. Nonetheless, Ferrer's execution caused a furore of protest in England. When the matter was raised in the House of Commons Belloc shouted 'Rubbish!', an inter-jection that earned him a good deal of hostile comment in the press and led to him being sent a flood of anonymous and threatening letters. Undeterred, he returned to the case as soon as the election was over, analysing it carefully in two articles in the *Dublin Review* in January and April 1910, as well as writing the pamphlet for the Catholic Truth Society.

By this time, Belloc's attitude to parliamentary politics had plumbed new depths of disillusionment. With contemptuous disregard for the institution of which he was a member, and with the noble and notable exception of the debate over female suffrage, he played little further part in the debates in the House of Commons. Instead he contented himself with making short, waggish speeches exposing the hypocrisy of politicians. These were, in the judgement of Elizabeth Haldane, 'full of wit, but irresponsible',[12] a view that must have been shared by most of Belloc's contemporaries in Parliament. A cartoon published in the *Evening Chronicle* depicted the Prime Minister, dressed as a huntsman, driving his hounds into the kennel for a crucial vote. Underneath was the caption, 'Mr Asquith's previous experience with Mr Belloc suggests a little difficulty.'[13]

Clearly Belloc's political future on the Liberal benches was becoming increasingly untenable. A parting of the ways was inevitable and when it became clear that there would be yet another general election so soon after the previous one, Belloc resolved that his days of playing the party game were over. He wrote to the local Liberals in Salford to say that he would only stand in the forthcoming election as an Independent. Informing George Wyndham of his decision, he predicted that those who controlled the caucus in Salford would not 'stand a candidate pledged to ridicule and criticize the Party System, and if they won't have me independent they shan't have me at all: if they will have me they will be idiots, for I shall be defeated and they will have paid for nothing'.[14]

Not surprisingly, and no doubt fully as Belloc had expected and possibly even hoped, the caucus refused to accept his conditions for standing again. A.C. Tait, a Socialist, urged him to contest the seat as an Independent, with or without the support of his former colleagues: '. . . your courage, your outspoken desire for straight politics and your advocacy of the democratic ideal have not gone unregarded in this land.'[15]

Belloc replied to Tait on 29 November 1910,[16] explaining his reasons for not seeking re-election.

> My retirement from Parliament at this moment is necessary under the present electoral law. Without a second ballot, without proportional representation, nothing but a very great expenditure or some particular hold upon the locality can give a man a chance against the two official candidates. Had I fought South Salford an official Liberal would have been put against me, and the sum of £600 to £1000 would have been put at his disposal, and an expenditure of £600 would have been necessary upon my side. The official Liberal would have received anywhere from a thousand to two thousand votes, proceeding from

convention, tradition, Non-Conformist opposition to a Catholic, and so forth. My quarrel would not have been that the Conservative would have got in, for it does not matter in this election who gets in, but that £600 on my side would have been thrown away. Moreover one must be inside the House to see how utterly futile is any attempt at representative action. It is all very well as advertisement, but it is without any practical consequence whatever, and it is like trying to feed on air to attempt to satisfy the appetite for action under such conditions.

I agree with you that realities may enter politics soon, and when they do I shall re-enter politics with them.[17]

Similar sentiments were expressed by Belloc at the end of November in his last-ever speech in the House of Commons: 'For myself, I repeat my own intentions as a declaration of faith, that I shall not be at pains to play the Party game ... If the machine will not let me stand as an Independent to represent my constituency and to do what my constituents want done in this House, then I think everyone will agree with me that even the most modest pen in the humblest newspaper is as good as a vote in what has ceased to be a free deliberative assembly.'[18]

As the threat of his 'modest pen' implied, Belloc's valedictory address to Parliament was by no means a farewell to politics. In fact, even as these words were being spoken, he was in the midst of writing *The Party System* with Cecil Chesterton, intended as an indictment of the undemocratic nature of parliamentary 'democracy'. On 24 July, Belloc had written to Cecil Chesterton proposing 'that we should write in collaboration a book upon the party system'.[19] 'My only feeling,' Chesterton replied on the following day, 'is one of considerable pride that you should think well enough of my work to make such a proposal.'[20]

'Cecil Chesterton wrote one half and I wrote the other,' Belloc informed George Wyndham on 27 December, 'just as the Hail Mary was written half by the Church and half by St Gabriel ... Dual authorship is seldom a success, but the Hail Mary pulled it off all right.'[21]

According to Robert Speaight, Cecil Chesterton was one of 'probably only two men who had any influence over Belloc after he had reached maturity', the other being Father Vincent McNabb.[22] Although such a judgement possibly overstates Cecil Chesterton's importance, or at least underestimates the importance of others who had influenced Belloc at least as much, his place in Belloc's life was certainly both potent and prominent while it lasted.

Temperamentally, Cecil Chesterton was very different from his brother. Like Belloc, he was a man of action, tempestuous and impulsive. 'I have known them on occasions set off at a moment's notice, without so much as a toothbrush and disappear into the void, *en route*, perhaps, for some interesting trees whose acquaintance Belloc had made the previous summer in Brittany or the Pyrenees,' wrote Ada Jones, a fiery young journalist who knew both men and who would later marry Cecil.[23]

A regular visitor to King's Land, Cecil Chesterton would argue and discuss religion and politics with Belloc deep into the night, their furious debates fuelled by the flow of wine and the glow of conviviality. Eventually, Cecil succumbed to Belloc's persuasive powers. Having been a Fabian socialist who had argued on political platforms against his brother and against Belloc, Cecil had since moved closer to them in ideology, rejecting collectivism in favour of Belloc's vision of social justice through distributism. He shared Belloc's contempt for the machinations of Parliament and was ideally suited as his collaborator on *The Party System*.

In his friendship and collaboration with Cecil Chesterton, Belloc had discovered a new and powerful ally. Furthermore, his alliance with this 'other Chesterton' would give birth to another Chesterbelloc that was set to shake the political establishment to such a degree that, in the months that followed, Belloc's 'modest pen' would be made to blush with a mixture of embarrassment and pride at his friend's reckless indiscretion and his courageous achievement in exposing the system they both despised.

EIGHTEEN

Eye-Witness to Scandal

IN THE WAKE OF the considerable controversy caused by the publication of *The Party System* in February 1911, its co-authors decided to launch a new radical weekly, financed by Charles Granville, of which Belloc would be editor and Cecil Chesterton his assistant. Belloc motored all over the country to recruit contributors, returning with promises of material from Shaw, G.K. Chesterton, H.A.L. Fisher and Algernon Blackwood. Originally, as Belloc informed W.S. Blunt, it was to be called simply *The Witness*,[1] until G.K. Chesterton suggested the *Eye-Witness* as a better alternative.[2] 'There is no need to say that it will have any particular policy,' Belloc informed Blunt, 'except that it will follow the lines which I have already associated myself with. People will know what that means . . . Also of telling the truth, so far as the police and the prison system of this country allow it.'[3]

The first issue of the *Eye-Witness*, published on 22 June 1911, included essays by Baring, Wells and Blackwood, dramatic criticism by Desmond MacCarthy, and a poem by Blunt, as well as contributions by Belloc himself. Cecil Chesterton set the combatively controversial tone that future issues would follow by writing, under the pseudonym of 'Junius', an 'Open Letter to the Prime Minister' on the subject of the sale of honours. Subsequent issues included articles or poems by G.K. Chesterton, A.C. Benson, E.S.P. Haynes, Edward Thomas, F.Y. Eccles, John Phillimore and Arthur Quiller-Couch. By the end of the year its circulation was still rising and was larger than any other weekly except *The Spectator*. The spirit with which the *Eye-Witness* was written and edited was recalled fondly by Arthur Ransome.

> This little paper was a pleasure to all of us and replaced the old
> *Week's Survey* in our affections. Tuesday was the meeting-day for its
> contributors . . . And there in a basement room [of the Adelphi Hotel]

we would hear them and find them, Belloc talking like his books (I used to listen for a reference to a 'bullet-headed French gunner'), G.K. Chesterton shaken by internal laughter, quivering like a gigantic jelly, and Cecil Chesterton, who could out-argue either of them, though he could not write so well, laughing until his eyes disappeared at things slid into the conversation by the much quieter Maurice Baring.[4]

In spite of its scathing attacks on the political system, the *Eye-Witness* was not without allies in Parliament. John Burns, the Labour politician long since admired by Belloc for his radicalism, bought two copies weekly and forced them on his colleagues in the Cabinet, much to the annoyance of the postmaster general, Herbert Samuel.[5] Belloc's increasingly robust opposition to socialism had not prevented him from continuing to have a high regard for Burns and, as a letter to Blunt on 18 April 1911 disclosed, he retained a fondness for that other great pioneer of the Labour Party, Keir Hardie.

> What I told you of Keir Hardie is reliable. The man has a larger dose of sincerity than most politicians: he suffers from a very touchy vanity which follows that kind of success, proceeding from such social origins: finally, he is not to be depended upon for active criticism of the Administration, because, in having produced the Labour Party his life's work is done and he is content, and on the side of the contented people in most things. But, as I have said, his love of justice is quite genuine and you will find that he is respected by men who are attached to that attribute.[6]

He was not so favourably disposed towards Ramsay MacDonald, the newly elected leader of the Labour Party, declaring with Wildean wit that MacDonald should beware 'lest I make you immortal with an epigram'.[7] In 1911 Belloc and MacDonald debated publicly over the ramifications of Lloyd George's National Insurance Bill. This Bill, so instrumental to the establishment of the welfare state, was welcomed by most socialists but was seen by Belloc as signifying the erosion of individual liberties. For Ramsay MacDonald the welfare state was a step towards the socialist state; for Belloc it was merely a euphemism for the servile state in which everyone was being forced to surrender their freedom to the power of politicians in return for 'insurance' against poverty. The debate between MacDonald and Belloc was printed as a pamphlet entitled *Socialism and the Servile State*, in which their respective speeches were published verbatim. In the following year Belloc would distil the arguments he had put forward in this debate in one of his most important books, *The Servile State*.

'I am going to ... tell my publishers to write and complain if *The Servile State* which I have just brought out, is not reviewed,' he wrote to G.K. Chesterton. 'There is no money in the book but I particularly want it to be widely read.'[8] Evidently, from a letter written to a friend five days later, Belloc had asked Chesterton to review it for the *Daily News*. 'I do hope the *Daily News* will allow Gilbert to review *The Servile State* although it is a book by a friend, because if he doesn't review it no one else will.'[9]

'The intellectual influence of *The Party System* and *The Servile State* is difficult to measure,' wrote Victor Feske in his study of British Liberalism from 1900 to 1939. Yet, he added, 'Belloc's dual critique sowed the seeds of doubt in the so-called Radical Liberals intent on harnessing the power of the modern state to their reformist policies ... If the arguments of *The Servile State* were correct, all of New Liberalism's assumptions were turned inside out ...'[10] Another academic, Michael Bentley, believed that *The Party System* and *The Servile State* had dealt a 'heavy blow' to progressivism and its enthusiasms.[11]

The Guild Socialist Maurice Reckitt was even more emphatic in his estimation of *The Servile State*'s influence.

> I cannot overstate the impact of this book upon my mind, and in this I was but symptomatic of thousands of others who had passed through the same phases as I had. Belloc argued, with a rigorous cogency and with forceful illustration, that the whole allegedly socialist trend, which the Fabians were so fond of boasting that they had grafted upon Liberalism, was leading not to a community of free and equal citizens, not even to any true collectivism, but to the imposition upon the masses, as the price of the reforms by which their social condition was to be ameliorated, of a servile state ...[12]

Similarly, Eric Gill's political and religious conversion possibly owed more to Belloc's *The Servile State* than to any other single factor. According to Eric's brother Cecil, in his unpublished *Autobiography*, Belloc 'contributed much to Eric's social formation with his *Servile State*'.[13] Gill, like Cecil Chesterton, was a former Fabian socialist who, under the influence of Belloc's persuasive arguments, was turning away from former influences such as Nietzsche and Wells towards the radical alternative offered by Belloc and the brothers Chesterton in the pages of the *Eye-Witness*.

More surprisingly, perhaps, is the apparent influence of *The Servile*

State on George Orwell. Discussing 'earlier writers' who had 'foreseen the emergence of a new kind of society, neither capitalist nor Socialist and probably based upon slavery', Orwell continued, 'A good example is Hilaire Belloc's book, *The Servile State* . . . it does foretell with remarkable insight the kind of things that have been happening from about 1930 onwards. Chesterton, in a less methodical way, predicted the disappearance of democracy and private property, and the rise of a slave society which might be called either capitalist or Communist.'[14]

Orwell, of course, would eventually write a bestselling novel about a slave society which could be either capitalist or communist, and it is tempting to detect the shadow of Belloc's *The Servile State* over his inspiration for *Nineteen Eighty-Four*. Yet Orwell was no great admirer of Belloc or Chesterton, both of whom were scathingly criticized by him on several occasions, most amusingly in his reference to 'Father Hilaire Chestnut's latest book of RC propaganda' in the opening chapter of his novel *Keep the Aspidistra Flying*. Yet, beguilingly, he irritated his Trotskyist friends during the 1930s by insisting that 'what England needed was to follow the kind of policies in Chesterton's *G.K.'s Weekly*'.[15]

Belloc's position as editor of the *Eye-Witness*, coupled with his authorship of *The Servile State* and co-authorship of *The Party System*, led to him being in ever greater demand as a public speaker in radical circles. He spoke to the Bristol and District Fabian Society on the party system and, in February 1911, to another meeting of the Fabians in Cambridge. At the latter engagement he stayed as the guest of A.C. Benson at Magdalene College.[16] As always, however, Belloc did not restrict himself to one subject area. He spoke on almost anything and everything to almost anyone and everyone, entertaining groups as diverse as the Hull Catholic Federation and the Hale Literary Society on subjects as varied as the Battle of Crécy and French poetry.

The multiplicity of subjects on which he chose to speak was merely a reflection of the multifarious subjects on which he chose to write. During 1911 and 1912 he published two novels, *The Girondin* and *The Green Overcoat*; a further volume of comic verse with Basil Blackwood entitled *More Peers*; historical studies such as *The French Revolution* and *The River of London*; several works of military history, including *The Battle of Blenheim, Waterloo, Crécy* and *Warfare in England*; his masterly genre-defying 'farrago' *The Four Men*; and yet more collections of his essays, *First and Last* and *This and That and the Other*, in which he discoursed on subjects as various as 'The Absence of the Past', 'St Patrick', 'Inns' and 'The Love of England'. 'If they won't buy one kind of book, then I write another,' he quipped to George Wyndham on 16 April 1911.[17]

On 11 June 1911, only days before the launch of the *Eye-Witness*, Belloc and Cecil Chesterton became embroiled on the fringes of an acrimonious dispute between their mutual friend Wilfrid Scawen Blunt and his cousin, Lord Alfred Douglas. Four days earlier, Blunt had written in his diary that the 'scoundrel Alfred Douglas has become a Catholic, after bringing a libel action not a year ago against a parson who stated that he had done so'. Douglas's conversion did not impress Blunt, who had long since lapsed from his own Catholic faith, and his attitude was hardly softened by the abusive nature of a letter received from Douglas on 10 June. Douglas referred to Blunt as 'a contemptible cad, whom most people considered a half crazy old gentleman, with a bee in his bonnet', adding in a tone clearly designed to cause the maximum offence that being 'known as your friend or associate has always been something in the nature of a social handicap'. Blunt recorded in his diary:

> Alfred Douglas writes me another abusive letter, which is what I expected and indeed intended, for I had rather have him as an enemy than a friend. His letter shows that, whatever he may have done by becoming a Catholic, it has not brought him to the point of repenting his sins. He is a swindler, a blackguard of the lowest type – the aristocratic swindler.

Blunt informed Belloc and Cecil Chesterton of 'Alfred's latest escapade' when the two men were his guests for dinner on the following evening:

> ... and they told me that among other of his blackmailing attempts ... he threatened the other Chesterton which caused them to get up the dossier of Alfred's connection with the Oscar Wilde trial and that armed with this they reduced Alfred to silence. They have got the dossier by them still ... But they consider him quite harmless to effect anything except annoyance.[18]

Apart from the suggestions of scandal surrounding Lord Alfred Douglas, the evening at Blunt's would have been dominated with talk of the *Eye-Witness*, to which Blunt had already agreed to contribute. Belloc, however, was never temperamentally suited to the role of editor and, on 2 July, within weeks of the appearance of the first issue, he was writing plaintively to George Wyndham, 'I find that I have to do the thinking, and the adding-up, and the judgement, which in a regiment would be spread among seven or eight men, and above half my energy is spent in something unknown to armies, which is the undoing of the ineptitude of others.'[19]

He was soon referring to the *Eye-Witness* as 'the wretched thing' and, in June 1912, after a year in which he had grown increasingly tired of the routine and the responsibility, he resigned the editorship to Cecil Chesterton. 'He will run the *Eye-Witness* in my place,' Belloc informed Blunt on 15 June 1912.

> I have given up putting my name outside the paper and accepting the legal responsibility of the editorship because it was steadily putting my other work into such arrears that my income was threatened. Had I independent means I would devote myself to the paper entirely. As it is the paper was eating into my other business, and pushing it further and further back ... and ... it naturally makes me anxious when I see so much being elbowed out by journalism. But I shall go on writing for this paper just the same and supervising it, only I shall not have that heavy strain of putting it together and being quite certain of every word that goes in, which was eating up my time.[20]

Four months after handing over the editorship to his assistant, Belloc wrote to Baring that the *Eye-Witness*, soon to be renamed the *New Witness*, 'continues to be conducted by Cecil Chesterton, always with vigour, not always with discretion'.[21] The words were prophetic. Ever since assuming the editorship, Cecil had vigorously pursued a war of attrition against Godfrey Isaacs, managing director of the Marconi Company, alleging that Isaacs was guilty of insider trading in his company's shares. The whole affair, as exposed in the pages of the *New Witness*, took on a potentially explosive nature, becoming known as the Marconi Scandal, after it was revealed that senior government officials had profited from the insider dealing in Marconi shares. The financial beneficiaries included the attorney general Rufus Isaacs, who was Godfrey Isaacs's brother, the chancellor of the exchequer Lloyd George, and the Master of Elibank, the government's chief whip.

Eventually, largely due to the 'pretty considerable agitation' that the *New Witness* had maintained, but also due to similar agitation on the part of the *National Review*, the *Morning Post* and certain sections of the financial press, a Select Committee of the House of Commons was appointed in an attempt to get at the truth of the whole affair. Cecil was summoned to appear before the Committee on 2 January 1913; Belloc four days later. Writing to Blunt on 5 January to cancel a prearranged appointment with him, Belloc wrote that it was 'most unfortunate' that 'the Marconi

Committee desiring to bully me tomorrow makes it necessary for me to go up tonight to London: I very much regret it! I always look forward to these opportunities of seeing you but this week it is cut off by these distressing parliamentarians with whom I am to tussle.'[22]

Meanwhile, presumably working on the principle that the best means of defence is attack, Godfrey Isaacs decided to sue Cecil Chesterton for criminal libel. Belloc attended the preliminary hearing at Bow Street on 28 February, accompanied by G.K. Chesterton, at which the defendant was committed for trial. Belloc reported to Maurice Baring that Cecil's speech had 'created a very powerful impression'.[23]

Belloc returned from a visit to Spain as soon as he received news of the commencement of the full trial at the Central Criminal Court on 27 May, and wrote excitedly to Blunt on 7 June as the case drew to a close.

> You may be interested in a personal impression of the Chesterton case, which I came back from Spain immediately to attend when I first saw a notice of it in a paper. I was in court pretty well all day yesterday and I further heard from Cecil Chesterton and from Gilbert what passed the day before when I was travelling . . .
>
> Maurice Baring's evidence was excellent. When he was asked whether it was consonant with the dignity of a literary man to say anything unpleasant about politicians he cited Junius . . . Gilbert Chesterton said in his evidence that he envied his brother's position in the dock upon such a charge . . . A crowd gathered outside the doors of the Old Bailey and cheered Chesterton as he left.
>
> I go up this Saturday morning by an early train to follow the last stages of the trial . . . and to be present in court throughout. I shall return in the evening, but not before I have decided upon the issue, in company with Gilbert Chesterton, what had better be done according as Cecil is acquitted or no.
>
> I write you this because I thought you would be interested to know how the whole matter struck an eye-witness . . . And my general conclusion is that whatever happens the thing has been well fought and will be morally successful . . .[24]

With prophetic foresight, Belloc also predicted in this letter to Blunt that the most likely outcome 'would be a verdict of guilty with the opportunity for giving only a nominal sentence'. The judge directed the jury that the case had nothing to do with the question of whether there had been unethical trading in Marconi shares but 'whether the individual Godfrey Isaacs, in his career as a company-promoter previous to the Marconi

Case, had been unfairly described by the individual Cecil Chesterton'.[25] Thus directed, the jury returned a guilty verdict. Yet the judge failed to impose the three-year prison sentence that many had expected Cecil to receive if found guilty. Instead he was only fined £100, a lenient sentence that was taken as being indicative of a moral victory that superseded the nominal defeat. Such was certainly Belloc's view as he wrote to Blunt on the day of the verdict of 'how important in my opinion the success is'.

> The other bit of news is that [R.B.] Haldane has told a friend of mine that the politicians are perfectly determined (he among them) to make [Rufus] Isaacs Lord Chief Justice, and that again I think is good news for it will reduce things to a farce. The truth is that the whole system is now in such a bad way that whatever they do it turns against them.[26]

This 'bit of news' subsequently proved entirely trustworthy. Less than two months after the public enquiry into the Marconi Scandal had disclosed that Rufus Isaacs had made a profit of £3,000 in a single day through selling his shares in his brother's company, he was made Lord Chief Justice and took the title of Lord Reading. Many besides Belloc and Chesterton were outraged by such chutzpah in defiance of public opinion, and Kipling's poem on that occasion reflected the views of many.

> Well done, well done Gehazi,
> Stretch forth thy ready hand,
> Thou barely scaped from Judgement,
> Take oath to judge the Land.
> Unswayed by gift of money
> Or privy bribe more base,
> Or knowledge which is profit
> In any market place.

The enmity that many in the government felt towards Belloc and Cecil Chesterton in the acrimonious aftermath of the Marconi Scandal was witnessed by the 24-year-old Duff Cooper in 1914, shortly after he had first begun working for the Foreign Office. Finding himself in the company of 'Mr McKenna, who was then Home Secretary, Mr Illingworth, the Liberal Chief Whip' and Winston Churchill, whom he had recently met for the first time, Cooper listened with growing indignation as 'they began to talk politics, assuming apparently that I thought as they did'.

> I should have been too shy to set them right, although when Illing-worth began to abuse Hilaire Belloc, whom I knew and loved, and

Cecil Chesterton, I felt that I could understand some of the difficulties experienced by St Peter in the house of Caiaphas. This led on to a discussion of the Marconi scandal, which was then fresh in people's memories, and I was delighted when Winston solemnly assured his colleagues that if that affair had been properly handled by the Opposition it might have brought down the Government.[27]

There was a strange postscript to the whole Marconi Scandal. In the middle of the trial, Cecil Chesterton had sought out the same Father Bowden at the Brompton Oratory who had received Maurice Baring into the Church four years earlier. Then, on 7 June, the eve of his conviction and with the prospect of prison staring him in the face, Cecil was received into the Catholic Church at Corpus Christi, Maiden Lane. But the final *coup de grâce* belonged to Godfrey Isaacs, the plaintiff in the case, who was himself received into the Catholic Church some years later. Such a convergence was as unlikely as the reception into the Church of the two litigants in an even more notorious libel action contested almost 20 years earlier. Nobody would have thought that Oscar Wilde, the arch-decadent, and his hated adversary the Marquis of Queensberry, the arch-atheist, would have been received on their respective deathbeds, within months of each other, into the Catholic Church; and the reconciliation within the same mystical Communion of Cecil Chesterton and Godfrey Isaacs was scarcely less surprising. Truth, it seems, is infinitely stranger than fiction.

According to Cecil's widow, his decision to be received into the Church was largely due to the 'long talks on the faith' that he had enjoyed with Elodie Belloc during his frequent visits to King's Land,[28] but it seems difficult to conceive that his long and friendly arguments with Belloc had not contributed to his decision also. Either way, there is little doubt that Belloc would have felt as 'profoundly grateful' for Cecil Chesterton's conversion as he had for Maurice Baring's. Perhaps, however, the final word on the Marconi Scandal and its curious aftermath should be left to G.K. Chesterton, who recorded his views about Godfrey Isaacs's conversion in his *Autobiography*.

And there is to be added to this a curious and ironic conclusion to the matter; for many years after my brother received the Last Sacraments and died in a hospital in France, his old enemy, Godfrey Isaacs, died very shortly after being converted to the same universal Catholic Church. No one would have rejoiced more than my brother; or with less bitterness or with more simplicity. It is the only reconciliation; and it can reconcile anybody. *Requiescant in pace.*[29]

Ghostly Secrets and Mortal Wounds

ANY TEMPTATION TO triumphalism in the wake of Cecil Chesterton's 'moral victory' at the Marconi trial was tempered by Belloc's sober analysis of Chesterton's failings as an editor. On 27 August 1913 Belloc wrote to Baring that he was 'a little in doubt whether the *New Witness* will manage to survive'. It was not sufficiently broad, diversified or witty and not 'even moderately business-like'.

> They do not seem to know who they pay, nor when they pay him. And Cecil never seems to get anybody in from outside a very small clique. Without the Marconi to feed on it may easily perish. I cannot give my time to it unrewarded . . . but more important still is the fact that if I dabbled in it people would make me responsible for its enormities; not enormities of daring, but enormities of mis-judgement.[1]

Belloc was particularly worried about the anti-Semitism displayed with monotonous regularity in the pages of the *New Witness*, and especially by Hugh O'Donnell's bigoted excesses.

> I have specially regretted the recent and increasing way the *New Witness* has got into of hitting blind. For instance, the detestation of the Jewish cosmopolitan influence, especially through finance, is one thing, and one may be right or wrong in feeling that detestation or in the degree to which one admits it; but mere anti-semitism and a mere attack on a Jew because he is a Jew is quite another matter, and I told him repeatedly that I thought the things he allowed O'Donnell to publish were unwise and deplorable.

He condemned the way in which O'Donnell's contributions and 'many other passages unsigned' had employed 'the national term "Jew" . . . simply as a term of abuse, much as Lower Middle-class Americans will use the term "Irish"'.[2]

On 30 October he informed Baring of his desire to distance himself publicly from the *New Witness*. 'I have thought of writing a letter which would testify to my disagreement in policy. I have had it in mind to do so now for six months, but I have always hesitated because it would look disloyal.'[3] Clearly, the awkwardness of Belloc's position with regard to the *New Witness* was exacerbated by his sense of loyalty to Cecil Chesterton.

At the end of 1913 he was once again collaborating with Cecil on another book, a volume of history which was far more scholarly, and therefore far more demanding of his limited time, than had been the propagandistic and polemical approach of *The Party System*.

Belloc had been commissioned by the Catholic Publication Society of America to write a supplementary eleventh volume, covering the period from 1689 to 1910, to John Lingard's celebrated 10-volume *History of England to 1688*. Lingard, a Catholic priest and scholar, had undertaken the research and writing of his *History*, published between 1819 and 1830, to counter the ingrained anti-Catholic bias of the Whig historians.

Lingard's scholarship was highly respected by academics of all persuasions. In 1913, G.P. Gooch described Lingard as a 'serious historian' who was 'studiously reserved in his judgements of people and events . . . how different was his cool Catholicism from the Ultramontane rigour that came in with Pius IX.'[4] Gooch, who had been a Liberal MP with Belloc from 1906 to 1910 before assuming the editorship of the *Contemporary Review* in 1911, would probably have been contemptuous of the fact that Lingard's 'cool Catholicism' was to be supplemented by an eleventh volume written with the 'Ultramontane rigour' of Belloc. How much more contemptuous would he have been had he known that large sections of the volume were being ghostwritten by Cecil Chesterton, who had recently been convicted of criminal libel and whose obvious inability to be 'studiously reserved in his judgements of people and events' was openly admitted even by his friends, including Belloc himself? It is perhaps little wonder, therefore, that Belloc was careful to keep Cecil's involvement a closely guarded secret.

Belloc's motive for recruiting Chesterton to help with the volume was born of necessity. His correspondence throughout 1913 is riddled with references to being overburdened with work and behind schedule with the meeting of publishers' deadlines. 'I have to catch up the arrears of months of ill-health,' he had complained to Baring on 27 August.[5]

Belloc's and Cecil Chesterton's collaboration on volume 11 of Lingard was at its most intense and most panic-driven during November and

December 1913. The book had been due at the publishers sometime in October or November, and it seems that Belloc might have turned to Chesterton in desperation. 'Don't forget about the Lingard please,' he wrote earnestly on 20 November.[6] Cecil replied from the *New Witness* offices on the following day to reassure him:

> I have been getting on with the Lingard and I send you what I have done to the end of Peel's government. It is, I should say, something between 6,000 – 7,000 words. I am now going to begin on the Irish Famine. I am gunning for 1867 – the date of Disraeli's Reform Bill – as the date to which I should take the narrative this month. That will leave me from then till 1900 for the last instalment.
>
> By the way, you are to do some 4,000 words about the Crimean War in its military aspects, aren't you? I shall be getting to it pretty soon. And do you also want to do anything about the military side of the Indian mutiny? [*sic*] which will immediately follow?[7]

On 6 December, Cecil sent 'about 10,000 words of the Lingard' to Belloc, which, with the two previous instalments despatched earlier, meant that he had now written 'rather over' 20,000 words, 'perhaps nearer 25,000'. 'I have got to let you have about 40,000 more before the end of the year, have I not, to complete the book? I have no doubt of being able to do this.'[8]

'I am in receipt of the Lingard,' Belloc wrote on 30 December, 'which I will have counted and which I will then re-do, as I have all of yours for the book. It is just what I want for it gives me all the facts.'[9] This letter might suggest that Belloc was reworking Chesterton's initial draft, placing Cecil more in the role of a researcher supplying the facts than that of an uncredited co-author. Yet a letter from Belloc to G.K. Chesterton, written 18 months later, shortly after Belloc's 'Lingard Volume XI' was published, states that Cecil had 'devilled', i.e. ghosted, much of the section dealing with the nineteenth century, 'and did it very well . . . He knows the names and actions of the Parliamentarians of Victoria. I don't, except Gladstone, Disraeli, Cobden, Peel and Lord John Russell . . .'[10] It seems, therefore, by Belloc's own admission, that Belloc wrote most of the first part of the volume, covering the period from 1689 to the end of the Napoleonic Wars in 1815, whereas Cecil Chesterton wrote most of the second part, covering the period from 1815 to 1910. Thus Lingard's *History of England Volume XI* was in fact the 'secret Chesterbelloc', a clandestine collaboration between Belloc and the 'other' Chesterton.

On 3 November 1913, Belloc wrote to Blunt of a mutual friend: 'People not in Parliament so exaggerate the importance of that tawdry place that they will judge him – or tend to – by its standards: & he was right above it altogether.'[11] The friend in question was George Wyndham, Conservative MP for Dover, who had died suddenly at the age of 50, from the passage of a blood clot through the heart, earlier in the year. Belloc loved Wyndham dearly and considered him the most intelligent man he had ever met.[12] He had learned of his friend's sudden death from a headline emblazoned on a newspaper placard, glimpsed as he was ambling down the Strand with Maurice Baring. He was struck with grief, and was haunted by his memories and by the deep sense of loss they engendered.

Only days before his death, Wyndham had visited the Bellocs at King's Land. He and Hilaire had walked in the surrounding woods and had discussed at length the problem of immortality. Wyndham declared his firm belief that the soul was immortal. Belloc responded that he shared such a belief, but that he could only do so through the cold acceptance of authority. Unlike Wyndham, he was not able to feel the truth of such a belief emotionally. A day or so later, Wyndham had written again to reiterate the beliefs he had affirmed during their talk. Confronted with the news of his death almost immediately thereafter, Belloc must have been struck by the unfathomable profundity of providence. A week later he wrote to Baring:

> It is clear that the whole conduct of human life must depend upon a man's decision in this matter [of immortality]. Those who are so blessed as to feel (and personally know) the high destiny of man I have always sought (those few I know well, those very few) and importuned them with questions as I have also you. I like to hear from the lips of others, as though it were a thing seen, that which I know I must defend but to which I have no access of my own.[13]

Questions of mortality must have struck Belloc with particular poignancy during the following weeks as he travelled to Lourdes, the Catholic shrine that attracts thousands of sick and dying pilgrims. He joined Elodie at the Hôtel de la Chapelle, where she had taken rooms for herself and their two daughters, now aged 14 and 12. The sight of so many seriously ill pilgrims merely exacerbated Belloc's sense of desolation at the death of his friend. 'I cannot get the Dead Man out of my thoughts,' he confessed to Baring.

Today in rattling through the prayers for the living in my head, at Mass, his name halted me suddenly and abominably: I remembered, or rather stumbled, and left it unspoken: it has to come later now in the much longer list of names one runs through in a chain night after night and at Mass, too; for whom we ask the three things, Refreshment, Light and Peace. We agreed and were continuing to agree more nearly in everything; he was the only man older than myself whom I sought, and I sought him eagerly always. I loved him with all my heart, and so surely as I have no horizon beyond that plain horizon of this world, so surely will some years of mine to come be full *desiderio tam cari capitis*.[14]

Soon after his return from Lourdes, Belloc was motoring with Elodie near Slindon when, passing Halnacker Hill, he was appalled to see the mill in ruins. The desolate sight, transfused with the devastating insight of mortality, was transformed creatively into 'Ha'nacker Mill', one of Belloc's most poignant and powerful poems. Physically and metaphysically, Halnacker Mill's 'desolation' is a metaphor for mortality. Physically, the ruined mill whose 'sweeps have fallen' is a symbol of England's decline and decay, her approaching death. Metaphysically, the mourning for the passing of apparently permanent things is a yearning for the comfort of verities amidst the erosion of Time. The briar grows blindly; the clapper is still; the sweeps have fallen; Sally is gone; spirits call but no one answers. The silence is not only deadening but deafening. A scream in a vacuum. In this stillness, this Real Absence, the heartfelt cry of a broken soul cannot be heard. Yet, not heard, it is felt crushingly. The desolate soul's hunger for consolation is palpable. The stillness is starving, striving for life. Desolation and desire are one.

As ever, Belloc sought practical relief from the melancholy musings of his mind and soul in the love and laughter of friends and family. Apart from regular meetings with old friends such as Baring, Blackwood and the Chestertons, he was making new acquaintances during his frequent sorties to London. The young Duff Cooper, who was just going in for the Foreign Office examination, Lady Diana Manners, Lady Juliet Duff, Arnold Lunn, the Jesuit C.C. Martindale and the Dominican Vincent McNabb were all new acquaintances destined to become lifelong friends. Belloc travelled to Lullenden, where the Churchills were then living, to help Winston Churchill bottle a barrel of wine he had recently purchased. He renewed his acquaintance with the prodigiously gifted priest-novelist R.H. Benson during a visit to Cambridge, where he sat between Benson and Cardinal Bourne at a gathering of Catholic undergraduates. Sadly, his friendship with Benson, with whom he had much in common, would be extinguished almost before it had begun by Benson's untimely death in the following year. His early death (he was 43, a year younger than Belloc) robbed English literature in general, and Christian literature in particular, of one of its finest novelists.

On the other extreme, politically and theologically, was Belloc's delightful friendship-in-enmity with George Bernard Shaw. At the start of the year he debated publicly with Shaw on the subject 'Property or Slavery?' at a sell-out public meeting, attended by Rupert Brooke and Arnold Bennett among others, organized under the auspices of the Fabian Society. 'Crammed, at concert prices,' Bennett recorded in his diary. 'Not a seat unsold. Shaw very pale with white hair, and straight. His wife beside him. Effect too conjugal for a man at work. Sidney and Beatrice Webb next to him. Effect also too conjugal here. Maurice Baring supporting Belloc, both very shabby . . . I have never seen Shaw emotional before, as he was then.'[15] Belloc's high regard for Shaw, as distinct from his low opinion of Bennett and Wells, was recalled amusingly by J.B. Priestley: 'Belloc once said that Wells was a cad who didn't pretend to be anything but a cad; that Bennett was a cad pretending to be a gentleman; that Shaw was a gentleman pretending to be a cad.'[16]

Back home in Sussex, the seventh anniversary of the family's arrival at King's Land was celebrated on 3 September 1913 by a fireworks party in the garden, much to the delight of the Belloc children. 'A piece called "Jack-in-the-Box", the point of which is an immense explosion, behaved like a speech by the late Duke of Devonshire and was disappointing in the extreme,' Belloc informed Baring.[17]

Belloc's friendship with Wilfrid Scawen Blunt, which stretched back a quarter of a century to his youthfully precocious attempts to persuade Blunt to write for the *Paternoster Review*, had deepened considerably since the two men had become neighbours. Belloc's frequent visits probably brought him into contact with other members of the literati, such as Yeats, Sturge Moore, Ezra Pound and Richard Aldington, all of whom were regular visitors to Blunt's home at Newbuildings. In September 1913, presumably with the recent vision of the ruins of Halnacker Mill fresh in his mind, Belloc wrote to Blunt 'that the topography of the Weald interests me more than any book and occupies a great deal of my thoughts'. As a means of regenerating the desolated economic life of his beloved Sussex, he tried to interest his friend in plans to persuade the authorities to reopen 'the old Canal' which 'would be a great benefit to the small farmers and to everybody else, and the ditch is there ready dug if only the Development Commission would give us a little to restore its working'.[18]

Elodie often accompanied Belloc on his regular visits to Newbuildings, and her friendship with their elderly and illustrious neighbour became as warm as that of her husband. Blunt often presented Elodie with copies of his books and the growing affection he felt for her can be gauged by the inscriptions he wrote in each of them. In the earliest they are signed formally 'to Mrs Belloc', but by 1913 he was signing them to 'dearest Elodie'.[19]

On 23 December 1913, Elodie fell suddenly and grievously ill, being unable to swallow her food. Five days later Belloc wrote to Blunt, cancelling their regular weekly meeting. 'I am afraid that I must not leave the house in the evening while this grave illness continues. I only go out for an hour's walk or so in the day & when I have to telephone to London or to fetch things from Horsham. Elodie has rallied a little . . .'[20]

On the day that Elodie fell ill, but presumably before she had done so, Belloc had written to Cecil Chesterton asking about tickets for 'the Mock Trial of John Jasper for the Murder of Edwin Drood', a charity event organized by the Dickens Fellowship due to take place at the King's Hall, Covent Garden on 7 January.[21] The 'trial' was inspired, of course, by *The Mystery of Edwin Drood*, Dickens's last, unfinished novel. Participants in the charity event included G.K. Chesterton as judge, Cecil Chesterton as counsel for the defence, and J. Cuming Walters for the prosecution. Witnesses included Arthur Waugh, father of Evelyn, who played Canon Crisparkle, and Ada Jones, Cecil's fiancée, who played Princess Puffer, the Opium Woman. Foreman of the jury was Bernard Shaw, and other jury members included W.W. Jacobs, G.S. Street and William Archer, but not, contrary to popular belief, Belloc.[22]

On 29 December, Cecil wrote apologetically to Belloc informing him that the Fellowship had been using his name in the publicity material, citing him as one of the jury. 'I hear the Dickens Fellowship people have been using your name without authority! Not my fault! . . . Apologies,' Cecil wrote, explaining that the Fellowship assumed he would be prepared to make up one of the jury 'as you have not read the book'.[23] Belloc replied on the following day that the 'only objection' to his name being used was 'that such a liberty can become a habit'. He still had hopes of being able to participate in the 'trial', but Elodie's illness made this doubtful. Cecil had sent Elodie some flowers and a card, for which Belloc thanked him, stating that she was a little better but that he and the family were still very anxious about her.[24] On the same day he informed Blunt, who had 'sent down for news' of Elodie's progress, that 'on the balance she has certainly gone forward & I shall hope for a better day today'.[25]

It seems that Elodie's condition deteriorated over the New Year, because Belloc wrote separately to both Chesterton brothers on 1 January to state that he would not be able to attend 'the Drood Trial'.[26] 'Two or three days ago Elodie fell ill and I now have to have two trained nurses in the house and constant visits of a doctor from London. Under these circumstances I am afraid it is quite impossible for me to be present upon the 7th.'[27]

Three weeks later, Belloc wrote desperately to Baring:

> Elodie gets no worse and no better; certain of the symptoms have improved, but others are more distressing and I am bound here very anxiously . . . Elodie is stronger *functionally* i.e. in digestion and nutrition but weaker *nervously*. She eats almost normally but she can see no one, she can read but very little and she sleeps more and more ill. I cry and pray God to take her to the *Sun*. The doctor won't let her move – not even out of bed – and it will be long, long. Priez pour elle et pour moi.[28]

In the event, it was not long. Presumably suffering from cancer, Elodie deteriorated rapidly. There are no further entries in Belloc's diary after 27 January as, numbingly, he began to contemplate the unthinkable. 'Today & tomorrow will be very anxious indeed,' he wrote to Blunt on 30 January.

> I am here continuously. The most critical moment so far was this morning about 8 to 9 when her pulse suddenly grew very rapid & the nurse thought her in Peril. I sent for the Doctor & the Priest. She had, to her great comfort, the Sacraments. The Doctor came when the Priest had gone & said the immediate peril was past. It might at any moment return. He comes back again tomorrow & I have sent for the children.[29]

In summoning the priest, and in summoning his children home from their various schools, Belloc was acting out the final moments of his living nightmare. Darkness descended and the abyss beckoned.

Elodie began to drift in and out of consciousness. Her delirious mumblings, no longer disguised by her carefully cultivated English accent, became once more unmistakably Californian.

'Elodie died tonight a little before midnight of the Purification,' Belloc wrote to Blunt. 'She died unconscious and without pain. I write this while I still have the power.' The short note was dated 'The Night of February 2–3, 1914'.[30] At the moment of death, he had become hysterical, throwing himself onto his wife's body, holding it to his in one last unrequited embrace.

Although for Elodie, so he and she believed, death was only the end of the beginning, for Belloc, his wife's death was more like the beginning of the end. Left alone, bereft, mourning and broken, the loss of 'my beloved Elodie', as he described her in a grief-stricken telegram to his sister,[31] had opened up a wound that would never heal. Elodie's death had left her husband mortally wounded. Painfully, she remained, omnipresent, during every day of his life without her, her ghostly presence a constant reminder of her absence. Her room was closed on the day of her death and never again used during Belloc's lifetime, an untouched, virginal shrine to the purity of her memory. Each night, on his way to bed, he would pause in front of the closed door and trace upon it the sign of the cross, a ritual reiteration of a passion that may have passed but was not spent. Transformed by the kiss of death, it was married in Belloc's Catholic conscience with the Passion at the broken heart of humanity.

TWENTY

'Where Darkness Is . . .'

> When you to Acheron's ugly water come,
> Where darkness is and formless mourners brood,
> And down the shelves of that distasteful flood
> Survey the human ranks in order dumb.

O N THE MORNING AFTER HER DEATH, Elodie's body was carried to the hall at King's Land where it lay surrounded by candles. Throughout the day, friends and neighbours arrived to pray beside it. Belloc wired the news of her death to his mother, adding, 'I shall need all your help.'[1]

On the same day he sent the following telegram to G.K. Chesterton: 'Elodie entered immortality yesterday the Purification a little before midnight unconscious blessed and without pain. Pray to God for her and for me and for my children.'[2] Frances and Gilbert Chesterton replied by return that they were 'grieved beyond words'.[3]

Belloc was helped in the first crisis of bereavement by Father Vincent McNabb, a recent acquaintance who had become one of his closest friends. McNabb had travelled to King's Land the moment he heard the news, walking with Belloc in the garden and offering him 'stars of comfort',[4] the value of which can be gauged by Belloc's words to a friend almost 20 years later: 'I envy you a retreat from Fr Vincent! It is a strange and profound experience to hear him speaking quietly upon the essential things . . . the effect is extraordinary; it is his personal holiness which comes out and the force of it is incalculable. There is no living man for whom I feel such awe and reverence . . .'[5] The same extraordinary effect was felt by G.K. Chesterton, who remarked of the Dominican's holiness that 'Father McNabb is walking on a crystal floor over my head'.[6]

Elodie's Requiem and funeral were arranged for 5 February at the little Catholic church at West Grinstead, not far from King's Land. It is clear, however, from a letter that Belloc wrote to Blunt, that he had hoped to have her buried in his family's tomb at La Celle St Cloud.

> It is not because She or I could expect or trouble anyone but only as a matter of courtesy that I write to tell you. If you are free & come it will be very good of you but you may not be able to come. It is at half past three on Thursday tomorrow at the little place at West Grinstead, the cemetery by the church there. I cannot take Her *straight* to France, the official red tape process too long. I will have her here in Sussex till She can go to my place.[7]

Belloc's friends did their best to console him. Gilbert and Frances Chesterton travelled to King's Land and 'found Hilaire in a disordered room, a broken man'.[8] Maurice Baring, cutting short a visit to Russia, hastened to Sussex, his visit being remembered by 14-year-old Eleanor.

> . . . a few weeks after beloved Mamma had died, I came into the dining-room at nightfall and there by candlelight my father and dear Maurice Baring were sitting together at the long oak table having a little food and wine. H.B. said, 'Oh darling! here is Uncle Maurice who has come all the way from Russia so as to comfort me.' There was something holy in that meeting; warmth and comfort filled the low room. I kissed Uncle Maurice and, tongue-tied with youth, stole away to leave them in their Christian feast of Hope and Consolation.[9]

In spite of such efforts, Belloc confessed to being 'abominably alone' in the weeks and months following Elodie's death, 'many months, in which on many nights awake I did not think I could endure the coming of day, and in which, during certain days, I did not think I could endure the coming of night'.[10] The suffering would become more durable with the passage of time, but he never for a moment ceased to mourn the loss of his beloved Elodie. For the rest of his life he dressed in the same black broadcloth as an outward sign of his inner grief, and the King's Land writing paper was thereafter always edged with black. Every year Mass was offered for the repose of Elodie's soul, sometimes on the Feast of the Purification, the anniversary of her death, and sometimes on 16 June, the anniversary of their wedding.

The impression that Belloc's desolate demeanour made on the nine-year-old daughter of his friend Charlotte Balfour was striking. Clare wrote in her memoirs:

The first time that I remember meeting Belloc was in London soon after his wife had died ... when I was nine years old. My mother and I met him after mass in Westminster Cathedral and walked with him to Victoria Station. He trotted along beside us with his tiptoe gait, dressed all in black with an Inverness cape and top-boots, and I was impressed by his look of great sadness and wondered how he could bear his widowhood. My mother was a widow, but I had the idea that it was far worse for a man.[11]

The loss of Elodie was also felt dreadfully by her children. Eleanor recalled:

[After] our beloved Mamma died, life for ... us five children was never the same again ... My father ... did his very best for us as far as he could, but without Mamma it must have been an intolerable burden at times. We missed her beyond measure and made up our minds to go on missing her, and we would never accept the guidance or help offered in her place by other kindly people. She had been the queen of our hearts and home ...[12]

Belloc's granddaughter Marianne Jebb believed that his children 'suffered indescribably' as a result of their mother's death.

He did his utmost to cherish them. He had a great and strong constitution and would say, 'Now my children, it's just right for sailing', and off they had to go to be knocked about by the boat in all weathers and hit by the boom. It was a tough life ... The children had a very difficult childhood without their mother and they really needed extra cherishing.[13]

Implicit in both these descriptions is a suggestion of unwilful neglect on the part of Belloc towards his children. In Eleanor's description there is also the suggestion that their pent-up anger over the loss of their mother spilled over into displays of rebelliousness. Neglect and rebellion were certainly in evidence in the memories of Charlotte Balfour's daughter, who recalled visiting King's Land shortly after Elodie's death. At nine years old, Clare Balfour was the same age as the youngest of the Belloc children, Peter. Louis, the eldest, was now 16 and was home during the holidays from Downside. Eleanor and Elizabeth, 14 and 13 respectively, were also home from their convent school in Staffordshire. Hilary, then 12, was, like Peter, still living at King's Land. According to Clare Balfour, she and her siblings 'soon discovered that companionship with the Belloc children was strenuous and alarming'.

They were given a freedom that few children were allowed and they took advantage of it to the utmost . . . As they liked risking their lives, travelling by rail without a ticket was one of their pleasures; the country trains were boarded at a bound outside the little railway halts as they gathered speed. The boys showed us a hole in a field caused by the explosion of a mine they had made themselves; and what other children that we knew so much as dreamed of possessing invisible ink?[14]

Similar stories abound. Clare Balfour remembered the frightening games invented by the Belloc children, with bloodcurdling names such as 'The Terrible Death', and the death-defying exploits on the adjacent windmill, which involved climbing the sails when they were at a standstill or dashing between them when they were in motion. These mini-Bellocian 'feats of courage' were 'far beyond the daring of us timid Balfours'.

At mealtimes, Edith, the housekeeper, tried in vain to keep order. 'Hilary would take some gunpowder out of his pocket, lay it in a trail from plate to plate, and set it alight. Or it might be Louis' turn to cry out "Hell!", at which the Bellocs would all take up their steel knives and grate them on their plates to simulate the sound of gnashing teeth.' Only occasionally, when their games became too noisy, did a rebuke from their father produce 'a sudden and awful silence'.[15] All too often, however, he was not around to wield authority or exert discipline and the children were left, quite literally, to run wild. Perhaps, as Eleanor insisted loyally, her father had done 'his very best . . . as far as he could' for his children. If so, his 'very best' was barely adequate.

In his grief, Belloc felt the need to escape for a time from his commitments, from his children and, perhaps, from himself, or at any rate from his suffering. Within three weeks of Elodie's death, he had set out by himself for Rome. He had a 'splendid' audience with Pope Pius X, who was 'looking older but less unhappy than when I saw him eight years ago'.[16] The ageing Pope, loved and respected by Belloc for his uncompromising stance towards the heresy of Modernism, would die a few months later, leaving his own epitaph in his will: 'I was born poor, I have lived poor, and I wish to die poor.' Following his death on 20 August 1914, Belloc would pay tribute to the Pope in an appraisal of his pontificate published in the British Review.

The note of Pius X's reign was simplicity. It stood composed of a few very clear principles like a carefully constructed classical thing of cut stone standing against a flood.

For as the note of that reign was simplicity of principle rigidly applied, so the note of society which it had to meet and subtly to dominate was one of very rapid and anarchic change.[17]

Having left money for Masses to be said for Elodie in Rome, the city she loved above all others, Belloc proceeded to Naples and thence to Sicily, walking the length of the island seeking solace in the landscape. Crossing to Tunisia, he reached the edge of the desert before the heat forced him to retrace his steps. He sailed to Marseilles, walked in Provence and travelled north into Lorraine to visit the house and village of St Joan of Arc before heading south again to Toul, his old garrison town. On St Patrick's Day, 17 March, he was writing to John Phillimore from Lyons, beseeching him 'to take such means as should be taken, whether by prayers or by Masses, or any other means for my preservation in this very difficult task'. He was, he wrote, 'in peril of my intelligence and perhaps of my conduct and therefore of my soul'.[18] Six days later, he was in Paris and apparently in a more settled frame of mind as he wrote to Blunt.

> It is very kind of you to have written to me as you have. I am most grateful for news from Sussex, especially as you tell me that the little boys [Peter and Hilary] seem well and happy during this rather prolonged absence of mine. The young woman who looks after them Edith Faires is a most admirable and devoted person and Elodie always had the highest opinion of her. I intend, if possible, to put the service of the house more or less under her care in future. I shall be returning now in quite a few days, exactly how long I do not know, but I should imagine about a week or even possibly less.[19]

Belloc returned home in time for Easter, spending it with his children. Shortly afterwards, at the insistence of his friend Auberon Lucas, who lent him a motorcar and a chauffeur, Belloc and the children toured England and Wales. They were accompanied by Ruby Goldsmith, Belloc's secretary, who remembered that 'Mr Belloc put up a good "front" of joviality and sang lustily as we travelled along'. At Auberon Lucas's country home in Hampshire, Belloc and Miss Goldsmith set about trying to answer 'the many hundred letters of sympathy and condolence which he had received'.[20]

The return of 'joviality' and song signalled the slow emergence of Belloc from the fogs of confusion that had clouded his mind in the days and weeks following Elodie's death. Even if, as Ruby Goldsmith had perceived, the joviality on the babbling surface was only a 'front' for the stillness of the melancholy depths, his return to song was still a return to life – a resurrection. 'My father told me,' wrote Eleanor, 'that after a great loss and an abiding grief there is always duty and toil left to pull us together and to enable us to start life again.'[21] It is, however, significant that Eleanor ended her memoir of her father with the death of her mother; significant also that Marie Belloc Lowndes, Belloc's sister, ended her memoir of her brother with the death of her sister-in-law. In both cases, there is a sense that something of Belloc had died with the death of his wife. The Belloc who emerges from the shadows of Elodie's death is an older and a sadder man, but also a newer and a wiser one.

The older, sadder, newer, wiser Belloc was most in evidence in *The Cruise of the Nona*, a book that recounted a cruise from Holyhead to Sussex on his yacht in May 1914. In the book's final pages, Belloc pays tribute to the healing power of the sea and illustrates how the cruise, undertaken so shortly after the most cataclysmic event in his life, had been not merely a voyage of self-discovery, but very much a voyage of recovery, during which he recovered not only his health but himself.

> The sea is the consolation of this our day, as it has been the consolation of the centuries. It is the companion and the receiver of men. It has moods for them to fill the storehouse of the mind, perils for trial, or even for an ending, and calms for the good emblem of death. There, on the sea, is a man nearest to his own making, and in communion with that from which he came, and to which he shall return . . . The sea is the matrix of creation, and we have the memory of it in our blood.
>
> But far more than this is there in the sea. It presents, upon the greatest scale we mortals can bear, those not mortal powers which brought us into being. It is not only the symbol or the mirror, but especially it is the messenger of the Divine.
>
> . . . All that which concerns the sea is profound and final. The sea provides visions, darknesses, revelations . . . The sea has taken me to itself whenever I sought it and has given me relief from men. It has rendered remote the cares and wastes of the land; for of all creatures that move and breathe upon the earth we of mankind are the fullest of sorrow. But the sea shall comfort us, and perpetually show us new things and assure us. It is the common sacrament of this world. May it be to others what it has been to me.[22]

In one of the love sonnets to Elodie, not published until 1923 but probably dating from his precocious youth, Belloc had imagined his beloved's death and her arrival at 'Acheron's ugly water . . . Where darkness is and formless mourners brood'. He had now discovered that 'darkness' is not with the dead but with the living who are left floundering in death's wake. In the endless days following Elodie's death, he had been the brooding mourner suffering in the place of grief 'where darkness is'.

The same youthful sonnet had concluded with his deceased beloved proceeding 'like a royal ghost', treading 'like Egypt or like Carthage crowned',

> Because in your Mortality the most
> Of all we may inherit has been found –
> Children for memory: Faith for pride;
> Good land to leave: and young Love satisfied.[23]

Deprived of his love's physical presence, and marooned with the omnipresence of his memories of her, he sought solace and gained sustenance from the children she had left him, the Faith they had shared, and the 'good land' at King's Land which remained as a shrine to the life they had built together. He would never regain the *joie de vivre* that was his before Elodie's death, but he would at least continue to derive strength and a degree of tranquillity from the children, the Church and the home that she had bequeathed to him.

TWENTY-ONE

War and Other Diversions

O N 29 JUNE 1914, during a break in his cruise on the *Nona*, Belloc
motored to Salisbury where he attended Mass.

> During the Mass, the priest . . . asked the congregation to pray for the
> soul of the Archduke Heir-Apparent of Austria, who had been mur-
> dered at a place called Sarajevo. I had never heard the name, and I had
> but a vague idea of who this archduke was, of his relationship to the
> Emperor, and of his heirship to the throne of Hapsburg-Lorraine. I
> came to the 'Nona', where she lay, and sailed out with her into the sea
> for some days. I had no conception that anything could be brewing.[1]

The assassination of Archduke Ferdinand set in motion a chain of events
that would lead within a few weeks to the outbreak of the First World
War. Belloc was in London on 4 August, the day that war was declared,
and decided right away that he must offer his services against the Prussian
foe. He approached General Macdonough at the War Office, but was told
that he was not needed. During the early months of the war, according
to his sister, Belloc 'made many determined efforts to join the British or
French Army as a liaison officer'.[2] His letters testify to his growing frustration. 'Not a sign of a staff for me to go to yet,' he wrote dejectedly to
Lady Juliet Duff on 12 September, 'not even a divisional one. It is an
abominable shame, and when I chuck it in disgust and try through the
French, it may be too late – they will wonder why I didn't ask before.'[3]
'They have not yet let me go to the War and I am correspondingly
peevish,' he complained to Baring on 8 October, 'but by dint of perpetual
effort I shall go . . .'[4]

A week later, Belloc was hearing first-hand accounts of the horrors
of the front from Lord Basil Blackwood.

> . . . one's safety or otherwise in this war is simply a mater of Fate. The
> Germans have specialized in shells and . . . who can scheme to escape

shells? Many guns have a range of eight miles, shells fall so impartially that they can't be dodged, one must simply await with resignation what fate has in store. The most horrible scene I have witnessed was one that followed the explosion of two shells of the largest calibre on our billets killing 24 & wounding 20. I was on the spot & helped to remove the shattered debris. I shall never never forget the hateful sight or the long drawn out melancholy business of digging graves . . .

Continuing with the same tone of gruesome realism, Blackwood requested 'a small bottle of morphia tabloids' for use in the case of wounded men in great pain when no doctor was available, 'a small bottle of permanganate tabloids to put in water to wash a wound, otherwise it is better not to wash it', and 'a tourniquet' to 'put over the artery to secure great pressure at that point'. On the assumption that his vivid depiction of the horrors of the front had not dampened Belloc's enthusiasm for active service, Blackwood concluded with reassurances that his friend should not be disheartened by his failure to secure enlistment.

> I can understand your extreme anxiety to take a direct part in this war but for your consolation let me say that as far as I can see there is no sort of hurry as there will be an abundance of opportunity in due course for all those who have been unsuccessful hitherto, to come, and secondly that you are probably of far greater use in England writing lecturing and illuminating. I must tell you that your articles in *Land and Water* are enormously appreciated here by the soldiers & it occurred to me at once to suggest to you that it might be worth your while to get the job of writing the official history. I expect it would be a goldmine . . .[5]

The articles to which Blackwood referred were written as a result of a visit to King's Land on 9 September by Murray Allison, the proprietor of *Land and Water*, a new weekly journal dedicated exclusively to coverage of the war. After a three-hour discussion, Allison had persuaded Belloc to sign a contract to write a weekly article for the magazine on the military situation as it unfolded. Since the circulation of *Land and Water* soon reached 100,000, Belloc's articles were destined to secure him a wider fame than ever, and would make him far wealthier during the years of the war than he had ever been before.

A letter from Spenser Wilkinson, a Professor of Military History, published in *Land and Water* on 26 December 1914, is typical of the respect in which Belloc's articles were held.

It appears to me that Mr Hilaire Belloc is rendering a great service to this country and to the cause of the Allies by his weekly articles on the war, published in *Land and Water*, of which I have read every word since they began. No other articles have been so helpful to me. They reveal a thorough knowledge of war and a military judgement of a high order, as well as an unrivalled grip of the geography of a theatre of war and of its significance. They are, moreover, so clearly written and so well illustrated that no one can fail to understand them.

'Belloc has been very fine in *Land & Water*,' wrote the artist William Rothenstein to Max Beerbohm. 'I love to be told by convincing & fine people that we are to win, to go on until we win & that Germany is to be beaten to her knees.'[6]

As was evident from these two responses to Belloc's articles, the role of military 'expert' was co-existent with, and was put to the service of, the patriotic duty to produce propaganda for the Allied cause. Belloc soon realized that his pen was mightier than his sword and that, as Blackwood had suggested, he was of 'far greater use to England' as a writer and lecturer than he could ever be as a liaison officer in the army. He abandoned any idea of military service and concentrated instead on fighting the war with his pen.

There is little doubt that Belloc allowed his expertise in military matters to be clouded by his wishful thinking on behalf of the Allies, and this led eventually to a growing cynicism on the part of many of his readers with regard to the accuracy of his judgements. Later in the war, trench-weary troops would wonder why the conflict continued to drag on interminably if as many Germans were being killed as Belloc claimed. On 6 September 1915, posters appeared in the streets emblazoned with the words 'Belloc's Fables' and listing the errors he had made in his weekly articles. A spoof book, entitled *What I Know about the War*, by Blare Hilloc, containing nothing but blank pages, was circulated widely.

In the early days, however, before public enthusiasm for the war had been blunted by the blood-soaked horror stories emerging from the front, *Land and Water* remained a fashionable journal and Belloc its most fashionable writer. By July 1915 he was being paid 40 pounds for his weekly contribution, an enormous sum for a single article. In the same month Arnold Bennett, writing to André Gide, referred to Belloc as 'my favourite military expert'.[7] Although Belloc was, of course, no war-profiteer, there is no denying that he profited greatly from the war. As early as September 1914 he had signed a contract with Nelson to publish his *Land and Water* articles in book form. These appeared in two volumes, in 1915 and 1916 respectively, as *A General Sketch of the European War*. It was indicative of the public's subsequent sense of disillusionment with the conflict's entrenched futility that there were no third or fourth volumes covering the years 1917 and 1918.

'It wouldn't ... be much good trying to see Belloc,' Rupert Brooke observed in a letter to a friend during New Year's leave at the start of 1915. 'When he's not in the London Library surrounded by Atlases, he's lecturing all over England. He'll be the richest man in the world by the end of the war: and swamp the Jews.'[8]

Considering Belloc's temporal fame and celebrity, there is a touch of irony in the fact that his most enduring legacy in relation to the war was not linked to his role as propagandist but to his influence as a poet. Many of the war poets were deeply indebted to him. In particular, Rupert Brooke's discipleship of Belloc was patently obvious in his two best-known poems. 'The Old Vicarage, Grantchester' reads in parts almost like a parody of Belloc, so much so that it is strikingly similar in effect, if not necessarily in intention, to the tongue-in-cheekiness of Squire or Beerbohm. Certainly, it is difficult to perceive the following lines as anything but a humorous hybrid of 'The South Country' and 'West Sussex Drinking Song'.

> For Cambridge people rarely smile,
> Being urban, squat, and packed with guile;
> And Royston men in the far South
> Are black and fierce and strange of mouth;
> At Over they fling oaths at one,
> And worse than oaths at Trumpington ...

Similarly, Brooke's 'The Soldier', a poem that was destined to acquire iconographic significance following the poet's death in 1915, reads like a poignant and passionate reworking of the untitled poem that begins 'He does not die that can bequeath' with which Belloc had concluded *The Four Men* – a book that Brooke had 'eagerly devoured' during a visit to Germany in 1912.[9] It is probable, therefore, that two of the most popular poems of the twentieth century would not have been written without the source of inspiration that Belloc had provided. Perhaps the words of Ivor Gurney, another war poet greatly influenced by Belloc, will serve as a footnote to Brooke's poetry: 'Belloc of course has influenced it, but what of that? It is jolly good Belloc at any rate, and none but a fool will grumble about such a Mentor.'[10]

Gurney's discipleship of Belloc was, if anything, even more pronounced than that of Brooke. In the list of those to whom he wished to dedicate his first book of verse, *Severn and Somme*, Gurney listed Belloc, 'whose *Path to Rome* has been my trench companion'.[11] Gurney's admiration 'for Hilaire, who has Faith and doesn't emit noisome darkness like a squid'[12] extended beyond Belloc's poetry to his politics also. '*Land and Water* is still very optimistic,' Gurney wrote on 28 June 1915:

> My thoughts go onward to the dim time after the war, and the politics in ten years time. Here is Belloc gaining a great following; who is a very strong opponent of the Party System, a Strong Anti-Socialist, and though once a Liberal MP with a strong contempt for it. He is certain to show large in public opinion, and there will be many and curious rows and large and generous bewilderment.[13]

As in Brooke's whimsical quip that Belloc would 'swamp the Jews', there is in Gurney's prophecy a suggestion that Belloc was being looked upon by many of the young generation as a crusading figurehead, a leader of ideas and of men. Belloc would probably have been horrified, or at least amused, at the prospect, but it seemed that there were many during the early years of the war who sought to thrust 'greatness', in its crypto-fascist mould, upon him.

A more benignly endearing disciple was G.K. Chesterton who, in the autumn of 1914, suffered a serious collapse in health. His condition deteriorated and on Christmas Eve, almost exactly a year after Elodie had fallen ill, he lapsed into a long and rarely broken coma. For a time his illness seemed life threatening, but the danger passed and the slow road to recovery commenced. 'When I first recovered consciousness, in the final turn of my long sickness,' Chesterton wrote in his *Autobiography*, 'I am told that I asked for *Land and Water*, in which Mr Belloc had already begun his well-known series of war-articles.'[14]

Chesterton was always jingoistic as far as the conduct of the war was concerned – his own contribution to the war effort being summed up succinctly, though hardly subtly, in *The Barbarism of Berlin*, the book he wrote before the onset of his illness – and he was more than happy to follow the Bellocian line, as outlined in *Land and Water*, unquestioningly. Certainly, in military matters, Chesterton was very much Belloc's disciple, a fact that could be discerned from the tone of a letter Belloc had written to him four years earlier. 'The French have by their aeroplanes quite changed the art of war,' Belloc had written, 'it sounds extravagant but is perfectly true: fighting henceforward will be a perfectly different thing. But do not alarm yourself. It will still be dangerous and extremely exciting.'[15] Before the war ended, Belloc would have cause to rue the naive romanticism of his vision of aerial warfare.

Like Chesterton, Ford Madox Ford was quite content, in an article for *Outlook* in January 1915, to 'begin by imitating Mr Hilaire Belloc'. He then proceeded, in pseudo-Bellocian fashion, to divide Europe into the 'Gallo-Latin', the 'Anglo-Saxon' and the 'Austro-German' civilizations. Finally, in a distant but distinct echo of Belloc's 'Europe of the Faith', Ford singled out adherence to the truths of Christianity as the defining elements of true civilization:

> For me, the first element of Occidental civilization is some tradition of Christianity, Eastern or Western . . . whatever may or may not be said against Russia, her fidelity to the Eastern Church at least cannot be questioned, and whatever may or may not be said for Prussia her fidelity to any form of Christianity has always been extremely questionable.[16]

There were, however, some notable dissenting voices. D.H. Lawrence, writing to Bertrand Russell on 2 June 1915, failed to share Belloc's optimism. 'Hilaire Belloc says, peace in two months. All the Bellocites are convinced. I am not. I think like you, more death, and ever more death, till the fire burns itself out.'[17]

If the outbreak of war had provided a perversely welcome diversion from the grief-laden months that had followed Elodie's death, the constant round of parties to which, increasingly, Belloc was being invited provided a welcome diversion from his work for *Land and Water* and from the lectures he was giving, seemingly endlessly, on military subjects. The underlying reason for his popularity as a dinner guest was explained most memorably by Lady Diana Manners, who described Belloc as 'perhaps with Winston Churchill the man nearest to genius I have known, one of the most complex, contradictory and brilliant characters ever to rumble, flash and explode across this astonishing world of ours . . . He was the "Captain Good" in life as well as the minstrel, the story-teller, the soothsayer, the foundation and the flush of the feast.'[18] Lady Cynthia Asquith recorded in her diary on 26 June 1915 that she had sat next to Belloc at a dinner party and that he had waxed eloquent on 'the corruption of politicians' and that he had 'sat up talking until nearly three'.[19]

In April 1916 Belloc escaped from the hectic routine in London, seeking physical respite and spiritual replenishment in the landscape of eastern England. On 7 April he wrote to Blunt from Lincoln, describing the city as 'very very fine . . . With Ludlow the only place with medieval continuity & external tradition in England. I have come up the East of England. Largely on foot.'[20]

Four days later he was back in London for what his sister described in her diary as 'the most remarkable Poets' Reading I have ever attended . . . held at Lord Byron's beautiful house in Piccadilly, lent by Lady d'Erlanger, in aid of the Star and Garter Home at Richmond'.[21] 'It was a most amusing idea,' wrote Cynthia Asquith, 'ten live poets reading their own poems.'[22] The 'live poets' in question were Belloc, Laurence Binyon, Émile Cammaerts, W.H. Davies, Maurice Hewlett, Walter de la Mare, Henry Newbolt, Owen Seaman, Margaret Woods and W.B. Yeats. Augustine Birrell was in the Chair and, to conclude the proceedings, G.K. Chesterton proposed the vote of thanks. Marie Belloc Lowndes described W.H. Davies as 'a strange tiny poet' who read four of his own poems. Yeats, according to Cynthia Asquith, 'recited four poems preciously, but really rather beautifully'. Possibly the most poignant moment was provided by an actor reading a 'beautiful poem' by Julian Grenfell, the promising young poet who had fallen in action during the previous year. Belloc read two of his own verses – 'Lines to a Don' and his sonnet 'The Poor of London' – and 'got a big reception'.[23]

Cynthia Asquith described Belloc's reading of his 'Lines to a Don' as 'very funny'[24] and it is easy to imagine the audience's amused response to Belloc's litany of insults to the don who 'dared attack my Chesterton'. His other choice, 'The Poor of London', was presumably selected for its aptness on such a charitable occasion, but one wonders whether he had also chosen its radical message as a means of haranguing the complacent rich who had gathered in such salubrious surroundings to be entertained 'for charity'. Cynthia Asquith recalled seeing Belloc 'making an unholy row' earlier in the evening, complaining that he had become the 'sport of the rich at forty-six', and it is clear that he both loved and loathed the 'high society' he was now keeping. Increasingly, throughout his years of widowhood, he would become the regular guest of a number of wealthy families, staying at their country homes and town houses. He enjoyed their friendship and their company, but he often felt uneasy and resentful at his dependence on a wealth that was not his.

In early June, Belloc visited the Italian front before proceeding to

Rome for a private audience with Pope Benedict XV. 'I had a long, long talk with him,' he informed Charlotte Balfour. 'He is a thoroughly good man ... he has something like Holiness in his expression and an intense anxious sincerity. He spoke of individual conversion as opposed to political Catholicism in a way which – with my temperament all for the Collective Church – profoundly impressed me. I was exceedingly glad to have seen him and to have got his blessing.'[25]

Back in England, Belloc's high profile as a writer for *Land and Water* continued to keep him in considerable demand as a lecturer. He could command as much as 20–30 pounds per lecture and sometimes gave as many as 10 a week. He lectured three times at the Queen's Hall in London, and on the first of these a total of 600 pounds was taken on the door. More than 2,000 people came to hear him at the Colston Hall in Bristol and, soon after his return from Rome, he gave the Lees-Knowles Lectures in Military History at Cambridge, his first academic distinction since leaving Balliol.

In July 1916 Louis Belloc, having left Downside the previous summer and subsequently enlisted with the Royal Engineers, was sent on active service to France. He was two months short of his nineteenth birthday. Belloc's concerns for his eldest son's safety must have been heightened by the deaths, in September and November respectively, of two of his closest friends, Raymond Asquith and Auberon Lucas. In the meantime, safe in London, Belloc continued to do whatever he could for the war effort. On 12 December 1916 he gave a charity lecture in London to raise money for a hospital for the French wounded in Brittany.[26] A few weeks later Belloc told his sister 'that the United States will do all in their power to maintain their neutrality', but added that they would end by being driven into the war. Marie recorded:

> On the other hand, he hopes the present situation will be prolonged because he believes it will be best for the Allies for America to be in a state of benevolent neutrality rather than at War. He is just off to see Haig and to stay at French Headquarters. He is convinced that by April the submarine menace will be thoroughly in hand.[27]

Not surprisingly perhaps, Marie Belloc Lowndes, both in her diaries and in her published memoirs, treats Belloc's analysis with respectful and unquestioning credulity, always working on the implicit assumption that her brother's knowledge and wisdom in such matters were faultless. Amongst the war-worn troops, however, his persistent optimism was becoming irksome. Sassoon wrote on 21 June 1917:

A long statement of the war-aims etc by Belloc in *Land and Water* leaves me quite unconvinced. He argues from the point of view of British rectitude: and it is that which I am questioning. Worst of all, he argues on the assumption that 'the next few months' will bring a military decision; he has done this since 1915, so one cannot put much faith in him.[28]

Similarly, Wilfred Owen complained in a verse of self-confessed cynicism:

> And if girls sigh, they sigh ethereally,
> And wish the Push would get on less funereally.
> Old Bill enlarges on his little jokes.
> *Punch* is still grinning at the Derby blokes.
> And Belloc prophecies [*sic*] of last year, serially.[29]

In spite of these protestations, Owen, like Brooke and Gurney, remained an admirer of Belloc, carrying around a 'battered copy of *Gems from Hilaire Belloc*'.[30] In June 1915 he had written to his mother, 'I thought much of H. Belloc; and have added much to my appreciation of Travel, since reading *Hills & the Sea*. Another thing: was it not Belloc's great forefinger which pointed out to me this passage of De Vigny: *If any man despairs of becoming a Poet, let him carry his pack and march in the ranks*.'[31]

In January 1916, writing to his sister, Owen reported that 'the Colonel gave a brilliant lecture on the causes of the War', adding that he was 'an expert after the style of Belloc'.[32] Even as late as June 1917, he was reporting to his mother that Belloc's *A Picked Company* was the last book he had read. Nonetheless, as his 'cynical' verse signified, he was losing patience with what was widely perceived as Belloc's blindness to the harsh realities of the war.

Belloc was, however, no more immune from those harsh realities than anyone else. In July 1917 he learned that his old friend Basil Blackwood had been killed, and in August he received news that Louis had been gassed on the Somme and had been sent to a military hospital in Manchester. On 5 September Belloc informed Blunt that 'the whole family went up with me to Manchester'. Louis was 'nearly all right again & to be released in a few days'.[33]

From Manchester, Belloc travelled with his other four children to Exmoor for a family holiday. 'Exmore mislikes me,' he wrote to Blunt. 'It is all hills, & every ravine *packed* with tourists of the worst & it all smells strongly of Charles Kingsley, who was a fanatical humbug . . . The children – who like Exmoor better than I do – send you their regards.'[34]

On the Feast of All Souls, 2 November, Belloc arranged to have a Requiem Mass said for Elodie in the chapel at King's Land.[35] The following month, on hearing of the death of Lady Wentworth, he commiserated with Blunt in words that must have echoed the sentiments he felt at Elodie's Requiem. 'You agree with me on the impossibility of dealing, not adequately indeed, but at all, with the circumstance that the affections & memories and aims of the human spirit are utterly out of scale with its habitation & limits here. The inequality of lives is the chief mark of that tragic circumstance.'[36]

By the end of 1917, Belloc was growing as weary of the war as everyone else.

> I cannot tell you how bored I am at having to rush over to France
> ... especially as my mission is of the most futile description. They
> merely want me to be able to say that I have seen the Americans
> drilling, but I can see that just as well with my mind's eye, without
> crawling through the war zone in trains that go about 10 miles an
> hour, and motoring in arctic weather.[37]

The war, however, trundled on relentlessly, and Belloc trundled on with it, equally relentlessly and increasingly reluctantly. In June he had met Marshall Foch – 'A *really* delightful man, full of genius and movement'[38] – and in December he met Pershing, the American General-in-Chief, who struck him as 'a man of determination and character' with whom he was 'greatly impressed'.[39] In May 1918, accompanied by 18-year-old Eleanor, he visited the Grand Fleet in the Firth of Forth as the guest of Admiral de Robeck.

Ironically, having been hopelessly optimistic in all his predictions since the war had begun, Belloc told his sister on 27 August 1918 that he did not think the war was likely to end 'before April or even *June*' of the following year. Marie preferred to believe the predictions of a 'French Saint' who 'says it will end before Christmas'.[40] In the event, the 'saint' was right and Belloc, predictably, was wrong.

On the day before his erroneous prediction, although he would not hear the news until several days later, Belloc's worst fears were realized. Following his recovery from the gas attack of the previous year, Louis Belloc had retrained with the Royal Flying Corps. In early August he left for France for his first tour of duty as a pilot. 'I parted from him with a heavy heart,' Belloc wrote to a friend on 14 August, 'but ... like myself at his age there was no escaping what youth so intensely desired.'[41] On

26 August, Louis's squadron set out to bomb the German transport columns. He never returned and his body was never found.

Belloc was devastated by the news that his son was missing, but refused to accept the worst. For months afterwards he clung desperately to the hope that Louis had survived and that he had been taken prisoner. He was filled with remorse for his perceived failings as a father, recalling Louis's life with nostalgic affection, 'especially his early childhood and the days before any disasters came'.[42] Only three weeks before Louis's death, in a letter to Blunt, Belloc had quoted two 'very beautiful' lines from Homer that must have returned to haunt him when he heard the dreadful news of his son's disappearance.

> The chief of Heroes, he ran up like a young tree
> And I myself nourished him, like a young tree in the corner of a
>   garden-field.[43]

Desperately, doggedly, during the dying months of the war, Belloc tried every avenue he knew to trace his son, hoping against hope that he had survived. The war ended and still Louis was not to be found. Eventually, the dying embers of his hope burned themselves out. 'The Vatican are now making enquiries about Louis for me,' he wrote to Blunt on 12 December, 'but the time is getting long and I have little hope.'[44]

TWENTY-TWO

A Private Friendship

THE ARMISTICE IN NOVEMBER 1918 offered scant comfort to the grieving Belloc. Like millions of others he was left to pick up the pieces of a broken life, fumbling through the fragments of bittersweet memories and guilt-ridden regrets. For him, as for countless others, the war had left a lingering aftertaste.

The war would also have one last sting in its tail. Within weeks of peace being declared, Cecil Chesterton died of the effects of trench fever at a field hospital in France. He was buried in a military cemetery on 6 December. A year earlier, he had written to Belloc *en route* for embarkation to France. 'I am writing this in the train going to Liverpool . . . By the way, if anything should happen to me – torpedoes or the like – you will have me remembered in your nice little chapel, won't you?'[1]

'Cecil Chesterton is dead,' Belloc wrote in a tribute article in the *New Witness* a week later. 'He has left the only place which we know and understand, and gone to better and more permanent things which we shall understand in our turn.' Remembering also, no doubt, the death of his beloved Elodie, and torn by the loss of his son, for whom his hopes were now fading, Belloc wrote of 'the intolerable sense of loss and grief which follows upon such a departure in us who remain'.

Belloc's obituary to Cecil Chesterton concentrated on Chesterton's editorship of the *New Witness* and his exposure, in its pages, of government corruption.

Nothing can replace him, nor exercise the function which he exercised, nor do what he did for his country . . .

It is the function exercised by the man who will bring out corruption into the air: oxydize it; burn it up. But the exercise of such a function in such times can be undertaken only by, at the best, a very small number of men . . . For this function requires a combination of three things, each rare, and in combination, of course, much rarer still. These three things are knowledge, the power of lucidity in expression, and, lastly, courage.[2]

Having declared that Chesterton embodied all these strengths, he emphasized the last of these. 'His courage was heroic ... He never in his life checked an action or a word from a consideration of personal caution, and that is more than can be said of any other man of his time.'

These eulogistic sentiments might have been appropriate to a panegyric, but they could not disguise the fact that, while his friend was alive, Belloc had often considered these examples of 'heroic courage' as a rashness and a recklessness of judgement. Two years earlier he had written impatiently to Baring, 'Cecil Chesterton has just done the silliest thing that even the recent history of the *New Witness* could show.' Referring to the case of Francis Oppenheimer, a German Jew who was acting as an Allied agent in Holland, Belloc had written that 'his service to this country has been of the utmost value'. Cecil Chesterton, presumably on the crudest anti-Semitic grounds, refused to publish Belloc's comments. 'The *New Witness* wouldn't print this, simply from ignorance. They said that Oppenheimer was a German Jew and that therefore they would not support him ...' Clearly frustrated, Belloc complained to Baring that if the *New Witness* 'goes in for the simple Jingoism, Jew baiting or any other crude emotion of the man in the street ... it has no reason at all for its existence, for it is not witty and it is not solid'.[3]

In the same month, August 1916, Belloc had protested against the conscription of Russian Jews, saying, 'It is against all my principles that Jews should be conscripted at all, and the idea of forcing that unfortunate people back to Russia is very wrong.'[4] Belloc's own view of the 'Jewish question', if not in itself confused, was certainly confusing to many readers. It would, however, be clearly wrong to equate his position on this thorny issue with the 'Jew baiting' that he explicitly condemned.

G.K. Chesterton was mortified by his brother's death, succumbing to uncharacteristic bitterness. He found it a cruel injustice that Cecil was dead while Rufus and Godfrey Isaacs, whom he perceived as his brother's persecutors at the Marconi trial, were still alive. In an open letter to Rufus Isaacs, Chesterton's pain spilled over into vitriol, verging on hatred. 'It would be irrational to ask you for sympathy but I am sincerely moved to offer it. You are far more unhappy; for your brother is still alive.' Eaten by a rancour fed with despair, Chesterton had entitled the open letter 'At the Sign of the World's End'. The title was singularly appropriate. For both Belloc and Chesterton – one mourning a son, the other a brother – the war's end must have seemed like the world's end. Life would go on, but not as they had known it. Behind were memories of loved ones lost; ahead was the post-war 'waste land' soon to be evoked by T.S. Eliot. The war would not end war, as the pre-war optimists had naively declared, but it would put an end to many other things.

In dutiful debt to his brother's memory, G.K. Chesterton assumed the editorship of the *New Witness*, urging Belloc to assist him in his endeavours. 'I never believed so strongly as I do at present that England needs an organ like the *New Witness*, as I think you and I could make it,' he wrote in May 1919.[5] By August, however, he was beginning to regret his decision. 'I should be honestly relieved to be clear of the *New Witness*, except as a contributor. Editing is about as much my job as tightrope dancing.'[6]

There were a few moments of joy amid the sorrows wrought by the war – oases of hope in a desert of desolation. The much publicized reception of Ronald Knox into the Catholic Church on 22 September 1917 was a great source of comfort. On 26 November that year, at the suggestion of Cardinal Bourne, Knox moved to the Brompton Oratory, where he would remain until the end of 1918. It was, therefore, presumably sometime during the final months of the war that Belloc had 'blown in' on him at the Oratory, as Knox reported to his sister, and exuberantly congratulated him on his conversion. The two men had met previously at Oxford and each shared a healthy respect for the other's abilities. Knox had re-read *The Path to Rome* twice in the months before his conversion. The book had long been a favourite and he had set himself the task of indexing it under more than 300 heads. Belloc, for his part, had written a letter to Knox as soon as news of his reception had reached him. He had, however, refrained from sending it. As he would confess to Knox six years later, the unsent letter had expressed his belief in Knox's importance to the Catholic revival in England. 'It is of importance to England today that every testimony should be given – and I cannot but think that if all your time and energies were free for the examination, the proclaiming of the Faith . . . they would be spent to the country's good. Such effort is needed, and very few are there to undertake it.'[7] Knox's conversion would bring the two men closer together and by 1921 their friendship had matured sufficiently for Knox to be a Christmas guest at King's Land.

Perhaps the most mature, and possibly the most valued, of all Belloc's friendships was that which he continued to enjoy with Wilfrid Scawen

Blunt, his ageing neighbour who was now approaching his eightieth year. On New Year's Eve 1918, Belloc wrote hopefully to Blunt about the coming year. 'I pray for an early spring. We all need it. The spirits of the world are down in the depths.'[8] Through all the depths of the previous years, Blunt's friendship had proved a powerful sustaining force. Clare Balfour, who, with her mother, was still a regular visitor to King's Land, recalled Blunt's arrival at Belloc's home one winter's day when the children were outside playing a 'wild and shrieking' game of football. He had driven up, 'sitting erect in a phaeton drawn by two Arab horses'.

> He came into the field and stood beside Belloc to watch us. The two men were both Sussex-born, both cradle Catholics, both unsuccessful Liberal politicians and both poets. In appearance they made a striking contrast – Belloc short, stout, clean-shaven, dressed all in black, and Wilfrid Blunt with a grey beard, magnificent in stature, tall and thin in a long yellow checked coat that came down to his ankles.[9]

Siegfried Sassoon, who visited Blunt in June 1919, gives an evocative account of the warmth of Belloc's friendship with the old man. Belloc was Blunt's 'most valued neighbour', who, in Sassoon's words, had 'for many years ... done much to sustain him by his brilliant powers as a talker and the gusto of his human companionship'. At Blunt's request, Sassoon walked the 'pleasant two miles by a field path' from Newbuildings to King's Land with the intention of asking Belloc to come over to Newbuildings later in the day. Upon his arrival, and although they had never previously met, Belloc received him with 'glowing hospitality' and introduced him to another visitor, the novelist E.W. Hornung – creator of 'Raffles, the gentleman burglar' – who was seated at a table with a tankard of beer.

> Belloc, full of anxiety to make me welcome, poured me a goblet of Burgundy and handed me a good-sized cigar, neither of which I had the heart to refuse. It would have been ungracious to explain that I seldom drank wine except at dinner; to confess that a bottle of ginger-beer would suit me better might have seemed disrespectful to his veneration of august vintages. As a result I was soon feeling somewhat stupefied, and could only produce feeble responses to his stimulating talk ... Altogether I felt that we had chosen the wrong time of day for acclimatization to an atmosphere of Burgundy and flushed conviviality. The circumstances created a social incompatibility which Belloc's geniality failed to put right ... Meanwhile I contrived to

discard my cigar, and Belloc took me to see the view from the top of his windmill. Proud of being a landed proprietor, he pointed out the boundaries of his estate. Broad and sturdy in his black clothes, he was eloquent about the Weald and its local customs and traditions. Observing his fine, ruddy, and uncompromising countenance, I was aware that nothing could be more delightfully Bellocian than his eulogizing of the Sussex landscape ...

Returning to the house and continuing his monologue, Belloc lamented his own failures as a writer and claimed that he had not achieved 'anything lasting'. 'Most of us,' Sassoon would counter many years later, 'would have been thankful to have written a tithe of his resonant prose,' adding that he believed Belloc's long poem 'In Praise of Wine', with its 'magnificently perfected couplets', would 'outlive most of the verse published by his contemporaries'.

Over the next 38 years Sassoon would continue to admire Belloc's poetry, prose and personality, but would continue to find the Catholic dimension beyond his comprehension. Then, in 1957, he was struck by some words of Belloc in a letter to Katherine Asquith, published in Robert Speaight's biography, which would prove crucial to his own conversion to the Catholic Faith. ' "Outcast and unprotected contours of the soul" is not *me* but beloved *Belloc*,' he informed a friend, explaining that the phrase appeared in Belloc's letter to Asquith, which he proceeded to quote at length:

> The Faith, the Catholic Church, is discovered, is recognized, triumphantly enters reality like a landfall at sea which first was thought a cloud. The nearer it is seen, the more it is real, the less imaginary: the more direct and external its voice, the more indubitable its representative character, its 'persona', its voice. The metaphor is not that men fall in love with it: the metaphor is that they discover home ... It is the very mould of the mind, the matrix to which corresponds in every outline the outcast and unprotected contour of the soul. It is Verlaine's 'Oh! Rome – oh! Mere!' And that not only to those who had it in childhood and have returned, but much more – and what a proof! – to those who come upon it from the hills of life and say to themselves, 'Here is the town.'[10]

'Belloc's magnificent words settled it, once and for all,' Sassoon wrote. 'My whole being was liberated.'[11] Sassoon's gratitude to Belloc was only tempered by a wistful wish that Belloc 'could have known it, foreknown it' all those years earlier when they had met. As a tribute, Sassoon chose Belloc's 'magnificent words' to Katherine Asquith as the epigraph to *The Path to Peace*, a selection of his own verse published in 1960.

None of this could be known or foreknown to either man on the hot summer's day in 1919 when Sassoon paid his visit to King's Land at Blunt's beckoning. Evidently, however, as his memoirs testify, Sassoon succeeded in persuading Belloc to visit Blunt later that day.

> There are moments in one's life-experience which never lose their felt and memorable freshness. One of them is before me now, seen as I saw it then. Mr Blunt, tired but reluctant to return to his room, had asked Belloc to sing something. Not having heard of his country songs, I was taken by surprise when, with complete naturalness, he trolled out a ditty in his high tenor voice. It was 'Ha'nacker Mill' that he sang, to a tune of his own, and he made it sound as if the words had come down through long-vanished generations. In fact I assumed it to be an old Sussex ballad, though in print it has more the quality of a modern poem, except, perhaps, in the first verse . . .
>
> But what returns to me in sunset light is the broad and bulky yet somehow boyish figure of the singer, sitting on a bench close by the old friend whom he was intent on pleasing, and Wilfrid Blunt, listening with half-closed eyes, his face touched to tenderness and regret by the power and pathos of the words. I see them thus together, and so shall always do, as though the moment could never be taken from them and might be re-enacted beyond the dream of earthly time.[12]

It would seem, from a letter dated six weeks later, that Blunt had not known Belloc's beautiful poem 'Ha'nacker Mill' prior to the haunting rendition of it that Belloc had given in Sassoon's presence at Newbuildings. 'I am so glad you liked Halnacker Mill,' Belloc wrote on 27 July. 'The thing is printed I will send you copies.'[13] The same letter detailed a recent voyage that Belloc had taken along England's south coast on his boat, the *Nona*, the first trip he had been able to make since before the war. 'I am just back off the sea where I have had a most excellent journey into the Solent, & I am off again this afternoon to take a clear four days. I hope to get my boat into the Channel for all that time. It is five years since she was last out! She is as old as me exactly, & I am 49 years old today.'

Belloc's wanderlust for the hills and the sea, always a comfort in times of desolation, was undiminished. Apart from rediscovering the joys of sailing, he was continuing to enjoy the pleasures of exploring the multifarious landscapes of Europe. In late May, shortly before the meeting with

Blunt that Sassoon would immortalize, he had travelled widely thr
Italy – first in the north, stopping at Turin, Milan, Verona and V
and then south to Ravenna, Florence, Orvieto and Rome, where he ı
Pope Benedict XV for the second time, almost three years after their
previous meeting. In October he travelled through France, refamiliarizing
himself with old haunts and haunted by old memories. He visited La Celle
Saint Cloud, 'to see whether my poor old house were worth restoring'.

> It was a strange experience to find it still standing and only deserted
> – though suffering from a life-time of emptiness. It is thirty years
> since I last lived and slept there and 20 perhaps since it was regularly
> inhabited: it was astonishingly full of reminiscence and childhood . . .
> it fell into less and less use and was abandoned, but never sold. I
> hesitate to sell it: it seems impious. But perhaps it could hardly be
> lived in again.[14]

From La Celle Saint Cloud he journeyed on foot 'down through Anjou
to the Loire'. The Loire valley lifted his spirits, but there were always
reminders of his own loss in the sense of loss he encountered in others.

> . . . in Liré, du Bellay's little town . . . three women were complaining
> of the dead: two very old women in caps, the third a woman of sixty
> who spoke of her son. Their complaint was that no one knew where
> the dead were lying and that no one could visit that earth. In a
> generation all this mighty society of Europe will re-arise transformed,
> but for the moment it is all mourning and intolerable desolation:
> until the little children become men.[15]

It is not difficult to imagine the pain that the women's conversation must
have caused Belloc, whose own son was lying in an unknown grave
somewhere in France. The melancholy spirit, so dominant in Belloc's life
at this time, was expressed with pathos and poignancy in a letter to
Professor Edward G. Browne, a Cambridge don, on 28 July 1920, the day
after Belloc's fiftieth birthday. 'I welcome every birthday because I find
it an approach to the grave . . . whereas few men seek death, all after a
certain age desire to be rid of life.'[16] 'Tarantella', one of Belloc's most
powerful poems, was written in this post-war period. It encapsulates, with
sublime nostalgic simplicity, this potent, almost omnipotent, sense of
doom and desolation.

'Tarantella' first appeared in January 1920 in the third issue of a new
magazine, the London Mercury, edited by Belloc's friend J.C. Squire. The
same issue contained poems by Thomas Hardy, Robert Nichols and Robert

Graves, and an essay by Walter de la Mare, indicative of the high quality of contributions that Squire had managed to secure for the journal. Belloc would continue to contribute both poetry and prose to the *London Mercury* throughout the twenties and thirties, and his friendship with Squire would remain a valuable source of conviviality and comfort. He also appears to have valued Squire's judgement with regard to wine, recording in his diary on 22 January 1920 that he had bought a supply of white port at Docman's on Squire's recommendation.[17]

Other friendships helped to lighten the gloom-laden days, particularly those of a number of young men who began as disciples of Belloc's literary personality and who would become friends of the most valued kind. As much as he enjoyed the companionship of his contemporaries, such as Baring and Chesterton, he loved the liveliness of the young generation who helped him recapture, in fleet and fleeting moments, the carefree spirit of his youth. With D.B. Wyndham Lewis, J.B. Morton and Douglas Woodruff, probably the most prominent of this new generation of fresh-faced Bellocians, he was reminded that life could be enjoyed on the babbling surface even when endured in the chillness and stillness of the depths.

Douglas Woodruff first met Belloc in Oxford in the autumn of 1920, having been introduced to him because he had been a friend and contemporary of Louis Belloc at Downside.[18] Wyndham Lewis and J.B. Morton, on the other hand, were not drawn by any family connection but by a fond familiarity with Belloc's work. Wyndham Lewis captured the nature of Belloc's influence on this new circle of young acolytes in an affectionate memoir published in the *Catholic Herald* more than 30 years later.

> It is difficult to express all that Belloc meant (and means) to those of us of a much younger generation, admitted to his friendship at a time when he had already achieved the greater part of his many-sided fame as a master of English prose, a brilliant talker ... a considerable poet, both serious and light, a delicious essayist, a formidable debater, an historian who drove the anti-Catholic opposition to fury, a satirist whom *The Times* has ranked with Maugham and Waugh, a traveller, a polemist, a citizen of Europe, the prophet of *The Servile State*, a great man in every sense.
>
> He treated us invariably as his intellectual equals, which was a regal compliment ... [He] never monopolized and never bored. Even his low spirits, as Chesterton said, were much, much more uproarious and enlivening than anybody else's high ones.

Thus he was always to a group of us young enough to be his sons, and any suspicion of what the French call a *chapelle*, or flattery-circle, may be instantly dismissed. No flattery could live in that atmosphere of mirth and irony.[19]

If Belloc was intolerant of flattery, he seems to have accepted an element of good-natured reverence on the part of his young friends. J.B. Morton modelled himself on Belloc, whom he always called 'the Master', to such a degree that, according to Belloc's grandson, his books were not only 'very similar' to his mentor's but that, in old age, he would eventually resemble him physically.[20] Flattery, it seems, was only tolerated in its sincerest form.

Partly due to Belloc's influence, Wyndham Lewis and J.B. Morton both became Catholics, Lewis in 1921 and Morton the year after. Both men were rising stars of Fleet Street. Morton took over Wyndham Lewis's highly popular 'Beachcomber' column in the *Daily Express* in 1924 and Wyndham Lewis later became 'Timothy Shy' in the *News Chronicle*. Together they established a satirical style of journalism which remained popular in spite of attacks from George Orwell and others who accused them of using their columns to write Catholic propaganda. 'From either a literary or a political point of view,' Orwell wrote scathingly, 'these two are simply the leavings on Chesterton's plate.'[21] In fact, they were more the leavings on Belloc's plate, and their gibes at politicians and other errant personalities owed more to the strident tradition of Cecil Chesterton than to the good-natured and rambling ruminations of his older brother.

Belloc was himself writing more 'Catholic propaganda' than ever at this time. In 1920 the Catholic Truth Society published his essay, *The Catholic Church and the Principle of Private Property*, and the same year also saw the publication of his hugely influential, and highly controversial, *Europe and the Faith*, one of the pivotal works of the Catholic Literary Revival. The controversial aspect of this particular book is epitomized in the oft-quoted final passage in which Belloc appears to state that the concept of Europe and the essentials of the Catholic Faith are mutually dependent.

> . . . our European structure, built upon the noble foundations of classical antiquity, was formed through, exists by, is consonant to, and will stand in the mould of, the Catholic Church.
> Europe will return to the Faith, or she will perish.
> The Faith is Europe. And Europe is the Faith.[22]

Not surprisingly, the final five words led to a great deal of misunderstanding, with many coming to the misleading conclusion that Belloc was implying that the Catholic Faith was dependent on Europe. Eventually, 16 years later, his name had become so synonymous with this provincial vision of Catholicism that he felt compelled to reassert his belief in the universality of the Church.

> I have never said that the Church was necessarily European. The Church will last for ever, and, on this earth, until the end of the world; and our remote descendants may find its chief membership to have passed to Africans or Asiatics in some civilization yet unborn. What I have said is that the European thing is essentially a Catholic thing, and that European values would disappear with the disappearance of Catholicism.[23]

G.K. Chesterton's eventual, and somewhat tardy, reception into the Catholic Church on 30 July 1922, three days after Belloc's fifty-second birthday, came as a surprise to almost nobody except Belloc himself. Unlike many others, who were not so much surprised by Chesterton's decision as by the length of time he had taken to reach it, Belloc had long since reached the conclusion that his friend would never take the final decisive step across the threshold of the Church. Although Chesterton had defended the Church with his pen ever since the publication of his *Orthodoxy* 14 years earlier, Belloc was convinced that he would never actually convert. As he explained to Baring on 25 August 1922, he had believed that Chesterton had the Catholic *mood* but that he lacked the *will* necessary for conversion.

> People said that he might come in at any time because he showed such a Catholic point of view and so much affection for the Catholic Church. That always seemed to me quite the wrong end of the stick. Acceptation of the Faith is an act, not a mood. Faith is an act of will and as it seemed to me the whole of his mind was occupied in expressing his liking for and attraction towards a certain mood, not at all towards the acceptation of a certain Institution as defined and representing full reality in this world. There is all the difference between enjoying military ideas ... and becoming a private soldier in a common regiment.[24]

Belloc's surprise at his friend's conversion was expressed in a series of letters to their mutual friend Father John O'Connor. 'It is very great news indeed!' he wrote on 12 August. 'I am overwhelmed by it.' Eleven days later he reported that he still remained 'under the *coup* of Gilbert's conversion. I had never thought it possible!' On 25 August, the day he expressed his bewilderment to Baring, he wrote again to Father O'Connor: 'The more I think on Gilbert the more astonished I become!' Finally, on 9 September, he wrote to tell Father O'Connor that he had seen Chesterton two days previously. 'I went to stop a night with him. He is very happy. In the matter of explanation you are right. But I have no vision.' At the bottom of the page, Belloc appended a sketch, a whimsically symbolic self-portrait, depicting a blind man led by a dog, and tapping with a stick.[25]

'I am not very much good at understanding what is going on in other people's minds,' Belloc confessed to Baring, 'and it turns out most happily that I was wrong.' He predicted that Chesterton would 'suffer in several ways' as a direct result of his conversion. 'He will now be labelled, and . . . his former colleagues, such as the *Church Times*, will say he is being influenced by all sorts of people, which is humiliating.'[26] Perhaps Belloc already foresaw the likelihood that he would be 'blamed' for 'influencing' Chesterton's conversion. Certainly, Max Beerbohm was not alone in the belief, recounted to Malcolm Muggeridge, that Chesterton had been 'dragooned into the Catholic Church by Belloc – as with Maurice Baring, and, if he had lived, George Wyndham'.[27]

Edward Shanks, in a pen portrait of Belloc published in the September 1921 issue of the *London Mercury*, had attained a more fairly proportioned estimate of the true relationship between the two halves of the Chesterbelloc. After alluding to the fact that some of Belloc's work 'resembles Mr Chesterton, with whom it is so usual to compare him', Shanks added that comparison between the two writers should not be overstated. 'The comparison holds good also in the general attitude of both towards the world – an attitude which it is probably incorrect to say that Mr Chesterton learnt from Mr Belloc, the one having rather found in the other a confirmation of what he himself had already guessed.'[28]

Shanks's comparison of Belloc's and Chesterton's similarities and differences illustrated a greater perceptiveness than that of many other critics, Beerbohm included. It is plainly more than a little simplistic to suggest that Chesterton's conversion was nothing more than an expression of his passive discipleship, and it would be truer to say that his reception into the Church was the confirmation of his kinship of spirit with Belloc. On the other hand, it would be erroneous to suggest that Belloc's presence in Chesterton's life had played no part whatever in his conversion. Indeed, there are echoes of Belloc's continuing influence in the very letter that he wrote to Chesterton on the occasion of his reception into the Church. Having explained to his friend that he was a sceptic by nature, but that he found 'the doubt of the soul . . . to be false: a mood: not a conclusion', he described 'the Faith' in typically uncompromising terms. 'My conclusion – and that of all men who have ever once seen it – is the Faith. Corporate, organized, a personality, teaching. A thing, not a theory. It.'[29]

A thing, not a theory. It . . . Seven years later Chesterton published a book of essays defending It, the Faith, under the title *The Thing*. After his conversion, as much as before, Chesterton would remain indebted to Belloc.

Even as Belloc's bombastic brand of evangelism was ushering young acolytes and old friends into the Church, he was displaying a more serene side of his character in his relationship with the rapidly ailing Wilfrid Scawen Blunt. As far back as 1916 Belloc had introduced Blunt to Father Vincent McNabb in the hope that the holy Dominican might help reconcile Blunt to the Catholic faith that he had long rejected. Blunt was well aware of Belloc's ulterior motive, but nonetheless accepted Father McNabb into his circle of friends. According to Elizabeth Longford, Blunt's biographer, 'The friendship with Father McNabb was a growing source of light in Blunt's darkness.'[30]

On 22 October 1921 Blunt was so ill that he made what he thought would be his last-ever diary entry. It was a cry for spiritual help, a scream in the dark. 'I should like to die worthily but I feel it is beyond my power. I go out into the darkness where no wisdom can avail. I would wish to believe in another life beyond, for my life here has been a happy one. I would wish to believe a good God loves us all.'[31] His health continued to falter, but he received an unexpected stay of execution. Both physically and spiritually he staggered on, recording in his diary on St Patrick's Day 1922 that Belloc had gone to Rome, bringing Blunt's homage to Pius XI who, only weeks before, had succeeded Benedict XV as Pope. 'How willingly would I believe if only I could but, woe is me, I cannot.' Belloc returned from Rome a week later, bringing a crucifix blessed for Blunt by the Pope. It was a decisive moment. 'It found me,' Blunt recorded, 'in a mood for conversion and an insistence on the necessity for me of a return to the Sacraments before I die.'[32]

Belloc assured him that, being already a Catholic and with no quarrel with the Church, he was entitled to ask for the sacraments. Any lingering doubts and hesitations were swept aside by Belloc's admission that he himself often went to the sacraments 'feeling little'. This was, to Blunt, a revelation, at once both paradoxical and powerful, a mystical moment springing from a sceptical statement. Depth in the dryness of dust. Suddenly Blunt perceived that the faltering, flickering candle of the sincere sinner was as much in need of the oxygen of grace as was the flaming faith of the saints. The very dimness of Belloc's natural scepticism was a light of hope to the old man groping in the dark; his very doubt an affirmation. Both men, the beleaguered believer and the would-be believer alike, were fumbling for faith in the shadows of doubt.

It is easy to imagine Belloc discussing the Catholic Faith with Blunt in much the same way that he had expressed it in his letter to Chesterton. Assured by Belloc that faith was an act of the will subject to the grace of God which did not require any 'feeling', Blunt requested that Father McNabb be sent for. Shane Leslie, in his account of Blunt's reconciliation with the faith of his childhood, vividly imagined the 'great moment' when the sheikh of Sussex and the Irish Dominican met in communion, 'both wearing white robes'.[33]

Blunt died on the morning of 10 September 1922, within weeks of his reconciliation with the Faith, and was buried beneath the soil of his own grounds. The monument erected over his grave included six lines from his sonnet 'Chanclebury Ring':

> Dear checker-work of woods, the Sussex Weald!
> If a name thrills me yet of things of earth,
> That name is thine. How often have I fled
> To thy deep hedgerows and embraced each field,
> Each lag, each pasture – fields which gave me birth
> And saw my youth, and which must hold me dead.

The similarity between these lines and several of Belloc's poems in praise of Sussex are a striking indication of the extent to which Blunt and Belloc were kindred spirits. Indeed, a letter written by Belloc in 1904 appears to suggest that Blunt's poetry had influenced his own. Thanking Blunt for sending him some of his new verses, Belloc wrote: 'I shall read them with that delight which ran through me fifteen years ago when I first was given your verses as a boy . . . In those days I learnt them by heart . . . I thank you, as must be doing hundreds of the younger men for writing us such lines.'[34] Their bond of friendship, stretching back three decades, went deeper than the soil of Sussex, and Sassoon, a child of Kent, knew that the real core of their friendship was best expressed in Sassoon's own favourite of all Blunt's verse, a poem which begins:

Love me a little, love me as thou wilt,
Whether a draught it be of passionate wine
Poured with both hands divine,
Or just a cup of water spilt
On dying lips and mine.

Belloc bid Blunt farewell, envious perhaps that his friend no longer felt that 'desire to be rid of life' which ate away at his own being. A thirsty traveller trudging doggedly and dogmatically through a spiritual desert, Belloc carried the burdens of bereavement with resignation. As he had confessed to Chesterton, grief had drawn the juices from life. In this he was not alone. Grief had drawn the juices from the lives of a whole generation. Yet the conversions of old friends and new, friends such as Chesterton, D.B. Wyndham Lewis and J.B. Morton, had brought a welcome relief and respite from the wasteland of hopes and desires.

One suspects, however, that none of these conversions gave as much joy to Belloc as the reconciliation with the Church of his old and dear friend Wilfrid Scawen Blunt. Those few who were privileged to see Belloc and Blunt together, as Siegfried Sassoon did, would not easily forget the poetry and passion of this most private of friendships.

What returns to me in sunset light is the broad and bulky yet somehow boyish figure of the singer, sitting on a bench close by the old friend whom he was intent on pleasing, and Wilfrid Blunt, listening with half-closed eyes, his face touched to tenderness and regret by the power and pathos of the words. I see them thus together, and so shall always do . . .

TWENTY-THREE

Popes, Dictators and Jews

THE BEGUILING MIXTURE of humility and bombast that made Belloc so endearing to some and so infuriating to others was in evidence in two letters written in 1922, one to Katherine Asquith, the other to Charlotte Balfour. Referring to the spate of converts who had been received into the Church, particularly in the previous year, 'those around me who have seen the Faith and practise it on every side', Belloc told Katherine Asquith that they had 'come into it with travail, and their example is worth ten times my own arguments'.[1] Katherine Asquith would be received into the Church herself two years later, indicating that Belloc's 'arguments' for the Faith were not as worthless as he maintained. In his relationship with her, as with his friendship with Blunt, he displayed a serenity seldom shown in his relations with the public at large.

Belloc's public persona was more in evidence in the letter to Charlotte Balfour in which, with seemingly self-righteous pomp, he discussed the prospect of his private audience with the new Pope on 11 March 1922. 'We are to have our Audience tomorrow, I believe. I want to tell the new Pope one or two things. I hope he believes them. The last one doubted me when I told him the Allies were certain to achieve, but this one has wider experience.'[2] These lines remind one irresistibly of Max Beerbohm's hilarious cartoon, published the previous year, entitled 'Mr Belloc's Visit to the Vatican'. Depicting a rotund Belloc holding a sheet of paper out to the lean and quizzical Pope, Beerbohm's cartoon is captioned with the following dialogue:

THE POPE: 'They tell me, my son, that you are a prophet.'
MR BELLOC: 'I am, Your Holiness. And also I have a talent for drawing very pretty diagrams. Here is one of them, showing that in England the national conversion will take place some time between May and July, 1923.'[3]

Bombast aside, real and imagined, Belloc's view of Pius XI was expressed in the letter to Blunt in which Belloc had informed his terminally ill friend of his gift of 'a small crucifix of no value but blessed by the new Pope for you'.

> I had a long conversation with him. He is a remarkable man – far superior to his predecessor. He is full of experience of Europe & knows England well – which is rather a rare advantage at the Vatican & should prove very useful in the near future. He reads English continually & familiarly and French & German as a matter of course. His questions to me were very central & to the point & he took a lively interest in the effects of the war on our society and government. I could only give him very gloomy replies, for indeed I see no hope of recovery . . .
>
>   There is something like a very definite pact – understood rather than expressed – between the Vatican now & the Italian government. The first great religious procession since 1870, through the streets of Rome took place while I was there: it was the carrying of the body of St Philip Neri through the streets on the third centenary of his canonization and hundreds of thousands turned out in honour of it: a most extraordinary sight! The French Embassy had a specially decorated balcony on the Palazzo Farnese – which is typical of this moment of transition in which we live – as was also the fact that they were all present in a special Tribuna at the High Mass at St Peter's.[4]

Similar sentiments were expressed on 28 June in a letter to Charlotte Balfour, who had also just returned from a pilgrimage to Rome.

> Were you not impressed in Rome (as I was) by the much greater position of Religion and the tiny dimensions to which the official world has been reduced? The most striking contrast was the procession of St Philip Neri. Something like half Rome was blocked to traffic by enormous crowds following the Saint, all the rest of the City was empty, and meanwhile the King, the Minister, and a handful of Free Masons were officially playing the fool unveiling a Mazzini monument which no one cared about and which no one goes to see.[5]

Considering Belloc's scarcely disguised contempt for the Italian government, it is hardly surprising that he supported the March on Rome by Mussolini's blackshirts a few months later which established the world's first fascist dictatorship. He informed a friend on 7 November that his mother, who was now 93 years old, was 'glad there has been a new revolution in Italy – and so am I . . .'[6] Earlier in the year he had written that 'our society' would be saved by the establishment of 'some new line of Dynasties sprung from energetic individual men who shall seize power'.[7] These views led him to offer his support to the French royalist movement, the *Action Française*, led by the charismatic figure of Charles Maurras, and he declared on 28 June 1922 that it 'has done an immense amount of good'.[8]

In offering his support to the French monarchists, Belloc had completed the transition from the ardent republicanism of his youth, which had inspired such early work as his studies of Danton and Robespierre. Although he continued to admire Napoleon, presumably as the archetype for the new generation of 'energetic individual men who shall seize power', his view of French history, and particularly his view of the Revolution, would henceforth be tinged with ambivalence.

Belloc's support for the *Action Française* was analysed eloquently and dispassionately by André Bordeaux, Professor of English Literature at the University of Tours.

> Belloc was anti-Protestant and anti-German; so was Maurras. Belloc denounced the corruption of the parliamentary system; so did Maurras. Belloc could hardly bear the Jews; neither could Maurras . . .
>
> Though Maurras was not a Christian and tended to consider the Catholic Church as a mere political ally, the fact that most Catholics in France supported his movement definitely strengthened Belloc's hope that the Action Française would be of great use to the Church and might ultimately bring about a revival of Catholicism in Europe as a whole.[9]

Clearly Belloc's belief in what would now be termed 'a third way', a political creed which rejected both capitalism and communism, was leading him into treacherous waters. His own political beliefs were expressed once again in 1922 in *Catholic Social Reform versus Socialism*, a reiteration of the distributism that he had long preached and which was itself merely an articulation of Catholic social doctrine. Enshrined within Belloc's distributism, and at the very heart of the Church's social teaching which had been Belloc's inspiration, was the principle of subsidiarity. This stipulated that political and economic power should begin with the family and that the usurpation of such power by big business or central government should be rectified by its devolution from larger to smaller institutions. Such a creed was essentially libertarian and did not sit comfortably with political dictatorship. Yet Belloc's desire for a 'Europe of the Faith' led him to support Mussolini in Italy and Maurras in France on the somewhat naive assumption, at least with the wisdom of hindsight, that their strong anti-capitalist and anti-communist stance would result in the resurrection of Catholic Europe. Significantly, he chose to ignore the fact that neither Mussolini nor Maurras were practising Catholics.

Belloc's general political position was summed up succinctly in the same letter in which he had called for the establishment of 'energetic' dictatorships. 'The present Parliamentary welter throughout Europe is not *viable*. It is everywhere thoroughly despised and at the same time it is oppressive and dreadfully corrupt. It means in practice government by a few rich men with an absurd preponderance of financial banking and largely Jewish power. That can't last.'[10] At the heart of such a view, rooted in Belloc's bitter experience of the party system, is a conceptual conundrum which, at best, is a paradox pointing to new political paradigms or, at worst, is nothing more than a contradiction arising out of a contorted view of political reality.

Seven years later, G.K. Chesterton sought to tackle this very conundrum in his analysis of Mussolini's regime in *The Resurrection of Rome*. His approach deserves consideration because it offers a valuable insight into Belloc's own political position. Chesterton had already openly declared himself a disciple of Belloc as far as their shared advocacy of the political philosophy of distributism was concerned. 'You were the founder and father of this mission; we were the converts but you were the missionary,' he wrote in an 'Open Letter' to Belloc, published in the *New Witness* on 27 April 1923. It is fair to assume, therefore, that Chesterton's own approach to the political questions of the day would be similar, possibly almost synonymous, with those of Belloc.

Having met Mussolini during a visit to Rome, and having been both charmed and impressed by the Italian dictator, Chesterton was nonetheless insistent that his discussion of the political situation in Italy should not 'be mistaken for a defence of Fascism'. He was, he insisted, more in sympathy with the pre-fascist Popular Party, 'which was specially the party of the Catholic Democrats' and which had been 'chiefly criticized for having been too democratic'.[11] In spite of this, he still felt that Mussolini's fascist syndicalism was preferable to the institutionalized plutocracy of multinational capitalism, or to the dictatorship of the proletariat recently unleashed in Bolshevik Russia.

Ultimately, Chesterton was frustrated that there only seemed to be two alternatives to plutocracy, namely communism or fascism, neither of which were very satisfactory. 'I wish there were in the world a real white flag of freedom, that I could follow, independently of the red flag of Communist or the black flag of Fascist regimentation. By every instinct of my being, by every tradition of my blood, I should prefer English liberty to Latin discipline.'[12]

It is possible that Belloc had more sympathy with 'Latin discipline' in general, and with the Latin dictatorship of Mussolini in particular, than did Chesterton. There is no doubt, however, that the two men shared the same passionate belief that the true Authority in Rome did not reside with Il Duce but with Il Papa. Neither believed that the Eternal City would be ruled eternally by fascism, any more than they would have believed Hitler's boasts about a 'Thousand Year Reich' a decade later. Fascism would fade away, but the Pope would remain. Hence, in a divine paradox that delighted Chesterton, thousands of goose-stepping black-shirts on the secular streets of Rome were not so powerful as a handful of Swiss Guards on the steps of St Peter's.

The same caution that is needed when dealing with Belloc's attitude to fascism should be exercised when dealing with his attitude towards Jews. The view that he was an anti-Semite persists. Frederic Raphael, writing on 'The Jewish Question' in *The Spectator* on 25 November 2000, observed, 'English fiction has made fools and scoundrels of the Jews, but it has rarely attributed the ills of the world to their very existence. It needed Hilaire Belloc and Ezra Pound and T.S. Eliot, none of them native Britons, to introduce to English literature the programmatic hatred that mere distaste was too lazy to confect.'

The suggestion that Belloc had a 'programmatic hatred' of Jews is patently absurd. He could be accused of prejudice, certainly, and some of his utterances, particularly if taken out of context, are clearly reprehensible. Hatred, however, is far too strong a word. According to Reginald Jebb, his son-in-law and admittedly a biased source, Belloc 'got on famously' with the Jews.

I have seen him in a drawing-room, surrounded by Jews all eagerly talking to him and obviously enjoying his company and – more surprising still – he was discoursing to them on the Jewish problem and explaining his views on it. It is a complete mistake to say that he disliked Jews personally ... There is no doubt ... that he saw the dangers in political Jewry, but for individual Jews he had no antipathy and numbered several among his friends.[13]

'As for me,' Belloc wrote, concurring almost word for word with his son-in-law's judgement, 'I get on famously with them.'[14] These words were written in 1941, after his attitude towards the Jews had softened in the wake of Nazi atrocities, but as early as 1924, nine years before the Nazis came to power, he was defending himself plaintively from allegations that he was anti-Semitic.

> There is not in the whole mass of my written books and articles, there is not in any one of my lectures (many of which have been delivered to Jewish bodies by special request because of the interest I have taken) there is not, I say, in any one of the great mass of writings and statements extending now over twenty years, a single line in which a Jew has been attacked as a Jew or in which the vast majority of their race, suffering and poor, has received, I will not say an insult from my pen and my tongue, but anything which could be construed even as dislike.[15]

Many of the allegations of anti-Semitism against Belloc were the result of the publication of his book *The Jews*, which appeared in February 1922. '*The Jews*,' wrote Robert Speaight, 'was anything but an anti-Semitic tract, and it is a tragedy that for a hundred people who know the rhyme about Lord Swaythling or the "little curly-headed men" there is not one who has read Belloc's sober examination of the problem.'[16] A similar complaint was made by Belloc's friend, J.B. Morton.

> Many times I have heard people quote 'How odd of God to choose the Jews,' and attribute it to Belloc. Once this happened in his presence, and he said, 'That's not the way I write.' But people continue to attribute it to him, probably because of the false idea that he was what is called 'anti-Semitic'. He liked or disliked a Jew as he liked or disliked any other man, and he wrote a book called The Jews, which those who called him an 'anti-Semite' should have taken the trouble to read.[17]

Belloc's friends and defenders – Jebb, Speaight and Morton – may or may not be justified in their defence of his position *vis à vis* the Jews, but they are certainly justified in their suspicion that the vast majority of those who accuse Belloc of anti-Semitism have never set eyes on his book *The Jews*. Clearly, any discussion of Belloc's alleged anti-Semitism should start, and quite probably should end, with a sober analysis of this volume. Primarily, it was intended as a warning of the dangers of not addressing the 'problem', a sort of 'Cautionary Tales for Adults'.

Significantly, the book was dedicated 'To Miss Ruby Goldsmith, My secretary for many years at King's Land and the best and most intimate of our Jewish friends, to whom my family and I will always owe a deep debt of gratitude'. The preface described the object of the book as a 'modest' discussion of 'the relation between the Jews and the nations around them'. Describing the whole issue as a 'vital political matter' and 'a pressing problem', it made no claims 'to any complete solution of it'. It proposed no 'detailed, still less, any positive legal solution' to the problem.

Belloc conceded that many would see the book as the result of 'odd and exaggerated fears', to which he responded that it was, for Jew and Gentile alike, 'an attempt at justice'. Perhaps it was both: an attempt at justice which was born out of odd and exaggerated fears, the same odd and exaggerated fears which would soon lead to one of the greatest of all historical injustices. It would, however, be wrong to equate the complex nature of Belloc's position too closely with the crude hatred of the Nazis, a hatred that he would condemn outright. On the contrary, the purpose of Belloc's book was to raise the issues surrounding the 'problem' without raising tensions between Jews and Gentiles.

> I will conclude by asking my Jewish, as well as my non-Jewish, readers to observe that I have left out every personal allusion and every element of mere recrimination. I have certainly avoided the mention of particular examples in public life of the friction between the Jews and ourselves and even examples drawn from past history. With these I could have strengthened my argument, and I would certainly have made my book a great deal more readable. I have left out everything of the kind because, though one can always rouse interest in this way, it excites enmity between the opposing parties. Since my object is to reduce that enmity, which has already become dangerous, I should be insincere indeed if from mere purpose of enlivening this essay I had stooped to exasperate feeling.
>
> I could have made the book far stronger as a piece of polemic and indefinitely more amusing as a piece of record, but I have not written it as a piece of polemic or as a piece of record. I have written it as an attempt at justice.[18]

There is no reason to doubt the genuineness of Belloc's motives in writing the book, but there is also little doubt that his principal thesis, that the Jews represent an alien body within the society they inhabit, had the inevitable effect of alienating many of his readers, Jew and non-Jew alike.

Nonetheless, his prediction on the very first page concerning the possible disastrous consequences of 'the recent and rapid intensification' of the antagonism between Jews and Gentiles reads, in the light of subsequent events, uncannily like prophecy. 'For if the quarrel is allowed to rise unchecked and to proceed unappeased, we shall come, unexpectedly and soon, upon one of these tragedies which have marked for centuries the relations between this peculiar nation and ourselves.'[19]

Surprisingly, perhaps, *The Jews* includes a chapter entitled 'The Anti-Semite' in which Belloc is at pains to distinguish between 'the anti-Semite' and those 'who are attempting to solve the problem'. 'It is the line dividing those whose motive is peace from those whose motive is antagonism.'[20] It is indeed a little odd that someone so often attacked for his anti-Semitism should write the following:

> The Anti-Semite is a man who *wants to get rid of the Jews*. He is filled with an instinctive feeling in the matter. He detests the Jew as a Jew, and would detest him wherever he found him. The evidences of such a state of mind are familiar to us all. The Anti-Semite admires, for instance, a work of art; on finding its author to be a Jew it becomes distasteful to him though the work remains exactly what it was before. The Anti-Semite will confuse the action of any particular Jew with his general odium for the race. He will hardly admit high talents in his adversaries, or if he admits them he will always see in their expression something distorted and unsavoury.[21]

Consider Belloc's cool and calm condemnation of anti-Semitism with the anti-Semitic rants in otherwise respectable newspapers, such as *The Times*, against the Jewish involvement in the Bolshevik Revolution. Robert Wilton, writing in *The Times* in September and October 1920, vented his spleen against the Jews with a shrillness of tone that would elicit a criminal prosecution if published today: 'the Jewish murderers were brought into Russia . . . the eagerness of the local Jews to anticipate the signal to start the butchery . . . the Jew Goloshchekin, to the Jew Sverdlov . . . so passed on power in the Jew-ruled Soviet . . . To accomplish the hellish design of the Jew-fiend Sverdlov . . .'

Similar unrestrained diatribes were printed in other newspapers, particularly in the *Morning Post*, in the years following the Russian Revolution. Neither were such sentiments the preserve of gutter-journalists. Winston Churchill wrote the following in an article on Zionism and Bolshevism in the *Illustrated Sunday Herald* on 8 February 1920.

The part played in the creation of Bolshevism and in the actual bringing about of the Russian Revolution by these international and for the most part atheistical Jews ... is certainly a very great one; it probably outweighs all others. With the notable exception of Lenin, the majority of the leading figures are Jews. Moreover, the principal inspiration and driving power comes from Jewish leaders ... The same evil prominence was obtained by Jews in [Hungary and Germany, especially Bavaria] ...

Although in all these countries there are many non-Jews every whit as bad as the worst of the Jewish revolutionaries, the part played by the latter in proportion to their numbers in the population is astonishing. The fact that in many cases Jewish interests and Jewish places of worship are excepted by the Bolsheviks from their universal hostility has tended more and more to associate the Jewish race in Russia with the villainies which are now being perpetrated.

Again, compared with the rabid rants of Wilton and the more restrained analysis of Churchill, Belloc's words in *The Jews* represent the height of moderation.

The Bolshevist Movement was a Jewish movement, but not a movement of the Jewish race as a whole. Most Jews were quite extraneous to it; very many indeed, and those of the most typical, abhor it; many actively combat it. The imputation of its evils to the Jews as a whole is a grave injustice and proceeds from a confusion of thought whereof I, at any rate, am free.[22]

Considering the turbulent and virulently anti-Semitic times during which it was written, Belloc's *The Jews* is, for the most part, an exercise in carefully considered and controlled restraint. He condemns the rise of anti-Semitism in Germany, dismissing the widely held and prejudiced assumption amongst many Germans that the Jews were to blame for the war and for the poverty that followed in its wake. Yet his own prejudices surface irritatingly on a number of occasions, weakening his argument, and the book's controversial theme was destined to anger those Jews who did not feel in the least bit 'alien'. Michael Coren, in his biography of Chesterton, wrote perceptively of his subject's prejudices towards the Jews in a manner that would be equally applicable to Belloc.

He did not realize, did not want to understand, that when European wars took place French Jews battled against and killed German Jews ... English Jews would die in the trenches, killed by some of the thousands of Jews who won so many medals and so much praise in the ranks of the German army. He rejected any advice about Russian Jewish war heroes, any historical facts about Jews in Nelson's navy and Wolfe's army at Quebec.[23]

In spite of Belloc's belief that he was being reasonable, and in spite of his best efforts to control his own passionate prejudices, there were many who found the line of reasoning in *The Jews* not merely wrong but offensive. He was both surprised and disappointed by 'the bad reception of my Jew book', believing that those who did not like what he had to say had simply misunderstood him.

> The point is that a Jewish adviser – one Benjamin – whom I trusted to judge wisely and to whom I submitted the proofs – has said that the book is unjust and that his people will refuse to read it or sell it, etc. It saddens me: for if the Jews don't accept a just solution in time they are doomed to a renewal of misery. I have put the case as justly as I could.[24]

Once again, Belloc's ominous foreboding that the Jews were 'doomed to a renewal of misery' if they did not heed the dangers inherent in the rise of anti-Semitism displayed a remarkable degree of prescience. Subsequently, the rise of Nazism would confirm his worst fears. In 1989 two British Jews, Anthony Read and David Fisher, wrote *Kristallnacht: The Nazi Night of Terror*, in which they documented the opening of the Nazi campaign of persecution. Seen in the horrifying light of real anti-Semitism, Read and Fisher were able to put Belloc's attitude towards the Jews into a balanced perspective.

> Belloc, like his friend Chesterton, like so many of the English middle class, was prejudiced against Jews. He did not like them . . . Nevertheless, he was not anti-semitic – certainly not in the Nazi sense and the idea of employing physical brutality against a single Jew would have appalled him. He was an honourable man, uneasily aware that there was something going on in Germany of which, in conscience, he could not approve.[25]

This judgement was echoed by Chesterton himself, who spoke of his and Belloc's disgust at the persecution of the Jews in Nazi Germany.

> In our early days Hilaire Belloc and myself were accused of being uncompromising anti-Semites. Today, although I still think there is a Jewish problem, I am appalled by the Hitlerite atrocities. They have

absolutely no reason or logic behind them. It is quite obviously the expedient of a man who has been driven to seeking a scapegoat, and has found with relief the most famous scapegoat in European history, the Jewish people. I am quite ready to believe now that Belloc and I will die defending the last Jew in Europe.[26]

The final word on Belloc's alleged anti-Semitism should be from his own pen. Years before Hitler came to power in Germany he wrote a book which, for all its weaknesses, should be seen as a remarkable work on a potentially explosive subject. His thinking might have been muddled, his conclusions inconclusive, but his raising of the issue to a heightened level of debate was surely, in the light of subsequent events, very much needed. Belloc's *The Jews* might indeed have been the product of prejudice, but it was also a work of both prescience and prophecy.

My solution may appear at the end of this generation as mildly inapplicable to the acute situation then arisen between the Jews and ourselves as appear today the old debates on the very tentative demand for Home Rule in the '80s. Let us act as soon as possible and settle the thing while there is yet time. For in the swirl and rapids of the modern world, which grow not less as towards a calm, but more intense as towards a cataract, every great debate takes on with every year a stronger form, a nearer approach to conflict; and none more than the immemorial debate, still unconcluded, between Islam and Christendom and the Beni-Israel.

But for my part, I say, 'Peace be to Israel.'[27]

TWENTY-FOUR

Friends and Family

THE YEAR IN WHICH *The Jews* was published was an especially eventful one. Apart from the meeting with the new Pope, the reception of Chesterton and J.B. Morton into the Church, and the reconciliation of Blunt to the Faith shortly before his death, the year was also memorable for the marriage of Belloc's elder daughter Eleanor. In the midst of so many mini-triumphs of the Faith, the news of his daughter's engagement was, however, to prove a disappointment.

'My engagement to Eleanor in 1922 came as something of a shock to Belloc,' wrote Reginald Jebb. 'A Protestant and a school master – that was a combination of attributes he would certainly not have chosen for his future son-in-law. His summing up of the situation was characteristic. "But, my darling child, that is almost as bad as marrying a parson."' Jebb also recalled 'the somewhat Victorian interview' with his future father-in-law in the drawing room at King's Land. They discussed the financial position and 'the difficulties that might arise when a Catholic marries a non-Catholic'. Belloc was slightly mollified to discover that his daughter's fiancé owned a small house in Horsham and that he was 'far from feeling any aversion to the Catholic Faith', but he remained less than enthusiastic. 'Well,' he muttered at the conclusion of the interview, 'I suppose we must go on with it.'[1]

Jebb's relationship with Belloc would improve considerably. Years later he would look back to the awkwardness of the initial interview with an affectionate understanding that he could scarcely have felt at the time.

> . . . as I came to realize when I got to know him better, and especially after I had been received into the Church, his stiffness of manner at this interview was the result of the profundity of his own faith and his anxiety lest anything should interfere with the faith of his daughter. Thereafter I never experienced from him anything but kindness, generosity, and friendly companionship.[2]

Father Vincent McNabb, who was 'like a mother hen with Belloc's children after Elodie's death',[3] shared his friend's concerns about the prospects of a mixed marriage. Belloc, however, was determined, after he had given his reluctant consent, to secure permission from the Archbishop for a nuptial Mass at Westminster Cathedral. It was unusual in the case of mixed marriages for permission to be granted, and it says something for Belloc's influence that he did receive the Archbishop's consent. In consequence, Reginald Jebb and Eleanor Belloc were duly married with all the pomp and grace of a full nuptial Mass, with 11 bridesmaids resplendently in attendance, at Westminster Cathedral on 1 August 1922.

Eleanor's marriage was destined to cause a good deal of disruption to family life at King's Land. In January 1921, Belloc had written to Charlotte Balfour, whose daughter Clare would be one of the bridesmaids at the wedding, that Eleanor was 'replacing her mother; maturing, of spiritual wisdom, full of life and altogether my household'.[4] Her marriage meant that her practical presence was lost to King's Land, forcing Belloc to run the household himself, albeit with the able assistance of Edith, the cook, and other domestic help.

His younger daughter Elizabeth had no desire to fill the role of surrogate homemaker vacated by her sister. Always a restless spirit, she had been only 13 when her mother had died and seems never to have recovered from the shock of the loss. Like Eleanor, she had been educated at the Dominican convent at Stone in Staffordshire, but she had little in common with her elder sister and they had failed to forge a strong or lasting bond. On the contrary, shortly before Eleanor's wedding there had been a major falling out between them, resulting in an estrangement that would never be healed. As a direct consequence of this mutual antagonism, Elizabeth made the decision to live away from her family. Thereafter, she would return to King's Land only rarely, and only if she were certain that Eleanor would not be present. She shared her father's literary gifts, having several of her poems published in the Jesuit monthly *America*, and she shared his wanderlust, travelling almost continually around England and the continent. Her restlessness was exacerbated by an unhappy love affair with Val Elwes, who later became a priest and chaplain at Oxford University. It is said that she sometimes lived rough on the streets of London, appearing unexpectedly at the homes of family friends to ask for handouts of food. Her restlessness, her poverty and her unpredictability were a great cause of concern to Belloc. His letters to her testify to his frequent gifts of money and to his anxiety as to her wellbeing and whereabouts.[5]

The break-up of family life at King's Land was completed in 1923 with the departure of the two surviving sons. Peter departed for Spain, seeking adventure at sea on a Spanish ship; Hilary, his elder brother, left for America, settling in California where he would make a fortune as an engineer building highways and shopping malls.[6] Peter would return and would become a great consolation to his father, joining him as one of the regular members of the crew of the *Nona*. Hilary, however, would seldom return. 'He couldn't get on with his father,' recalls Belloc's granddaughter Zita Caldecott, who retained fond memories of 'Uncle Hilary'.

> They were such powerful personalities and so much alike. You can't have two stags on one hill ... Once I went for lunch with Uncle Hilary at a restaurant on the King's Road. We were still there when they began serving dinner. He was holding forth in the manner of his father and everyone in the restaurant was gathered round our table. He was sent down from Balliol for wild behaviour of some sort or other. He ended up qualifying in a US university as an engineer and became very rich. He married a cousin of Elodie's family and, in the mid-thirties, adopted a son who was named 'Martin Luther Belloc' to annoy his father.[7]

According to J.B. Morton, the dispersion of his family left Belloc feeling 'very lonely'.[8] 'For my part,' he told Charlotte Balfour in 1922, 'my cancer of loss gets worse and worse with every year and I grow fixed in the void of my wife and my son; to this, new poverty and anxiety for the home add greatly.'[9] King's Land, devoid of his children's presence, lost some of its homely attraction and he spent more and more time in London, or at the homes of friends around the country, returning to Sussex at weekends only.

In the absence of family, Belloc's friends became ever more important. With Morton, he began to frequent lively literary lunches at a pub near the offices of the *London Mercury*, where they would meet with J.B. Priestley, Robert Lynd and the well-known journalist James Bone, talking for two hours over ale or Burgundy, 'sometimes with wit, sometimes banality, and just occasionally verbal violence'.[10] It was at one of these gatherings that he first met the young A.P. Herbert, the writer and humorist who was soon to join the staff of *Punch*.

Herbert, who described Belloc as one of his 'prime heroes, who alarmed me a little',[11] was invited by Belloc to sail with him on the *Nona*. Herbert readily agreed and the two men, accompanied by J.C. Squire, set sail from Torquay, heading up-Channel. Herbert recalled Belloc at the tiller, clad like an old salt in 'a peaked cap, an old blue jersey, and jacket', sounding forth on a variety of subjects as his two companions listened, their attention freshened by the Channel breezes. 'When the sun shone and the wind was fair there might be a little lecture on the glories of the Tudors; when it was foul we heard about the machinations of the Jews.' Presumably he was discoursing on the latter subject when, noticing black clouds gathering ominously ahead, he steered discreetly into West Bay, Bridport, rather than face the hazards of rounding Portland Bill – which he respectfully referred to as 'William'.

Having landed on the shores of Wessex, Squire suggested that they should pay their respects to the octogenarian Thomas Hardy at Dorchester, 16 miles away. Belloc agreed to the idea of visiting 'that atheist novelist' and the three men crammed into a taxi. When they arrived at Hardy's 'modest villa', Squire went ahead to ascertain whether they would be welcome. 'Do you mean that Catholic journalist?' Hardy enquired when Belloc's name was mentioned.

Although he was suffering from the after-effects of attempting to cycle several miles, and was recovering 'from this excess', Hardy readily agreed to receive his visitors. It was wonderful, wrote Herbert, to see Belloc 'who had been lording it along the coast', bullying harbour officials and others, 'enter the little drawing-room, cap in hand, and bow reverently before the Master'. Herbert's weighted account aside, it is far more likely that Belloc's stately bow was little more than an act of courteous deference towards his host's hospitality and seniority of age. Certainly there is nothing to suggest any reverence on Belloc's part to Hardy's position as 'the Master', and Belloc's correspondence to Katherine Asquith about this particular voyage omits any mention of the visit to Hardy.[12]

In fact, Squire recalled that Belloc and Hardy engaged in lively talk, evidently as equals, 'both passionate about history' and both taking as their chief topic 'a great legendary storm off Portland Bill'. Their lively dialogue was uninterrupted by either Squire or Herbert, both of whom listened in respectful silence.[13] There is something soothingly reassuring about this apparently warm encounter between the 'atheist novelist' and the 'Catholic journalist'. Hardy had been shocked out of his lifelong agnosticism by the horrors of the First World War, and was seeking in the final years of his life some form of rapprochement between science and religion. Belloc, on the other hand, although he would always cling doggedly and dogmatically to his lifelong faith, felt a natural affinity with the desolation of any sceptic-souled spirit groping for an understanding of truth. The chasm between the two men was, therefore, not as wide as Squire and Herbert – nor, indeed, as Hardy and Belloc – might have believed.

Belloc was a regular guest at the annual dinners of Squire's cricket team, the Invalids, held at the Cheshire Cheese on Fleet Street. Chesterton, E.V. Lucas and E.C. Bentley were other regular guests at these uproarious evenings, at which Belloc's verse 'The Winged Horse' was always sung and those foolhardy enough to attempt to make a speech were accompanied by sporadic outbursts of song and insult. According to Morton, anyone hearing the succession of sea shanties, French marching songs and Spanish folk songs being sung by the assembled revellers would never have guessed that cricket was the ostensible excuse for the gathering.[14]

Such ribaldry and revelry further confirmed the role of the Chesterbelloc in placing the 'boozy halo' around Catholicism of which Wells had complained. New generations of Oxford undergraduates were intoxicated by Belloc's and Chesterton's enticing cocktail of wine, religion and song. 'There was more drinking in the Oxford of the 1920s than there is today,' wrote Christopher Hollis, 'and the influence of Belloc and Chesterton was potent in giving an appearance of consecration to Catholic alcoholic consumption – Cathalcoholism as Douglas Woodruff called it in a Union speech ... We read Chesterton's *Flying Inn* and united to bawl together the songs of *Wine, Water and Song*.'[15] Hollis, like Morton, D.B. Wyndham Lewis and others of the young generation, was also a disciple of the political creed of distributism as espoused by the Chesterbelloc. 'My opinions – such as I had then – were those of a follower of Hilaire Belloc and G.K. Chesterton, of the denunciation of the Servile State and the advocacy of a wide distribution of property. I took it on myself to denounce impartially all established political parties and indeed the whole system and to proclaim myself independent.'[16]

Belloc was destined to prove instrumental in Hollis's conversion. Having arrived at Balliol 'like the majority of public schoolboys, an unbeliever', wrote Hollis, he began to question his own unbelief in the heady surroundings of Oxford. 'I was in those days a great disciple and hero-worshipper of Hilaire Belloc, who was a frequent visitor to his old college, Balliol.' It was hardly surprising, therefore, that Hollis, later to rise to prominence as a writer, publisher and Member of Parliament, eventually had the opportunity to meet his mentor. 'To young companions – myself among them – he always was full of generosity, encouragement and kindness. I came to owe much to this remarkable man.' 'The Faith is never truly held unless it is held in challenge,' Belloc told Hollis. 'The young man must get rid of what he has been merely taught and then rediscover it for himself. If he doesn't do that it isn't really his. It's not worth having.'[17]

A good description of Belloc in the early 1920s, as seen through the eyes of one of his young disciples, was given by J.B. Morton.

> He looked considerably older than his fifty-two years ... The black clothes, black tie, and old-fashioned, stiff, stick-up collar made him look like the Frenchmen of my boyhood. But the ruddy complexion and the broad, square shoulders and massive body gave him the air of an English farmer. His eyes were blue, and when spoken to or speaking he would move his head sharply, and look straight at you, as though he were not only carrying on a conversation but reading a character.[18]

In the spring of 1922, for the first time in a decade, Belloc published a work of fiction. *The Mercy of Allah*, described by Robert Speaight as 'undoubtedly ... the most effective' of Belloc's satires,[19] had as its theme the subject of usury. 'We must give away the secret of Mr Belloc's little joke without more ado and admit that *The Mercy of Allah* has more to do with London and New York than with Baghdad, its ostensible scene,' wrote a reviewer in the *Times Literary Supplement*. 'It is, in fact, a large-scale parable.'[20] Following so swiftly on the heels of his book on the Jews, few had any doubts that Belloc's parable, ostensibly about a Muslim, was in fact a thinly veiled attack on Jewish financiers. 'Mr Belloc can make his wrong-headedness amusing,' wrote the *TLS* reviewer, 'but it remains wrong-headedness all the same.'

The ghosts of Belloc's 'wrong-headedness' were to return to haunt him during a lecture tour of the United States during February and March 1923. 'I am rather afraid the Jews may attack me,' he wrote to his former secretary and old friend Ruby Goldsmith on 30 January, shortly before setting sail. 'They do not seem to mind being violently abused nearly so much as a severe analysis of the situation. I regret this. I think that the security and happiness of the Jewish community in the future depends almost entirely on their facing the facts ... the differences between the two races need not lead to hatred or bitterness ...'[21]

'The Jew question is a fearful bore over here,' he wrote to Charlotte Balfour on St Patrick's Day, 17 March. 'People talk of it morning noon and night.'

Those who know I have written a book on it take it for granted that I am in approval of a general massacre – which is the usual extreme confusion Americans reach when they have worked themselves up on the matter, while the very much smaller number who have actually read my book, disagree with its judicial tone: they want blood and thunder ... all ... everywhere rave and howl against the Jews ... it makes the life of the mass of Jews here – who are poor – very hard. Magistrates are ... biased against them – they are insulted in public and refused entry to Clubs and even hotels and in general made to feel that they are enemies. What a life! Fancy some wretched man coming with his family from, say, Poland, and landing into this! For the American had no tradition or habit in the matter and never appreciates complexity. He feels the racial friction and reacts in the shape of violent revulsion.[22]

When Belloc arrived in New York, a Jewish friend whom he had first met in France during the war, Major Louis Henry Cohn, gave a luncheon for him at the Jewish Club. Many of the Club's members expressed indignation that Cohn should have invited someone who was generally regarded as an anti-Semite onto the Club's premises as an honoured guest, and one eminent Jewish judge even made a speech calling on Belloc to be deported. Cohn, however, was undaunted and his friendship with Belloc emerged unscathed. A year later, on 6 February 1924, Belloc wrote to Cohn expressing his disdain for anti-Semitic intellectuals, such as Nester Webster.

The Cause of World Unrest is a book written by a woman called Webster. In my opinion it is a lunatic book. She is one of those people who have got one cause on their brain. It is the good old Jewish revolutionary bogey. I think people are great fools who do not appreciate what a part the Jew has played in revolutionary movements, but people are much bigger fools who get it on the brain and ascribe every revolutionary movement to Jews and secret societies. The prime cause of revolution is injustice ... But there is a type of unstable mind which cannot rest without morbid imaginings, and the conception of single causes simplifies thought. With this good woman it is the Jews, with some people it is the Jesuits, with others Freemasons and so on. The world is more complex than that. Many of the facts quoted are true enough, but the inferences drawn are exaggerated ...[23]

Apart from the controversial aspects of the Jewish question, Belloc found the United States much as he had done during his last visit in 1898. 'I have just given my first lecture here in Boston,' he wrote to Chesterton on 22 February. '... I do not find the States much changed since I was last here 25 years ago, but I find the change in myself alarming.'[24] From New York, on 27 March 1923, Belloc wrote to an American friend, Carl Schmidt, about his impressions of the United States.

> The essential point in the moral world is the cleavage between the Catholic Church and the rest. In Europe this is so clear by this time that the continuance of our civilization in its worthy form depends upon Catholicism. I am not sure that is the case over here ... you will either have Catholicism developed or a new religion. And if you have a new religion you will have a totally different civilization from that of the Old World.[25]

The differences between Europe and the United States, the Old World and the New, inflamed Belloc's imagination to such a degree that, as soon as he returned to England, he set about writing *The Contrast*, his book on the nature of these differences.

The Contrast, for all its intuitive insights, would be eclipsed in importance by the publication of *Sonnets and Verse* by Duckworth & Co., a collection that would further secure Belloc's reputation as a poet. According to Maurice Baring, as expressed in a letter to Ethel Smyth on 27 November 1923, Belloc's verse was 'in relation to contemporaries ... *of the stuff that will endure*'.[26] This general view was expanded upon in an essay by Baring, written in 1923 and published in *Punch and Judy and Other Essays* in September of the following year.

> Nothing is more hazardous, more full of possible pitfalls and errors than to write a considered judgement on contemporary verse ... The question is further complicated when the contemporary author happens to be a personal friend; not because ... the critic is too easily biased in favour of his friend's writing, but, on the contrary, because he is liable to check his spontaneous praise and admiration, to understate his case ...

Baring, though a friend, was not a sycophant, a fact that was signified clearly by his critical judgement of Belloc's sonnets.

> Personally – noble as the work in these sonnets is, stern as is the stuff they are made of, and priceless their fitful gleams of vision – I do not think that it is in the sonnet that Mr Belloc is most successful. His sonnets have sometimes the complexity of Shakespeare's without their

fundamental ease and lucidity, and at moments the baldness of Wordsworth without the supreme sweep of simplicity that in Wordsworth carries you off your feet.

It was in the lyrical poems and ballads that Baring believed his friend had attained 'technical mastery . . . complete and complex'. In the most successful of these, such as 'The South Country', 'the elf of poetry is definitely caught in the net'.

> He does the same trick to my mind in a higher degree in the poem called 'Ha'nacker Mill', which has not only lilt, but an undefinable [*sic*], vague, haunting suggestion of poetry, sadness, and doom about it. It says what it has got to say quite perfectly, but it suggests at the same time a great deal more than it says. It has magic. The same could be said of the poem which follows it in the book, 'Tarantella'.[27]

Belloc was one of 52 guests who attended a dinner at the Royal Albion Hotel in Brighton on 27 April 1924 to celebrate Baring's fiftieth birthday. Others in attendance included Chesterton, E.V. Lucas, Duff Cooper, J.C. Squire and 'lots of sailors and airmen'.[28] Baring made a rhyming speech while several other guests, including Chesterton and Duff Cooper, gave more prosaic addresses. The evening reached a riotous climax on the beach. 'After dinner Maurice insisted on bathing. They all tried to stop him and there was a free fight on the beach. I said that he ought to be allowed to bathe if he wanted to and I fought on his side. He finally got into the water and an energetic sailor stripped stark naked and plunged in after him.'[29] In his autobiography, Chesterton paid homage to the 'godlike joy of life that induced a gentleman to celebrate his fiftieth birthday in a Brighton hotel at midnight by dancing a Russian dance with inconceivable contortions and then plunging into the sea in evening dress'.[30]

It was at such moments, fully alive in the company of friends and sharing their 'godlike joy of life', that Belloc seemed to come to life himself. Yet, as he confessed to Baring during a visit to Strasbourg in November 1923, the simpler joys of youth were passing away. 'When I was 23 years of age I climbed to the top of Strasbourg spire by the staircase and scratched on the top my name, battery and regiment. But now I am 53 and that is 30 years ago and I do nothing any more.'[31] He might indeed have been feeling his age, but his idea of doing nothing was singular to say the least. Throughout the 1920s he would continue to write prodigiously, producing several books and dozens of essays every year; he would continue to make friends and infuriate enemies; he would travel and travail as though he were a man many years younger.

Ford Madox Ford, spotting Belloc in a town in France in 1923, was amazed at his energy and irrepressibility. In his 'not more than ten hours' in the town, 'some of which must have been devoted to sleep', Belloc had visited the cattle market, where Ford had seen him 'talking to a farmer and punching a fat bullock as if he had been a grazier all his life'. He then checked out of his hotel and left the town before Ford had the opportunity to meet him, but not before he had collected enough material to write an essay. 'How did he do it?' Ford wondered.[32] If, as Chesterton suggested, Belloc's low spirits were far more uproarious than other people's high spirits, it seemed that his idea of 'doing nothing' involved doing much more than most men half his age.

TWENTY-FIVE

War of the Wells

I N JULY 1923 Belloc accompanied his son Peter on a walking tour of France. Revisiting old haunts, he felt himself a spiritual exile amid the modernity sweeping across post-war Europe.

> I mourn here for the past, in Paris, and tell Peter the world has gone bad. But he assures me it is old age and that every generation does that. He says his generation like the world enormously. *Libre à eux* – I find it like a garden into which beasts have broken. Perhaps they will go out by a gap in the hedge and we may put things straight again, all the little onions in neat rows, and, in some prodigious time, grow trees again.[1]

The same mournful melancholy surfaced in a letter to Katherine Asquith, written in Marseilles. 'Already Europe is half barbarized, with guttersnipes in the high places and tradition breaking.'[2]

Such sentiments might indeed be 'anti-progressive' but, contrary to what Peter Belloc had seemed to imply, they were not merely the reactionary rantings of the older generation against the younger. As Belloc's vociferous circle of young disciples proved, his belief that post-war Europe was a 'half barbarized' wasteland was widely held. Christopher Hollis was received into the Church by Monsignor Barnes in the late summer of 1924, having been influenced hugely in his progress to Rome by Belloc's *The Servile State* and *Europe and the Faith*. He was 24. His friend and contemporary at Oxford, Evelyn Waugh, had sought to dissuade him from becoming a Catholic, arguing from the perspective of a muscular agnosticism. Several years later, Waugh would reject his own arguments against the Church and would become a Catholic himself, at the age of 26.

Waugh's reception caused consternation and confusion. It seemed inconceivable that the popular young novelist who was known principally, in the words of a writer in the *Daily Express*, for his 'almost passionate adherence to the ultra-modern' could have joined the Catholic Church. His reasons for conversion, outlined in an article in the *Express* entitled 'Converted to Rome: Why It Has Happened to Me', were expressed in words which could have been written by Belloc himself.

> It seems to me that in the present phase of European history the essential issue is . . . between Christianity and Chaos . . .
>
> Today we can see it on all sides as the active negation of all that western culture has stood for. Civilization – and by this I do not mean talking cinemas and tinned food, nor even surgery and hygienic houses, but the whole moral and artistic organization of Europe – has not in itself the power of survival. It came into being through Christianity, and without it has no significance of power to command allegiance. The loss of faith in Christianity and the consequential lack of confidence in moral and social standards have become embodied in the ideal of a materialistic, mechanized state . . . It is no longer possible . . . to accept the benefits of civilization and at the same time deny the supernatural basis upon which it rests.[3]

Apart from the obvious echoes of Belloc's *Europe and the Faith*, which would influence Waugh as it had influenced Hollis, there were obvious parallels with Eliot in Waugh's rejection of chaos and desire for order. Waugh, like Eliot, had rejected the 'waste land' of post-war modernity and had turned his back on the 'hollow men' that it was producing. These two young writers, Eliot and Waugh, the 'ultra-modern' poet and the 'ultra-modern' novelist, were following the trail of dynamic orthodoxy that Belloc and Chesterton had blazed 20 years earlier. They were not alone. Commenting on Waugh's conversion, the *Bystander* observed that 'the brilliant young author' was 'the latest man of letters to be received into the Catholic Church. Other well-known literary people who have gone over to Rome include Sheila Kaye-Smith, Compton MacKenzie, Alfred Noyes, Father Ronald Knox and G.K. Chesterton.'[4] The list was far from exhaustive. As the century progressed, the tide of Roman converts was becoming a torrent. By the 1930s there would be some 12,000 converts a year in England alone.

Not surprisingly, Belloc greeted what he perceived as the turning of the tide with barely restrained joy, verging on triumphalism. Nowhere was this more in evidence than in the preface he wrote to Dom Hugh G. Bevenot's *Pagan and Christian Rule*, published in 1924.

It is sufficiently clear to those who survey Europe in the mass and follow the full outline of their time, that our civilization must return to the Faith or be destroyed.

It is a conclusion arrived at in a hundred ways by observation, by instinct, by history. There stands in support of it the evident formation, insistent throughout the West, of growing intellectual superiority upon the Catholic side: so that today no one is worthy to stand as an equal against the Catholic controversialist save that rare being the pure sceptic. We have today against the full and convincing system which Catholicism permanently presents, opponents, who, for the most part, do not know what they are attacking, and, therefore, in their attack can do little more than abuse. The moral and the intellectual tide of the moment is clearly with the return of that philosophy which is more than a philosophy; that fullness in which alone the human spirit is at rest and the mind of man finds its home: that living thing which is called the Catholic Church: that Sufficient Community which at the same time enfranchises, decides, and nourishes.[5]

Belloc was under no illusions that Chesterton's conversion, in particular, had been hugely influential in establishing 'the intellectual superiority upon the Catholic side'. If, as Eliot's poetry intimated so powerfully, the post-war world was a spiritual wasteland, then Chesterton's was a clear, if paradoxical, voice crying in the wilderness. 'I love G.K.C. and hate the Catholicism of Belloc and Rome,' wrote H.G. Wells. 'If Catholicism is still to run about the world giving tongue, it can have no better spokesman than G.K.C. But I begrudge Catholicism G.K.C.!'[6]

A clue as to why Wells loved Chesterton and hated Belloc can be gleaned from an incident in 1922. Following Wells's announcement that he intended to stand for Parliament as a Liberal candidate, the *Daily News* invited both Belloc and Chesterton to give their comment on his candidature. Their respective replies offer a penetrating insight into the huge difference in temperament between the two friends, Chesterton's charitable affability contrasting starkly with Belloc's chafing bellicosity.

CHESTERTON: I wish Wells all possible luck, but I can't say that is exactly the same as wishing he will get into Parliament. The question is not whether Wells is fit for Parliament, but whether Parliament is fit for Wells. I don't think it is. If he had a good idea, the last place in the world where he would be allowed to talk is the House of Commons. He would do better to go on writing.

BELLOC: Of the effect of election upon Mr Wells's style I am not competent to pronounce. But in morals, temperament, instruction, and type of oratory, I know him to be admirably suited for the House of Commons.[7]

A further example of the spirit of enmity which existed between Belloc and Wells was witnessed by Siegfried Sassoon at the Reform Club on 29 June 1923.

Last night H.G. Wells joined me as I was beginning my dinner at the Reform ... Belloc (who went round America lecturing against H.G. last winter) came and sat at the next table. When H.G. got up to depart, Belloc snorted and prepared to cut him. H.G. strolled across and slapped him on the back, exclaiming 'Why, Belloc, you're getting fat!' Belloc could say nothing. H.G. remarked to me 'It's a great advantage, when dealing with pompous people, to be a cad!'[8]

This embittered exchange, and Belloc's earlier gibe at Wells's suitability for Parliament, came in the midst of the increasingly acrimonious controversy between the two men that had arisen following the publication of Wells's *Outline of History*. Originally, Wells's book was published in separate sections, the first of which appeared in 1920, and each of which was attacked vehemently and vociferously by Belloc.[9]

The whole of Wells's vision of history was anathema to Belloc. He objected to its tacitly anti-Christian stance, epitomized by the fact that Wells had devoted more space in his 'history' to the Persian campaign against the Greeks than he had given to the figure of Christ. Belloc's principal objection, however, was to the philosophy of materialistic determinism that had shaped Wells's historical 'outline'. Wells believed that human 'progress' was both blind and beneficial; unshakeable, unstoppable and utterly inexorable. History was the product of invisible and immutable evolutionary forces that were coming to fruition in the twentieth century. Human history had its primitive beginnings in the caves, but was now reaching its climax in the modern age with the final triumph of science over religion. The emergence of science from the ashes of 'superstition' heralded a new dawn for humanity, a brave new world of happiness made possible by technology.

Wells's 'outline' had been, to Belloc, like a red rag to a bull. Predictably, he charged. His first attacks against *The Outline of History* were published in the *London Mercury* and the *Dublin Review*, where he lambasted Wells for his inaccuracies and for writing 'howlers'. Thereafter he clinically dissected Wells's *History* in a long series of articles in *The Universe*. Commencing with 'Mr Wells and the Creation of the World (Man)', he continued with 'Mr Wells and the Fall of Man', 'Mr Wells and God', 'Mr Wells and the Incarnation', 'Mr Wells on Priesthood', and so on. In fact, the reference to Belloc as a charging bull is not wholly accurate. He was not so much a bull as a bulldog, biting hard and refusing to let go.

Belloc accused Wells of a prejudiced provincialism, complaining that his adversary had 'not kept abreast of the modern scientific and historical work' and that he had 'not followed the general thought of Europe and America in matters of physical science'. Furthermore,

> in history proper, he was never taught to appreciate the part played
> by Latin and Greek culture, and never even introduced to the history
> of the early Church . . . With all this Mr Wells suffers from the very
> grievous fault of being ignorant that he is ignorant. He has the strange
> cocksureness of the man who only knows the old conventional text-
> book of his schooldays and mistakes it for universal knowledge.[10]

The controversy reached a conclusion and a climax in 1926, when Belloc's articles for *The Universe* were collected into a single volume and published as *A Companion to Mr Wells's 'Outline of History'*. Wells responded with *Mr Belloc Objects*, to which Belloc, determined to have the last word, replied with *Mr Belloc Still Objects*. At the end of the six-year struggle, Belloc claimed to have written over 100,000 words in refutation of the central arguments of Wells's book.

The war of words proved hugely beneficial to a new publishing company, Sheed & Ward, which published Belloc's two volumes. Tom Burns, later to make a name in publishing in his own right, was a young man working for Sheed & Ward when the Belloc–Wells controversy approached its climax.

> The first excitement in the office was the publication of Hilaire Belloc's
> *A Companion to H.G. Wells' Outline of History* in 1926. Wells was very
> much in vogue at the time and *Outline of History* was his secularist
> prophecy. Belloc's *Companion* was sharply personal in tone: Wells
> was uneducated, insular, ignorant of foreign languages, lower middle
> class and untrustworthy. Wells replied with a witty pamphlet, *Mr
> Belloc Objects*, where he suggested that Mr Belloc had apparently been
> born all over Europe. Belloc came up fighting in the third round, *Mr
> Belloc Still Objects*. The whole affair launched Sheed & Ward into the
> limelight.[11]

An intriguing account of Belloc's frame of mind at the height of his war with Wells was provided by the writer Beverley Nichols, who interviewed him 'in the gloomiest of all surroundings – the hall of the Reform Club' sometime during 1926.

I write at a time when the Belloc–Wells controversy is still at its height. The controversy began when Belloc hoisted the flag of Orthodoxy to rally round him those whom he considered to have been misled by Wells's *Outline of History*. It is a controversy of reasoned Faith against reasoned Doubt. And Belloc gave me, in one sentence, the whole of his personal defence of Faith.

He said: 'Wells, being without Faith – or, at any rate, being a former Bible Christian who has lost his God – imagines that people who have Faith are hypnotizing themselves into having it: either out of fear or the narrowness of their traditions, or, as far as I can see, out of pure cussedness. I am not hypnotizing myself. Faith is a gift . . .'

With certain trepidation I took from my pocket a copy of *Mr Belloc Still Objects* – a reply to Mr Wells's *Mr Belloc Objects*. Almost at random I opened it at the chapter where he plunges into what he describes as Mr Wells's 'Great Rosy Dawn' – i.e., the Wellsian ideal of Utopia. He plunges, I say, into this Dawn, breathes its mist fiercely through his nostrils, and finds it no dawn at all, but a twilight preceding a universal darkness. And in the course of this discovery he throws out, into the darkness, a great many of Mr Wells's assertions, echoing them with a contemptuous but disturbing retort of his own.

Now, I disagreed with some of those retorts, and I said so . . .

So, at the outset, a yawning chasm separated us. But even across that chasm Belloc loomed as a large, if somewhat unwieldy figure. Even across that chasm he had a certain capacity to disturb . . . I, like the rest of us, had been brought up to regard the Darwinian system as a fundamental fact. Yet here was Belloc quoting, in the name of Common Sense as much as in the name of the Church, authority after authority to prove that it was nothing of the sort.[12] Almost in a bombardment the names of countless European professors, with their considered verdicts against the theory of natural selection, all neatly dated and docketed, were hurled at me. The hall of the Reform Club echoed to the sound of Doctor von this and Professor von that. The result was humiliating. I seemed to be left naked in my ignorance, though soothed by the knowledge that I was not alone in it . . .

. . . as I bade farewell to that black-coated figure, I felt sorry for two people. I felt sorry for him because I still felt that he had nailed at least some of his colours to the wrong mast. And I felt sorry for myself because I had no colours to nail to any mast at all, and the world seemed singularly grey.[13]

Arnold Lunn, like Beverley Nichols, was an unbeliever at the time of the Belloc–Wells controversy. Unlike Nichols, however, Lunn found himself, albeit reluctantly, agreeing with Belloc.

In his famous controversy with H.G. Wells all my sympathies were with Belloc, though I was still an agnostic. Even then I knew that Wells, with his 'Existence impresses me as a perpetual dawn', had far less claim to be considered a prophet than Belloc, who replied that Wells's 'dawn' was nothing more than the 'shoddy remnant of the Christian hope, and when it is gone there will return to us, not the simple paganism of a sad world, but sheer darkness; and strange things in the dark'.[14]

These words, published in Lunn's memoirs many years later, were merely a reiteration of the words he had written in a private letter to Belloc at the height of the controversy.

I have just read with the liveliest of interest and admiration your magnificent reply to H.G. Wells. I am not a Catholic, but I none the less rejoice to see you disposing completely of Wells's utterances. Quite apart from the merits of the actual issue, I regard your book as one of the finest books of controversial writing that I have ever read.[15]

As the conflict between Wells and Belloc became increasingly bitter, their attacks became increasingly personal. 'H.G. Wells has written a very strong letter indeed saying that I am a wicked man and an attacker of the innocent which is himself,' Belloc wrote to Lady Lovat on 17 June 1926.[16] Meanwhile, Wells, 'with a sort of malicious amusement', complained to J.B. Morton that 'talking with Belloc is like trying to break into a hailstorm'.[17] 'Poor old H.G. Wells found it was like arguing with the winds to argue with H.B.,' wrote Eleanor Jebb, 'for every time Wells put his nose out H.B. pounced again and wore Wells into silence. But if only Wells had continued a little longer I think H.B. would have become bored and also busy with some other opponent.'[18]

Browbeating someone into submission is not necessarily the same as winning the argument, but Belloc, in his postmortem of the affair, appeared to believe that in doing the one he had achieved the other.

Wells ... published a popular outline of history by way of attack upon the Christian religion. I skinned him carefully and slowly ... showing that he had read little, knew nothing and could not think. I published my criticism serially in a number of syndicated small papistical papers which nobody ever sees. Nevertheless Wells went mad and published a very violent pamphlet against me calling me all manner of names, and saying particularly that I had invented the attack on Darwinism and that there were no European World authorities opposed to Natural Selection. I took up the challenge and printed a list of such authorities, enough to convince a blind man that Natural Selection was dead. He has now retired bandaged, is telling everybody that he refuses to read my pamphlet, also that he is sick of the whole affair, which I can well believe. But he will yet take his revenge perhaps by the aid of bravos or perhaps by tripping me up on a dark night.[19]

There is little in this unrepentant and self-righteous analysis to suggest that Belloc 'was genuinely sorry that he hurt Wells' or, as his daughter later maintained, that he 'would have liked to put the personal side to rights'.[20] It does seem, however, that he was as weary of the struggle as his adversary. 'I am tired of controversy and quarrelling,' he confessed to Lady Lovat, in the same letter in which he had complained of Wells's 'very strong letter' attacking him, 'and desire (a) refreshment, (b) light, and (c) peace. But I make this my condition; that the refreshment shall be of the grape and not chemical, that the light shall be of the sun or wax candles, and not electric, and that the peace shall not be of Versailles.'[21]

As the dust settled, and the fog of acrimony cleared, it was left to J.B. Morton to put Belloc's role in the controversy into perspective.

Both as a man and as a writer he was in fierce opposition to the world of his time and, more particularly, to the shallow and absurd philosophy of what was called progress. The triumph of physical science, coinciding with the decay of religion, had produced that mood of arrogance of which H.G. Wells was the most popular exponent. Belloc saw in this baseless confidence in a splendid future, not only lack of intelligence and reasoning power, but immediate peril.[22]

The lasting legacy of the war of words between Belloc and Wells is its timely and timeless embodiment of the conflict between 'progress' and tradition. 'The orgy of irresponsible innovations and inventions – which

... now threatens to become a Gadarene stampede of headlong and irresistible impetus – was regarded as something beneficial and called "progress", which it certainly is, being downhill and completely without brakes: the most rapid and disastrous "progress" ever witnessed,' wrote the Catholic poet, Roy Campbell.[23]

Campbell's words had the benefit of hindsight, being written in 1949, after the atrocities of Hitler and Stalin and the dropping of nuclear bombs on Hiroshima and Nagasaki had shocked and shaken the world out of its 'progressive' dementia.

Belloc had foreseen that a credulously optimistic faith in scientific 'progress' could lead to 'sheer darkness' and 'strange things in the dark', whereas Wells could only see a bright future and a brave new world of enlightened scientific thinking. In 1934 Wells had an audience with Stalin, declaring to the Soviet leader that 'at the present time there are in the world only two persons to whose opinion, to whose every word, millions are listening – you and Roosevelt'. With the incredible gullibility that Wells displayed throughout his life, he told Stalin how he had seen 'the happy faces of healthy men and women' on the streets of Moscow and knew 'that something very considerable is being done here'. Blinded by his own credulous optimism, it would take the horrors of the Second World War to open his eyes to the evils that could be unleashed by science in the service of 'progressive' ideologies. His last book, written before his death in 1946, was full of the desolation of disillusionment and was entitled, appropriately, *The Mind at the End of its Tether*. In the end, Wells's 'progressive' optimism was defeated, not by Belloc, but by reality.

TWENTY-SIX

Reformed Characters

THE VERBAL DUEL between Belloc and Wells over the latter's *Outline of History* – one of the most famous, and certainly one of the most bitter, literary disputes of the century – was indicative of Belloc's increasing preoccupation with historical questions. 'In history we must abandon the defensive,' he wrote in 1924. '. . . We must make our opponents understand not only that they are wrong in their philosophy, nor only ill-informed in their judgement of cause and effect, but out of touch with the past: which is ours.'[1] Two years earlier, in one of his last letters to Blunt before the latter's death, Belloc had expressed his passion for writing on historical subjects. 'I am just completing a book on the campaign of 1812. I find it fascinating work. Literary work should be composed for the love of it – it is a bad thing as a profession.'[2]

The Campaign of 1812, published in 1924, was as fascinating to read as it evidently had been to write. Tightened with good scholarship but loosened with the eloquence of evocative prose, it carried the reader forward on the narrative flow of its own exuberance. Belloc would, however, from the mid-1920s onwards, be less concerned with European history than with the history of England in the sixteenth and seventeenth centuries. There were notable exceptions, such as *Joan of Arc* in 1929, *Richelieu* in 1930 and *Napoleon* in 1932, but in general Belloc now concentrated his attention and his passion on aspects of English history. His motivation was a desire to redress the anti-Catholic bias of the Whig historians in their treatment of the Reformation.

Twenty years earlier, as a great admirer of R.H. Benson's historical novels, Belloc had written of his hopes that Benson would turn his attention to a serious study of the history of the Reformation in England. 'It is quite on the cards that he will be the man to write some day a book to give us some sort of idea what happened in England between 1520 and 1560.'[3] Benson's untimely death in 1914 had put an end to these hopes and, from 1925, Belloc embarked on the work himself. Commencing with the first of four volumes of *A History of England*, he also wrote specific books on many of the main characters and key events surrounding the English Reformation. These included *Oliver Cromwell* (1927), *James the Second* (1928), *How the Reformation Happened* (1928), *Wolsey* (1930), *Cranmer* (1931), *Charles the First* (1933), *Milton* (1935) and *Characters of the Reformation* (1936).

As usual, however, Belloc did not restrict himself to one particular field of interest. In the year in which the first volume of his *History of England* was published, he also published a novel, *Mr Petre*, and, most memorably, his wonderfully discursive and ever-popular farrago, *The Cruise of the Nona*. He was disappointed with the novel, declaring to Katherine Asquith that he loathed it, but he was enthusiastic about Chesterton's illustrations for it.

> He is marvellous! He is far better with his pencil than his pen. In a line he gives you a whole human being: and it is sane full European stuff ... He did eight in an hour and a half. But if I hadn't forced him he'd never have done them at all. I delight in the talents of my fellow men: and his drawing of the human face is amazing.[4]

Belloc's dependence on Chesterton's illustrations was revealed graphically in a letter to Chesterton in which it is clear that he was reliant on his friend's artistic gifts as much-needed inspiration.

> I am absolutely at the end of my tether in the matter ... of my book ... The book cannot come out unless these few extra drawings are done, and I know they would not take more than an hour and a half for I have all the subjects and could deal with them at once. Our minds have always jumped together, and your hand has genius in its rapidity.[5]

Probably in recompense for Chesterton's work on the illustrations for *Mr Petre* and the other Chesterbelloc novels, Belloc agreed to write for *G.K.'s Weekly*, Chesterton's magazine, the first issue of which was published on 21 March 1925. Later in the year he spoke in support of Chesterton's candidacy in the rectorial election at Glasgow University. Already embroiled in his war with Wells, Belloc seemed to relish the added controversy surrounding Chesterton's candidature. He spoke twice in the Men's and once in the Women's Union, as well as contributing regularly to *G.K.C.*, the daily news-sheet produced by Chesterton's student supporters.

'Chesterton is a poet and a great poet,' Belloc told his student audience at a raucous meeting in the Debating Hall on 15 October. 'He has written the best poem within living memory . . . To read and understand a great poet always demands thought, and thought inevitably brings discomfort.'[6]

There was also controversy in May 1925 after Belloc became involved in the furore that followed the unveiling by the Prime Minister, Stanley Baldwin, of Jacob Epstein's *Rima* in Kensington Gardens. The bas-relief tablet, a memorial to the naturalist W.H. Hudson who had died the previous year, was attacked for its Art Deco crudity. 'Take this horror out of the Park!' was the headline in the *Daily Mail* following the unveiling. One outraged MP described it as 'the bad dream of the Bolshevist in art', and Belloc, evidently agreeing with the populist outcry, was a signatory to a letter, published in the *Morning Post* and signed by, among others, Sir Arthur Conan Doyle, demanding its removal. In response, Bernard Shaw, Arnold Bennett, Ramsay MacDonald and Augustus John signed a letter demanding that it remain.[7]

On 23 March 1925 Belloc's mother died, age 95. She died as peacefully as she had lived for the previous 30 years. 'It was as simple and easy as going to sleep,' Belloc wrote to a friend four days later.

> She simply ceased to breathe. I am profoundly grateful that she had so prolonged a life of complete and unbroken happiness. For the last 35 years she lived in her own way, quite contented on the tiny income which survived the wreck of our fortune and seeing all whom she desired to see and in absolute peace and plenitude. Her death was consonant with all this. It is rare indeed that such long happiness and such a quiet passage out of this detestable world is granted. It was a reward . . .[8]

At the time of his mother's death, only Eleanor, of Belloc's four children, was in England. Peter was in Spain, Elizabeth in Switzerland and Hilary in California. He gained great delight from his granddaughter Marianne, who had been born in 1923, the first of Reg and Eleanor Jebb's children. 'She wears little white woollen breeches and a green coat and hat which ravish my heart with Joy,' he told Katherine Asquith.[9] A year later he was gaining similar joy from his grandson Philip, 'smiling simply and wholly in his crib like the blessed of God'.[10]

Consolation and delight were also to be found, as ever, in the company of friends, old and new. In April 1925 he met Max Beerbohm at the home of Lady Colefax, informing Maurice Baring that he seemed to get 'nicer and nicer as he grows older'.[11] His friendship with Baring was as warm as ever, and he seemed to admire Baring's novels as much as he admired Chesterton's poetry and drawings. *Cat's Cradle* presented 'the cross-purposes and despairs and maimed effort of human life', he wrote to Lady Lovat on 30 October 1926. 'Yet he managed to suggest the Fatherhood of God and the Incarnation and Redemption behind it all. Masterpiece – masterpiece – masterpiece!'[12] Years later, Belloc would confess his feelings of inferiority to Baring in the art of writing fiction. Having informed Baring that he was re-reading his novel *The Coat without Seam* and was 'absorbed' by it, he compared Baring's achievement in fiction with his own inadequacies. 'The reason I am absorbed is that your style is direct. You say what you have to say, I wish I could do that! My own method is circumlocution pushed to an extreme. It is a grave defect; but I am too old to remedy it now.'[13]

Belloc and Chesterton continued to frequent the dinners of Squire's cricket team at the Cheshire Cheese, and continued, it seemed, to be the life and soul of the party. Writing to Edmund Blunden in October 1926, Squire commented that the dinners were 'very successful' and that 'both Belloc and Chesterton turned up at the last one and sang like larks'.[14]

Earlier in the year, the General Strike had highlighted Belloc's differences with many of his wealthy friends, the hostile attitude of whom towards the strikers was typified by the doom-laden account of the strike given by Lady Diana Cooper in her memoirs.

> I remember depressed huddled little lunches at Gower Street, with Maurice unnaturally despondent and the normally robust plunged into gloom. Belloc alone seemed totally unmoved and in the highest spirits. The wireless for the first time became to us a necessity. The sky in memory seems dark, pitch-dark at noon. Every day increased the vast hordes of strikers, but, as always in full crisis, the sinews stiffened. All despondency evaporated ... The club boys became special constables. My brother was on night duty from nine to six a.m. Some foolhardies were driving buses and trains. I was a freelance ... taking stranded workers home in my car, telephoning Max Beaverbrook for news and being connected to him by Edwina Mountbatten and Jean Norton, who were operating the *Daily Express* switchboard.[15]

Lady Diana's husband, the Conservative MP Duff Cooper, wrote of the strike in similar terms, remarking that Belloc remained in good spirits 'and cheered us all up'.[16] It is doubtful that he had done so by singing with ironic gusto the song that he had made up about the strike – 'Rally round the rich, boys; up the millionaires!' – which J.B. Morton remembered him singing in the Temple Bar.[17] The truth was that Belloc's natural sympathies were with the strikers, as they had been during the Dock Strike of 1889 when he had first heeded Cardinal Manning's assertion that 'all human conflict is ultimately theological'. In particular, he lamented the fact that his friends were so blinded by the fear of Bolshevism that they had lost all sight of questions of justice or charity.

> We are in a state of permanent and sullen civil war, modified by general patriotism and terror of the police and the troopers. The rich are seeing to it that these divisions shall grow more acute. God has blinded them. I have not met one single gentleman or lady on the side of the poor in this crisis. That's ominous![18]

'When a nation is divided against itself,' he wrote, 'settlement is the duty and not victory.'[19] It was, therefore, scarcely surprising that he failed to share the jubilation of most of his friends when the strikers were eventually defeated. 'Yes, the Miners have lost the Strike all right,' he lamented in November, 'principally through the treason of a so-called Labour-leader called Thomas.'[20] He further complained: 'The Mind of Big Business is deplorably manifest in the Press. Every one of the little news sheets is crowing over the victory, and assuring the workmen that they must have their faces ground and must return to their old conditions or worse.'[21]

The General Strike had represented 'an exceedingly grave moment, in my opinion graver than the worst moments of the war'. Its gravity, however, was not in the magnitude of the conflict but 'in the inability of men to perceive the nature of the problem'.[22] Increasingly frustrated by the myopic failure of most people to see beyond the twin materialist options of capitalism and the 'detestable heresy' of communism, Belloc, like Chesterton, continued to plead for the sanity of distributism. Chesterton was now President of the Distributist League, which would later publish Belloc's An Essay on the Restoration of Property, a masterfully succinct appraisal of 'the nature of the problem' and, indeed, of the practicalities of the solution.

The League was also responsible for organizing a public debate between Chesterton and Shaw at the Kingsway Hall in London in late October 1927. Chaired by Belloc and broadcast live by the BBC, the debate featured Shaw and Chesterton discussing the theme, 'Do We Agree?' Needless to say, they did not. Shaw still argued for socialism, Chesterton for distributism, and never the twain did meet. There was something almost stale about the stalemate until Belloc stole the show with his summing up. After reciting a poem of his own composition in which he described modern industrial civilization as a 'lump of damnation, without any soul', which was 'built upon coal' and would soon 'float upon oil', he continued with the grave solemnity of a prophet: 'I am surprised that neither of the two speakers pointed out that one of three things is going to happen ... The industrial civilization, which, thank God, oppresses only the small part of the world in which we are most inextricably bound up, will break down and therefore end from its monstrous wickedness, folly, ineptitude, leading to a restoration of sane, ordinary human affairs, complicated but based as a whole upon the freedom of the citizens. Or it will break down and lead to nothing but a desert. Or it will lead the mass of men to become contented slaves, with a few rich men controlling them. Take your choice.'[23]

In spite of these diversions into prophecy, Belloc remained preoccupied, not with the problems of the present, nor with predictions about the future, but with the truth about the past. Indeed, he felt that the present problems and future difficulties were the result of the mistakes of the past, and were only soluble through a correct understanding of where our ancestors had gone wrong. In 1927 the second volume of *A History of England* was published, as well as *The Catholic Church and History* and a biography of Oliver Cromwell. The following year would see the publication of the third volume of his *History*, as well as a life of James II and his panoramic *How the Reformation Happened*.

In an essay entitled 'If', published in *A Conversation with an Angel and Other Essays* in 1928, Belloc described how the present had been shaped by decisions and actions taken in the past. If we misunderstood how and why people acted in the past, we would not understand how and why the world is as it is today. After citing the obvious example of the Battle of Hastings, and the tactical decisions made by William the Conqueror, he proceeded to a discussion of the more recent history of the United States. 'I suppose of all modern decisions nothing has made more difference to the history of the world than the decision of the English Cabinet not to recognize the Southern States as an independent nation during the American Civil War.' As always, however, Belloc's principal preoccupation was with the Reformation and with the characters who had given it shape.

But to return to the 'if'. If Calvin had not written his book there would have been no organized counter-Church in France. The confused original movement would not have had a nucleus and a framework, and 'The Religion', as they called it, would hardly have had corporate existence. From that a whole train of consequences would have arisen which would have meant a completely different history for Europe in the seventeenth and eighteenth centuries.[24]

If history was so important, the writing of history became important by association. If it was done badly, the present would be deprived of the lessons of the past.

The worst fault in [writing] history, infinitely worse than mechanical inaccuracy, and worse even than lack of proportion, is the fault of not knowing what the spiritual state of those whom one describes really was. Gibbon and his master Voltaire, the very best of reading, are for that reason bad writers of history. To pass through the tremendous history of the Trinitarian dispute from which our civilization arose and to treat it as a farce is not history. To write the story of the sixteenth century in England and to make of either the Protestant or the Catholic a grotesque is to miss history altogether.[25]

Belloc's frustration at this widespread chronological snobbery, by which the present continually judged the past superciliously from a position of presumed superiority, was in evidence in a letter to Maurice Baring.

There is an enormous book called Volume 1 of a *Cambridge History of the Middle Ages*. It is 759 pages in length of close print ... It does not mention the Mass once. That is as though you were to write a history of the Jewish dispersion without mentioning the synagogue or of the British Empire without mentioning the City of London or the Navy ...[26]

In a letter to his daughter, Belloc complained that 'most people are still steeped in that false official history which warps all English life',[27] a complaint to which he returned in his book *The Crisis of Our Civilization*, in which he described the omnipresence of this warped 'official' history in the experience of every educated Englishman. 'The historians whose works he had been given as textbooks, those who inform the fiction he knows, the classics of his tongue, the body of the literature with which he is familiar, are the historians in opposition to ourselves. Write down half a dozen names: Macaulay, Carlyle, Gibbon, Mommsen, Old Freeman, Motley, and the modern writer Trevelyan.'[28] It was, therefore, as something of a personal crusade that Belloc took on the 'weary work [of] fighting this enormous mountain of ignorant wickedness' that constituted 'tom-fool Protestant history'.[29]

'Gibbon from beginning to end is an anti-Catholic pamphlet,' he complained, 'extremely well-written and, as a presentation of historical development, grossly unhistorical.'[30] Macaulay, another *bête noire*, was dismissed in private correspondence to Katherine Asquith as 'a bold and resolute liar'[31] and, more circumspectly, in an essay published in 1928.

> Now when a man is arguing as a lawyer to a brief, though he be arguing for a cause in which he believes, yet is he drawn as by ropes towards making everything support his client. He will suppress, distort, and misstate – but all for the right side – and that is Macaulay's excuse.
>
> It is a subtle point in moral theology (which those may discuss who are interested in that science) how the very certitude of a major truth may lead a man to a lot of lying. But, at any rate, Macaulay was, in that largest matter of his creed, transparently sincere; and as a writer he has triumphantly survived.[32]

It could, of course, be argued that this was a clear case of the proverbial pot calling the kettle black. Certainly, most of Belloc's critics assumed that he was doing exactly what he had accused Macaulay of doing. However 'transparently sincere' he might be, Belloc was arguing the case for the Catholic version of history and was, it was implied, prone to 'suppress, distort, and misstate' those aspects of history that failed to place the role of the Church in a favourable light. 'Mr Belloc urges the view of history that the Vatican would urge if the Vatican were as enlightened and as free as Mr Belloc,' wrote Shaw.[33] Similarly, G.M. Trevelyan complained to John Buchan that 'non-professional historians so often have bees in their bonnets, like Wells and Belloc'.[34]

Desmond MacCarthy, a more sympathetic critic, still felt compelled to allude to Belloc's biased approach. 'As an historian and biographer he interprets the Reformation, the Cromwellian rebellion and the revolution of 1688 from a Catholic point of view. He cannot be reckoned among the impartial historians, but his own bias constantly makes us aware of the bias in judgements which we regard as impartial simply because they are so familiar.'[35] Aside from any dispute as to Belloc's objectivity of judgement, MacCarthy's words elucidate the indisputable value of Belloc's role as a historian. At the very least, he acts as the counsel for the defence after more than a century in which the Whig historians had acted as the prosecution in their anti-Catholic and pro-Protestant bias. Belloc had at least raised the whole issue of bias in the writing of history. As a conscientious objector to the monolithic monologue of 'official history', he had enabled conscientious students to see both sides of the story.

Perhaps, however, Belloc deserves recognition as being more than merely a much-needed counterbalance to the bias of previous 'official' historians. Perhaps he deserves to be seen as a true historian, that is, a historian who sought objectivity in his judgements to such a degree that he tried sincerely to overcome his own prejudices in the service of historical accuracy and truth. Philip Guedalla, possibly the most distinguished and certainly the most popular historian of Belloc's generation, believed that Belloc was 'a historian of unusual eloquence'.[36] Guedalla had readily sought Belloc's advice in his own research and remained a great admirer of his work.[37]

Guedalla's praise of Belloc was ratified more recently by Norman Stone, Professor of Modern History at Oxford, who wrote in the *Sunday Times* on 4 October 1992 that he considered Belloc a more perceptive historian than G.M. Trevelyan. 'I think that, in the end, I shall go to Trevelyan's enemies, Hilaire Belloc or Lord Acton, both Catholics, for an understanding of modern England.' Such posthumous praise from such a prestigious source serves as a fitting tribute to Belloc's ground-breaking historical studies of the leading characters of the Reformation, the 'weary work' that came to dominate the later years of his life.

TWENTY-SEVEN

A Final Flourish

I N J U N E 1927 Belloc sat for the artist James Gunn at his London studio. Gunn wrote to his sister that Belloc was 'one of the finest of men, & a great poet & . . . a man of great heart & kindliness'.[1] It would appear that this was the first time the artist and the poet had met, although Gunn had sent Belloc a gift in November 1923, to which the latter had responded with the following amusing note. 'Words will not express my gratitude! It is the most valuable and amusing present I have ever had in my life: which is a tall order: as I have had (A) a Mug which plays *Madame Angot* when you take it up full of beer; (B) £100 from a forgotten debtor.'[2]

The two men became firm friends. A few years later, Belloc would introduce Gunn to Baring and Chesterton, the result of which would be Gunn's celebrated group portrait of Belloc, Baring and Chesterton which now hangs in the National Portrait Gallery in London. This famous painting, which Chesterton referred to jokingly as being a portrait of 'Baring, Over-Bearing and Beyond-Bearing', serves as a timeless celebration of one of the most famous and fruitful literary trinities of the century. The friendship had already endured for three decades, in the case of Belloc and Baring, and for almost as long in the case of Belloc and Chesterton. For one who felt the melancholy force of mortality and decay as acutely as Belloc, such friendships were like pillars of permanence, as resolute and as reliable as the love of Sussex he had celebrated at the dawn of the century in his book *The Four Men*.

> . . . it has been proved in the life of every man that though his loves are human, and therefore changeable, yet in proportion as he attaches them to things unchangeable, so they mature and broaden.
>
> On this account . . . does a man love an old house, which was his father's, and on this account does a man come to love with all his heart, that part of earth which nourished his boyhood. For it does

not change, or if it changes, it changes very little, and he finds in it the character of enduring things.[3]

In this light, it is easy to imagine Belloc's sense of loss when he was forced, with great reluctance, to part with the *Nona* in the summer of 1927. She, also, was an old friend, having been acquired by Belloc in 1901. He wrote of the loss to Katherine Asquith.

> Alas! She has lived her life, and all the rest is mere waiting for dissolution and the end. I have loved her well; I love her still. But there is no more sailing in her. Her age is upon her ... A better sea boat never was. But teak and oak are mortal and must pass ... Lord! What times I have had with her! She also enjoyed it, though she never confessed as much (a modest craft) and we understood each other very well. But now that great friendship is interrupted and the end has come.[4]

Being unable to sell her, he gave her away to a friend, gaining a degree of consolation in the belief that 'she will have a kind home'.[5] He was, however, only delaying the inevitable. Two years later, on 3 October 1929, he reported that the *Nona* was 'even now being broken up having gone to pieces with age'.[6]

At the same time that Belloc was reluctantly accepting the death of the *Nona*, he was overseeing the resurrection of the old mill at King's Land. 'I have had my mill put all new again at a ruinous cost,' he told Lady Lovat, 'and it has, for the first time, ground six sacks of corn!'[7]

In November 1927, answering the perennial call of his wanderlust, Belloc travelled to North Africa where, at El Kantara on the edge of the Sahara desert, he found an unlikely location to complete the writing of his life of James II. By early December he was in Provence amid olive trees, cypresses, pines and mountain peaks. 'I could stay here for many years writing history which no one will read,' he wrote to Lady Lovat. 'But I may not, I must go North.'[8] He was back at King's Land for the customary festivities at Christmas, but was soon travelling again. By the end of February he was driving through the deserts of Tunisia; in March he was in Sardinia; in June he was in Poland, making a pilgrimage to the Marian shrine of Our Lady of Czestochowa.

Amid these wanderings, he still found time for literary work. His 'Heroic Poem in Praise of Wine' was finished in 1928 and published in the *London Mercury*. It had taken him several years to write and is considered by many to be his highest achievement in verse. None was more fulsome in its praise than Robert Speaight, who considered parts of the 'Heroic Poem' to possess 'exactly the quality of marble; the strength and delicacy of a frieze'.

> No other poem so resumes Belloc's personality and spiritual lineage; his high spirits and his sense of exile; his courage and his near despair. Nothing so fine in the heroic couplet had been achieved by a modern English poet, if we except certain poems by Mr Roy Campbell. For most people it will stand as Belloc's monument; the quintessence of a European mind, at once humble and combative.[9]

On 20 July 1928, Belloc informed Maurice Baring that he had 'finished *Belinda* – a fearful sweat – like sawing marble – but worth it. It is the only thing I ever finished in my life and the only piece of my own writing that I have liked for more than 40 years.'[10] Belloc modified his judgement slightly, declaring to an American friend, Carl Schmidt, two years later that it was 'certainly the book of mine which I like best since I wrote *The Path to Rome*'.[11] Either way, he clearly felt that *Belinda* was a work with which he could feel satisfied, itself a unique judgement with regard to his works of fiction. Previously his novels had been little more than a source of disappointment to him and had been the object of his self-critical scorn. He loathed them and believed them inferior to, and unworthy of, Chesterton's illustrations. At last, with *Belinda*, he felt that he had achieved something worthwhile and enduring. 'I go over it word for word, like a mosaic,' he told Katherine Asquith on 1 July, three weeks before its completion, 'changing, fitting in, adapting, dictating, erasing, spatch-cocking, caressing, softening, enlivening, glamouring, suppressing, enhancing and in general divinizing this my darling treasure.'[12]

Belloc's enthusiasm while writing *Belinda*, which he had been working on since December 1923, was recalled by his son-in-law Reginald Jebb. Belloc would call in at his and Eleanor's house in Horsham,

> bringing with him sheets of the *Belinda* manuscript that he had just completed and read them out to us with obvious relish. That was an unusual thing for him to do. I cannot recall any other occasion when I heard him read aloud from his manuscripts, though he often quoted his own verse from memory. I think he realized that in *Belinda* he had achieved something he had set out to do.[13]

Similar memories were recalled by J.B. Morton, who remembered Belloc reading aloud from the book after it had been published and 'laughing loudly' as he read the passage containing Horatio's farewell to the shores of England. Morton shared his friend's high opinion of *Belinda*.

> It is a mistake to think that it is all pastiche. Jostling the most amusing parodies of the idiom of another day are passages of great beauty, and before you have finished laughing, you are deeply moved, and then you are laughing again. The description of Horatio and Belinda falling in love is exquisitely done. So is the yearning of old Sir Robert to go back through the years, when he meets his first love . . .[14]

Jebb concurred, declaring:

> Any sympathetic reader will find in it much more than a satire of upper-class conventions of the early nineteenth century. It is certainly that, but there is at the same time a compassionate – almost a nostalgic – feeling for the two young lovers and their fight against fate. Through the satire – so admirably clothed in the language of the more romantic nineteenth-century novelists – a very genuine beauty keeps appearing. And I think it must be these two contrasting themes, so perfectly fused, that makes *Belinda* one of the books that Belloc really enjoyed writing.[15]

These positive appraisals of *Belinda*'s merits were not the preserve of Belloc's friends and relatives. A reviewer in *The Times* was equally effusive:

> Mr Belloc goes back to the mood of parody, but of parody decked out with gracious ornament. His new book occasionally reminds us in form of *Zuleika Dobson* or *The Happy Hypocrite*, but its ebullient humour is not that of those famous fantasies. Belinda, daughter of a richly landed baronet, is an early Victorian heroine, whose love story of tears quickly quenched in splendid marriage is related with the lusciousness that the romantic Victorian novelists of 'high life' like to impart to their style. Only, Mr Belloc has the skill to see that an ornate style, insipid in the hands of a bungler, can be made as attractive as a good piece of baroque architecture in the hands of a master. If we get all the absurdity of which he is master in the angry interview between Belinda and her haughty father on the subject of her love for Horatio Maltravers . . . we get real beauty, of a Renaissance quality, in such an episode as Venus's apparition to bless the lovers in the great park. And Mr Belloc's brevity is admirable: the novelists he satirizes were not so wise . . .[16]

Bearing in mind Belloc's own high opinion of *Belinda*, he must have rejoiced greatly at such praise. Similarly, he must have been enormously satisfied to receive the following laudatory lines from the well-known Anglican monk, Father Waggett.

> My dear and dearest Belloc, Your *Belinda* is unspeakably beautiful. I thank God for a fresh unfolding of your genius, a fresh date for the life of our prose exquisite in spirit and in form. Every word is lovely. The humour of the convention moves within the limits of an accomplished harmony. And what you give us in your music is a deep consolation. We have had too much of affection that is hindered & crippled, moving between rash impulses and nameless regrets. In the delicately tinted image of Belinda, now the owner of my devotion, you have shown the love, hindered by circumstance, but in itself at once free and safe; a little sister of the Love that casteth out Fear. If this is what our grandparents knew how worthily you have reminded us of what they knew.[17]

Perhaps the most poignant and perceptive of all the critical judgements of *Belinda* was that offered by Robert Speaight in his biography of Belloc.

> Of all Belloc's works in prose *Belinda* is the most perfect, the most original, the most timeless, and therefore perhaps the most secure. It is also the most difficult to define. If we call it 'pastiche', we realize at once that we have employed too light and artificial a word. Artificial in a sense it is, and no one could describe it as heavy; but deep feeling underlies the artifice and the humour has the weight of Belloc's own *gravitas*. The book grinds no axe and proves no point. It is a gratuitous, disinterested and quite impersonal essay in romantic irony. Small in scale and purposely conventional in subject, it still leaves an impression of grandeur; fine, not finicky; hard as a diamond and delicate as wrought iron.[18]

The greatest irony about Belloc's writing of *Belinda* is that it appears to contradict what he himself had written in his essay 'On Irony' in 1910. 'Irony is a sword, and must be used as a sword,' he had written. In *Belinda* irony is not wielded as a weapon, but flourished like a feather. It is not used to bludgeon its victim senseless, but to tickle him with an affectionate sensibility. It is not an irony that is iron-shod and hardened by its own heartlessness, but one that is fleet of foot and on a flight of fancy. *Belinda* belies categorization – and belies any categorizing of Belloc amongst the ranks of the artistically or aesthetically insensitive.

'My stock is going up,' Belloc wrote delightedly to Katherine Asquith in January 1929. 'Hal Fisher wanders about England telling everyone that

Belinda is the best novel written in English and the summit of all prose and lyrism.'[19] Certainly, *Belinda* served to remind those who might other-wise have been tempted to forget, that Belloc was a writer of the foremost rank. Arnold Bennett, writing in the *Evening Standard* on 13 June 1929, placed him in illustrious company when he recommended 'as models for young writers such men as T.H. Huxley, Matthew Arnold, Cardinal Newman, Hilaire Belloc, D.H. Lawrence, Max Beerbohm, Sterne'. Bennett, however, had never doubted Belloc's powers, either as an essayist or as a poet. Discussing the 'influence of journalism on the art of literature', he wrote on 8 December 1927 how 'many of the finest essays – beautiful short masterpieces, by especially Chesterton, Lynd and Belloc' owed their existence to newspaper commissions.[20] As to Belloc's position as a poet, Bennett criticized the critic A.C. Ward for his curious appraisal of the poetry of 'Chesterton, Masefield, Noyes, Flecker, Rupert Brooke and Belloc ... He overpraises most of these poets, though not Belloc, who is the best of them when in the vein.'[21]

If Belloc's *Belinda* achieved the accolades that its artistic subtlety and originality merited, his next book, published in April 1929, sank largely without trace. *Survivals and New Arrivals* is perhaps Belloc's most under-rated work. It was certainly one of his most ambitious. It set out to analyse the various heterodox philosophies vying for supremacy in the modern world, some of which were 'survivals' from the past while others were 'new arrivals', relatively speaking, in the historical development of thought. It was a perfect example of Belloc's assertion that the lessons of the past, properly understood, could be used as a weapon in the struggles of the present.

> Now the historical period in which we have most practical interest is our own. To grasp the situation of the Catholic Church *today* we must appreciate which of the forces opposing her are *today* growing feeble, which are *today* in full vigour, which are *today* appearing as new antagonists, hardly yet in their vigour but increasing.
>
> As for the Faith itself it stands immovable in the midst of all such hostile things; they arise and pass before that majestic presence:–
>
> *Stat et stabit, manet et manebit: spectator orbis.*[22]

Amongst the philosophies and intellectual movements that Belloc places under his metaphysical microscope are: the Biblical attack, Materialism, the 'Wealth and Power' argument, the Historical argument, Scientific Negation, Nationalism, Anti-Clericalism, the 'Modern Mind' and Neo-Paganism. In each case his reason, his logic, his eye for historical and philosophical perspective, are unerring. As an exposition of the Catholic philosophical position, and its opposition across the centuries, it represents a truly remarkable achievement.

His motivation for writing the book could be gleaned from his general attitude to religious controversy, as expressed in *The Cruise of the Nona*. 'The orthodox seem to feel, in approaching the sceptics, that they are dealing with superiors. It ought to be just the other way. The people who are in the tradition of Europe, who have behind them the whole momentum of civilization, who have humour and common sense as the products of Faith, ought to approach their contradictors as inferiors.'[23]

Belloc's general thesis, and his attitude towards the 'survivals' and the 'new arrivals' alike, was summed up with succinctness, three years after the book's publication, in a letter to Carl Schmidt.

> ... the present anti-Catholic mood of pseudo-scientific fatalism will not last, but will give rise to some new false religion. It is the characteristic of opposition to the Catholic Church that it takes on all sorts of new forms as the centuries proceed. The new false religion will necessarily be some form of worship of humanity by itself – nationalism is an instance in point ... I think ... that there will be no complete victory on either side or the other. The Catholic forces are very much more powerful than their enemies imagine and I think that those who live in an anti-Catholic society may fail to gauge that fact; for we have on our side the considerable forces of history, and the power to reason closely. I do not think we shall be overwhelmed.[24]

Survivals and New Arrivals was, without doubt, Belloc's most ambitious, and most accomplished, sortie into the world of popular apologetics. It is, to him, what *Orthodoxy*, *The Everlasting Man*, *The Thing* or *The Well and the Shallows* were to Chesterton, or what *Mere Christianity* was to C.S. Lewis. It is curious, therefore, that it is so often overlooked. Its fate, ironically, could be described in the words that Belloc ascribed to Chesterton's *The Thing*, which was published in the same year as *Survivals and New Arrivals*. *The Thing* was Chesterton's 'best piece of work', wrote Belloc. 'Of all his books it is by far the most profound and the most clear.' Nonetheless, Belloc mused, its intrinsic merits did not guarantee either critical or popular success. 'I am curious and even meditative upon its probable fate. If it is read by the generation now rising, that will mean England is beginning to think. If it is forgotten, that will mean that thought is failing; for nowhere has there been more thorough thinking or clearer exposition in our time.'[25]

Although Belloc would have been too modest to have said so, even assuming that he believed it to be true, his words were equally applicable to *Survivals and New Arrivals*. It is his most underrated book, superior in many respects to the far more famous and celebrated works of apologetics by Chesterton, C.S. Lewis and others. It is, in parts, difficult to read, sometimes almost too difficult to read. Its approach is sometimes laboured, at least seemingly so on first perusal. Yet its apparently lethargic, chugging style is surprisingly effective. Throughout the book's pages, Belloc is driving a slow, relentless, ten-ton steamroller over the world's 'heresies'. His prose does not float, sting, dance or sing like Chesterton's, but he nonetheless squashes the 'heretics' under the wheels of his inexorable, unanswerable logic. While Chesterton, as a Catholic apologist, cuts a dashing figure, swashbuckling his way to victory with his sword of truth, Belloc comes trundling over the horizon in a tank.

The publication of *Survivals and New Arrivals* brought to an end a remarkable year in which, creatively, Belloc had surpassed himself – an *annus mirabilis* in which he had carved with marbled precision the 'Heroic Poem', believed by many to be his finest achievement in verse; in which he had finished *Belinda*, his finest novel, crafted with filigreed and feathered finesse; and, last but emphatically not least, a year in which he had written a history of the human mind in its relation to objective truth that, in words he applied to another, was 'of all his books . . . by far the most profound and the most clear'.

Years earlier, lamenting that he would never again attain the literary heights he had reached in *The Path to Rome*, Belloc had written, 'Alas! I never shall so write again!'[26] His judgement was premature. If, however, he had written the same words in 1929, they would have rung true. Following his *annus mirabilis*, he never would so write again. Good books would follow, but nothing to warrant a place among the greats of twentieth-century literature. 'The Heroic Poem in Praise of Wine', *Belinda* and *Survivals and New Arrivals* were written in the final flourish of his genius.

TWENTY-EIGHT

Farewell to the Chesterbelloc

I N THE SPRING OF 1929, the young Evelyn Waugh met Belloc, Baring and Max Beerbohm, 'each an idol of mine', for the first time. Still a relative unknown, his first novel having been published in the previous September, Waugh was in self-confessed awe of their presence.¹ Although he would state that, of the three, Beerbohm was pre-eminent in his affections, describing him as 'an idol of my adolescence to whom every year had deepened my devotion',² Waugh's debt to Belloc was nonetheless considerable. According to A.L. Rowse, Belloc was Waugh's 'model and mentor'. 'What a model,' Rowse added in parenthesis, 'what a mentor!'³

The enduring friendship between Beerbohm and Belloc was witnessed by J.B. Morton, who was struck by the immense pleasure that the former evidently derived from the latter's company during a memorable evening at a Soho restaurant. 'Belloc was at his most tempestuous, and Max Beerbohm sat chuckling quietly, and only occasionally putting in a word. He was enjoying himself thoroughly ... There was a twinkle in his eye while he listened.'⁴ A visit by Beerbohm to King's Land during 1929 inspired a short verse, 'In the Store Room at King's Land', in which Beerbohm, with affectionate wit, paid homage to his friend.

Not everyone was as amused or as enamoured with Belloc as Waugh and Beerbohm. In March 1929, the anti-Catholic controversialist J.W. Poynter published *Hilaire Belloc Keeps the Bridge*, subtitled 'An Examination of his Defence of Catholicism'. Poynter's hostility to Belloc and the Church was evident in his preface: 'We are reminded ... of the legend of how Horatius Cocles held the bridge against the enemies of Rome. Mr Belloc seems, in England, to be holding the bridge. There is, however, a difference. The hero of old was defending a Rome which loved freedom and truth; Mr Belloc defends a Rome which is wedded to despotism and obscurantism.'⁵

Whatever Poynter's intentions were, one can scarcely imagine Belloc being anything other than flattered by the comparison with the famous solitary hero of ancient Rome immortalized by Macaulay. Neither, one suspects, would he have been too offended, though perhaps heartily amused, by the closing sentence of Poynter's 'Examination' of his efforts to defend the Church.

> When we see so able a man, as Mr Belloc is, devoted to the promotion of the cause of such a conception of life, we cannot avoid asking – not, of course, with any meaning implying lack of recognition and respect for sincerity and learning, which indeed all must admire, but because of the contrast between the ability of the advocate and the intellectual weakness of the cause: Is it worthy of you, Mr Belloc?[6]

Had he condescended to respond, Belloc would have replied, no doubt, that it was the unworthiness of the advocate, not of the cause, which was at issue.

Belloc's genuine self-effacement, masquerading as mock-humility, was evident in a letter to James Gunn, dated 29 April 1929, in which Belloc alludes to his delight that Gunn's portrait of him was being exhibited at the Fine Art Society.

> Joy. Fun. Excellent. Admirable . . . And to me it is particularly gratifying. I want the advertisement. Time presses. I'm 59 [sic]. I shall put on a mask, and go and listen to the comments of the public. When does it open? . . . It is a great thing to have one's portrait painted by a man of genius like you because posterity then knows all about it. They say 'nothing is known of the man save his magnificent portrait by Gunn'. Or they say 'Portrait of an Unknown Person, by Gunn'. Sometimes they go as far as to say 'Portrait of a gentleman'. They can only do that by the clothes.[7]

James Gunn was one of the guests at an extravagant birthday party to celebrate Belloc's sixtieth birthday on 27 July 1930, at which the idea of Gunn's *Conversation Piece* was first mooted.[8] The birthday dinner at the Adelphi Hotel was organized by A.D. Peters, Belloc's literary agent, with 24 specially invited guests in attendance.[9] These included G.K. Chesterton, who chaired the proceedings, Maurice Baring, Peter Belloc, A.P. Herbert, Reginald Jebb, Robert Lynd, D.B. Wyndham Lewis, J.C. Squire, Douglas Woodruff, Christopher Hollis, Duff Cooper, E.C. Bentley, H.S. Mackintosh, J.J. Hall, E.S.P. Haynes, Edward Shanks and J.B. Morton.[10] The evening's conviviality has passed into the realm of literary legend, largely due to the graphic account given by Chesterton in his autobiography. 'To me it was that curious experience, something between the Day of Judgement and a dream, in which men of many groups known to me at many times, all appeared together as a sort of resurrection . . . and the renewed comradeship stirred in me the memory of a hundred controversies.'[11]

It was decided from the outset that no speeches would be allowed to impede the spontaneous flow of conversation, but Chesterton, as chairman, was permitted to say a few words in presenting Belloc with a golden goblet inscribed with lines from his 'Heroic Poem in Praise of Wine'.

I merely said a few words to the effect that such a ceremony might have been as fitting thousands of years ago, at the festival of a great Greek poet; and that I was confident that Belloc's sonnets and strong verse would remain like the cups and the carved epics of the Greeks. He acknowledged it briefly, with a sad good humour, saying he found that, by the age of sixty, he did not care very much whether his verse remained or not. 'But I am told,' he added with sudden reviving emphasis, 'I am told that you begin to care again frightfully when you are seventy. In which case, I hope I shall die at sixty-nine.'[12]

The golden rule with regard to speeches was waived towards the end of the evening when someone suggested to Chesterton that he should thank A.D. Peters for organizing the birthday celebration. He did so, to which Peters replied that the real credit should go to J.B. Morton. Morton, however, answered solemnly that he owed the idea to J.C. Squire, who was seated on his right. Catching on to the joke, Squire declared that the person on *his* right deserved the credit. Each and every member of the party rose to the occasion, paying tribute to the person seated next to them in tones of ever-increasing absurdity. A.P. Herbert impersonated a town councillor, Duff Cooper pretended to be a Liberal politician, and so it went on until everyone had praised his neighbour. The highlight of the evening, at least in the delightful image it presents to posterity, was provided by Maurice Baring, who recited a Horatian ode to 'Hilario Belloc' which had been composed in Latin by Ronald Knox especially for the occasion, while balancing a glass of Burgundy on his bald head in defiance of the best efforts of certain irreverent guests to dislodge it with pellets of bread.[13]

'At this time,' wrote J.B. Morton, 'Belloc looked much older than his sixty years. Overwork, lack of sleep, and no settled way of living were telling on him more and more. Yet in the years that followed he worked even harder than before, pouring out novels and essays and articles and books of all kinds.'[14] He acquired a new boat, but confessed to his son in April 1932 that the effects of age were reducing his appetite for the sea. 'I am afraid ... that I shall not do very much sailing after this year ... I get older every year, oddly enough, instead of staying the same as one does between 20 and 60.'[15]

His physical decline did not prevent Belloc seeking consolation, as ever, in the comforts of friendship. In 1931 he gave a drunken oration at a dinner of the Saintsbury Club which was described by those present as being witty, brilliant and eminently memorable – memorable, that is, to everyone except the speaker himself, who confessed next morning that he could not recall a single word he had said.[16] He continued to meet regularly with old companions such as J.C. Squire, A.D. Peters and H.S. Mackintosh, with whom, on 22 April 1931, he rendezvoused to 'drink some of that wine I discovered'.[17] He also painted the town red with newer and younger friends such as Tom Burns, who recalled an evening in Soho, also in 1931, during which he and Belloc consumed lager and oysters before proceeding to a restaurant for 'a splendid meal' accompanied by a plentiful supply of wine.[18]

In the midst of all the merry-making the work continued apace. In the spring of 1931 Belloc was working on his life of Cranmer, writing to Ronald Knox that he was 'dealing with Cranmer's admirable prose, crapulous cowardice, sincere Moloch worship, heroic death and the rest of it'.[19]

If the approach of old age had not dimmed Belloc's *joie de vivre* in the company of friends, neither had it lessened his wanderlust. He continued to travel widely throughout Europe and in March 1932 he found himself in Leipzig at the time of the presidential elections in which Hitler emerged as a powerful force. Describing Hitler as 'wretched', he lamented the number of Catholics who had failed to vote for Hindenburg and had chosen to vote for either Hitler or the communists instead, 'though the Nationalists are openly anti-Catholic and Communism is abhorrent to the Catholic temper'.[20]

Returning to England from Germany, Belloc was delighted by the success of Gunn's *Conversation Piece* at the Academy Summer Exhibition. 'I am glad you like Jimmy Gunn's picture,' Belloc wrote to a friend on 20 March 1932. 'I think it is quite first-rate, especially the way he has caught Gilbert Chesterton. I am horrified to see the accumulation of wickedness in my own face – it is due to the length of years ...'[21] On 11 May, *Punch* captioned a cartoon of the portrait in a way that encapsulated the public's lingering perception of the Chesterbelloc: 'Mr Chesterton takes a note of another Sussex tavern, discovered by Mr Belloc, where they sell very good ale.'

Belloc, Baring and Chesterton had sat for Gunn's group portrait at his studio at 12 Bedford Gardens in Kensington during the final weeks of 1931 and the early weeks of 1932. During one of these sittings, on 15 February 1932, the three sitters collaborated on the composing of a Ballade. According to Gunn, the 'Ballade of Devastation' was composed by Baring and Chesterton 'with interjections by Hilaire Belloc'.[22] It was signed 'GKMBC', a clear indication of Belloc's relatively peripheral role in its composition, and was published in *The Times* two days after its composition.

In November 1947, James and Pauline Gunn gave one of the preliminary sketches for the *Conversation Piece* to Princess Elizabeth as a wedding gift on the occasion of her marriage to the Duke of Edinburgh. The future Queen replied on 16 December to offer 'our most sincere thanks for the delightful picture of Mr Chesterton, Mr Belloc and Mr Maurice Baring . . . I think it perfectly charming, and much look forward to hanging it in my house.'[23] It is intriguing to conjecture whether she ever did so; whether, even now, the triumvirate of writers overlooks some corner of one of the royal residences, or whether the picture gathers dust unheeded in a neglected storeroom.

On 30 May, Belloc wrote to Gunn that he had looked into the Academy 'just for a moment the other day to see the picture, which I remembered so well from the studio . . . It has been enormously admired as you know, and more and more as time goes on.' He added that he had been 'so queer lately that I have had hardly any time in London: I have overworked myself badly . . .'[24] As this letter suggests, Belloc's ailing health was becoming more of a concern. His eyesight was failing, forcing him with reluctance to resort to the typewriter instead of handwriting correspondence, and prompting him, with whimsical wistfulness, to wish in a letter to a friend at the beginning of 1932 that she had sent him 'some new eyes for Christmas'.[25] Insomnia, recurrent throughout his life, was another problem. It was best, he told a friend on 14 November 1932, not to struggle to get to sleep. 'I used to get myself into a frenzy of effort to seize on sleep, but now I just lie awake and bear it and I find it wearies me less.'[26]

These problems paled into relative insignificance in September 1932 after he suffered what appears to have been a minor stroke. 'It was a dreadful thing that happened,' he informed his son Peter.

I completely lost my memory. I had a very bad night and when I got up this morning I was rather dazed and I remained so during the morning. I tried to do some work in the library of the Reform Club and I went on till half past one and then went off to lunch with my mind quite empty. This sort of thing has happened to me once or twice in the last two or three years. It does not seem to get more frequent but it is really alarming when it does happen and distresses me a great deal. It comes of having done more work than I ought to have done at my age.[27]

Similar blackouts would follow. He informed Charlotte Balfour on 18 February 1933:

All these lapses of consciousness are due to circulation. I have had more than one, as you know – and I have no idea how long they last. I had one the other day in the middle of my illness. I had got up to come down to table, where I was dining alone reading a paper, when I found myself coming to on the stone floor with one foot caught up in the table rail![28]

The 'illness' to which Belloc referred had been dismissed two weeks earlier in a letter to H.S. Mackintosh as nothing worse than a bad case of influenza. 'I've had flu badly & I'm not recovered yet, worse luck.'[29] He was more candidly forthcoming in a letter to Charlotte Balfour two days later.

All my life I have been so strong in body and mind that with this *défaillance* I feel like another person – like a sheep or a wet rag. I cannot recognize myself for being myself, but all misfortune has this good that it helps one to understand other people and their troubles.

Desmond [MacCarthy] took my place yesterday at a lecture which I was to have given for the Hospital. I was going to lecture on the breakdown of Art and Literature. But on account of my illness I could not do so. He lectured, oddly enough, on me, and, I am told, very flatteringly. He read out my poem on Wine and they all began to cry, which is Glory indeed. But to tell you the truth I am more keen on salvation now, and ultimate repose than Fame . . .

When we are young we are on adventure and seeking new things and often discovering the right, but when we know how the world is made and what a doom there is on all and what mortality means, we are concerned rather with avoiding the things oppressive and difficult.[30]

He also confessed to Charlotte Balfour that he thought himself twice near death during the illness, prompting him to go through all his private papers 'in case I should be cut off suddenly'. His recovery, however, was swift and, apparently at least, complete. By the end of April he was putting the finishing touches to his biography of William the Conqueror and, a month later, was working on his life of Charles I. If, as he clearly believed, his illness had been the result of overwork, he was doing precious little to prevent further relapses.

The return to health inevitably meant a return to vigorous physical activity. He sailed across the Channel to France at the end of July, only days before his sixty-third birthday, informing his son-in-law that he 'found everybody there peaceful [?] & laughing at the mad German'.[31] The 'mad German' was, of course, Hitler, who had become Chancellor of Germany in January and had engineered the burning of the Reichstag a month later.

As was customary, Belloc spent Christmas 1933 at King's Land with his children and grandchildren. As was also customary, Father Vincent McNabb spent Christmas with the Bellocs, saying Midnight Mass for the family in the small chapel upstairs. The grandchildren remained a great source of delight and consolation. Marianne Jebb, now Sister Emmanuel Mary of the Canonesses of St Augustine, remembered Belloc taking her to Mass at West Grinstead church, with her brother Philip. She also remembered him visiting her at her school at Westgate-on-Sea, near Ramsgate in Kent, travelling there by train and taxi. She recalled his 'small little footsteps' as he took her out to a café. He bought her an ice cream and asked her whether she would like another before walking her back to school. Sister Emmanuel Mary believed that this would have been in 1935 or 1936 when she was about 11 or 12 years old, but a letter to her father, written by Belloc on 12 July 1934, suggests that it was a year or two earlier. 'I saw Marianne yesterday, and Hester Balfour. Marianne was blooming! We went out together, and she had an ice. We also looked at the sea, and I was shown over the convent and its delightful garden.'[32]

Marianne also remembered how she was singled out as Belloc's grand-daughter whenever a priest or some other notable visitor arrived at the school, which was run by Ursuline nuns. 'It was a feather in their cap.' At the time, she complained to her friends that such celebrity was embarrassing, but inside she was very proud. Many years later, when Marianne was visiting her parents' grave, her brother Philip asked her: 'Can you remember how grandpapa loved you?' The question prompted feelings of guilt. 'I hadn't loved him back enough.'[33] Another of the Belloc grand-children to be educated at Westgate, Zita Caldecott, the daughter of Peter and Stella Belloc, remembered that Belloc had told the nuns to stop forcing her to write with her right hand. 'If God has made her left-handed, leave her be,' he told them, much to Zita's delight.[34]

On 4 August 1934, three weeks after his journey to Westgate to visit Marianne, Belloc met his daughter-in-law, Stella, and her children at Paddington station. He took them by cab to a restaurant for lunch and then to the zoo.[35]

Belloc might have gained consolation in the hopes for the future enshrined in his grandchildren, but his heart still pined for his past life with Elodie. 'Tomorrow (Friday) is the Day of the Dead when we have an early Mass for Mamma at West Grinstead,' Belloc reminded his son on 31 October 1934.[36] The reminder was scarcely necessary. Every year, on All Souls' Day, the same early Mass was offered for the repose of Elodie's soul at the small village church in which she was buried.

Apart from the perennial sense of loss and loneliness, there was also the perennial presence of poverty, the combined effects of which prompted Belloc, in November, to invite his daughter and son-in-law, and their children, to move into King's Land.

> I do want you to consider my proposal that you and Eleanor should be under this roof as your own after Christmas. Edith is leaving me early in December, with her husband: I am selling my car; I shall be alone while I am here, and I have to be a great deal away, often for many weeks at a time. If you and Eleanor could take over the house ... with your children round you, it would be an inestimable boon to me ...
>
> And I ought to add that this arrangement would be a very great advantage to me materially. I cannot run the household myself and I have no desire to do so: I shall not be earning as much as I have in the past few years, I am (as I said) selling my car, and if I may have the occasional use of yours to go to the station and back it will be one very great lowering of expense. So will a dozen other items which, shared under one roof, halve expenditure.

The letter concluded, pathetically, with a confession that the only alterna-tive was a future consumed with loneliness. In the past, he had always been the master of King's Land. 'But all that is changed now; my old age is upon me ...'[37]

Reginald Jebb readily accepted Belloc's offer. He was himself in some financial difficulty after the failure of the Catholic prep school he had tried to establish and was as relieved as his father-in-law at the lowering of expenditure. Consequently, in January 1935, Belloc could write that he now had 'not only all my grandchildren . . . here, but five cats also under my roof . . . and the two little kittens who are useful for the young grandchildren. Kittens and children go together like strawberries and cream . . . That again is innocence, on which for my part I lay great store. I have always wanted to recover my own . . .'[38]

No sooner had the Jebbs arrived at King's Land than Belloc departed for one of the most extensive journeys he had made for many years. Between February and May 1935 he travelled to the United States, Cuba, Spain and Palestine. 'I always like being in America, and find it most amusing,' Belloc wrote to his son from New York on 27 February. 'The newspapers tell one very little about Europe. The similarity of the language makes them sometimes talk about England as though they knew it better than other countries, but it is just as foreign to them as all the others. The real gulf is between Europe and the United States, and not between the different European nations.'[39]

Two months later, having lectured extensively in the United States, he arrived in the Holy Land, visiting Nazareth, the Sea of Galilee, Bethlehem, and finally Jerusalem where, on pilgrimage to the Church of the Holy Sepulchre, he bought his granddaughter a rosary.[40]

For all his intermittent bouts of ill health and his complaints that he was becoming too old to work, Belloc continued much as before. 'I should not do much lecturing,' he had written to his daughter on board the MS *Lafayette, en route* for the United States on 13 February. 'I am too old for it.'[41] Yet, in blatant contradiction or defiance of his own words, he would boast in a letter to his son three months later that he had made 'two crossings of the Atlantic and all the Mediterranean both ways – 10 thousand miles of sea' and that he had been 'lecturing and writing nearly all the time' in places as diverse as New York, Boston, Philadelphia, Washington, Baltimore, Miami, Nassau, Vigo, Bayonne, Pau, Marseilles, Cannes, Naples, Messina, Athens, Constantinople, Aleppo, Antioch, Tripoli, Beirut, Damascus, Nazareth, Jerusalem, Bethlehem, Haifa, Foggia, Bari, Pescara, Ravenna, Vicenza, Milan and Lucerne, 'and it is not over yet'.[42]

If Belloc's recovery from a series of minor strokes was little short of remarkable, the two friends with whom he was portrayed by Gunn in *Conversation Piece* were faring less well. Maurice Baring had been struck down by the onset of the Parkinson's disease that would eventually kill him and would publish his last novel, *Darby and Joan*, in 1935. Over the next 10 years, increasingly incapacitated by the debilitating effects of his illness, he would cope heroically with the inexorable decline in his health. His bravery in these years was encapsulated by 'a friend', probably Lady Lovat, in a letter to *The Times* shortly after his death.

> ... it was his faith that inspired the courage which withstood all the suffering and physical humiliation of his last years. Never – even when he grew very weak and his mind sometimes wandered – was he known to utter a word of complaint; and in such fortitude as his there surely is something given that pays the ransom of the world. Life never became a habit with him, it was always a miracle; the inevitable was accepted by his unfailing qualities of gentleness and strength.[43]

The key, perhaps, to Baring's fortitude in the face of suffering could be found in the words of a character from *Darby and Joan*: 'One has to accept sorrow for it to be of any healing power, and that is the most difficult thing in the world ... A Priest once said to me, "When you understand what accepted sorrow means, you will understand everything. It is the secret of life."'

Chesterton's health was also beginning to suffer. At the beginning of 1936 he was too ill to work. There was a partial recovery, but he found his weekly journalistic commitments more of a struggle and any remaining energy was expended in the writing of his *Autobiography*. He died on 14 June 1936. On the day of his funeral the church in Beaconsfield was filled to overflowing with his friends and admirers. Those in attendance included Max Beerbohm, Eric Gill, D.B. Wyndham Lewis, Aldous Huxley, Fulton J. Sheen, Douglas Woodruff, Desmond MacCarthy, Ronald Knox, E.C. Bentley, Frank Sheed, Maisie Ward, Vincent McNabb, Thomas Derrick, Émile Cammaerts, C.C. Martindale, Ignatius Rice, A.G. Gardiner and, of course, Hilaire Belloc.

Maurice Baring, unable to attend because of his own illness, wrote several letters to Chesterton's widow which were almost illegible. 'Too paralysed with neuritis and "agitance" to hold pen or pencil ... All my prayers and thoughts are with you. I'm not allowed to travel except once a week to see doctor, but I'll have a Mass said here.'[44] The following day he wrote again. 'There is nothing to be said, is there, except that our loss, and especially yours, is his gain? ... O, Frances, I feel as if a tower of strength had vanished and our crutch in life had broken.'[45] The same intense desolation was felt by Belloc, who was found after Chesterton's funeral weeping tears of disconsolate isolation into a pint of beer outside the Railway Hotel in Beaconsfield.

'I am finishing a story,' Chesterton had written in his *Autobiography*, 'rounding off what has been to me at least a romance, and very much a mystery-story . . . But for me my end is my beginning, as Maurice Baring quoted of Mary Stuart . . .' For Belloc, weeping into his beer, Chesterton's death marked not so much the end of the beginning, but the beginning of the end.

TWENTY-NINE

The Last Rally

OLLOWING CHESTERTON'S DEATH, Belloc agreed to take over the editorship of *G.K.'s Weekly*, the magazine that Chesterton had edited since 1925. Belloc informed his son Peter of his 'anxious work' for the magazine and requested articles from him. 'Send us short stuff ... under whatever pen name you use. We pay nothing: I get nothing: we all are in the soup: but it's great fun. Bevan [Wyndham Lewis] and Johnny [Morton] are both sending stuff & Maurice Baring some verse.'[1] Contributions were also secured from Evelyn Waugh, who wrote in his diary on 6 November 1936 that he had written 'free stuff for Belloc'.[2] Belloc discussed with his son-in-law, Reginald Jebb, a new column 'of extracts from the press and from public speeches' for the magazine. 'Not a bad title for the column would be "Fun"; then I could have a standing motto for it, "We hobble through this difficult world with the aid of two crutches, Fun and Beauty."'[3]

As with his editorship of the *Eye-Witness* 24 years earlier, however, Belloc's enthusiasm began to wane almost immediately. 'To add to my woes I have taken over Gilbert Chesterton's little weekly paper so as to try and keep it alive,' he wrote to Evan Charteris, complaining, 'I have to write about half of it myself.'[4] He wrote to Charteris again, five days later, detailing how much work without remuneration was required in keeping the paper afloat. 'I am sweating blood to get the little review really interesting and readable and to put it on its legs again, but ... there is not capital and no one is paid. I do it all for nothing. The great thing was not to let it die when Chesterton died.'[5] As with the *Eye-Witness*, Belloc relinquished the editorship of *G.K.'s Weekly* after only a year at the helm. His relief at off-loading the burden on to Hilary Pepler and Reginald Jebb was clear in a letter to Lady Phipps in September 1937. 'I am glad I am no longer responsible for *G.K.'s Weekly*. I promised to write for them regularly, but it's a magnet for cranks, has no capital and can hardly survive.'

In the same letter he spoke of the perennial threat of penury that loomed over the family finances.

> The trouble is that I get so fearfully tired nowadays. That American strain rather broke my back, but it was necessary to put the family in funds. In England I can earn nothing except by writing books, and that won't last for ever. Writing books, hack-work to order, is a most burdensome business: but as the newspapers won't take any stuff from me it is the only way of earning by my pen.[6]

These words were echoed in a letter to Carl Schmidt, written on 8 July 1936.

> I have often wished that I had had fortune and leisure in order that I might have reserved myself for the important matters only and not wasted the greater part of my life upon hack-work. But one always must remember that people of fortune and leisure hardly ever do any serious work at all – so perhaps it is just as well.[7]

He had put the matter more whimsically in the preface he wrote to Maurice Baring's *Dead Letters* in 1935. 'Well there it is. I will not go on writing, for criticism is not my trade; nor writing either, for that matter. I have been compelled to take to writing from early youth as a drowning dog with a brick round its neck is compelled to treading water; but I was never born for it.'[8]

In the letter to Schmidt, Belloc divided his work into two categories: 'hack-work which I do for a living and which is in expense of energy seven-eighths of the whole; and teaching work, which I do for the instruction of those who know less than I do. The latter of course brings in no money at all.' His writing of *An Essay on the Restoration of Property* fell into the latter category. Published by the Distributist League in 1936, this essay remains one of the most important and one of the most neglected of Belloc's works. As an accompaniment to his earlier work *The Servile State*, and as a volume to complement Chesterton's *The Outline of Sanity*, it represents a lucid exposition of the distributist creed. Its influence crossed the Atlantic, where it would inspire the work of Dorothy Day and Peter Maurin during the formative years of the Catholic Worker Movement.[9]

As the letter to Lady Phipps indicated, financial necessity forced Belloc to return to the United States early in 1937 to give a series of lectures at Fordham University in New York, which would be published later in the year by Cassell as *The Crisis of our Civilization*. On 25 February he wrote plaintively to Reginald Jebb that it was 'very difficult to get work done over here on account of the enormous amount of time taken up travelling. All the distances are so great, and involve great fatigue as well, which I am feeling more than I used to.'[10] On 9 April he wrote again to Jebb, this time giving his impressions of Hertford, Connecticut and explaining that he had been 'astonished to find that three quarters of the town was Catholic'.[11] He sent money home to alleviate the pecuniary position of his family, mailing 43 pounds and 10 shillings to his daughter-in-law on 11 March,[12] and also wrote affectionately to his granddaughter, Gabrielle.

> My darling little Gabrielle
>   Thank you so much for your nice letter! And tell Zita & Barbara from me how much I love them & how much I wish I had been home for Zita's birthday!
>   This town in which I am is 3,000 miles away from England and has very high houses indeed. I send you a picture of one house which is 35 stories high; and there is another which is more that 1,000 feet high! Taller much than the Downs at home!
>   It is sea all the way between where I am & England. The sea is called the Atlantic. I am coming across in a few days.
>   God bless you
>   from
>   Grand-papa[13]

The highlight of the visit was a private audience with the President, Franklin D. Roosevelt. 'I liked him,' Belloc reported to a friend on 15 April. 'He is intelligent and well-bred. Also he flattered me, and anyone who flatters me is my friend.'[14] 'He seems to me to have more integrity than most men and plenty of intelligence as well,' he wrote to Duff Cooper, 'and considerable knowledge of the past – which is a good test of a man's cultivation . . . I like him. I was closeted with him for over an hour and it was not wasted.'[15]

Belloc returned to England at the end of May, temporarily wealthier and temperamentally wearier than before he had left for the United States more than three months earlier.[16] On 27 July 1937, he celebrated his sixty-seventh birthday by sailing across the Channel to Ostend with his son and several other 'young men'. 'I am too old to go to sea in small boats that jump up and down. And every year I say I won't go again. And every year I go for a "once more" and I get stiffer and stiffer every time.'[17]

Politically, like many of his co-religionists, Belloc supported Franco in the civil war that was raging in Spain. In a letter to Reginald Jebb on 9 August he wrote contemptuously of 'the Red Government' and voiced his support for the pro-Franco stance taken by Arnold Lunn.

> Arnold Lunn gave a lecture on the Spanish Anti-Catholics with Lord FitzAlan in the Chair. He then went back to Cumberland Lodge, which is where FitzAlan lives in Windsor Park. When he got there he found the old Catholics, and especially Lady FitzAlan, cursing the Spanish Catholics so freely that he packed his bag and left the house. An amusing incident greatly to his credit.[18]

Since his reception into the Church, largely under Belloc's enduring influence, in July 1933, Lunn had become one of the most vociferous Catholic controversialists in the English-speaking world. In fact, although he would never match Belloc as a writer, he largely assumed his mentor's mantle as a robustly acerbic defender of the Faith. As Belloc's powers waned, and as he wearied of controversy, Lunn would take up the cudgels on behalf of the Church. It was little wonder, therefore, that Belloc could nod approvingly in Lunn's direction with an almost paternalistic mixture of amusement and pride.

Belloc's support for Franco in the Spanish Civil War did not indicate any sympathy for Hitler's regime in Germany. On the contrary, a visit to Berlin at the end of August 1937 only heightened his loathing for the Third Reich. He wrote to Reginald Jebb from the British Embassy on 30 August regarding an article on 'French Communism',[19] but it was the all-pervasive power of the Nazis that was uppermost in his mind as he surveyed life in Hitler's Reich. 'It is a blessing to be out of Germany,' he wrote to Jebb from Lucerne in Switzerland on 4 September, 'where the yelling & the tearing up & down of military cars is almost a more offensive nuisance than the all pervading despotism – which Germans adore, because they feel it their guarantee against a native sentimental chaos & because they vaguely hope for some future victory in arms: probably in Bohemia.'[20]

Belloc's impressions of Germany, fresh and bitter in his mind, were published in an article in the *Catholic Herald* on 24 September.

> Those who now govern (with despotic power) in Germany are convinced that what they would call 'Christianity' (a very vague term, but we all know what they mean) is disappearing so rapidly from the European mind, and particularly from the German mind, that what

is left is no more than an encumbrance to reaching the goal they have in view, which goal, as we all know, is the union of all Germans in one great State.

They have a religion, as indeed all men must have a religion, for men cannot live without something to worship. That religion is the worship of the German race as the highest thing on earth, and of what we can only translate as Germanism as the supreme human good.

First of all they would amalgamate into one body all those who are by speech and tradition capable of becoming members of such a State. Next they would trust to the power, not only in numbers but in morals, intelligence and technical achievement, of such a State to dominate the world. It is not fair to say that they clearly envisage wars of conquest, but it is understood that they take the ultimate supremacy of this ideal German state of theirs for granted!

Having left Germany, Belloc spent some weeks in Italy and France before returning to England. In early December he was back in France, 'lecturing at the Sorbonne and to the rich in clubs',[21] and writing to his daughter Elizabeth that he was making progress on his study of Louis XIV, which would be published in 1938.[22] Other books published that year, the last in which his pen would work so productively, included *The Great Heresies*, *Return to the Baltic*, *The Question and the Answer*, *The Case of Dr Coulton* and, last but not least, a new edition of his *Sonnets and Verse*, which contained additional poems, previously unpublished or uncollected, the most notable of which were 'Twelfth Night', 'The Islands', the 'Ballade of Illegal Ornaments', a host of new epigrams and several sonnets to Lady Diana Cooper.

The Case of Dr Coulton arose out of Belloc's long-standing duel with the historian Professor G.G. Coulton, a Fellow of St John's College, Cambridge. They had first met face to face in a hostile exchange of views at the Cambridge Union on 15 November 1924. Thereafter they had engaged in a bad-tempered game of controversial cat and mouse, each accusing the other of distorting history to suit their own prejudices. In bellicosity, Belloc had met his match in Coulton, of whom someone remarked that 'the law of correspondence with Dr Coulton is the survival of the rudest'.[23]

In October 1929, Coulton had concluded an attack on 'Mr Hilaire Belloc's Apologetics' with the accusation that his adversary was guilty of 'ignorance in its widest sense; *ignorantia affectata*, as the schoolmen called it, plays with him almost as conspicuous a part as the natural ignorance of a man who writes and talks so much that he has no real time for study'.[24] In the previous year they had crossed swords acrimoniously in *The Nation and Athenaeum* until Belloc had retired from the debate, wearied if not necessarily defeated. 'It is very kind of you to have sent me the proof of Dr Coulton's letter, which I return. I do not propose, myself, to add anything more to this interminable correspondence. I must also thank you for your courtesy in having printed so many letters of mine in connection with it.'[25]

The 'interminable correspondence' resumed in the pages of *The Universe* in March 1929 and continued sporadically thereafter. Its acrimonious climax was sparked off by a statement in the *Daily Telegraph* in June 1937 alleging that the early Church had permitted divorce and remarriage. Ronald Knox asked for documentary justification of such a claim and Belloc and Coulton were drawn into the ensuing debate. The controversy culminated in the publication of two pamphlets, *Divorce, Mr Belloc and 'The Daily Telegraph'* by Coulton, and *The Case of Dr Coulton*, Belloc's reply.

The personal nature of Coulton's assault on Belloc's reputation was epitomized by the following extraordinarily vindictive assertion.

> I have the unenviable distinction of having been first to descend seriously into his arena and to soil my hands with him. It is like taking a double-barrelled gun to a rat; but, when the creature is breeding, the job may be worth while. And Mr Belloc is indeed breeding: he bids fair, like Abraham, to become a father of many nations. Already a whole group of young Romanists have caught his spirit, and discovered how easy it is to flood the market with specious historical propaganda . . .[26]

It was rudeness of this sort that had prompted Belloc to write in *The Universe*:

> A fanatic is one whose hatred of another man's religion has made him lose all sense of proportion. In Mr Coulton's case this loss of balance has led him (as it usually does in the worst cases) to a loss of decent manners in debate . . . He has already called me a Welsher, an ape-man, a charlatan, a bully and a liar . . . I can hardly be expected to engage further with a man who has fallen into these habits of mind and speech.[27]

Belloc, however, could rarely resist provocation and Coulton's pamphlet prompted an instant riposte. He enjoyed writing *The Case of Dr Coulton* and derived great pleasure from 'the mixture of learning and insult which I hope I have achieved'.[28] 'It is amusing to chastise the insolent and this time he has got it good and hot,' Belloc informed a friend in September 1938.[29]

Coulton's principal tactic in debate was to wear his opponent down with a deluge of correspondence, telegrams and solicitor's letters, Belloc wrote, but in dealing with antagonists of this sort 'one should never let go. One should get them on the run and, having got them on the run, one should keep them on the run. But,' he added tellingly, 'it is an awful strain.'[30]

On 27 May 1938, having finished his act of vengeful catharsis, Belloc wrote with an air of evident satisfaction, verging on smugness, to J.B. Morton.

> I am sending you by this same post my pamphlet on Coulton. I hope it will amuse you. I have a higher opinion of it than I usually have of my own work. It seems to me learned, clear, and telling. I think he is bowled out. The great thing to remember in dealing with dons is that they think that people outside their own body are as ignorant as the unfortunate boys who are compelled to attend their lectures. They have no idea that critics with a wider range of experience can make fools of them and run rings round them. It is a very good thing to expose work of Coulton's kind because the great mass of people think that a thing has only got to come from a University to be revered.[31]

Coulton, of course, never conceded defeat. He never considered himself 'bowled out' by Belloc's pamphlet, nor that Belloc had run rings round him. Amid the insults were points of fact, alleged or otherwise, with which each bombarded the other. A few diligent scholars might have been prompted to check the sources that each of the adversaries wielded as weapons, but most of those who read the two pamphlets were content to be amused or horrified by the sight of two elderly men exchanging insults. It might not have been edifying, but it was certainly entertaining.

Belloc's battle with Coulton served as a welcome respite from the 'hack-work' that he found ever more loathsome and tedious. Four days after his triumphalist letter to Morton about the pleasure he had derived from writing *The Case of Dr Coulton*, he was writing dejectedly to his son about his efforts to finish his latest historical biography. 'I shall be immensely relieved when I have got through this horrible book on Louis

XIV. I never wanted to undertake such a hackneyed subject, which I have never properly read up, but the publishers will accept no other hack-work.'[32]

Amid Belloc's public battle with Coulton, and his private struggle with 'hack-work', events in the wider world were becoming ever more threatening. In March, the *Anschluss*, Hitler's occupation of Austria, had prompted Belloc to write an alarming – though in the light of subsequent events scarcely an alarmist – article for the *Catholic Herald*.

> Austria, taken as a whole, was the core and rallying point of Catholic influence among Germans. *On this account, more than any other, the survival of Austria was a stumbling block to the new despotism erected by Hitler and his little clique . . .*
>
> Therefore the interest of the latest developments in this rapid change, the interest of the fall of Austria and its occupation by the North German Government of Berlin and its spirit, lies in the heavy blow it delivers to the Catholic tradition among the Germans.

The Catholic youth of Germany, seduced by National Socialism, were falling away from the Faith of their fathers. The fall of Austria would further weaken the ability of the Church to counter the rise of Nazism: 'It is the older people who still strongly adhere to the Faith, and the younger people who have been swept off their feet by the new religion of race; that is, by the new religion of self-worship.'[33] The same pessimism was evident in a letter to Reginald Jebb, written from Paris on 2 August.

> The French have made up their mind that they cannot hope for serious reinforcement from England. They quite appreciate that all hope of creating a serious English Army must be abandoned . . . But it is a sad thing that people at home will not learn. One cannot live forever on bluff. The silence of the Press on the realities of our time is certainly astonishing. I don't suppose there has ever been anything like it in the past.[34]

Perhaps it was not altogether surprising, in the midst of such doom-laden thoughts, that Belloc began to lapse ever more frequently into reveries of wistful nostalgia. 'The number of people left now who remind me of my earlier life is getting less and less,' he wrote to a friend on 7 May 1938. 'I was only 45 *[sic]* when the war broke out and now I am not very far from 70 and the people who I had known when I was young are most of them gone . . .'[35] The same nostalgia was evident in a letter to Evelyn

Waugh on 13 June, although the wistfulness was tempered by Belloc's genuine delight in his young friend's latest satirical novel.

> My dear Evelyn,
>
>   I have just read 'Scoop'. It is very good! I have not read anything comic like that for heaven knows how long and I was grateful for it. It is even true that I laughed out loud eight or nine times. My opinion may be worthless or valuable according to two criteria. I read hardly anything outside that I have to read for my detestable hack-work. Therefore I am a bad comparer. On the other hand when I read anything I nearly always put it down again in two minutes because I cannot understand or value the things now printed in this country. Therefore if I not only understand but value your book it is an original emotion; and very strong ... I hope it has sold like a mill-race. It deserves to! ... I am going to Denmark where I hear the people are happy, if I find they are indeed so I shall be indeed enriched but I cannot believe that reputation to be true. I have known happy places in my life, but that was a long time ago and I thought that by this time they had all disappeared.[36]

Belloc was in Denmark and Sweden throughout late June and early July. It was the first time he had visited either country for 45 years and, as he told a friend upon his return, what he found 'most remarkable' was 'the striking increase of the difference between Sweden and Denmark' since his previous visit as an undergraduate with Lord Basil Blackwood in 1893.[37] The same letter, written on the morning of his return, already spoke of his plans for further trips abroad. He might, as he approached his sixty-eighth birthday, have grown tired of life, but he had clearly not grown tired of travel. The wanderlust remained, as insistent and as insatiable as ever.

In March 1939, following the death of Pope Pius XI, Belloc travelled to Rome for the coronation of his successor, Pius XII. He stayed for two nights at the English College, borrowing candles from his old friend Father H.E.G. Rope by which to read in the evenings,[38] before settling in a quiet hotel in Albano, south of Rome. The city was awash with writers sent by sundry press agencies and newspapers to cover the coronation, and Belloc mixed convivially in the company of Tom Driberg, Alfred Noyes and Hugh Walpole.[39]

He also met the poet Roy Campbell, and discussed with him the recent triumphs of the Nationalist forces in Spain. Both men were delighted that the British and French governments, on 27 February, had officially recognized the legitimacy of Franco's regime. Belloc had visited the battle-fields of the civil war shortly before his arrival in Rome, and had met General Franco, whom he described unequivocally as 'the man who has saved us all'.[40] Campbell had also visited the Spanish battlefields and his *Flowering Rifle*, a viciously satirical poem that combined an impassioned defence of Franco with an equally impassioned attack on his enemies, had been published on 6 February. Belloc had read and admired the poem, declaring with dogmatic bombast and dubious critical judgement that Campbell's other work would not count beside it in the long term. It is likely that Belloc had actually read very little of Campbell's previous work, and equally likely that he would not have made such a sweeping judgement had he done so. Campbell, however, was delighted at Belloc's praise and apparently unconcerned by such a casual dismissal of his other work. He wrote to his mother:

> I don't know if I told you, that in Rome Hilaire Belloc turned up (a wonderful old man!) . . . He is a very great writer and with Maurras and Daudet in France, and his friend Chesterton, they have all been forerunners of the Right movement. He thinks I have done a really good thing with *Flowering Rifle*, and that my other work will not even count beside it in the long run. His word is worth more than the whole of Fleet Street.[41]

The coronation of Pope Pius XII on 12 March impressed Belloc greatly. 'The crowd stretched all the way from St Peter's to the Tiber and beyond – just like a vast flood, and the inside of St Peter's was choc-a-bloc. One had to get up at half past four and the doors were open at six and the thing wasn't over until after one. But it was worth it.'[42] 'The Pageant was one of the finest things I have ever seen,' Belloc told Baring. 'It was perfectly astonishing! I am, indeed, glad I was there.'[43] The new Pope, whom Belloc had met many years earlier when, as Cardinal Pacelli, he had been secretary of state to the Holy See, was 'not only the obvious and the only possible' choice, 'but he is just what was wanted'.

> He has become holy in the course of years and he is a first-rate diplomatist. He is one of those people who can manage to get things done without offense [*sic*] and without friction. But the elements of the situation are lamentable. The German power can recruit itself now from numbers not far short of 100 million. The Italians are alienated, and the French political situation is deplorable.[44]

The portents of war that overshadowed the Pope's coronation were domi-
nating everyone's thoughts by the spring of 1939. 'This new German
monstrosity was brought into being by the Bank of England under the
orders of which our politicians also helped to build up the new Germany,
and now they must take the consequence,' Belloc opined to his daughter
from Paris on 23 March.[45] In other correspondence he wrote that Hitler
was 'touched with lunacy', that he was suffering from 'religious megalo-
mania' and that he was 'a lachrymose windbag'.[46] He was, however, more
ambivalent in his attitude towards Mussolini. As late as 4 August he could
still write that the Italian dictator was 'a very sane and well-balanced
man',[47] whereas four months earlier he had lamented the 'injustice and
folly of the anti-Jewish policy in Italy'.[48] Belloc was particularly concerned
for the future of Max Beerbohm, who lived in Rapallo with his Jewish
wife.

> I am particularly sorry for Max Beerbohm, of whom I am very fond,
> and who was so well fixed at Rapallo where he had counted on
> finishing his old age in a good climate and at peace with his admirable
> wife. I have often told you about her. She was a Miss Cohen, a Jewish
> actress, high Anglican, I gather, in religion, like Max's own sister.[49]

On 12 May, Belloc wrote to congratulate his daughter Elizabeth on the
publication of her poem 'Four Rivers' in a recent edition of the Jesuit
journal *America*. 'It is a frightfully good poem! . . . write as much verse
as you can.' He also alluded to his own work on a study of Charles II,
which would be published the following year as *The Last Rally*. He was,
however, finding the lack of 'leisure or quiet' an obstacle to his work. 'It
is much easier to write abroad than in England . . .'[50]

Evidently frustrated at the endless distractions, Belloc travelled to Paris
to finish the book. The heat was 'appalling, with the thermometer hovering
round 90 for days, which makes the narrow streets hardly habitable and
the broad avenues worse still'. Yet, as he told his son Peter on 8 June, he
had succeeded in doing a great deal of work.

> I am just finishing an enormous amount of work which I have done
> more easily because, here in Paris, I am cut off from all interruption.
> I have a little, very cheap room from which I sally out, working all
> day dictating and correcting my manuscript, which grows apace. My
> history book, which has to be delivered shortly, is thus piling up
> quickly under my hands, and that is a great relief to me, because I
> had got it rather into arrears. It is about Charles II, and the main

object is to undo the horrible lies of our official history on him and the whole of his period. It was the moment when the English people lost their land and their independence as private owners and what was left of their religion, but nobody has ever been told this. They are only told that it was a glorious period of enlightenment and liberty.[51]

Not for the first time, although almost for the last, Belloc's efforts to counter and correct the 'official' history of England had become a personal crusade against falsehood, real and alleged. He seemed, in old age, as indomitable as he had been in youth. Certainly, as he approached his seventieth year, he appeared as irrepressible as ever. Appearances, however, can be deceptive. Never again would he write so prolifically; never again would he raise his head above the parapet in bad-tempered controversy. In fact, the title of his study of Charles II, *The Last Rally*, was as appropriate to the author as it was to his subject. Belloc was rallying his own creative forces for the last time. With the commencement of the Second World War in September 1939, he would effectively take his bow and leave the field to others. Although the world did not know it, and although, indeed, it had more pressing matters with which to concern itself, it was witnessing Belloc's Last Rally. His exit, however, would be slow and protracted. Old Thunder was not about to die, but he would begin to fade away.

THIRTY

Decline without Fall

WITHIN DAYS OF THE OUTBREAK of the Second World War, Belloc returned to an old war of his own. H.G. Wells had claimed in his latest book that he remained 'puzzled' by Belloc's adherence to the Catholic Faith. Belloc replied with an open letter to Wells, published in *The Universe* on 15 September. He began:

> It seems (unless I misunderstand the reviewers) that you cannot understand how a man can be of my sect or persuasion (or whatever term you use in connection with religion) if he have enough intelligence to be what you call a 'scoffer' – that is, I suppose, a person who laughs at shams – and capable of appreciating evidence and rational processes of thought.

Belloc proceeded to dissect Wells's materialism along much the same lines as he had adopted many years earlier, but his overall tone was amicable and devoid of the acrimony that had soured their previous conflict. Certainly, the near serenity of his approach, tinged with only the slightest hint of sarcasm, was very much at variance with the wounding bitterness of his attacks on Professor Coulton in the previous year. Perhaps Belloc's softer tone was aimed at securing some sort of reconciliation, because, in the words of his daughter, he was 'genuinely sorry that he hurt Wells and would have liked to put the personal side to rights'.[1] The more conciliatory approach to Wells was evident in a letter to Baring two years later. Discussing Wells's 'defects', Belloc wrote that his old enemy had 'a clear mind and a first rate clarity of style'.

> But he knows hardly anything yet wants to think that he knows all that there is to know. This seems to be a common defect in those who have been bred up on physical science. And I think the reason is that physical science tells one a lot of facts, but nothing else ... He can explain quite clearly something which he has been

dogmatically taught – such as a third rate materialism of modern English physical science, but he can't explain the problem let alone the solution of the religious appetite in mankind . . . But he is most sincere and straightforward, and his vanity does not offend me for I think it natural for men who have had certain successes to be vain.[2]

The wistful desire to reconcile differences and rectify wrongs was also present in a charming essay Belloc wrote for the *Sunday Times*, 'On New Years & New Moons', published on New Year's Eve 1939.

A New Year has this useful thing about it . . . it makes man remember and regret his follies and his sins. Never forget the great saying that when a man comes towards the end of the downward slope and sees before him the open gates of the marble tomb, he finds on either side of him two groups of companions. They talk to him continually and leave him no peace: on the right side his follies; on the left his sins. If we did not become familiar and conversant with these ultimate companions we should make very poor wayfaring with them at the end. And as, before the end, we lose all other friends and fellowships, let us at least be conversant with these and learn to know them each by name . . .

On 4 January 1940 Belloc's article 'The Test is Poland' was published in the *Weekly Review*, as *G.K.'s Weekly* was now called. It was reminiscent in many respects of the sort of analysis he had written for *Land and Water* in the previous war, a beguiling cocktail of military history and contemporary politics.

A free and sufficiently independent Polish state is the condition of civilized Western influence in Central Europe. It is the necessary counterbalance to the Prussian spirit . . . If history were taught among us; if our governing class were given in youth some general idea of what Europe is, of how Europe arose and how Europe may die – or were even made to understand that England is a province of Christendom and of Europe and that, with the failure of the West, England quite certainly goes under – the essential importance of Poland at this moment would be grasped by those who conduct our destinies . . .

The 'resurrection of Poland' was, Belloc insisted, the 'one central criterion of value and success': 'The determination to save Poland, which is a determination not only to defeat Prussia but to oust the vile and murderous Communism of Moscow, is the moral condition of victory. If we waver we are lost.'

On 11 February, in the course of a review of *The Last Rally* in the *Observer*, Arthur Bryant praised Belloc's achievements, comparing him favourably with the most illustrious of his contemporaries.

> Mr Belloc is the most versatile of all living prose writers. Now that Hardy, Kipling, Galsworthy, and Chesterton are dead, he is unquestionably one of the three or four greatest. But unlike Mr Wells and Mr Shaw he has always taken the unpopular view of the problems of his age. His readers have probably never been a tenth as numerous as Mr Wells's. After his death the reverse may become true. Like Chesterton he may come to be remembered as a prophet and a man in advance of his age, while Mr Wells ... will almost certainly be neglected for having been so peculiarly well attuned to the intellectual and social fashions of his own day. For these, like all their forerunners, will presently be outmoded and pass.

For an article that was ostensibly a book review, Bryant's words read peculiarly like an obituary. Paradoxically, even as he was being lauded as 'a man in advance of his age', Belloc was being seen as a remnant of an earlier age. 'Old Belloc looks so much aged, I was quite surprised,' wrote the poet and artist David Jones in early August. Jones, one of Belloc's young disciples from the previous war, had not seen him 'for some years' and was shocked by his physical decline.[3] On 24 April 1940 Belloc wrote to a friend:

> It is all due to Old Age, which is, I do assure you, the most horrible lingering (and incurable) disease ever pupped or calved. It's funny that the books lie so horribly about it! To read the books one would think that old age was a lovely interlude between the pleasures of this life and the blaze of Beatitude. The books represent Old Age seated in a fine old comfortable dignified chair, with venerable snowy locks and fine, wise, thoughtful eyes, a gentle but profound smile, and God-knows-what-and-all! But the reality is quite other. Old Age is a tangle of Disappointment, Despair, Doubt, Dereliction, Drooping, Debt, and Damnable Deficiency and everything else that begins with a D.[4]

There seems little doubt that the Nazi invasion of France had hastened Belloc's decline. J.C. Squire told Edward Marsh that he had seen Belloc twice in 1940, 'first just before and then just after the collapse of France'. The second time, according to Squire, 'he looked 20 years older'.[5] According to Eleanor Jebb, the fall of France was the cause of the stroke that would effectively end Belloc's ability to work.[6] This, however, might be overstating the case. The stroke would not come until January 1942, fully 18 months after the French collapse. Certainly Belloc seems to have taken the devastating news of the French capitulation with a degree of stoicism, continuing, outwardly at least, much as before.

A young trainee nurse, Teresa Brading, who came to stay at King's Land for a couple of weeks in 1940, recalled Belloc as 'a kind and gentle man, very sad at times and beginning to become rather eccentric. With the loss of his wife . . . and then seeing his much loved France fall to the Germans . . . I think was all too much for him . . .' She recalled his spending 'long hours in his study' before emerging at four o'clock each day for his tea, which consisted, typically, of a light meal 'and a bottle of French red wine'.[7] His granddaughter Marianne Jebb recounted with fondness his nightly routine when he was at home at King's Land.

> Every night when going upstairs to bed, he would call in to the little chapel, only the length of a corridor away from his bedroom, to say his night prayers. Some nights my brothers and I were in the darkening garden, shutting the chickens up or some such, and I remember so vividly seeing his bearded old face through the uncurtained chapel windows, lit up by a candle, bent in prayer. As he made his way along to his bedroom, passing the door of his dearly loved wife . . . he would stoop and kiss it gently. I don't think we youngsters appreciated these gestures until we grew older.[8]

A less gentle Belloc was recalled by his grandson Anthony Jebb, now Dom Philip Jebb of Downside Abbey, who remembered his grandfather waving his blackthorn stick menacingly and driving off a platoon of soldiers who, in the summer of 1940, had started putting up a barbed-wire entanglement at the end of the vegetable garden at King's Land without first seeking permission.

> And woe betide anyone (usually some unwary French-Canadian soldier from camp in the woods around Knepp Castle) if he was found sitting in Elodie Belloc's pew in the church at West Grinstead: he would get a sharp rap over the legs as he was driven forth with that ever-present blackthorn. Then would come the creaks and groans as he settled into his place and followed the Mass in an immense Roman missal (which must once have had its place on an altar), muttering the responses half under his breath in those Tridentine days when only Dutch Modernists would have dreamt of a dialogue Mass.[9]

In spite of the fall of France, Belloc remained optimistic about the prospects of an Allied victory – a view which few, perhaps, would have shared in the dark days between the evacuation of Dunkirk and the victory of the Royal Air Force at the Battle of Britain. 'I believe the Boche *has* decided against invasion,' he wrote to his daughter-in-law on 3 August 1940, '& what is more we shall henceforward bomb him harder & harder – which is cheerful news. The Boche was a silly ass to take on this war – but then he always was a silly ass.'[10] Possibly these sentiments were little more than the products of wishful thinking, but even so, they would prove prophetic in the long term. In the short term, however, it was 'the Boche' who was bombing harder and harder. 'I was appalled at the sight of London after 10 days absence,' Belloc wrote to a friend on 16 October, shortly after the start of the Blitz.[11] Three days later, an edition of *Picture Post* carried an 'Open Forum' feature entitled 'Should We Have an Alliance with Russia?' Pat Sloan, a leading communist propagandist, argued to the affirmative while Belloc, on the facing page, replied in the negative: '. . . the Communist political idea is no different from the Nazi idea. It is our deadly enemy.'[12]

Belloc suffered a further setback towards the end of 1940, the impact of which probably hastened his decline in health as much as had the defeat of France. He had been contributing a weekly article for the *Sunday Times* on the military situation, similar in intent although not always as successful in execution as those he had written for *Land and Water* in the previous war. He found the commitment onerous, since it entailed him being in London every Friday night to finish his article and necessitated an overnight stay so that he was available on the following morning to read it over prior to it going to press. He complained that he 'had to deal with millionaires and idiots' and that, unlike 'the *Land and Water* days of the Great War', he had no control himself but had to 'consider others who control, and are incapable of intelligent control'.[13] Nonetheless, he was dependent on these articles for a great part of his income and was devastated when he was told that the contract was being terminated. 'The articles in the *Sunday Times* have come to an end!' he informed Elizabeth Herbert:

> And those in *Truth* are under notice to end in a few days. As those two papers were all the work I had and provided for my various families and dependents . . . I am suddenly plunged into the Consommé or Bisque: a cheerful prospect! . . . Do you think I can ever get back to writing legibly again? I doubt it! As life goes on – especially these last two years – frailties increase and faculties decline.[14]

In the 'sudden and total disappearance' of his income, there is a sense that Belloc saw himself facing a penurious abyss, 'for there is no prospect of any income whatsoever ahead'.[15] On 3 December, his sister Marie found him 'rather mournful' over the loss of the contract with the *Sunday Times*. 'He is very feeble,' she wrote to her daughter, 'which distresses me.'[16] On 16 December, Belloc lamented to his daughter over the lost contract, stating bitterly that 'they wouldn't renew it because they said they – which means the London suburbs – wanted something more cheerful!'[17] In similar vein, he wrote to another friend on 28 December that 'the *Sunday Times* told me they couldn't print me because I was not gay enough'.[18]

In desperation, Belloc was forced to return to the despised 'hack-work'. He gained a commission to write a book on Elizabeth Tudor, 'the wretchedly unhappy Queen of England',[19] which, as *Elizabethan Commentary*, published in 1942, would be the penultimate book from his pen. He was also destined to write one last poem of merit, inspired by the tragic death of Lady Lovat's daughter Rose Fraser, aged 14, in August 1940. 'I think continually of Rose,' Belloc wrote to Lady Lovat on 28 January 1941. 'I have always believed that thinking continually of those in beatitude is a sign of communion with them.'[20] His short poem to 'Rose', privately printed in 1942, would not only be his final word in verse, but one of his finest. Its sweet simplicity and unsaccharined sentimentality served as a fitting swansong.

According to Robert Speaight, the French collapse 'broke one half of Belloc's heart'.[21] The other half was broken on 2 April 1941 by the death of his son Peter, who was on active service with the Royal Marines. Dorothy Collins, Chesterton's former secretary who had once again taken on some light secretarial work for Belloc, was staying at King's Land when news of his son's death was brought to him by Father Riley, the parish priest at West Grinstead. Outwardly, the dreadful news was accepted stoically. 'There is nothing to be said and nothing to be done,' he told J.B. Morton when he arrived with his wife to offer his condolences on the following day. 'His command over himself was complete, and this added to our own distress,' wrote Morton. 'It required little effort of the imagination to realize his desolation.'[22] 'It is an awful blow & must be endured as best one may,' Belloc wrote to his daughter Elizabeth on 3 April.[23]

Peter Belloc was buried beside his mother, with full military honours, at West Grinstead church. During the interment, Belloc stood a little apart from the rest of the mourners, stricken and silent in his grief. 'It is a fearful thing this sacrifice of these young lives solely to satisfy Prussian vanity,' he wrote to Elizabeth. 'We are paying a fearful price for that ididic [sic] policy of supporting Prussia for so many years!'[24] Belloc had certainly paid a fearful price personally, losing his eldest and his youngest sons in the two wars against Prussia. His daughter Eleanor told J.B. Morton that it was after the death of his youngest son that he began to lose his memory, sometimes confusing Peter with Louis.[25]

Marie Belloc Lowndes was deeply concerned by the creeping senility with which her brother was afflicted. 'I am very unhappy about H.,' she wrote to Morton. 'I think Peter's death dealt him a mortal blow.'[26] Similar concerns were expressed in a letter to her daughter.

> Uncle H. left today ... He lives in a world so remote from reality, and has no idea of what people say, believe, and invent. Nothing will change him, of course. He is quite unaware how famous, in a sense, he is, both here and in America, and the interest taken in his personality. Did I tell you that three separate Americans went to La Celle to see the place and ask questions about him.[27]

In early June 1941 he suffered a further minor stroke, resulting in a good deal of confusion – including the apparent loss of a manuscript. 'I have had a disaster in the way of manuscript,' he wrote to Maurice Baring.

> The whole of my MSS of Elizabeth Tudor, called *Elizabethan Commentary* has disappeared! I had two days black-out while I was at Oxford, forgetting both what I had done and what I had to do and when my memory became more normal I was still blank about half the things I ought to have done. I have written to various places such as the Union and Balliol where I might have left it, but no trace of it. The loss is really serious, not only because three years' work has disappeared, but also the bulk of current income.[28]

The manuscript was eventually recovered and the book was duly published in the following year, but the latest stroke shook Belloc's fragile health still further and was an ominous foreshadowing of the near-fatal stroke that would soon follow.

A broken man, Belloc now began, as never before, to fear for himself, for the surviving members of his family, and for his home. 'Winston Churchill has just made a speech in which he tells us that the enemy will fall upon us in gigantic numbers. This has alarmed me a great deal. I am naturally timid and my dear home is within short range of the south coast, as you know.'[29] These words, written in June 1941, contrasted dramatically with the defiant and fearless optimism of his letter to his daughter-in-law 10 months earlier in which he had mocked the 'Boche' contemptuously and dismissed the idea of a German invasion. Rarely would he recover the tempestuously irrepressible spirit and the consoling *joie de vivre* that had been his mainstay in the past. The old Belloc had passed away, buried without fuss with the body of his son. All that remained were fragmented and fragmentary memories of a fading past.

His increasing senility meant that any flashes of insight were coloured as never before by his theological and historical obsessions. When Belloc's daughter visited Father John O'Connor – Chesterton's old friend who had been the original inspiration for the character of 'Father Brown' – in Yorkshire in July 1941 she had taken the opportunity to visit the home of the Brontë sisters in Haworth. 'The Brontës,' Belloc told her, 'were the special fruit of Calvinism, a philosophy which profoundly affected the less happy of the Victorians . . . It is astonishing what can be accomplished by one man's writing! Calvin introduced a sort of diabolism into European thought which has done a great deal of work and all to the bad.'[30]

The deteriorating state of Belloc's health and the death of his son cast a gloomy shadow over the birthday party organized in his honour at the Savoy Hotel on 29 July that year. Duff Cooper was in the chair and Desmond MacCarthy proposed the toast,[31] but those present could not help but compare the relative sombreness of the occasion with the rumbustious party 11 years earlier. According to H.S. Mackintosh, the only redeeming feature was 'a brilliant speech by Duff Cooper'.[32] Reginald Jebb was not even mollified by memories of Duff Cooper's speech, declaring that 'the few formal speeches' had 'none of the spontaneity and gaiety of 1930'.[33] Belloc himself walked up to the high table leaning on the arm of his son-in-law. He looked 'exceedingly tired . . . He made a short reply to Duff Cooper's speech in praise of his work, and then left early in the evening, as he was anxious to catch his train to Horsham. It was, I thought, a sad evening, and there were no songs. He seemed to have grown much older.'[34]

On 30 January 1942, Belloc suffered a stroke at the Reform Club and was discovered unconscious by Sir William Beveridge. He was brought back to King's Land on the following day and lapsed into a serious illness. At one point his condition was considered so grave that it was thought he would not survive the night. He received the Last Sacraments on 3 February. Such were the fears for his life that Marie Belloc Lowndes told Edward Marsh that he was dying.[35] Father Vincent McNabb was present at King's Land during the worst days of the illness, and Belloc's grandson

and granddaughter both recalled seeing him leaning over their grandfather, praying for him constantly and whispering '*sancte* Belloc' under
his breath.[36]

The path to recovery was tediously slow. Belloc was out of danger
after a week or so, but remained in bed until the end of April. When he
finally descended the stairs for the first time in almost three months, his
mind was confused and disorientated. He would never fully recover his
concentration or his grasp of current affairs, although the past retained
its potency.

By mid-May he was well enough to travel and began to make plans
to resume contact with his friends and family in various parts of the
country. 'I am going to pay some visits to the west and among them will
be a visit to you,' he wrote to his son's widow. 'Perhaps you will come
into Oxford with me. I always like going into that dirty and hypocritical
place because it reminds me of my youth.'[37] Possibly it was during this
visit that he met Barbara Wall and Auberon Herbert 'in a restaurant in
war-time Oxford', an encounter recalled by Wall. 'Belloc arrived in a
black cloak, large hat and in a bad temper. He refused all hospitality and
said all he wanted was a boiled egg for his supper.'[38]

For the most part, however, Belloc's dotage was not characterized by
cantankerousness but by blissfully oblivious mental re-enactments of his
past. He was never the same after his stroke, recalled J.B. Morton, 'but
the gaiety was still there and the good talk on every subject . . .'[39] Morton
visited Belloc most weeks in the final years of the war, picking him up
from King's Land by hired car and taking him into Horsham, normally
to the Black Horse, for lunch. Belloc's granddaughter Zita also retained
fond memories. 'I saw him through the eyes of a child and we led such
a sheltered life during the war that I grew up thinking that all grandfathers
were vastly entertaining, wrote funny verse and taught one music hall
songs. It was only when I went up to Oxford that I discovered how
colourless and quiet most people are!'[40] Another granddaughter, Marianne
Jebb, recalled an amusing incident that exhibited Belloc's generosity, as
well as his mental decline.

> Once during the war, when we were not very well-off, my mother
> had taken us out shopping in the car; as we were returning and there
> came into view the door of H.B.'s study that gave onto the garden,
> we saw that a gypsy had been asking him for financial help and H.B.
> was gradually handing out £1 notes. When my mother went quickly
> to see about the situation she found, to her horror, that he had already

given away £30! She became frantic, saying 'please give it back, he doesn't know what he's doing, he's had a stroke'. I understand my mother's reaction – but actually what I carried away deep in my young heart was his great and ever-present generosity.[41]

Lady Diana Cooper, to whom Belloc in healthier days had addressed several memorable sonnets, remembered him in the years after his stroke as being 'wonderfully detached from events of dread, still singing and discoursing and rollicking and concealing his Christ-like attributes'.[42] Such words, the fruits of fondness and friendship, erred on the side of charity. Yet, although Belloc was still capable of bellicose outbursts that were anything but Christ-like, his slow and inexorable decline was characterized for the most part by a growth in the virtue of patience. As his condition continued to deteriorate he coped, sometimes heroically, with his failing powers. His final years would see continuing decline but no significant fall.

THIRTY-ONE

The Fading

IN 1943 WINSTON CHURCHILL ASKED BELLOC if he would accept the Companionship of Honour. Belloc glanced down the list of those who already had it, rested his eyes on Astor, Attlee and Bondfield, and politely declined. As a man of honour, he had no intention of accepting such companions.[1] In the same year his friend and confessor Father McNabb died. In spite of his delicate health, Belloc insisted on travelling to London for the Dominican's Requiem. For many years the priest had travelled to King's Land each Christmas Eve, celebrating Midnight Mass in the small family chapel before slipping away 'very early, about three or four in the morning'.[2] The special place that he held in Belloc's heart was evident from a short tribute, 'To the Undying Memory', that Belloc wrote shortly after Father McNabb's death. It was, he said, 'astonishing . . . to have discovered so profound a simplicity united to so huge a spiritual experience'.

> I have known, seen and felt holiness in person. In that presence all other qualities sink away into nothingness. I have seen holiness at its full in the very domestic paths of my life, and the memory of that experience, which is also a vision, fills me now as I write – so fills me that there is nothing more to say. Men of this calibre are better known in their absence than in their presence. With that absence the rest of my life will, I think, be filled.

Across the chasm of the years, Belloc recalled one 'intimate personal experience' of the Dominican's holiness. 'Vincent McNabb was with me walking in our garden here in Sussex (which he knew so well!) on the chief occasion of my life, a moment, like all such moments, when the soul was in the presence of death and therefore of eternity.'[3] As he recalled the death of his wife almost 30 years earlier, and the consoling presence of the priest, he was recalling the greatest of all absences in his life, an absence that had filled the years with its silent presence.

The lucidity displayed in Belloc's valedictory address to Father McNabb would rarely be repeated. Seldom would he write again. Certainly there was no question of him emulating the example of Chesterton, who had taken his bow from literary life, shortly before his death, with the writing of an autobiography. Replying to an enquiry from an admirer on 22 June 1943, Belloc wrote that he had no intention of writing his own life.

> I should find it difficult to distinguish between personal matters and others; and I had better leave the whole thing alone. In my experience, people who write about themselves either say nothing worth hearing or tell the outside world too much. So I have never attempted an Autobiography and I don't think anyone has lost by the lack of it . . .[4]

The war, for the most part, was passing Belloc by. J.B. Morton recalled that it was the one subject on which he had lost all grasp of reality. He was, however, 'very badly shaken' when a fighter plane crashed in the grounds of King's Land, in the field that had once been the tennis court, only yards from the house. The dead pilot was carried into the house, reminding Belloc gruesomely of the horrors of war and perhaps haunting him with a vision of his long-lost son Louis, whose own plane had crashed in France a quarter of a century earlier. At other times, Belloc seemed positively to relish the proximity of danger. Arnold Lunn, visiting Belloc at King's Land in 1944, recalled a German bomber unloading as it fled from its pursuers. 'A stick of six bombs fell uncomfortably close with a curiously enlivening effect [on Belloc]. He leaped to his feet and lumbered through the door, and seemed disappointed that there was no further sign of action in the sky – for the plane had long since disappeared.'[5]

Although old friends – such as Ronald Knox, who spent a day at King's Land in 1944[6] – would occasionally visit Belloc in Sussex, his absence from the literary life of London was having a detrimental effect on his reputation. 'It is curious how certain men so famous *then* are forgotten now,' wrote Marie Belloc Lowndes to her daughter on 12 August 1944. '. . . Uncle Hilary never mentioned now. But his future place secure as a poet. His verse is *constantly* quoted in House of Commons, House of Lords, *The Times* and public speeches.'[7]

The increasing rarity of Belloc's visits to London was epitomized by a short feature in *The Universe* on 20 July 1945:

> Londoners saw Mr Belloc on Friday for the first time for nearly two years. He had left his country seclusion to honour the memory of

Cardinal Newman, the centenary of whose conversion was being celebrated by the Oratory School, his foundation.

Mr Belloc, now bearded and grey, is one of the school's most distinguished old boys. He attended the luncheon following High Mass at the Oratory, but he was not among the speakers.

The rare visits to London were treasured by his friends, but were marked by feelings of nostalgia for the vibrant Belloc of past years. Desmond MacCarthy wrote to the bedridden Maurice Baring in the summer of 1944 of a luncheon in Chelsea at which Belloc, after 'a glass or so' of port, had burst into song. He had sung with 'a voice perhaps a little less resonant ... but with the perfect rhythm and wagging of head and finger we remember so well. Wouldn't you like, Maurice, to have over again one of those luncheons at the Mont Blanc or elsewhere?'[8]

Baring's death in 1945 meant that Belloc, although the oldest, was the sole survivor of the triumvirate of writers immortalized by Sir James Gunn in *Conversation Piece*. J.B. Morton recalled that he and Belloc 'talked a great deal' of Baring's 'slow and edifying death'.[9] Belloc was particularly inspired by 'the strength and cheerfulness with which Baring bore his sufferings'.[10] Belloc's own sufferings were softened by senility. 'H.B. is very well but very aged & full of blessed forgetfulness,' Eleanor Jebb informed a correspondent on 20 August 1946.[11] His granddaughter Marianne Jebb recalled that, on the day she entered the priory of the Canonesses of St Augustine at Haywards Heath in 1945, Belloc had written her a cheque for five pounds. 'It was a very sweet gesture. I was very moved. He didn't connect that I was taking a vow of poverty. In his muddled mind he simply wanted to give me something.'[12]

A fascinating insight into Belloc's 'muddled mind' was provided by Hesketh Pearson and Hugh Kingsmill, who visited King's Land in June 1946. Belloc began by asking for 'news from town' before proceeding to denounce the dons and to bemoan his failure to secure a Fellowship more than half a century earlier. There followed a riotous procession of pithy put-downs of his contemporaries. F.E. Smith was 'superficial' – 'No brains. A politician.' Lloyd George was 'a little country solicitor who got on. Made a lot of money but didn't know how.' Kipling 'wrote trash' and, although he loved France, 'knew nothing about it. The ordinary English gentleman knows nothing about it, but Kipling knew less than nothing.' Gladstone also 'knew nothing' – 'Talked nonsense in a magnificent way. The official style of the period.'

There was also, however, some pithy praise as an antidote to the invective. Churchill was 'a genial fellow', although 'a Yankee, of course'. Asquith had a 'good, straightforward brain', although he 'knew nothing about France. No English politician does.' More surprisingly, perhaps, Shaw was praised as 'one of the kindest men alive ... Very generous to all kinds of persons one knows nothing about.' 'By the way,' he added, 'is it true that H.G. Wells is eighty years old? I can't believe it.' Wells, in fact, would die that year, disillusioned with his own scientific optimism, his mind at the end of its tether, but still as alienated from Belloc as ever. The enemies were never destined to be reconciled.

Belloc's re-emergent antagonism towards the Jews was the least pleasant aspect of the muddle-headedness. Oblivious, apparently, of the recent experience of the Jews in Europe, Belloc was still fighting the Dreyfus case of 50 years earlier. 'It was the Dreyfus case that opened my eyes to the Jew question. I'm not an anti-Semite. I love 'em, poor dears. Get on very well with them ... Poor darlings – it must be terrible to be born with the knowledge that you belong to the enemies of the human race.'

'Why,' asked Kingsmill, 'do you say that the Jews are the enemies of the human race?'

'The crucifixion,' replied Belloc.

If Belloc was still dogged by the ghost of Dreyfus, he was also haunted by the 'hack-work' that had been the bane of his life. This emerged in the short exchange that followed a question from Pearson about whether he was going to write an autobiography. 'No,' Belloc replied. 'No gentleman writes about his private life. Anyway, I hate writing. I wouldn't have written a word if I could have helped it. I only wrote for money. *The Path to Rome* is the only book I ever wrote for love.'

PEARSON: Didn't you write *The Four Men* for love?
BELLOC: No. Money.
PEARSON: *The Cruise of the Nona*?
BELLOC: Money.
KINGSMILL: I love the poetry in your essays, especially in the volume On Nothing.
BELLOC: Quite amusing. Written for money.
PEARSON: What profession would you have liked to follow?
BELLOC: I was called to the Bar. But what I wanted to be was a private gentleman. Lazing about doing nothing. Farm as a hobby, perhaps. Keep someone to run it.[13]

There was surely an element of deliberate self-parody in Belloc's terse dismissal of his life's work. The 'hack-work' that he had always found so irksome could not eclipse the many good works of literature that he had carved with his pen. He knew this to be the case, and must surely have been playing to the gallery and seeking to shock his audience. He was playing the wag, ragging his guests, and at the same time, no doubt, amusing himself. Even at its most muddled, Belloc's mind was capable of brilliant self-mockery.

In conversation with close friends, it was evident that he cared very much about his literary achievement. 'He talked sometimes about his work, and always said that he wanted his verse to endure,' recalled J.B. Morton. 'He thought a good deal about his verse, and was always wondering whether it would survive.'[14] 'I am distressed at not being able to finish my verse,' Belloc had written to Maurice Baring in 1941. 'There is still a good deal of it unfinished and I feel the time is short. Verse is the only form of activity outside religion which I feel to be of real importance: certainly it is the only form of literary activity worth considering.'[15] His grandson recalled Belloc looking at the bookcase full of his own works at King's Land and declaring, with heavy irony, 'What a fine fellow I am.'[16] In old age, overcome with nostalgia, he began to read his own books regularly, 'looking back on his vigour'.[17]

On 27 July 1947, his seventy-seventh birthday, there was, in the words of Eleanor Jebb, relaying the news to a friend, 'a swarming mass of a party here today with telegrams and general happy confusion!'[18] In this year Belloc lost his sister, who – in spite of writing bestselling crime stories and popular volumes of autobiography – had always lived in her brother's controversial shadow. Wilfred Meynell, whom Belloc had known since the late 1880s, died in the following year, just four years short of his hundredth birthday. Belloc was too ill to attend the funeral in Sussex. He was visited, however, by Barbara Wall, in the company of either Tom Burns or Father Ignatius Rice, who had decided to call on him on their way back to London from the funeral. Like many of his other friends who had not seen him for some time, they were shocked by the physical evidence of his decline. Wall recalled that he 'looked very old and dirty with food stains on his jacket'.[19]

Christmas 1948 was celebrated with the customary Dickensian festivity at King's Land. Around 40 villagers 'came to my father's Christmas Tree,' wrote Eleanor Jebb, 'and the turkey was glorious, so also the pudding to which we set fire after hot brandy had been poured over it. Everyone kept well & it seemed as if the Festival went on and on until I was dazed with cooking and washing-up!'[20]

In the summer of 1949, Belloc was once again having his portrait painted by James Gunn. This time, however, Gunn travelled to Sussex. Belloc sat in his favourite armchair, positioned by the fireplace, while Gunn worked. A short report in the 'Peterborough' column of the *Daily Telegraph* declared that the artist was 'pleased with his work and as greatly impressed as ever by the personality of his subject'.[21] For his part, Belloc thoroughly enjoyed Gunn's company while the portrait was being painted.[22]

Shortly after work on the portrait commenced, Belloc travelled to London to have lunch with Gunn, J.B. Morton and their respective wives. He was in fine form throughout the meal, but his friends were concerned by the air of uncertainty and confusion that overcame him after they drove him to Victoria station to catch his train back to Horsham.

> He was very tired and seemed overwhelmed by the noise and bustle of the station. He looked round him uncertainly, and stopped once or twice. We saw him into the train, and the guard who knew him well, made him comfortable. Though he was to be met at Horsham, we were alarmed at his helplessness, and at his obvious unfitness for journeys. I could not get used to that air of bewilderment.[23]

Gunn's portrait was unveiled at the Oxford Union by Duff Cooper on 30 November 1950. Its depiction of a sedate and stately old gentleman, staring solemnly at the viewer through the sadness of the years, was a stark reminder of the weary path travelled by Belloc since his fiery days as President of the Union 55 years earlier. The 'grizzlebearded' old man seemed distant in many ways from the Poet and the Sailor celebrated in *The Four Men*. Somewhere within, however, there remained 'Myself', infusing the trinity of Poet-Sailor-Grizzlebeard with a transcendent unity. The University of Oxford, which had spurned the Poet, was now happy to honour Grizzlebeard, and the unveiling ceremony was conducted with a degree of pomp and publicity. It received national newspaper coverage and the proceedings were broadcast by the BBC's Third Programme. Belloc was too frail to travel to Oxford himself, although several of his descendants were present.

In July of that year a glorious birthday party had been held at King's Land to celebrate Belloc's eightieth birthday. It contrasted happily with the sombreness of the party nine years earlier. Physically, Belloc had declined considerably in the intervening years, but his many friends were determined to make it an occasion to remember. H.S. Mackintosh, one of the guests, had the impression that there were 'several hundred' at the height of the party.[24] It was 'a beautiful summer day, and the party went on throughout the afternoon'.

> He greeted everyone with grave Gallic politeness, shaking hands and bowing slightly. He was always punctilious in such matters. But, in a moment when he was not surrounded, he asked testily: 'Who are all these people?' Someone answered: 'Your friends, Mr Belloc.' 'Nonsense! Who invited them?' 'I think most of them just came, Mr Belloc.' 'Damn fools! I can't understand what all the fuss is about – it's perfectly normal for a man to be eighty!' In spite of the exhaustion of meeting all these guests, he finished up the evening drinking wine and singing his favourite songs.[25]

A report in *The Tablet* described the party as 'an excellently arranged and very pleasant affair ... the patriarch ... receiving the guests, and later, singing his songs, and generally enjoying the lively party, and the guests mingling in and out of doors, taking refreshment under the trees, while the field across the lane gradually became a little car-park'.[26] Telegrams were received from the Apostolic Delegate, the Abbot of Downside, the Archbishop of York, the Bishop of Chichester and from Mr and Mrs Churchill. One of the guests, Douglas Hyde, the former leading communist whose conversion to Catholicism had been influenced to a large degree by Belloc's and Chesterton's writings, wrote movingly of his debt to the old man of Shipley.

> I have always been glad that I was among those privileged to be at Belloc's 80th birthday party and that I was able to use the opportunity to tell him that I was there to pay a debt to him.
>
> Indeed, one felt that almost everyone present on that memorable afternoon was there for the same reason. In a sense we were there for our own sakes more than his – to have the satisfaction of saying 'thank you' for help given.[27]

'That party got "out of hand"!' Eleanor Jebb wrote to a friend on 31 July. 'The glorious thing was that H.B. enjoyed it all. He sang all his songs at evening time to his grandchildren & us!'[28]

Belloc's songs were broadcast by the BBC at this time, performed by the young folk-singer and broadcaster Bob Copper. An admirer of Belloc since his childhood, Copper had written to Belloc to inform him of the impending broadcast, only to be crestfallen to receive a note from Eleanor

Jebb telling him that 'Mr Belloc never listens to the radio'.[29] If this was so, Belloc would also have missed Desmond MacCarthy's warm tribute to him as the 'most various of living authors', broadcast by the BBC Home Service to commemorate his eightieth birthday,[30] and also, presumably, the coverage of the unveiling of his portrait at the Oxford Union by the BBC Third Programme in November.

Domestically, Belloc rejoiced in the company of his grandchildren. In the summer of 1949 Peter Belloc's eldest daughter, Gabrielle Elodie, was married and in the following year his second daughter, Barbara, was also married. Belloc attended both weddings. Great-grandchildren followed and, thereafter, King's Land resonated with the cacophonous blend of four generations. The third of Peter Belloc's daughters, Zita Mary, brought her fiancé Andrew Caldecott to visit her grandfather at King's Land in 1950, and the two men discussed their shared interest in the campaigns of Napoleon.[31]

In August 1950, Anthony and Philip Jebb followed in their grandfather's footsteps, undertaking their own 'path to Rome' – although they took the easier option of travelling by car. 'Anthony and Pippa are revelling in Rome,' wrote their mother. 'They went in that ancient "Morris" and slept "rough" and washed in the Rhone! Anthony slept each night . . . in H.B.'s ancient fur-lined moth-eaten motoring coat!'[32]

Sadly, Julian Jebb, always something of a loner, failed to share the affection felt by his brothers for their grandfather. His jaundiced view has often been quoted to illustrate the less-flattering aspects of Belloc's dotage.[33] 'Julian Jebb was cruel to Belloc,' recalls Zita Caldecott. 'He wouldn't let him sit in the drawing-room. Julian was very strange. It wasn't Belloc's fault that he looked dishevelled and wore dirty shirts. He wasn't given a clean one! I considered Belloc saintly for the way he coped with all this.'[34]

Anthony Jebb, like his sister, followed a religious vocation, becoming a Benedictine monk at Downside and, as Dom Philip Jebb, would become headmaster of Downside School and Father Prior of the Abbey. Philip 'Pippa' Jebb became a successful architect. Julian Jebb worked for the BBC and made literary documentaries on figures such as Virginia Woolf. Tragically, and emulating the sorry example of Woolf herself, he took his own life.

Occasionally, Marie Belloc Lowndes's grandchildren would visit their great-uncle at King's Land, retaining memories of his 'big fuzzy beard', his singing and his complaints about the lack of wine.[35]

In December 1950, Malcolm Muggeridge, visiting King's Land in the company of Auberon Herbert, provided posterity with an evocative –

perhaps some would say provocative – portrait of the ageing Belloc in the pages of his diary.

> Belloc's house fairly roomy, but shabby, rather desolate ... Belloc came shuffling in, walks with great difficulty because he has had a stroke, inconceivably dirty ... mutters to himself and easily forgets what he said, heavily bearded, fierce-looking and angry ... Sucked on a pipe, said that he had been prevented from getting a Fellowship at Oxford because he was a Roman Catholic and against Dreyfus. This was sixty years ago, and it seemed very pitiful that such a grievance should survive so long. Wondered whether in old age I'd have such a grievance myself. Not at all a serene man. Although he has written about religion all his life, there seemed to be very little in him ... Reminded me oddly of Churchill ... the fearful wilfulness of the very old when they are not reconciled. The will still beating against the bars, and the strokes becoming more and more frenzied and futile as they become feebler ... thought of King Lear. Belloc occasionally hummed snatches of French songs, and then burst into what must have been a music hall song when he was young – 'Chase me girls, I've got a banana, oh what a banana!' This song pleased him hugely ... When his daughter and grandson were out of the room, he turned to Auberon and me and said: 'They're longing for me to die,' and then laughed gleefully ...
>
> At home found Bridget Lunn – very sweet, the exact opposite of Belloc, truly religious and gentle, intends to be a nun.[36]

Again, there is little doubt that Belloc was playing up to his audience, as he had done so provocatively when Kingsmill and Pearson had visited four years earlier. With strangers, or at least with those not counted as intimates, he seemed intent on behaving shockingly, an unattractive combination of incorrigible schoolboy and cantankerous octogenarian. Certainly the impression gained by those who witnessed his performance on such occasions was hardly sympathetic, as Muggeridge's candid account testifies.

Ironically, Muggeridge would eventually become a great admirer of Belloc after he, too, had reached old age. By that time, he had dropped the acerbic agnosticism that had animated his reaction to Belloc in 1950 and had been received into the Catholic Church himself. Thereafter, he was fond of quoting Belloc's religious aphorisms. A few years after his conversion, Muggeridge suffered several minor strokes which led to a condition known as multi-infarct dementia, essentially the same condition from which Belloc suffered in his final years, although in Muggeridge's case the condition was even more pronounced. It was, perhaps, an example of what Muggeridge would have called 'fearful symmetry' that his undignified dotage, lost in the mists of senile dementia, was so akin to Belloc's.

Father Paul Bidone, Muggeridge's friend and confessor, and the priest who received him into the Church,[37] was present both at Belloc's eightieth birthday party at King's Land and at Muggeridge's eightieth birthday party, organized by Richard Ingrams, at the Garrick Club in March 1983. It is intriguing, therefore, to compare Father Bidone's impressions of the ageing Belloc with those of Muggeridge.

> I knew Hilaire Belloc at the end of his life, when my only experience of his deeds was a guess. But his serenity, his calm, his determination, his faith were sufficient revelations of his greatness . . .
>
> I remember him vividly in his Chapel. He would ascend the narrow staircase and take his place at the priedieu. The religious silence would be broken only by the creaking of his bones when kneeling or rising from prayer. Before Communion he would light a candle and hold it, to express his reverence for Christ and as an act of faith in the 'light of the world' . . .
>
> He cherished his Chapel . . . To Belloc, faith meant the substance and form of things that exist: meant directions, inspirations, courage, vitality, forbearance, suffering, joy, consolation . . .
>
> During the long hours spent in conversation with him, I had many opportunities of studying all his moods and learnt much from them . . . As he grew older, it was obvious that his memory was beginning to fail, but his alertness and agility of mind remained perfect to the end . . .[38]

Possibly, Father Bidone's account was as sickly sweet as Muggeridge's had been bitterly sour. It serves, nonetheless, as a timely reminder that there was more to Belloc than met the cynical eye.

A sympathetic though mercilessly accurate eye was cast on Belloc at the end of September 1952 when Evelyn Waugh paid a visit to King's Land. His diary entry, like that of Muggeridge, was intricately descriptive and tinged with tragi-comic observation.

> Sounds of shuffling. Enter old man, shaggy white beard, black clothes garnished with food and tobacco. Thinner than I last saw him, with benevolent gleam. Like an old peasant or fisherman in French film . . . Shuffled to chair by fire. During whole visit he was occupied with unsuccessful attempts to light an empty pipe . . .

He could not follow anything said to him, but enjoyed pronouncing the great truths which presumably he ponders.[39]

The wittiest comment with regard to his visit was made by Waugh in a letter to Nancy Mitford. 'Laura & I went to visit the old Belloc yesterday by elaborate prearrangement with children and grand children. I have known him quite well for nearly 20 years. It was slightly disconcerting to be greeted with a deep bow & the words: "It is a great pleasure to make your acquaintance, sir."'[40]

Waugh's words could have belonged in one of his own works of fiction. With grimly amusing irony, Belloc, who had so admired Waugh's novels, laughing heartily at their caustic absurdities, had almost become a character in one of them. The comedy and the irony of the situation would no doubt have amused Belloc greatly; the tragedy, however, was that both the comedy and the irony were now beyond his grasp.

In March 1953 Belloc was visited by Sir William Haley, editor of *The Times*, and by H.S. Mackintosh, his old friend and admirer. 'We had heard,' wrote Mackintosh, 'that Belloc was showing increasing signs of decline and we little expected that the event would be a gay one. The old man was, however, in great form, and before lunch started he was already reciting his own verse and singing his own songs.' During lunch he discussed a variety of topics 'and, though his memory was failing and he became abstracted from time to time, his courtesy never faltered. Both Sir William and I are grateful for the memory of that last pilgrimage.'[41]

On 12 July, Eleanor Jebb discovered her father lying near the fireplace in a smoke-filled room. He had apparently fallen while poking the fire and had stumbled into the burning embers. Suffering from burns and from shock, he was taken to the Mount Alvernia nursing home of the Franciscan Missionaries at Guildford. A statue of the Blessed Virgin was taken from King's Land and placed in his room where he could see it. On the evening of 13 July he received the Last Sacraments. Two days later, on the Feast of Our Lady of Mount Carmel, Belloc died, a few days short of his eighty-third birthday.

The funeral took place at West Grinstead parish church on 20 July. Following the Requiem Mass, Belloc's body was lowered beneath the soil of his beloved 'South Country' and beside the body of his beloved wife. After a separation of almost 40 years, they were once more together. Parted by death's devastation, they were now reunited by its embrace.

The tributes poured in from friends and enemies alike. His co-religionists hailed the death of a hero. *The Tablet* devoted an entire issue to his memory with contributors such as Douglas Woodruff, Ronald Knox, Christopher Hollis, James Gunn, Frank Sheed and the Bishop of Southwark queuing up to pay homage. To Knox he was 'a Master of English Prose', to the Bishop of Southwark a 'Champion of the Church'.[42] 'Christendom has lost a great swordsman,' lamented his old friend D.B. Wyndham Lewis in the *News Chronicle*, 'more rigorous and sustained in attack than Chesterton, less chary of wounding an opponent's feelings, better equipped than his friend perhaps for duelling *à outrance* by reason of his French blood . . .'[43] The paying of homage was not, however, the preserve of Catholics for, as the headline of the *Catholic Herald* proclaimed proudly, 'The Nation Pays Tribute to the Master.'[44] Macdonald Hastings, writing in the *Daily Express*, declared that 'Hilaire Belloc was the last of the giants of the golden age of English literature.'[45] The *Daily Mail* concurred, declaring him 'the last of the giants'.[46] The leader-writer in *The Times* placed Belloc 'somewhere between Mr Pickwick and Dr Johnson', echoing Father Martin D'Arcy's dubbing of Belloc as the 'Catholic Dr Johnson'.

Perhaps Belloc was as oblivious to the mountains of praise heaped on him in death as he would have been had they been heaped on him in his dotage. During the long years of his decline, the light of earthly life had been fading from him even as he had been fading from it. He hoped and believed, nonetheless, that a brighter light would be kindled thereafter. Whether he be right or wrong, Belloc's attitude to the many posthumous tributes had already been stated in his study of Chesterton's place in English letters.

> In the appreciation of a man rather than of a writer virtue is immeasurably more important than literary talent and appeal. For these last make up nothing for the salvation of the soul and for an ultimate association with those who should be our unfailing companions in Beatitude; the Great Company. Of that Company he now is; so that it is a lesser and even indifferent thing to determine how much he shall also be of the company, the earthly and temporal company, of the local and temporarily famous.[47]

Such was his belief. As for his epitaph, he had written his own, almost half a century earlier, in the final quatrain of one of his verses.

> I challenged and I kept the Faith,
> The bleeding path alone I trod;
> It darkens. Stand about my wraith,
> And harbour me, almighty God.

NOTES
BIBLIOGRAPHY
INDEX

NOTES

One: Cradle Refugee

1 Robert Speaight, *The Life of Hilaire Belloc*, New York: Books for Libraries Press, 1970, p. 14.
2 Marie Belloc Lowndes, *The Young Hilaire Belloc*, New York: P.J. Kenedy & Sons, 1956, p. 1.
3 Birth certificate, quoted in a letter from Veronique Guyonnaud, Deputy Mayor of La Celle St Cloud, to Madame Flonriant, 29 January 1996; copy in author's possession courtesy of Kim Leslie, West Sussex Record Office, Chichester.
4 Belloc Lowndes, *The Young Hilaire Belloc*, p. 1.
5 Marie Belloc Lowndes, *A Passing World*, London: Macmillan & Co. Ltd, 1948, p. 20.
6 Marie Belloc Lowndes, *I, Too, Have Lived in Arcadia*, London: Macmillan & Co. Ltd, 1942, p. 11.
7 Speaight, *The Life of Hilaire Belloc*, p. 3.
8 Belloc Lowndes, *The Young Hilaire Belloc*, p. 31.
9 Bessie Rayner Belloc, *In a Walled Garden*, p. 17; quoted in A.N. Wilson, *Hilaire Belloc*, Harmondsworth, Middlesex: Penguin, 1986, p. 4.
10 Ibid.
11 Ibid., p. 209; quoted in Wilson, *Hilaire Belloc*, pp. 4–5.
12 Ibid.
13 Belloc Lowndes, *I, Too, Have Lived in Arcadia*, p. 3.
14 Ibid., p. 106.
15 Ibid., p. 115.
16 Ibid., pp. 183–4.
17 Ibid., p. 195.

Two: An Anglo-French Childhood

1 Belloc Lowndes, *I, Too, Have Lived in Arcadia*, pp. 214–15.
2 Ibid., p. 225.
3 Belloc Lowndes, *The Young Hilaire Belloc*, p. 19.
4 Belloc Lowndes, *I, Too, Have Lived in Arcadia*, p. 244.
5 Ibid., p. 245.
6 Ibid., p. 243.
7 Ibid., p. 246.
8 Speaight, *The Life of Hilaire Belloc*, p. 10.
9 Belloc Lowndes, *The Young Hilaire Belloc*, p. 22.
10 Belloc Lowndes, *I, Too, Have Lived in Arcadia*, p. 356.
11 Belloc Lowndes, *The Young Hilaire Belloc*, p. 23.
12 Speaight, *The Life of Hilaire Belloc*, p. 12.
13 Belloc Lowndes, *I, Too, Have Lived in Arcadia*, p. 265.
14 Ibid., p. 266.
15 Belloc Lowndes, *The Young Hilaire Belloc*, p. 55.
16 Ibid., p. 60.
17 Ibid., p. 61.
18 Ibid., p. 63.
19 Ibid., pp. 63–4.
20 Letter and poem published in *The Tablet*, 25 July 1970.
21 Belloc Lowndes, *The Young Hilaire Belloc*, pp. 66–8.
22 Belloc Lowndes, *I, Too, Have Lived in Arcadia*, p. 388.
23 Belloc Lowndes, *The Young Hilaire Belloc*, p. 56.
24 Ibid., p. 35.
25 Belloc Lowndes, *I, Too, Have Lived in Arcadia*, p. 303.

26 Robert Speaight (ed.), *Letters from Hilaire Belloc*, London: Hollis & Carter, 1958, p. 161.

27 Belloc Lowndes, *The Young Hilaire Belloc*, p. 68.

28 Ibid.

29 Speaight (ed.), *Letters from Hilaire Belloc*, pp. 269–70.

30 Birmingham Oratory Archives.

31 Belloc Lowndes, *The Young Hilaire Belloc*, p. 69.

32 Marie Belloc Lowndes, *Where Love and Friendship Dwelt*, London: Macmillan & Co. Ltd, 1943, p. 120.

33 Belloc Lowndes, *The Young Hilaire Belloc*, p. 8.

34 Belloc Lowndes, *Where Love and Friendship Dwelt*, pp. 44–5.

Three: First Love

1 Quoted in *The Tablet*, 25 July 1970.

2 Ibid.

3 Ibid.

4 Ibid.

5 Belloc Lowndes, *The Young Hilaire Belloc*, p. 72.

6 *The Tablet*, 25 July 1970.

7 Speaight, *The Life of Hilaire Belloc*, p. 32.

8 Ibid.

9 Belloc Lowndes, *The Young Hilaire Belloc*, pp. 73–4.

10 Ibid., p. 74.

11 Ibid., pp. 79–80.

12 Speaight, *The Life of Hilaire Belloc*, p. 23.

13 Belloc Lowndes, *The Young Hilaire Belloc*, pp. 65–6.

14 Ibid., pp. 83–4.

15 Hilaire Belloc to Minna Hope, undated [1887]; Belloc Collection, Boston College.

16 Minna Hope to Hilaire Belloc, 6 May 1887; Belloc Collection, Boston College.

17 Robert Speaight dates these letters as May 1884, but other sources suggest that Belloc's relationship with Minna Hope remained intense, at least on his part, until three years later. It also seems more likely that the sentiments expressed are those of a youth of 16, not those of a 13-year-old boy. The legibility of the date on Minna Hope's letter is inconclusive, but Kim Leslie, agreeing with the judgement of the present author, believes that a date of 1887 is 'distinctly possible'.

18 Her presence at the convent remains a mystery.

19 Speaight, *The Life of Hilaire Belloc*, p. 26.

20 Minna Hope to Hilaire Belloc, 6 May 1887; Belloc Collection, Boston College.

21 Hilaire Belloc, draft of letter to Minna Hope, undated [May 1887]; Belloc Collection, Boston College.

22 Belloc Lowndes, *The Young Hilaire Belloc*, pp. 83–4.

23 Ibid., p. 84.

24 Ibid., pp. 85–6.

25 Ibid., p. 86.

26 Ibid., p. 85.

27 Ibid., p. 87.

28 Speaight (ed.), *Letters from Hilaire Belloc*, p. 293.

Four: 'Youth Gave You to Me'

1 Belloc Lowndes, *The Young Hilaire Belloc*, p. 87.

2 Ibid.

3 Speaight, *The Life of Hilaire Belloc*, p. 34.

4 Belloc Lowndes, *The Young Hilaire Belloc*, p. 89.

5 Speaight (ed.), *Letters from Hilaire Belloc*, p. 20.

6 *Irish Monthly*, No. 185, Vol. XVI, November 1888.

7 Ibid., No. 189, Vol. XVII, March 1889.

8 Speaight, *The Life of Hilaire Belloc*, pp. 37–8.

9 Belloc Lowndes, *The Young Hilaire Belloc*, p. 93.

10 Ibid., p. 94.

11 Ibid.

12 Hilaire Belloc, *The Cruise of the Nona*, London: Constable, 1925, pp. 54–5.

13 Ibid.

14 Speaight, *The Life of Hilaire Belloc*, p. 44.

15 Wilson, *Hilaire Belloc*, p. 26.

16 Belloc, *The Cruise of the Nona*, pp. 232–4.

17 Elodie Hogan, diary, 1889; Belloc Collection, Boston College. There is, in fact, a degree of confusion as to whether this diary was written by Elodie or by her sister Elizabeth. It was written in a diary for 1883 that had once belonged to Elizabeth and is signed by her at the beginning. Yet the entries are definitely from 1889 and seemingly in a different hand (though this of course could be explained simply by the six-year interval between the entries). The diary was discovered amongst Elodie's possessions in King's Land and the author has assumed, tentatively, that the diary was written by the younger of the sisters. Since, however, the entries relate to occasions at which both sisters were present, the authorship is only of academic interest.

18 Belloc Lowndes, *The Young Hilaire Belloc*, pp. 98–9.

19 Quoted in Speaight, *The Life of Hilaire Belloc*, p. 55.

20 Ibid.

21 Elodie Hogan to Hilaire Belloc [undated, 1890?]; Belloc Collection, Boston College.

Five: Editor and Tramp

1 Hilaire Belloc to Elodie Hogan, 6 August 1890; Belloc Collection, Boston College.

2 Quoted in Speaight, *The Life of Hilaire Belloc*, p. 46.

3 Hilaire Belloc to Wilfrid Scawen Blunt [July 1890]; the Blunt Papers, West Sussex Record Office.

4 Belloc Lowndes, *The Young Hilaire Belloc*, p. 95.

5 Speaight, *The Life of Hilaire Belloc*, pp. 47–8.

6 Hilaire Belloc to Wilfrid Scawen Blunt [1890]; the Blunt Papers, West Sussex Record Office.

7 Belloc Lowndes, *The Young Hilaire Belloc*, p. 96.

8 Ibid., p. 97.

9 Speaight, *The Life of Hilaire Belloc*, p. 57.

10 Elodie Hogan to Hilaire Belloc [1890]; Belloc Collection, Boston College.

11 Hilaire Belloc to George Wyndham, 5 February 1910; Belloc Collection, Boston College.

12 Wilson, *Hilaire Belloc*, p. 37.

13 Edward Northcote, conversation with the author, 7 November 2000.

14 Hilaire Belloc, *The Path to Rome*, London: George Allen, 1902, p. 146.

15 Ibid., pp. 68–9.

16 Belloc Lowndes, *The Young Hilaire Belloc*, p. 101.

17 Ibid., p. 102.

18 Elodie Hogan to Hilaire Belloc, 19 July 1894; Belloc Collection, Boston College.

19 Speaight (ed.), *Letters from Hilaire Belloc*, p. 129.

20 Belloc Lowndes, *The Young Hilaire Belloc*, p. 102.

21 Speaight (ed.), *Letters from Hilaire Belloc*, p. 20.

22 Belloc Lowndes, *The Young Hilaire Belloc*, p. 102.

Six: Soldier and Scholar

1 Belloc Lowndes, *The Young Hilaire Belloc*, p. 102.

2 Ibid., p. 103.

3 Speaight, *The Life of Hilaire Belloc*, p. 63.

4 Ibid., p. 65.

5 Belloc Lowndes, *The Young Hilaire Belloc*, p. 108.

6 Ibid., p. 111.

7 Ibid., p. 114.

8 Speaight, *The Life of Hilaire Belloc*, p. 73.

9 Belloc Lowndes, *The Young Hilaire Belloc*, p. 109.

10 Ibid., p. 115.

11 Ibid., p. 116.

12 *Catholic Herald*, 27 July 1950.

13 Speaight, *The Life of Hilaire Belloc*, pp. 80–1.

14 *Tribune*, 10 August 1906.

15 Dom Philip Jebb, interview with the author, 5 December 2000.
16 Speaight, *The Life of Hilaire Belloc*, pp. 85–6.
17 Ibid., pp. 84–5.
18 *The Universe*, 24 July 1953.
19 John Moore, *The Life and Letters of Edward Thomas*, London: William Heinemann, 1939, pp. 42–3.
20 Speaight, *The Life of Hilaire Belloc*, p. 88.
21 *Sunday Times*, 9 June 1946.
22 *Isis*, 28 October 1893; quoted in Wilson, *Hilaire Belloc*, p. 50.
23 Speaight, *The Life of Hilaire Belloc*, p. 87.
24 *Isis*, November 1894; quoted in Wilson, *Hilaire Belloc*, pp. 49–50.
25 Belloc Lowndes, *The Young Hilaire Belloc*, p. 127.
26 Ibid., p. 125.
27 *Pall Mall Gazette*, 12 June 1893.
28 *The Universe*, 24 July 1953.

Seven: Survivals and New Arrivals

1 Speaight, *The Life of Hilaire Belloc*, p. 96.
2 Ibid., p. 95.
3 Wilson, *Hilaire Belloc*, p. 61.
4 Ibid.
5 Elodie Hogan to Hilaire Belloc, 1 January 1894; Belloc Collection, Boston College.
6 Ibid., 10 March 1894.
7 Ibid., 19 July 1894.
8 Ibid., 6 April 1895.
9 Speaight, *The Life of Hilaire Belloc*, p. 101.
10 Elodie Hogan to Hilaire Belloc, 1 February 1896; Belloc Collection, Boston College.
11 Belloc Lowndes, *The Young Hilaire Belloc*, p. 135.
12 Speaight, *The Life of Hilaire Belloc*, pp. 101–2.
13 Elodie Hogan to Hilaire Belloc, Good Friday 1896; Belloc Collection, Boston College.
14 Speaight, *The Life of Hilaire Belloc*, p. 102.
15 Belloc Lowndes, *The Young Hilaire Belloc*, pp. 135–6.
16 Speaight, *The Life of Hilaire Belloc*, p. 103.
17 Hilaire Belloc to Elodie Hogan, 7 June 1896; Belloc Collection, Boston College.
18 Ibid., 8 June 1896.
19 Marriage certificate; copy courtesy of the West Sussex Record Office.
20 Belloc Lowndes, *The Young Hilaire Belloc*, p. 136.
21 Marie Belloc Lowndes, *The Merry Wives of Westminster*, London: Macmillan & Co. Ltd, 1946, p. 28.
22 Ibid.
23 Belloc Lowndes, *The Young Hilaire Belloc*, p. 137.
24 Belloc Lowndes, *The Merry Wives of Westminster*, pp. 28–9.
25 Belloc Lowndes, *The Young Hilaire Belloc*, p. 137.
26 Speaight, *The Life of Hilaire Belloc*, p. 108.
27 Maurice Baring, *The Puppet Show of Memory*, London: William Heinemann Ltd, 1930, p. 223.
28 Speaight, *The Life of Hilaire Belloc*, p. 112.
29 Belloc Lowndes, *The Young Hilaire Belloc*, p. 139.
30 Ibid.
31 Hilaire Belloc to Elodie Belloc, November 1896; Belloc Collection, Boston College.

Eight: Baring and Buchan

1 Speaight, *The Life of Hilaire Belloc*, p. 117.
2 Ibid., p.118.
3 *Isis*, 20 March 1897.
4 Speaight, *The Life of Hilaire Belloc*, p. 118.
5 Quoted in Victor Feske, *From Belloc to Churchill*, Chapel Hill, North Carolina, USA: University of North Carolina Press, 1996, p. 28.
6 Ibid.
7 Belloc Lowndes, *The Young Hilaire Belloc*, p. 144.
8 Ibid.

9 A fine collection of Belloc's sketches was acquired by the University of Notre Dame in Indiana in 1978 from the estate of Belloc's friend, Douglas Woodruff. These include sketches of French and English landscapes, dating from April to October 1889; monochromatic drawings of the American landscape, dating from Belloc's first visit to the US in 1891; and a series of watercolours of French landscapes and buildings, dating from 1893–4.

10 *The Chesterton Review*, Vol. XIX, No. 1, p. 67.

11 Baring, *The Puppet Show of Memory*, pp. 222–3.

12 Ibid., p. 223.

13 Speaight (ed.), *Letters from Hilaire Belloc*, pp. 1–2.

14 Baring, *The Puppet Show of Memory*, p. 224.

15 Ibid., p. 223.

16 Ibid., p. 222.

17 Belloc Lowndes, *A Passing World*, p. 197.

18 Baring, *The Puppet Show of Memory*, p. 225.

19 Speaight (ed.), *Letters from Hilaire Belloc*, p. 225.

20 Belloc Lowndes, *The Young Hilaire Belloc*, p. 145.

21 Ibid., p. 144.

22 Ibid.

23 Ibid., p. 145.

24 Speaight, *The Life of Hilaire Belloc*, p. 115.

25 H. Montgomery Hyde, *Lord Alfred Douglas: A Biography*, London: Methuen, 1984, p. 124.

26 Quoted in Douglas Murray, *Bosie: A Biography of Lord Alfred Douglas*, London: Hodder & Stoughton, 2000, p. 112.

27 Maurice Baring to Hilaire Belloc, 15 November 1898; Belloc Collection, Boston College.

28 Speaight, *The Life of Hilaire Belloc*, p. 121.

29 Ibid., p. 120.

30 Ibid., p. 122.

31 Father Rope's memories of Belloc were published in *Belloc 70: A Conference to Celebrate the Centenary of the Birth of Hilaire Belloc at Spode House, Rugeley, Staffordshire*, Earley, Reading, Berkshire: Louis Schroeder, 1970, p. 38.

32 Wilson, *Hilaire Belloc*, p. 82.

33 Janet Adam Smith, *John Buchan: A Biography*, London: Rupert Hart-Davis, 1965, p. 70.

34 Ibid., p. 72.

35 Ibid., p. 73.

36 Ibid., pp. 61–2.

Nine: Baring and Chesterton

1 Belloc Lowndes, *The Young Hilaire Belloc*, p. 149.

2 Hilaire Belloc to Elodie Belloc, 18 December 1899; Belloc Collection, Boston College.

3 Hilaire Belloc to Elodie Belloc, 19 December 1899; Belloc Collection, Boston College.

4 Speaight, *The Life of Hilaire Belloc*, p. 147.

5 Ibid.

6 Ibid.

7 Maurice Baring to Blanche Warre-Cornish, 7 February 1900; quoted in *The Chesterton Review*, Vol. XIX, No. 1 (February 1988), p. 66.

8 Maurice Baring to Hubert Warre-Cornish, 9 February 1900; quoted ibid., pp. 66–7.

9 Speaight (ed.), *Letters from Hilaire Belloc*, p. 254.

10 Maurice Baring to Edward Marsh, [July] 1899; quoted in *The Chesterton Review*, op. cit., p. 66.

11 Maurice Baring to Ethel Smyth, 29 August 1925; quoted ibid., p. 70.

12 Maurice Baring, *Have You Anything to Declare?*, London: William Heinemann Ltd, 1936, p. 147.

13 Maurice Baring to Hubert Warre-Cornish, 9 February 1900; quoted in *The Chesterton Review*, op. cit., p. 66.

14 Speaight, *The Life of Hilaire Belloc*, p. 155.

15 Elodie Belloc to Hilaire Belloc, undated [spring 1900]; Belloc Collection, Boston College.

16 Maisie Ward, *Return to Chesterton*, London: Sheed & Ward, 1952, p. 52.

17 W.R. Titterton, *G.K. Chesterton: A Portrait*, London: Alexander Ouseley Ltd, 1936, p. 48.

18 Joseph Pearce, *Wisdom and Innocence: A Life of G.K. Chesterton*, London: Hodder & Stoughton, 1996, p. 48.

19 Maisie Ward, *Gilbert Keith Chesterton*, London: Sheed & Ward, 1944, pp. 211–12.

20 G.K. Chesterton, *Autobiography*, London: Hutchinson & Co., 1936, p. 116.

21 Ibid., pp. 116–18.

22 C. Creighton Mandell and Edward Shanks, *Hilaire Belloc: The Man and his Work*, London: Methuen & Co. Ltd, 1916, pp. vii–ix.

23 Speaight, *The Life of Hilaire Belloc*, p. 149.

24 Titterton, *G.K. Chesterton*, p. 49.

25 Ward, *Gilbert Keith Chesterton*, p. 114.

26 Speaight, *The Life of Hilaire Belloc*, p. 149.

27 *The Tablet*, 25 July 1953.

Ten: Romeward Bound

1 Belloc Lowndes, *The Young Hilaire Belloc*, p. 152.

2 Ibid.

3 Speaight, *The Life of Hilaire Belloc*, p. 156.

4 Speaight (ed.), *Letters from Hilaire Belloc*, p. 3.

5 Speaight, *The Life of Hilaire Belloc*, pp. 151–2.

6 Hilaire Belloc, *Hills and the Sea*, London: Methuen & Co., 1906, pp. 269–70.

7 Speaight, *The Life of Hilaire Belloc*, p. 157.

8 Edward Northcote, conversation with the author, 7 November 2000.

9 Belloc, *The Path to Rome*, pp. 7–8.

10 Speaight, *The Life of Hilaire Belloc*, p. 159.

11 Hilaire Belloc to Elodie Belloc, 18 June 1901; Belloc Collection, Boston College.

12 Ibid.

13 Ibid.

14 Speaight, *The Life of Hilaire Belloc*, p. 159.

15 Ibid.

16 Hilaire Belloc to Elodie Belloc, undated, postmarked 20 June 1901; Belloc Collection, Boston College.

17 Belloc, *The Path to Rome*, p. 283.

18 Ibid., p. 286.

19 Hilaire Belloc to Elodie Belloc, undated, postmarked 20 June 1901; Belloc Collection, Boston College.

20 Hilaire Belloc to Elodie Belloc, undated [23 June 1901]; Belloc Collection, Boston College.

21 Ibid.

22 Ibid.

23 Hilaire Belloc to Elodie Belloc, undated, postmarked 24 June 1901; Belloc Collection, Boston College.

24 Hilaire Belloc to Elodie Belloc, undated, postmarked 24 June 1901; Belloc Collection, Boston College.

25 Ibid.

26 Ibid.

27 From Belloc's personal copy of *The Path to Rome*, in the possession of Dom Philip Jebb of Downside Abbey.

28 Hilaire Belloc to Elodie Belloc, undated, postmarked 25 June 1901; Belloc Collection, Boston College.

29 Belloc, *The Path to Rome*, p. 345.

30 Hilaire Belloc, *One Thing and Another*, London: Hollis & Carter, 1955, p. 138.

31 Ibid., p. 139.

32 Ibid.

33 Ibid., pp. 139–40.

34 Ibid., pp. 141–3.

35 Hilaire Belloc to Elodie Belloc, undated [30 June 1901?]; Belloc Collection, Boston College.

36 Hilaire Belloc to Elodie Belloc, undated [7 July 1901]; Belloc Collection, Boston College.

37 Quoted in Wilson, *Hilaire Belloc*, p. 107.

38 Speaight, *The Life of Hilaire Belloc*, p. 161.

39 Dom Philip Jebb, interview with the author, 5 December 2000.
40 Speaight, *The Life of Hilaire Belloc*, p. 161.
41 Ibid., p. 163.
42 From Belloc's personal copy of *The Path to Rome*.

Eleven: The South Country

1 Elodie Hogan to Hilaire Belloc, 10 March 1894; Belloc Collection, Boston College.
2 Speaight, *The Life of Hilaire Belloc*, p. 167.
3 Eleanor Jebb, in her reminiscences of her father in *Testimony to Hilaire Belloc* (London: Methuen and Co. Ltd, 1956), gives the name of the farm as 'Godsmark', yet Belloc's correspondence from the farm is clearly marked 'Gossmarks'.
4 Eleanor and Reginald Jebb, *Testimony to Hilaire Belloc*, p. 112.
5 Hilaire Belloc to Wilfrid Scawen Blunt, 7 July 1902; the Blunt Papers, West Sussex Record Office.
6 Ibid.
7 Hilaire Belloc, *The Four Men*, London: Thomas Nelson and Sons, 1912, p. 3.
8 Hilaire Belloc to Maurice Baring, 4 December 1909; quoted in Speaight, *The Life of Hilaire Belloc*, p. 325.
9 Belloc, *The Four Men*, pp. vi–vii.
10 *Chicago Evening Post*, 2 May 1903.
11 Speaight, *The Life of Hilaire Belloc*, p. 188.
12 Patrick Howarth, *Squire: 'Most Generous of Men'*, London: Hutchinson, 1963, p. 29.
13 Ibid., pp. 81–2.
14 Clare Sheppard, *Lobsters at Littlehampton*, Padstow, Cornwall: Tabb House, 1995, p. 144.
15 Jebb, *Testimony to Hilaire Belloc*, p. 114.
16 Maurice Baring in the dedication to Belloc at the commencement of his novel, *Cat's Cradle*, London: William Heinemann Ltd, 1925.
17 Harris Wilson (ed.), *Arnold Bennett and H.G. Wells: A Record of a Personal and a Literary Friendship*, London: Rupert Hart-Davis, 1960, pp. 98–9.
18 Jebb, *Testimony to Hilaire Belloc*, p. 117.
19 Belloc Lowndes, *The Young Hilaire Belloc*, p. 153.
20 Jebb, *Testimony to Hilaire Belloc*, p. 118.
21 Hilaire Belloc to Wilfrid Scawen Blunt, 26 October 1903; Blunt Papers, West Sussex Record Office.
22 Belloc Lowndes, *The Young Hilaire Belloc*, p. 153.
23 Ibid., p. 154.
24 Speaight, *The Life of Hilaire Belloc*, p. 193.
25 Frances Chesterton, diaries; the Chesterton Collection, Plater College, Oxford.
26 Speaight, *The Life of Hilaire Belloc*, p. 195.
27 Ibid., pp. 195–6.

Twelve: The Chesterbelloc

1 Speaight, *The Life of Hilaire Belloc*, p. 192.
2 Chesterton, *Autobiography*, p. 116.
3 Ward, *Return to Chesterton*, p. 52.
4 Sketch map, drawn by Chesterton; the Chesterton Collection, Plater College, Oxford.
5 Frances Chesterton, diaries; the Chesterton Collection, Plater College, Oxford.
6 Jebb, *Testimony to Hilaire Belloc*, p. 110.
7 Ibid., p. 111.
8 R.H. Mottram, *For Some We Loved: An Intimate Portrait of Ada and John Galsworthy*, London: Hutchinson, 1956, p. 30. *See also*: Frederick R. Karl, *Joseph Conrad – The Three Lives: A Biography*, London: Faber & Faber, 1979, pp. 721–2; Max Saunders, *Ford Madox Ford: A Duel Life, Volume 1: The World Before the War*, Oxford University Press, 1996, p. 211; James Gindin, *John Galsworthy's Life and Art*, London: Macmillan, 1987, p. 148; and Arthur Mizener, *The Saddest Story: A*

Biography of Ford Madox Ford,
London: The Bodley Head, 1972,
p. 107.

9 Speaight, *The Life of Hilaire Belloc*,
p. 178.

10 Belloc Lowndes, *The Young Hilaire
Belloc*, p. 160.

11 Speaight, *The Life of Hilaire Belloc*,
pp. 192–3.

12 Ibid., pp. 190–1.

13 Ibid., p. 191.

14 Ibid., p. 188.

15 Ibid., pp. 191–2.

16 Ibid., p. 192.

17 Lord Basil Blackwood to Hilaire
Belloc, 10 November 1904; Belloc
Collection, Boston College.

18 Robert Brainard Pearsall, *Rupert
Brooke: The Man and Poet*,
Amsterdam: Rodopi N.V., 1974, p. 31.

19 Ibid.

20 Christopher Hassall, *Rupert Brooke: A
Biography*, London: Faber & Faber,
1964, p. 171.

21 Ibid.

22 Belloc, *One Thing and Another*,
pp. 172–3.

23 Pearce, *Wisdom and Innocence*, p. 95.

24 John O'Connor, *Father Brown on
Chesterton*, London: Frederick Muller
Ltd, 1937, p. 143.

25 Hilaire Belloc, *On the Place of Gilbert
Keith Chesterton in English Letters*,
London: Sheed & Ward, 1940, p. 72.

Thirteen: The Party System

1 Zita Caldecott, interview with the
author, London, 27 March 2001.

2 Speaight, *The Life of Hilaire Belloc*,
pp. 243–4.

3 See Chapter 11.

4 Jebb, *Testimony to Hilaire Belloc*, p. 121.

5 Speaight, *The Life of Hilaire Belloc*,
p. 204.

6 Chesterton, *Autobiography*, pp. 298–9.

7 Speaight, *The Life of Hilaire Belloc*,
p. 205.

8 Ibid., p. 207.

9 Ibid.

10 John P. McCarthy, *Hilaire Belloc:*

Edwardian Radical, Indianapolis:
Liberty Press, 1978, p. 102.

11 Speaight, *The Life of Hilaire Belloc*,
pp. 210–11.

12 Mike Hennessy, 'Belloc's first session
(1906): A Summary', unpublished
document. It is worth noting that
Hansard's rigorous verbatim record of
parliamentary proceedings did not
begin, in the form that we now know
it, until 16 February 1909. I am
grateful, therefore, to Mike Hennessy
for allowing me access to his own
exhaustive research into Belloc's
parliamentary career prior to that date.

13 Ibid.

14 McCarthy, *Hilaire Belloc: Edwardian
Radical*, p. 102.

15 Hennessy, 'Belloc's first session (1906):
A Summary'; and Speaight, *The Life of
Hilaire Belloc*, p. 209.

16 Laura Lovat, *Maurice Baring: A
Postscript*, London: Hollis & Carter,
1947, p. 50.

17 *Punch*, 25 July 1906.

18 Hennessy, 'Belloc's first session (1906):
A Summary'; and Speaight, *The Life of
Hilaire Belloc*, pp. 211–12.

19 Hilaire Belloc to Wilfrid Scawen Blunt,
9 November 1906; Blunt Papers, West
Sussex Record Office.

20 Hilaire Belloc to Wilfrid Scawen Blunt,
27 January 1907; Blunt Papers, West
Sussex Record Office.

Fourteen: Friends and Disciples

1 Belloc Lowndes, *The Young Hilaire
Belloc*, p. 167.

2 Ibid., p. 168.

3 Speaight, *The Life of Hilaire Belloc*,
p. 214.

4 Ibid., p. 215.

5 Ibid., pp. 217–18.

6 Ibid., p. 218.

7 Hilaire Belloc to G.K. Chesterton, 6
October 1921; Belloc Collection, Boston
College.

8 Lovat, *Maurice Baring*, p. 50.

9 Ibid., pp. 54–5.

10 Ibid., p. 50.

11 Jebb, *Testimony to Hilaire Belloc*, p. 127.

12 Speaight, *Letters from Hilaire Belloc*, pp. 7–8.

13 Ibid., p. 161.

14 Ibid., pp. 9–10.

15 Hilaire Belloc, postcard to 'Master Peter Belloc', 30 September 1906; property of Zita Caldecott and on loan to the author.

16 Jebb, *Testimony to Hilaire Belloc*, pp. 125–6.

17 Speaight, *The Life of Hilaire Belloc*, pp. 219–20.

18 Hilaire Belloc, *Audit the Party Funds*, Aylesford, Kent: The Aylesford Press, 1992, p. 8.

19 Speaight, *The Life of Hilaire Belloc*, p. 260.

20 Arnold Lunn, *And Yet So New*, London: Sheed & Ward, 1958, p. 62.

21 Ibid., pp. 60–1.

22 Ibid., p. 61.

23 Ronald Knox, *A Spiritual Aeneid*, London: Burns & Oates, 1958, p. 52.

24 Geoffrey Keynes (ed.), *The Letters of Rupert Brooke*, London: Faber & Faber, 1968, pp. 84–5.

25 Ibid., p. 45.

9 Speaight, *The Life of Hilaire Belloc*, pp. 222–3.

10 Ibid., pp. 250–1.

11 Ibid., p. 251.

12 J.G. Riewald (ed.), *The Surprise of Excellence: Modern Essays on Max Beerbohm*, Hamden, Connecticut: Archon Books, 1974, p. 128.

13 Ibid.

14 Ibid., p. 148.

15 J.G. Riewald (ed.), *Beerbohm's Literary Caricatures*, London: Allen Lane, 1977, p. 113.

16 Pearce, *Wisdom and Innocence*, p. 54.

17 H.G. Wells to Hilaire Belloc, 12 October 1908; Belloc Collection, Boston College.

18 *New Age*, 15 February 1908.

19 Pearce, *Wisdom and Innocence*, p. 47.

20 Chesterton, *Autobiography*, p. 118.

21 Ibid., p. 216.

22 Elodie Belloc's diary entry, Friday, 3 January 1908; Belloc Collection, Boston College.

23 Chesterton, *Autobiography*, pp. 216–17.

24 Ibid., pp. 217–22.

25 Jebb, *Testimony to Hilaire Belloc*, pp. 127–8.

26 Ward, *Return to Chesterton*, p. 71.

Fifteen: Love and Laughter

1 Hilaire Belloc to Elodie Belloc, 28 March 1907, written on G.K. Chesterton's notepaper; courtesy of Grahame Clough, Hilaire Belloc Study Centre, Sussex.

2 Speaight, *The Life of Hilaire Belloc*, p. 246.

3 Ibid., p. 247.

4 Ibid., p. 246–7.

5 Dom Philip Jebb, interview with the author.

6 Belloc Lowndes, *The Young Hilaire Belloc*, p. 173.

7 Hilaire Belloc to an indiscernible correspondent, 8 March 1907; courtesy of Grahame Clough, Hilaire Belloc Study Centre, Sussex.

8 Belloc, *One Thing and Another*, pp. 68–9.

Sixteen: Religion and Politics

1 Joseph Pearce, *Literary Converts*, London: HarperCollins, 1999, p. 45.

2 From Belloc's personal copy of *The Path to Rome*.

3 Speaight, *The Life of Hilaire Belloc*, p. 227.

4 Ibid., p. 250.

5 Hilaire Belloc to G.K. Chesterton, 2 March 1912; Belloc Collection, Boston College.

6 Hilaire Belloc to Wilfrid Scawen Blunt, 28 June 1909; Blunt Papers, West Sussex Record Office.

7 Hilaire Belloc to Wilfrid Scawen Blunt, 10 December 1907; Blunt Papers, West Sussex Record Office.

8 Hilaire Belloc, *The Church and Socialism*, London: Catholic Truth Society, 1909, pp. 5–6.

9 Ibid., p. 13.
10 Ibid., p. 16.
11 *New Witness*, 27 April 1923.
12 *Observer*, 13 December 1925.
13 Chesterton, *Autobiography*, p. 291.
14 *Belloc 70*, p. 38.
15 Speaight, *The Life of Hilaire Belloc*, p. 236.
16 Ibid., p. 237.
17 Ibid., pp. 237–8.

Seventeen: Farewell to Parliament

1 Speaight, *The Life of Hilaire Belloc*, p. 245.
2 Speaight (ed.), *Letters from Hilaire Belloc*, p. 24.
3 Dennis Shrubsall and Pierre Coustillas, *Landscapes and Literati: Unpublished Letters of W.H. Hudson and George Gissing*, Salisbury, Wiltshire: Michael Russell, 1985, p. 95.
4 Speaight, *The Life of Hilaire Belloc*, p. 240.
5 Ibid., pp. 280–1.
6 Cecil Chesterton to Hilaire Belloc, 16 January 1910; Belloc Collection, Boston College.
7 Hilaire Belloc to Mr Robinson, 18 January 1910; Hilaire Belloc Study Centre, Sussex.
8 Hassall, *Rupert Brooke*, p. 175.
9 Adrian Wright, *Foreign Country: The Life of L.P. Hartley*, London: André Deutsch, 1996, p. 37.
10 Saunders, *Ford Madox Ford: A Duel Life, Volume 1*, p. 278.
11 Speaight, *The Life of Hilaire Belloc*, p. 271.
12 Ibid., p. 285.
13 Ibid.
14 Ibid., p. 293.
15 Ibid.
16 Speaight, p. 293, gives the date of this letter as 28 November, presumably an error. The typed copy in the files at the Hilaire Belloc Study Centre clearly has the date as 'November 29, 1910'.
17 Hilaire Belloc, letter to A.C. Tait, 29 November 1910; Hilaire Belloc Study Centre, Sussex.
18 Speaight, *The Life of Hilaire Belloc*, p. 295.
19 Hilaire Belloc to Cecil Chesterton, 24 July 1910; Belloc Collection, Boston College.
20 Cecil Chesterton to Hilaire Belloc, 25 July 1910; Belloc Collection, Boston College.
21 Speaight, *The Life of Hilaire Belloc*, p. 301.
22 Ibid., p. 297.
23 Mrs Cecil Chesterton, *The Chestertons*, London: Chapman & Hall Ltd, 1941, p. 55.

Eighteen: Eye-Witness to Scandal

1 Hilaire Belloc to Wilfrid Scawen Blunt, 2 May 1911; Blunt Papers, West Sussex Record Office.
2 Hilaire Belloc, letter published in the *New Witness*, 4 May 1923.
3 Hilaire Belloc to Wilfrid Scawen Blunt, 2 May 1911; Blunt Papers, West Sussex Record Office.
4 From Arthur Ransome's *Autobiography*; quoted in Pearce, *Wisdom and Innocence*, p. 289.
5 Speaight, *The Life of Hilaire Belloc*, p. 308.
6 Hilaire Belloc to Wilfrid Scawen Blunt, 18 April 1911; Blunt Papers, West Sussex Record Office.
7 J.B. Morton, *Hilaire Belloc: A Memoir*, London: Hollis & Carter, 1955, p. 32.
8 Hilaire Belloc to G.K. Chesterton, 3 November 1912; Belloc Collection, Boston College.
9 Hilaire Belloc to Miss Allport, 8 November 1912; Belloc Collection, Boston College.
10 Feske, *From Belloc to Churchill*, p. 37.
11 Michael Bentley, *The Liberal Mind, 1914–1929*, Cambridge University Press, 1977, p. 164.
12 Maurice Reckitt, *As It Happened: An Autobiography*, London: J.M. Dent, 1941, pp. 107–8.
13 Cecil Gill, *Autobiography*, unpublished ms., p. 343; quoted in Pearce, *Literary Converts*, p. 63.

14 George Orwell, *Collected Essays and Journalism, 1945–1949*, London: Secker & Warburg/Octopus, 1980, p. 756.

15 Bernard Crick, *George Orwell: A Life*, London: publisher?, 1992, p. 270.

16 Hilaire Belloc to Mr Low [?], 9 February 1911; Hilaire Belloc Study Centre, Sussex.

17 Speaight, *The Life of Hilaire Belloc*, p. 330.

18 Montgomery Hyde, *Lord Alfred Douglas*, pp. 174–5.

19 Speaight, *The Life of Hilaire Belloc*, p. 307.

20 Hilaire Belloc to Wilfrid Scawen Blunt, 15 June 1912; Blunt Papers, West Sussex Record Office.

21 Speaight, *The Life of Hilaire Belloc*, p. 308.

22 Hilaire Belloc to Wilfrid Scawen Blunt, 5 January 1913; Blunt Papers, West Sussex Record Office.

23 Speaight (ed.), *Letters from Hilaire Belloc*, p. 54.

24 Hilaire Belloc to Wilfrid Scawen Blunt, 7 June 1913; Blunt Papers, West Sussex Record Office.

25 *Rex v. Chesterton*; quoted in Michael Ffinch, *G.K. Chesterton: A Biography*, London: Weidenfeld & Nicolson, 1986, p. 216.

26 Hilaire Belloc, to Wilfrid Scawen Blunt, 8 June 1913; Blunt Papers, West Sussex Record Office.

27 Duff Cooper, *Old Men Forget*, London: Rupert Hart-Davis, 1953, p. 46.

28 Mrs Cecil Chesterton, *The Chestertons*, p. 97.

29 Chesterton, *Autobiography*, p. 208.

Nineteen: Ghostly Secrets and Mortal Wounds

1 Speaight, *The Life of Hilaire Belloc*, p. 363.

2 Ibid., p. 311.

3 Ibid., pp. 363–4.

4 G.P. Gooch, *History and Historians in the Nineteenth Century*, London: Longmans, Green, 1913, p. 284.

5 Speaight, *The Life of Hilaire Belloc*, p. 363.

6 Hilaire Belloc to Cecil Chesterton, 20 November 1913; Belloc Collection, Boston College.

7 Cecil Chesterton to Hilaire Belloc, 21 November 1913; Belloc Collection, Boston College.

8 Cecil Chesterton to Hilaire Belloc, 6 December 1913; Belloc Collection, Boston College.

9 Hilaire Belloc to Cecil Chesterton, 30 December 1913; Belloc Collection, Boston College.

10 Hilaire Belloc to G.K. Chesterton, 17 July 1915; Chesterton Study Centre, Plater College, Oxford.

11 Hilaire Belloc to Wilfrid Scawen Blunt, 3 November 1913; Blunt Papers, West Sussex Record Office.

12 Speaight (ed.), *Letters from Hilaire Belloc*, p. 161.

13 Speaight, *The Life of Hilaire Belloc*, p. 331.

14 Ibid.

15 Newman Flower (ed.), *The Journals of Arnold Bennett 1911–1921*, London: Cassell & Company Ltd, 1932, pp. 57–8; also Pippa Harris (ed.), *Song of Love: The Letters of Rupert Brooke and Noel Olivier, 1909–1915*, New York: Crown Publishers, 1991, p. 229; Dan H. Laurence (ed.), *Bernard Shaw: Collected Letters 1911–1925*, London: Max Reinhardt, 1985, pp. 128–9; Frank Swinnerton, *Swinnerton: An Autobiography*, London: Hutchinson & Co., 1937, pp. 86–8; Ward, *Return to Chesterton*, pp. 60 and 128.

16 J.B. Priestley, 'Thoughts on Shaw', *New Statesman and Nation*, 28 July 1956.

17 Speaight (ed.), *Letters from Hilaire Belloc*, p. 57.

18 Hilaire Belloc to Wilfrid Scawen Blunt, 18 September 1913; Blunt Papers, West Sussex Record Office.

19 Zita Caldecott, interview with the author. Mrs Caldecott is now the proud possessor of these books.

20 Hilaire Belloc to Wilfrid Scawen Blunt,

28 December 1913; Blunt Papers, West Sussex Record Office.

21 Hilaire Belloc to Cecil Chesterton, 23 December 1913; Belloc Collection, Boston College.

22 The present author, in *Wisdom and Innocence*, his biography of G.K. Chesterton, repeats the oft-cited error that Belloc was one of the jury at this celebrated literary 'trial'. In fact, as the correspondence cited here demonstrates, Belloc was not at the trial. The January 1914 issue of the *Dickensian* states that Belloc would be a jury member, repeating the claims of the publicity material for the 'trial'. The February issue, however, includes a full report of the proceedings, including a list of the jury members, and it is clear from this that Belloc was not present.

23 Cecil Chesterton to Hilaire Belloc, 29 December 1913; Belloc Collection, Boston College.

24 Hilaire Belloc to Cecil Chesterton, 30 December 1913; Belloc Collection, Boston College.

25 Hilaire Belloc to Wilfrid Scawen Blunt, 30 December 1913; Blunt Papers, West Sussex Record Office.

26 Hilaire Belloc to Cecil Chesterton, 1 January 1914; Belloc Collection, Boston College.

27 Hilaire Belloc to G.K. Chesterton, 1 January 1914; Belloc Collection, Boston College.

28 Speaight, *The Life of Hilaire Belloc*, p. 341.

29 Hilaire Belloc to Wilfrid Scawen Blunt, 30 January 1914; Blunt Papers, West Sussex Record Office.

30 Hilaire Belloc to Wilfrid Scawen Blunt, 3 February 1914; Blunt Papers, West Sussex Record Office.

31 Belloc Lowndes, *The Young Hilaire Belloc*, p. 181.

Twenty: 'Where Darkness Is . . .'

1 Belloc Lowndes, *The Young Hilaire Belloc*, p. 180.

2 Hilaire Belloc to G.K. Chesterton, undated [3 February 1914]; Belloc Collection, Boston College.

3 Frances and Gilbert Chesterton to Hilaire Belloc, 3 February 1914; Belloc Collection, Boston College.

4 'Sayings of Our Lord must be remembered again and again; and we will find they will never come into our mind without bringing their attendant stars of comfort with them.' Vincent McNabb, OP, *Stars of Comfort: Retreat Conferences*, London: The Catholic Book Club, 1958, epigraph.

5 Speaight (ed.), *Letters from Hilaire Belloc*, pp. 239–40.

6 Ward, *Return to Chesterton*, p. 206.

7 Hilaire Belloc to Wilfrid Scawen Blunt, 4 February 1914; Blunt Papers, West Sussex Record Office.

8 W.R. Titterton, 'Belloc – He Loved England Well Enough to Fight Her', *The Universe*, 24 July 1953.

9 Jebb, *Testimony to Hilaire Belloc*, p. 151.

10 Speaight (ed.), *Letters from Hilaire Belloc*, p. 62.

11 Sheppard, *Lobsters at Littlehampton*, p. 145.

12 Jebb, *Testimony to Hilaire Belloc*, pp. 168–9.

13 Notes taken by Kim Leslie of the West Sussex Record Office during a conversation with Sister Emmanuel Mary (Marianne Jebb) at Our Lady's Priory, Sayers Common, Sussex, October 1993.

14 Sheppard, *Lobsters at Littlehampton*, pp. 146–7.

15 Ibid., pp. 150–1.

16 Speaight (ed.), *Letters from Hilaire Belloc*, p. 60.

17 Hilaire Belloc, 'The Reign of Pope Pius X', originally published in the *British Review* in 1914, republished in *The Tablet*, 2 June 1951.

18 Speaight, *The Life of Hilaire Belloc*, p. 344.

19 Hilaire Belloc to Wilfrid Scawen Blunt, 23 March 1914; Blunt Papers, West Sussex Record Office.

20 Speaight, *The Life of Hilaire Belloc*, p. 345.

21 Jebb, *Testimony to Hilaire Belloc*, p. 169.
22 Belloc, *The Cruise of the Nona*, pp. 346–7.
23 Hilaire Belloc, *Complete Verse*, London: Pimlico, 1991, p. 17.

Twenty-One: War and Other Diversions

1 Belloc, *The Cruise of the Nona*, p. 145.
2 Belloc Lowndes, *A Passing World*, p. 21.
3 Speaight, *The Life of Hilaire Belloc*, p. 347.
4 Speaight (ed.), *Letters from Hilaire Belloc*, p. 65.
5 Lord Basil Blackwood to Hilaire Belloc, 15 October 1914; Belloc Collection, Boston College.
6 Mary M. Lago and Karl Beckson (eds), *Max and Will: Max Beerbohm and William Rothenstein: Their Friendship and Letters 1893–1945*, London: John Murray, 1975, p. 96.
7 James Hepburn (ed.), *Letters of Arnold Bennett, Volume II, 1889–1915*, Oxford University Press, 1968, p. 366.
8 Keynes (ed.), *The Letters of Rupert Brooke*, p. 651.
9 Nigel Jones, *Rupert Brooke: Life, Death and Myth*, London: Richard Cohen Books, 1999, p. 263.
10 R.K.R. Thornton (ed.), *Ivor Gurney: Collected Letters*, Manchester: Carcanet Press, 1991, p. 441.
11 Michael Hurd, *The Ordeal of Ivor Gurney*, Oxford University Press, 1978, pp. 113–14.
12 Thornton (ed.), *Ivor Gurney*, p. 101.
13 Ibid., p. 25.
14 Chesterton, *Autobiography*, p. 250.
15 Hilaire Belloc to G.K. Chesterton, 18 September 1910; Belloc Collection, Boston College.
16 *Outlook*, Vol. XXXV, pp. 140–2 (30 January 1915).
17 George J. Zytaruk and James T. Boulton (eds), *The Letters of D.H. Lawrence, Volume II*, Cambridge University Press, 1981, p. 353.
18 Wilson, *Hilaire Belloc*, p. 221.
19 Lady Cynthia Asquith, *Diaries 1915–1918*, London: Hutchinson, 1968, p. 48.
20 Hilaire Belloc to Wilfrid Scawen Blunt, 7 April 1916; Blunt Papers, West Sussex Record Office.
21 Susan Lowndes (ed.), *Diaries and Letters of Marie Belloc Lowndes 1911–1947*, London: Chatto & Windus, 1971, p. 71.
22 Asquith, *Diaries 1915–1918*, p. 152.
23 Lowndes (ed.), *Diaries and Letters of Marie Belloc Lowndes*, p. 71.
24 In fact, the published volume of Lady Cynthia Asquith's *Diaries* reads as follows: 'I heard him say his "Doris" [sic] – very funny.' This, however, is surely a case of Lady Cynthia's handwriting being misread – 'Dons' being mistaken for 'Doris'! Marie Belloc Lowndes confirms that Belloc read his 'Lines to a Don' at this particular Poets' Reading.
25 Speaight, *The Life of Hilaire Belloc*, pp. 358–9.
26 Hilaire Belloc to 'My dear Foster'[?], 24 November 1916; Belloc Study Centre, Sussex.
27 Lowndes (ed.), *Diaries and Letters of Marie Belloc Lowndes*, p. 80.
28 Rupert Hart-Davis (ed.), *Siegfried Sassoon: Diaries 1915–1918*, London: Faber & Faber, 1983, p. 176.
29 Dominic Hibberd, *Wilfred Owen: The Last Year 1917–1918*, London: Constable, 1992, p. 34.
30 Ibid., p. 24.
31 Harold Owen and John Bell (eds), *Wilfred Owen: Collected Letters*, Oxford University Press, 1967, p. 342.
32 Ibid., p. 376.
33 Hilaire Belloc to Wilfrid Scawen Blunt, 5 September 1917; Blunt Papers, West Sussex Record Office.
34 Ibid.
35 Hilaire Belloc to Wilfrid Scawen Blunt, 29 October 1917; Blunt Papers, West Sussex Record Office.
36 Hilaire Belloc to Wilfrid Scawen Blunt, 21 December 1917; Blunt Papers, West Sussex Record Office.

37 Hilaire Belloc to Wilfrid Scawen Blunt, 26 November 1917; Blunt Papers, West Sussex Record Office.

38 Speaight (ed.), *Letters from Hilaire Belloc*, p. 84.

39 Hilaire Belloc to Wilfrid Scawen Blunt, 8 December 1917; Blunt Papers, West Sussex Record Office.

40 Lowndes (ed.), *Diaries and Letters of Marie Belloc Lowndes*, p. 85.

41 Speaight, *The Life of Hilaire Belloc*, p. 371.

42 Ibid., p. 372.

43 Hilaire Belloc to Wilfrid Scawen Blunt, 6 August 1918; Blunt Papers, West Sussex Record Office.

44 Hilaire Belloc to Wilfrid Scawen Blunt, 12 December 1918; Blunt Papers, West Sussex Record Office.

Twenty-Two: A Private Friendship

1 Cecil Chesterton to Hilaire Belloc, undated [probably June or July 1917]; Belloc Collection, Boston College.

2 *New Witness*, 13 December 1918.

3 Speaight (ed.), *Letters from Hilaire Belloc*, p. 73.

4 Quoted in Louis Jebb, 'Belloc's genius at sea with the Jews', *Catholic Herald*, 23 March 1984.

5 G.K. Chesterton to Hilaire Belloc, 3 May 1919; Belloc Collection, Boston College.

6 Ibid., 25 August 1919.

7 Speaight (ed.), *Letters from Hilaire Belloc*, p. 148.

8 Hilaire Belloc to Wilfrid Scawen Blunt, 31 December 1918; Blunt Papers, West Sussex Record Office.

9 Sheppard, *Lobsters at Littlehampton*, p. 162.

10 Speaight, *The Life of Hilaire Belloc*, p. 377.

11 D. Felicitas Corrigan (ed.), *Siegfried Sassoon: Poet's Pilgrimage*, London: Victor Gollancz, 1973, pp. 181–2.

12 Siegfried Sassoon, *Siegfried's Journey, 1916–1920*, London: Faber & Faber, 1945, pp. 158–9.

13 Hilaire Belloc to Wilfrid Scawen Blunt, 27 July 1919; Blunt Papers, West Sussex Record Office.

14 Speaight (ed.), *Letters from Hilaire Belloc*, pp. 95–6.

15 Ibid., p. 96.

16 Pearce, *Literary Converts*, p. 112.

17 Jebb, *Testimony to Hilaire Belloc*, p. 15.

18 Douglas Woodruff, 'Belloc, Man of Integrity', *The Month*, July 1970.

19 D.B. Wyndham Lewis, 'Deo Gratias for Hilaire Belloc', *Catholic Herald*, 24 July 1953.

20 Dom Philip Jebb, interview with the author.

21 Sonia Orwell and Ian Angus (eds), *George Orwell: The Collected Essays, Journalism and Letters, Vol. III*, London: Secker & Warburg, 1968, p. 175.

22 Hilaire Belloc, *Europe and the Faith*, London: Burns & Oates., 1962, p. 192.

23 Hilaire Belloc, letter to the *Catholic Herald*, 1936; quoted in Speaight, *The Life of Hilaire Belloc*, p. 387.

24 Speaight (ed.), *Letters from Hilaire Belloc*, p. 124.

25 O'Connor, *Father Brown on Chesterton*, pp. 141–2.

26 Speaight (ed.), *Letters from Hilaire Belloc*, p. 124.

27 John Bright-Holmes (ed.), *Like it Was: The Diaries of Malcolm Muggeridge*, London: Collins, 1981, p. 395.

28 Edward Shanks, 'Mr Belloc: Some Characteristics', *London Mercury*, Vol. IV, No. 23, September 1921.

29 Speaight, *The Life of Hilaire Belloc*, p. 374.

30 Elizabeth Longford, *A Pilgrimage of Passion: A Life of Wilfrid Scawen Blunt*, London: Weidenfeld & Nicolson, 1979, p. 420.

31 Ibid., p. 421.

32 Ibid., p. 422.

33 Ibid. Leslie is here referring to Blunt's predilection for Arab dress.

34 Hilaire Belloc to Wilfrid Scawen Blunt, 4 February 1904; Blunt Papers, West Sussex Record Office.

Twenty-Three: Popes, Dictators and Jews

1 Speaight (ed.), *Letters from Hilaire Belloc*, p. 128.
2 Ibid., p. 120.
3 Reproduced in Riewald (ed.), *Beerbohm's Literary Caricatures*, p. 115.
4 Hilaire Belloc to Wilfrid Scawen Blunt, 20 March 1922; Blunt Papers, West Sussex Record Office.
5 Speaight (ed.), *Letters from Hilaire Belloc*, p. 122.
6 Ibid., p. 129.
7 Ibid., p. 122.
8 Ibid.
9 André Bordeaux, 'A Man of Two Nations', *The Tablet*, 25 July 1970.
10 Speaight (ed.), *Letters from Hilaire Belloc*, p. 122.
11 G.K. Chesterton, *The Resurrection of Rome*, London: Hodder & Stoughton, 1930, p. 242.
12 Ibid., p. 283.
13 Jebb, *Testimony to Hilaire Belloc*, p. 17.
14 Wilson, *Hilaire Belloc*, p. 188.
15 Ibid.
16 Speaight, *The Life of Hilaire Belloc*, pp. 452–3.
17 Morton, *Hilaire Belloc*, p. 8.
18 Hilaire Belloc, *The Jews*, London: Constable & Co., 1922, pp. vii–ix.
19 Ibid., p. 3.
20 Ibid., p. 155.
21 Ibid., p. 148.
22 Ibid., p. 55.
23 Michael Coren, *Gilbert: The Man who was Chesterton*, London: Jonathan Cape, 1989, p. 203.
24 Speaight (ed.), *Letters from Hilaire Belloc*, p. 116.
25 Anthony Read and David Fisher, *Kristallnacht: The Nazi Night of Terror*, London: Michael Joseph Ltd, 1989, p. 183.
26 Quoted in the *Sunday Times*, 18 August 1957.
27 Belloc, *The Jews*, pp. 307–8.

Twenty-Four: Friends and Family

1 Jebb, *Testimony to Hilaire Belloc*, p. 13.
2 Ibid.
3 Sister Emmanuel Mary (Marianne Jebb), interview with the author.
4 Speaight, *The Life of Hilaire Belloc*, p. 507.
5 These somewhat sketchy details of Elizabeth Belloc's life, about which precious little is known, have been gleaned from the 'Hilaire Belloc–Elizabeth Belloc Correspondence', deposited as a Special Collection at Georgetown University, Washington DC, and from conversations with surviving friends and relatives of the Belloc family, particularly with Zita Caldecott, Belloc's granddaughter, and with Chloë Blackburn, daughter of the artist Sir James Gunn, whose mother, Pauline Miller, was a bridesmaid at Eleanor's wedding.
6 Morton, *Hilaire Belloc*, p. 29; and Zita Caldecott, interview with the author, London, 27 March 2001.
7 Zita Caldecott, interview with the author.
8 Morton, *Hilaire Belloc*, p. 29.
9 Speaight, *The Life of Hilaire Belloc*, p. 512.
10 Vincent Brome, *J.B. Priestley*, London: Hamish Hamilton, 1988, p. 69.
11 Reginald Pound, *A.P. Herbert: A Biography*, London: Michael Joseph, 1976, p. 77.
12 Speaight (ed.), *Letters from Hilaire Belloc*, pp. 123–6.
13 Pound, *A.P. Herbert*, pp. 77–8.
14 Morton, *Hilaire Belloc*, p. 73.
15 Christopher Hollis, *The Seven Ages*, London: The Catholic Book Club, 1975, p. 60.
16 Ibid., p. 45.
17 Ibid., pp. 51–2.
18 Morton, *Hilaire Belloc*, p. 26.
19 Speaight, *The Life of Hilaire Belloc*, p. 474.
20 *Times Literary Supplement*, 11 May 1922.
21 Hilaire Belloc to Ruby Goldsmith, 30

January 1923; Belloc Collection, Boston College.

22 Speaight, *The Life of Hilaire Belloc*, pp. 454–5.

23 Ibid., p. 456.

24 Hilaire Belloc to G.K. Chesterton, 22 February 1923; Belloc Collection, Boston College.

25 Hilaire Belloc to Carl Schmidt, 27 March 1923; Special Collection, The O'Shaugnessy-Frey Library, University of St Thomas, St Paul, Minnesota, USA.

26 Ethel Smyth, *Maurice Baring*, London: William Heinemann, 1938, p. 320.

27 Maurice Baring, 'Mr Belloc's Poems' in *Punch and Judy and Other Essays*, London: William Heinemann, 1924, pp. 283–93.

28 Diana Cooper, *The Light of Common Day*, London: Rupert Hart-Davis, 1959, p. 37.

29 Ibid.

30 Chesterton, *Autobiography*, p. 228.

31 Speaight (ed.), *Letters from Hilaire Belloc*, p. 146.

32 Max Saunders, *Ford Madox Ford: A Duel Life, Volume II, The After-War World*, Oxford University Press, 1996, p. 132.

Twenty-Five: War of the Wells

1 Speaight (ed.), *Letters from Hilaire Belloc*, p. 144.

2 Ibid., p. 154.

3 *Daily Express*, 20 October 1930.

4 *Bystander*, 8 October 1930.

5 Dom Hugh G. Bevenot, OSB, *Pagan and Christian Rule*, London: Longmans, Green & Co., 1924, pp. v–vi.

6 Pearce, *Wisdom and Innocence*, p. 275.

7 Speaight, *The Life of Hilaire Belloc*, pp. 397–8.

8 Rupert Hart-Davis (ed.), *Siegfried Sassoon: Diaries 1923–1925*, London: Faber & Faber, 1985, pp. 41–2.

9 It should perhaps be noted that serious doubts have been cast upon Wells's authorship of *The Outline of History*. A Canadian academic, A.B. McKillop, has argued forcefully that Wells had largely plagiarized an unpublished manuscript by an unknown writer, Florence Deeks. See A.B. McKillop, *The Spinster & The Prophet: A Tale of H.G. Wells, Plagiarism and the History of the World*, London: Aurum Press, 2001.

10 Michael Coren, *The Invisible Man: The Life and Liberties of H.G. Wells*, London: Jonathan Cape, 1993, pp. 162–3.

11 Tom Burns, *The Use of Memory*, London: Sheed & Ward, 1933, p. 32.

12 It is important to remember that Belloc differentiated between the general theory of Evolution and the specific theories put forward by Darwin. Thus, for instance, in a letter to the *Manchester Guardian* on 21 September 1926, he wrote: 'The whole of Vialleton's book is one continuous series of closed detailed proofs advanced, not against Evolution, of course, but against Darwinism.'

13 Beverley Nichols, *Are They the Same at Home?*, London: Jonathan Cape, 1927, pp. 30–3.

14 Lunn, *And Yet So New*, p. 68.

15 Arnold Lunn to Hilaire Belloc, 10 December 1926; Belloc Collection, Boston College.

16 Speaight (ed.), *Letters from Hilaire Belloc*, p. 170.

17 Morton, *Hilaire Belloc*, p. 90.

18 Jebb, *Testimony to Hilaire Belloc*, p. 149.

19 Hilaire Belloc to Hoffman Nickerson, 11 November 1926; Belloc Collection, Boston College.

20 Jebb, *Testimony to Hilaire Belloc*, p. 149.

21 Speaight (ed.), *Letters from Hilaire Belloc*, p. 171.

22 Morton, *Hilaire Belloc*, p. 119.

23 Roy Campbell, 'Books in Britain', *Enquiry*, London, Vol. 2, No. 3 (September 1949); quoted in Joseph Pearce, *Bloomsbury and Beyond: The Friends and Enemies of Roy Campbell*, London: HarperCollins, 2001, p. 292.

Twenty-Six: Reformed Characters

1 Hilaire Belloc, Preface to Bevenot, *Pagan and Christian Rule*, p. ix.

2 Hilaire Belloc to Wilfrid Scawen Blunt, 8 July 1922; Blunt Papers, West Sussex Record Office.

3 C.C. Martindale, *The Life of Robert Hugh Benson, Vol. Two*, London: Longmans & Co., 1916, p. 45.

4 Speaight (ed.), *Letters from Hilaire Belloc*, pp. 164–5.

5 Hilaire Belloc to G.K. Chesterton, 17 June 1926; Belloc Collection, Boston College.

6 G.K.C., student paper, 16 October 1925; quoted in the *Chesterton Review*, vol. XII, no. 2, and in Pearce, *Wisdom and Innocence*, pp. 314–15. The poem to which Belloc refers as the best within living memory is Chesterton's 'Lepanto' which he praised on several occasions, most notably in his essay *On the Place of Gilbert Keith Chesterton in English Letters*, p. 78.

7 Bevis Hillier, *Young Betjeman*, London: John Murray, 1988, p. 134.

8 Speaight (ed.), *Letters from Hilaire Belloc*, p. 162.

9 Ibid., p. 165.

10 Speaight, *The Life of Hilaire Belloc*, p. 509.

11 Speaight (ed.), *Letters from Hilaire Belloc*, p. 162.

12 Speaight, *The Life of Hilaire Belloc*, p. 491.

13 Hilaire Belloc to Maurice Baring, 30 September 1941; Belloc Collection, Boston College.

14 Howarth, *Squire*, p. 191.

15 Diana Cooper, *The Light of Common Day*, p. 62.

16 Duff Cooper, *Old Men Forget*, p. 150.

17 Morton, *Hilaire Belloc*, pp. 71–2.

18 Wilson, *Hilaire Belloc*, p. 296.

19 Ibid., p. 295.

20 Ibid.

21 Ibid., p. 296.

22 Ibid., p. 295.

23 Pearce, *Wisdom and Innocence*, pp. 326–7.

24 Hilaire Belloc, *A Conversation with an Angel and Other Essays*, London: Jonathan Cape, 1928, pp. 80–1.

25 From 'On Witchcraft', ibid., pp. 166–7.

26 Speaight (ed.), *Letters from Hilaire Belloc*, p. 75.

27 Hilaire Belloc to Elizabeth Belloc, undated; Hilaire Belloc–Elizabeth Belloc Correspondence, Special Collection, Georgetown University, Washington DC.

28 Hilaire Belloc, *The Crisis of Our Civilization*, New York: Fordham University Press, 1937, p. 238.

29 Hilaire Belloc to Hoffman Nickerson, 13 September 1923; Belloc Collection, Boston College.

30 Speaight (ed.), *Letters from Hilaire Belloc*, pp. 79–80.

31 Ibid., p. 182.

32 Belloc, 'On Macaulay' in *A Conversation with an Angel and Other Essays*, p. 203.

33 *The Nation*, 19 February 1921; reprinted in *The Works of Bernard Shaw, Volume 29: Pen Portraits and Reviews*, London: Constable & Co., 1931, p. 141.

34 Smith, *John Buchan*, p. 359.

35 Desmond MacCarthy, 'Most Various of Living Authors', *The Listener*, 27 July 1950.

36 Philip Guedalla, 'Mr Belloc: A Panorama' in *Essays of Today and Yesterday*, London: George G. Harrap & Co., 1926, p. 54.

37 An unpublished letter from Belloc to Guedalla, dated 14 March 1912 (Hilaire Belloc Study Centre), illustrates not merely that Guedalla had sought Belloc's advice as a historian of repute but also that, contrary to popular assumption, Belloc was himself diligent in his own research.

Twenty-Seven: A Final Flourish

1 James Gunn to Sylvia Gunn, [undated but probably written on 27 June 1927]; courtesy of Chloë Blackburn.

2 Hilaire Belloc to James Gunn, 14 November 1923; courtesy of Chloë Blackburn.

3 Belloc, *The Four Men*, pp. v–vi.
4 Speaight, *The Life of Hilaire Belloc*, p. 476.
5 Speaight (ed.), *Letters from Hilaire Belloc*, p. 179.
6 Hilaire Belloc to 'Mr [?] Smith' [name illegible], 3 October 1929; Hilaire Belloc Study Centre.
7 Speaight (ed.), *Letters from Hilaire Belloc*, p. 178.
8 Ibid., p. 191.
9 Speaight, *The Life of Hilaire Belloc*, p. 495.
10 Ibid., p. 500.
11 Hilaire Belloc to Carl Schmidt, 16 May 1930; Special Collection, O'Shaugnessy-Frey Library, Minnesota.
12 Speaight, *The Life of Hilaire Belloc*, p. 500.
13 Jebb, *Testimony to Hilaire Belloc*, p. 34.
14 Morton, *Hilaire Belloc*, p. 135.
15 Jebb, *Testimony to Hilaire Belloc*, p. 34.
16 *The Times*, 14 December 1928.
17 Father Waggett to Hilaire Belloc, 1 February 1929; Belloc Collection, Boston College.
18 Speaight, *The Life of Hilaire Belloc*, pp. 500–1.
19 Ibid., p. 502.
20 *Evening Standard*, 8 December 1927.
21 Ibid., 31 May 1928.
22 Hilaire Belloc, *Survivals and New Arrivals*, London: Sheed & Ward, 1929, p. 12.
23 Belloc, *The Cruise of the Nona*, p. 333.
24 Hilaire Belloc to Carl Schmidt, 19 February 1932; Special Collection, O'Shaugnessy-Frey Library, Minnesota.
25 Belloc, *On the Place of Gilbert Keith Chesterton in English Letters*, pp. 66–7.
26 Written by Belloc in his personal copy of *The Path to Rome*.

Twenty-Eight: Farewell to the Chesterbelloc

1 Evelyn Waugh, 'Max Beerbohm: A Lesson in Manners', originally published in the *Atlantic Monthly* in September 1956; reprinted in Riewald (ed.), *The Surprise of Excellence*, p. 93.
2 Ibid.
3 Richard Ollard, *A Man of Contradictions: A Life of A.L. Rowse*, London: Allen Lane/The Pengun Press, 1999, p. 262.
4 Morton, *Hilaire Belloc*, pp. 88–9.
5 J.W. Poynter, *Hilaire Belloc Keeps the Bridge*, London: Watts & Co., 1929, p. vii.
6 Ibid., p. 59.
7 Hilaire Belloc to James Gunn, 29 April 1929; courtesy of Chloë Blackburn.
8 *Sir James Gunn 1893–1964*, published in 1994 by the Trustees of the National Galleries of Scotland for the exhibition held at the Scottish National Portrait Gallery, Edinburgh, 3 December 1994 – 26 February 1995, p. 37.
9 Chesterton, with characteristic vagueness, put the figure at 'about forty', but H.S. Mackintosh stated specifically in an article entitled 'Memories of Hilaire Belloc' in *The Listener* on 8 October 1953 that 'twenty-four persons were there'.
10 This list has been compiled principally from signatures on the back of H.S. Mackintosh's invitation, a copy of which was sent to the author by Miranda Mackintosh, his daughter, and also from various published accounts of the sixtieth birthday celebration, including those given by Chesterton, J.B. Morton, Reginald Jebb, J.J. Hall and H.S. Mackintosh.
11 Chesterton, *Autobiography*, p. 303.
12 Ibid., p. 304.
13 J.J. Hall, 'Belloc the Sailor', *John O'London's Weekly*, 21 July 1950; and Speaight, *The Life of Hilaire Belloc*, p. 480.
14 Morton, *Hilaire Belloc*, p. 79.
15 Hilaire Belloc to Peter Belloc, 24 April 1932; courtesy of Zita Caldecott.
16 Speaight, *The Life of Hilaire Belloc*, p. 469. According to Morton, *Hilaire Belloc*, p. 138, this particular speech was described by Maurice Healy as 'the best speech he had ever listened to' – no mean feat considering the speaker could not recollect his own words on the following morning.

17 Hilaire Belloc to H.S. Mackintosh, 13 April 1931; courtesy of Miranda Mackintosh.

18 Burns, *The Use of Memory*, p. 33.

19 Hilaire Belloc to Ronald Knox, 9 March 1931; Belloc Collection, Boston College.

20 Speaight (ed.), *Letters from Hilaire Belloc*, p. 227.

21 Hilaire Belloc to James Murray Allison, 20 March 1932. Extract of letter published in the Christie's (New York) catalogue, 15 December 1995, p. 15.

22 Note by James Gunn attached to some drawings made by Chesterton during the sittings and to a rough copy of the Ballade, written in Baring's hand; courtesy of Chloë Blackburn.

23 HRH Princess Elizabeth, later HM Queen Elizabeth II, to Pauline Gunn, 16 December 1947; courtesy of Chloë Blackburn.

24 Hilaire Belloc to James Gunn, 30 May 1932; courtesy of Chloë Blackburn.

25 Speaight, *The Life of Hilaire Belloc*, p. 515.

26 Ibid.

27 Hilaire Belloc to Peter Belloc, 15 September 1932; courtesy of Zita Caldecott.

28 Speaight (ed.), *Letters from Hilaire Belloc*, p. 236.

29 Hilaire Belloc to H.S. Mackintosh, 2 February 1933; courtesy of Miranda Mackintosh.

30 Speaight (ed.), *Letters from Hilaire Belloc*, pp. 235–6.

31 Hilaire Belloc to Reginald Jebb, 27 July 1933; Belloc Papers, West Sussex Record Office.

32 Sister Emmanuel Mary (Marianne Jebb), interview with the author; and Hilaire Belloc to Reginald Jebb, 12 July 1934; Belloc Papers, West Sussex Record Office.

33 Sister Emmanuel Mary, interview with the author.

34 Zita Caldecott, interview with the author.

35 Hilaire Belloc to Stella Belloc, 23 July 1934; courtesy of Zita Caldecott.

36 Hilaire Belloc to Peter Belloc, 31 October 1934; courtesy of Zita Caldecott.

37 Hilaire Belloc to Reginald Jebb, 8 November 1934; Belloc papers, West Sussex Record Office.

38 Wilson, *Hilaire Belloc*, p. 332.

39 Hilaire Belloc to Peter Belloc, 27 February 1935; courtesy of Zita Caldecott.

40 Hilaire Belloc to Marianne Jebb, 6 June 1935; Belloc papers, West Sussex Record Office.

41 Hilaire Belloc to Elizabeth Belloc, 13 February 1935; Special Collection, Georgetown University, Washington DC.

42 Speaight (ed.), *Letters from Hilaire Belloc*, pp. 251–2.

43 *The Times*, 19 December 1945.

44 Pearce, *Wisdom and Innocence*, p. 483.

45 Ibid.

Twenty-Nine: The Last Rally

1 Hilaire Belloc to Peter Belloc, 19 September 1936; courtesy of Zita Caldecott.

2 Michael Davie (ed.), *The Diaries of Evelyn Waugh*, London: Weidenfeld & Nicolson, 1976, p. 412.

3 Hilaire Belloc to Reginald Jebb, 2 July 1936; Belloc Collection, Boston College.

4 Speaight (ed.), *Letters from Hilaire Belloc*, p. 258.

5 Speaight, *The Life of Hilaire Belloc*, p. 482.

6 Speaight (ed.), *Letters from Hilaire Belloc*, p. 265.

7 Hilaire Belloc to Carl Schmidt, 8 July 1936; Special Collection, the O'Shaugnessy-Frey Library, Minnesota.

8 Maurice Baring, *Dead Letters*, London: William Heinemann Ltd, 1935, p. xii.

9 Conrad Pepler OP, *Dorothy Day and the Catholic Worker Movement*, London: Catholic Truth Society, 1986, p. 8.

10 Hilaire Belloc to Reginald Jebb, 25 February 1937; Belloc Collection, Boston College.

11 Hilaire Belloc to Reginald Jebb, 9 April 1937; Belloc Collection, Boston College.

12 Hiliare Belloc to Stella Belloc, 11 March 1937; courtesy of Zita Caldecott.

13 Hilaire Belloc to Gabrielle Belloc, 21 May 1937; courtesy of Zita Caldecott.

14 Speaight (ed.), *Letters from Hilaire Belloc*, p. 264.

15 Speaight, *The Life of Hilaire Belloc*, pp. 457–8.

16 It is curious that Selina Hastings, in her biography of Evelyn Waugh (London: Minerva, 1994, p. 364), states that Belloc was one of the witnesses at Evelyn Waugh's wedding on 17 April 1937. Since Belloc was speaking in Boston on that day, his presence at the nuptial Mass in London is either a miraculous case of bilocation or, more likely and more mundanely, a simple case of mistaken identity.

17 Speaight (ed.), *Letters from Hilaire Belloc*, p. 265.

18 Hilaire Belloc to Reginald Jebb, 9 August 1937; Belloc Collection, Boston College.

19 Ibid., 30 August 1937.

20 Ibid., 4 September 1937.

21 Speaight (ed.), *Letters from Hilaire Belloc*, p. 268.

22 Hilaire Belloc to Elizabeth Belloc, 5 December 1937; Special Collection, Georgetown University, Washington DC.

23 Dr J.B. Lyons, 'The Don who Tangled with Belloc', the *Irish Medical Times*, 14 June, year unknown; reprinted in *The Bellocian*, Vol. 2, No. 2 (Summer 1998), p. 5.

24 *The Review of the Churches*, October 1929.

25 *The Nation and Athenaeum*, 26 May 1928.

26 G.G. Coulton, *Divorce, Mr Belloc and 'The Daily Telegraph'*, privately published, 1937, p. 13.

27 Quote in Lyons, 'The Don who Tangled with Belloc'.

28 Speaight, *The Life of Hilaire Belloc*, p. 416.

29 Ibid.

30 Ibid.

31 Hilaire Belloc to J.B. Morton, 27 May 1938; Hilaire Belloc Study Centre.

32 Hilaire Belloc to Peter Belloc, 31 May 1938; courtesy of Zita Caldecott.

33 *Catholic Herald*, 25 March 1938.

34 Hilaire Belloc to Reginald Jebb, 2 August 1938; Belloc Collection, Boston College.

35 Hilaire Belloc to James Murray Allison, 7 May 1938; Christie's (New York) Catalogue, 15 December 1995.

36 Hilaire Belloc to Evelyn Waugh, 13 June 1938; Belloc Collection, Boston College.

37 Hilaire Belloc to H.S. Mackintosh, 11 July 1938; courtesy of Miranda Mackintosh.

38 H.E.G. Rope, 'Belloc the Catholic', in *Belloc 70*, p. 38.

39 Rupert Hart-Davis, *Hugh Walpole: A Portrait of a Man, an Epoch and a Society*, London: Rupert Hart-Davis, 1952, pp. 400–1.

40 *The Tablet*, 15 July 1939.

41 Pearce, *Bloomsbury and Beyond*, pp. 217–18.

42 Speaight, *The Life of Hilaire Belloc*, p. 516.

43 Hilaire Belloc to Maurice Baring, 21 March 1939; Belloc Collection, Boston College.

44 Hilaire Belloc to Peter Belloc, 16 March 1939; courtesy of Zita Caldecott.

45 Hilaire Belloc to Elizabeth Belloc, 23 March 1939; Special Collection, Georgetown University, Washington DC.

46 Wilson, *Hilaire Belloc*, p. 362; and Hilaire Belloc to James Gunn, 28 April 1939; courtesy of Chloë Blackburn.

47 Hilaire Belloc to Bonnie Soames, 4 August 1939; Belloc Collection, Boston College.

48 Hilaire Belloc to Maurice Baring, 25 March 1939; Belloc Collection, Boston College.

49 Ibid.

50 Hilaire Belloc to Elizabeth Belloc, 12 May 1939; Special Collection, Georgetown University, Washington DC.

51 Hilaire Belloc to Peter Belloc, 8 June 1939; courtesy of Zita Caldecott.

Thirty: Decline without Fall

1 Jebb, *Testimony to Hilaire Belloc*, p. 149.
2 Hilaire Belloc to Maurice Baring, 30 September 1941; Belloc Collection, Boston College.
3 Rene Hague (ed.), *Dai Greatcoat: A Self-Portrait of David Jones in His Letters*, London: Faber & Faber, 1980, p. 100.
4 Speaight (ed.), *Letters from Hilaire Belloc*, p. 289.
5 Christopher Hassall (ed.), *Ambrosia and Small Beer: The Record of a Correspondence between Edward Marsh and Christopher Hassall*, London: Longmans, 1964, p. 347.
6 Sister Emmanuel Mary (Marianne Jebb), interview with the author.
7 Teresa Brading, unpublished memoir of Belloc; West Sussex Record Office.
8 Sister Emmanuel Mary (Marianne Jebb), 'Some Memories of Grandpapa – Hilaire Belloc', unpublished manuscript; West Sussex Record Office.
9 Dom Philip Jebb, 'Hilaire Belloc as a Grandfather', *Downside Review*, Vol. 88, No. 293 (October 1970).
10 Hilaire Belloc to Stella Belloc, 3 August 1940; courtesy of Zita Caldecott.
11 Speaight (ed.), *Letters from Hilaire Belloc*, p. 296.
12 *Picture Post*, 19 October 1940.
13 Speaight (ed.), *Letters from Hilaire Belloc*, p. 291.
14 Ibid., p. 290.
15 Ibid.
16 Lowndes (ed.), *Diaries and Letters of Marie Belloc Lowndes*, p. 208.
17 Hilaire Belloc to Elizabeth Belloc, 16 December 1940; Special Collection, Georgetown University, Washington DC.
18 Speaight (ed.), *Letters from Hilaire Belloc*, p. 298.
19 Ibid., p. 290.
20 Ibid., p. 298.
21 Speaight, *The Life of Hilaire Belloc*, p. 521.
22 Morton, *Hilaire Belloc*, p. 160.
23 Hilaire Belloc to Elizabeth Belloc, 3 April 1941; Special Collection, Georgetown University, Washington DC.
24 Ibid., undated.
25 Morton, *Hilaire Belloc*, p. 160.
26 Ibid., p. 161.
27 Lowndes (ed.), *Diaries and Letters of Marie Belloc Lowndes*, pp. 217–18.
28 Hilaire Belloc to Maurice Baring, 6 June 1941; Belloc Collection, Boston College.
29 Speaight (ed.), *Letters from Hilaire Belloc*, p. 300.
30 Hilaire Belloc to Elizabeth Belloc, 19 & 29 July 1941; Special Collection, Georgetown University, Washington DC.
31 Speaight states that Brendan Bracken, who was then the Minister of Information, presided at the dinner (*The Life of Hilaire Belloc*, p. 522). The printed menu for the evening, however, states specifically that 'The Rt Hon. A. Duff Cooper' was 'in the chair' and makes no mention of Bracken.
32 H.S. Mackintosh, 'Memories of Hilaire Belloc', *The Listener*, 8 October 1953.
33 Jebb, *Testimony to Hilaire Belloc*, p. 22.
34 Morton, *Hilaire Belloc*, p. 161.
35 Hassall (ed.), *Ambrosia and Small Beer*, p. 204.
36 Dom Philip Jebb and Sister Emmanuel Mary, interviews with the author.
37 Hilaire Belloc to Stella Belloc, 23 May 1942; courtesy of Zita Caldecott.
38 Barbara Wall, interview with the author, 18 October 2000.
39 Morton, *Hilaire Belloc*, p. 162.
40 Zita Caldecott, letter to the author, 17 January 2001.
41 Sister Emmanuel Mary, 'Some Memories of Grandpapa', and interview with the author.
42 Diana Cooper, *The Light of Common Day*, p. 252.

Thirty-One: The Fading

1 Douglas Woodruff, 'Belloc, Man of Integrity', *The Month*, July 1970. Also, Speaight, *The Life of Hilaire Belloc*, p. 525.

2 Sister Emmanuel Mary, interview with the author.

3 Ferdinand Valentine, OP, *Father Vincent McNabb, OP: Portrait of a Great Dominican*, London: Burns & Oates, 1955, pp. 207–9.

4 Hilaire Belloc to Percy Naldrett, 22 June 1943; Hilaire Belloc Study Centre.

5 Lunn, *And Yet So New*, p. 67.

6 Evelyn Waugh, *Ronald Knox*, London: Fontana Books, 1962, p. 247.

7 Lowndes (ed.), *Diaries and Letters of Marie Belloc Lowndes*, p. 251.

8 Speaight, *The Life of Hilaire Belloc*, p. 524.

9 Morton, *Hilaire Belloc*, p. 75.

10 Ibid., p. 165.

11 Eleanor Jebb to Denis Dooley, 20 August 1946; Hilaire Belloc Study Centre.

12 Sister Emmanuel Mary, interview with the author.

13 Hesketh Pearson and Hugh Kingsmill, *Talking of Dick Whittington*, London: Eyre & Spottiswoode, 1947, pp. 209–13.

14 Morton, *Hilaire Belloc*, pp. 167 and 173.

15 Hilaire Belloc to Maurice Baring, 6 June 1941; Belloc Collection, Boston College.

16 Dom Philip Jebb, interview with the author.

17 Ibid.

18 Eleanor Jebb to Percy Naldrett, 27 July 1947; Hilaire Belloc Study Centre.

19 Barbara Wall, interview with the author.

20 Eleanor Jebb to Percy Naldrett, undated but probably Christmas 1948; Hilaire Belloc Study Centre.

21 *Daily Telegraph*, 25 June 1949.

22 Eleanor Jebb to Percy Naldrett, 17 June 1950; Hilaire Belloc Study Centre.

23 Morton, *Hilaire Belloc*, p. 171.

24 Reginald Jebb, who lived at King's Land and would, therefore, presumably have a better idea than most of the numbers present, put the figure at more than 400; Jebb, *Testimony to Hilaire Belloc*, p. 23.

25 *The Listener*, 8 October 1953.

26 *The Tablet*, 5 August 1950.

27 *Catholic Herald*, 24 July 1953.

28 Eleanor Jebb to Percy Naldrett, 31 July 1950; Hilaire Belloc Study Centre.

29 Bob Copper, conversation with the author, 4 November 2000.

30 *The Listener*, 27 July 1950.

31 Zita Caldecott, interview with the author.

32 Eleanor Jebb to Percy Naldrett, 24 August 1950; Hilaire Belloc Study Centre.

33 Most particularly by A.N. Wilson in his biography of Belloc.

34 Zita Caldecott, interview with the author.

35 The Earl of Iddesleigh, conversation with the author, 1 November 2000; and Edward Northcote, conversation with the author, 7 November 2000.

36 Bright-Holmes (ed.), *Like It Was*, p. 420.

37 Father Bidone assisted the Rt Rev. Cormac Murphy O'Connor, then the Bishop of Arundel, now the Cardinal Archbishop of Westminster, at Muggeridge's reception into the Church on 27 November 1982.

38 Father Paul Bidone, FDP, 'A Great Crusader', *The Bridge: Official Organ of the Sons of Divine Providence*, Summer 1970, pp. 11–12.

39 Davie (ed.), *The Diaries of Evelyn Waugh*, pp. 703–4.

40 Charlotte Mosley (ed.), *The Letters of Nancy Mitford and Evelyn Waugh*, London: Hodder & Stoughton, 1996, p. 291.

41 *The Listener*, 8 October 1953.

42 *The Tablet*, 25 July 1953.

43 *News Chronicle*, 17 July 1953.

44 *Catholic Herald*, 24 July 1953.

45 *Daily Express*, 17 July 1953.

46 *Daily Mail*, 17 July 1953.

47 Belloc, *On the Place of Gilbert Keith Chesterton in English Letters*, p. 83.

BIBLIOGRAPHY

I. *Books and Pamphlets by Hilaire Belloc*

The following list of Belloc's publications is taken from *The English First Editions of Hilaire Belloc* by Patrick Cahill.

1896   *Verses and Sonnets.* Ward and Downey.

1896   *The Bad Child's Book of Beasts.* Oxford: Alden and Co., Bocardo Press; London: Simpkin, Marshall, Hamilton, Kent and Co.

1897   *More Beasts (for Worse Children).* Edward Arnold.

1898   *The Modern Traveller.* Edward Arnold.

1899   *Danton.* James Nisbet and Co.

1899   *A Moral Alphabet.* Edward Arnold.

1899   Extracts from the Diaries and Letters of HUBERT HOWARD with a Recollection by a Friend. (Edited by H.B.). Oxford: Horace Hart.

1900   *Lambkin's Remains.* Oxford: The Proprietors of the J.C.R.

1900   *Paris.* Edward Arnold.

1901   *Robespierre.* James Nisbet and Co.

1902   *The Path to Rome.* George Allen.

1903   *Caliban's Guide to Letters.* Duckworth and Co.

1903   *The Great Inquiry.* Duckworth and Co.

1903   *Why Eat?* A Broadside.

1903   *The Romance of Tristan and Iseult.* Translated from the French of J. Bédier by H.B. George Allen.

1904   *Avril.* Duckworth and Co.

1904   *Emmanuel Burden.* Methuen and Co.

1904   *The Old Road.* Archibald Constable and Co.

1906   *Esto Perpetua.* Duckworth and Co.

1906   *An Open Letter on the Decay of Faith.* Burns and Oates.

1906   *Sussex.* Adam and Charles Black.

1906   *Hills and the Sea.* Methuen and Co.

1907   *This Historic Thames.* J. M. Dent and Co.

1907   *Cautionary Tales for Children* Eveleigh Nash.

1908   *The Catholic Church and Historical Truth* (Catholic Evidence Lectures, No. 3). Preston: W. Watson and Co.

1908   *On Nothing.* Methuen and Co.

1908   *Mr. Clutterbuck's Election.* Eveleigh Nash.

1908   *The Eye-Witness.* Eveleigh Nash.

1908   *An Examination of Socialism.* Catholic Truth Society.

1909   *The Pyrenees.* Methuen and Co.

1909   *A Change in the Cabinet.* Methuen and Co.

1909   *Marie Antoinette.* Methuen and Co.

1909   *On Everything.* Methuen and Co.

1909   *The Church and Socialism.* Catholic Truth Society.

1910   *The Ferree Case.* Catholic Truth Society.

1910   *On Anything.* Constable and Co.

1910   *Pongo and the Bull.* Constable and Co.

1910   *On Something.* Methuen and Co.

1910   *Verses.* Duckworth and Co.

1911   *The Party System*, by Hilaire Belloc and Cecil Chesterton. Stephen Swift.

1911   *The French Revolution.* Williams and Norgate.

1911   *The Girondin.* Thomas Nelson and Sons.

1911   *More Peers.* Stephen Swift.

1911   *Socialism and the Servile State.* A Debate between Messrs. Hilaire Belloc and J. Ramsay MacDonald, M.P. The South West London Federation of the Independent Labour Party.

1911   *First and Last.* Methuen and Co.

1912   *The Four Men.* Thomas Nelson and Sons.

1912   *The Green Overcoat.* Bristol: J. W. Arrowsmith; London: Simpkin, Marshall, Hamilton, Kent and Co.

1912   *This and That.* Methuen and Co.

1912   *The Servile State.* T. N. Foulis.

1915   *Land & Water Map of the War*, drawn under the direction of Hilaire Belloc. *Land & Water.*

1915   *The History of England* (in eleven volumes). Vol. XI is by H. B. Sands and Co.; New York: The Catholic Publication Society of America.

1915   *A General Sketch of the European War: The First Phase.* Thomas Nelson and Sons.

1916   *A General Sketch of the European War: The Second Phase.* Thomas Nelson and Sons.

1916   *The Second Year of the War*. Reprinted by permission from *Land and Water*. Burrup, Mathieson and Sprague.

1920   *The Catholic Church and the Principle of Private Property*. Catholic Truth Society.

1920   *Europe and the Faith*. Constable and Co.

1922   *Catholic Social Reform versus Socialism*. Catholic Truth Society.

1922   *The Jews*. Constable and Co.

1922   *The Mercy of Allah*. Chatto and Windus.

1923   *On*. Methuen and Co.

1923   *The Road*. Manchester: Charles W. Hobson.

1923   *Sonnets and Verse*. Duckworth and Co.

1923   *The Contrast*. J. W. Arrowsmith (London) Ltd.

1924   *Economics for Helen*. J. W. Arrowsmith (London) Ltd.

1924   *The Campaign of 1812*. Thomas Nelson and Sons.

1925   *The Cruise of the 'Nona'*. Constable and Co.

1925   *A History of England: Vol. I*. Methuen and Co.

1925   *England and the Faith*. A Reply published in the *Evening Standard* to an article by Dean Inge in the same journal. Catholic Truth Society.

1926   *Mrs. Markham's New History of England*. The Cayme Press.

1926   *The Emerald*. Arrowsmith.

1926   *A Companion to Mr. Wells's 'Outline of History'*. Sheed and Ward.

1926   *Mr. Belloc Still Objects*. Sheed and Ward.

1927   *The Catholic Church and History*. Burns Oates and Washbourne.

1927   *A History of England: Vol II*. Methuen and Co.

1927   *The Haunted House*. Arrowsmith.

1927   *Oliver Cromwell*. Ernest Benn.

1928   *A History of England: Vol. III*. Methuen and Co.

1928   *James the Second*. Faber and Gwyer.

1928   *How the Reformation Happened*. Jonathan Cape.

1928   *But Soft—We are Observed*. Arrowsmith.

1928   *A Conversation with an Angel*. Jonathan Cape.

1928   *Belinda*. Constable and Co.

1929   *Survivals and New Arrivals*. Sheed and Ward.

1929   *Joan of Arc*. Cassell and Co.

1929   *The Missing Masterpiece*. Arrowsmith.

1930   *Richelieu*. Ernest Benn.

1930   *Wolsey*. Cassell and Co.

1930   *The Man Who Made Gold*. Arrowsmith.

1930 *New Cautionary Tales*. Duckworth.

1931 *A Conversation with a cat*. Cassell and Co.

1931 *Essays of a Catholic*. Sheed and Ward.

1931 *A History of England: Vol. IV*. Methuen and Co.

1931 Cranmer. Cassell and Co.

1932 *The Postmaster–General*. Arrowsmith.

1932 *Napoleon*. Cassell and Co.

1933 *William the Conqueror*. Peter Davies.

1933 *Becket*. Catholic Truth Society. (Published also by Sheed and Ward (1933) in 'The English Way', a collection of essays by various authors.)

1933 *Charles the First*. Cassell and Co.

1934 *Cromwell*. Cassell and Co.

1934 *A Shorter History of England*. George G. Harrap and Co.

1935 *Milton*. Cassell and Co.

1936 *The County of Sussex*. Cassell and Co.

1936 *An Essay on the Restoration of Property*. The Distributist League.

1936 *Characters of the Reformation*. Sheed and Ward.

1936 *The Hedge and the Horse*. Cassell and Co.

1937 *An Essay on the Nature of Contemporary England*. Constable and Co.

1937 *The Crusade*. Cassell and Co.

1937 *The Crisis of Our Civilization*. Cassell and Co.

1938 *Sonnets and Verse*. Duckworth. New edition, with additional poems.

1938 *The Great Heresies*. Sheed and Ward.

1938 *The Question and the Answer*. Longmans, Green and Co.

1938 *Monarchy: A Study of Louis XIV*. Cassell and Co.

1938 *The Case of Dr. Coulton*. Sheed and Ward.

1939 *On Sailing the Sea*. Methuen and Co.

1940 *The Last Rally*. Cassell and Co.

1940 *The Catholic and the War*. Burns Oates.

1940 *On the Place of Gilbert Chesterton in English Letters*. Sheed and Ward.

1941 *The Silence of the Sea*. Cassell and Co.

1942 *Elizabethan Commentary*. Cassell and Co.

1942 *Places*. Cassell and Co.

INDEX